Policing and Misconduct

❖

KIM MICHELLE LERSCH

University of South Florida

Editor

M. L. DANTZKER

Series Editor

Upper Saddle River, New Jersey 07458

Library of Congress Cataloging-in-Publication Data

Policing and misconduct/Kim Michelle Lersch, editor.
    p. cm.—(Prentice Hall's policing and ... series)
    Includes bibliographical references.
    ISBN 0-13-027016-4
        1. Police misconduct—United states. 2. Police ethics—United States. I. Lersch, Kim
    Michelle. II. Series.
HV8138 .P673 2002
363.2'3'0973—dc21   2001034377

Publisher: Jeff Johnston
Executive Acquisitions Editor: Kim Davies
Editorial Assistant: Korrine Dorsey
Assistant Editor: Sarah Holle
Copy Editor: Louanne Dreyer Elliott
Managing Production Editor: Mary Carnis
Production Liaison: Barbara Marttine Cappuccio
Production Editor: Janet Bolton
**Director of Manufacturing
    and Production:** Bruce Johnson
Manufacturing Buyer: Cathleen Petersen

Creative Director: Cheryl Asherman
Senior Design Coordinator: Miguel Ortiz
Cover Design: Blair Brown
Cover Photograph: Paul Edmondson/© Tony
    Stone
Composition: Janet Bolton
Electronic Art Creation: Mark Ammerman
Marketing Manager: Ramona Sherman
Printing and Binding: Phoenix Book Tech
Proofreader: Maine Proofreading Services

Pearson Education LTD.
Pearson Education Australia PTY, Limited
Pearson Education Singapore, Pte. Ltd.
Pearson Education North Asia Ltd.
Pearson Education Canada, Ltd.
Pearson Educacion de Mexico, S.A. de C.V.
Pearson Education—Japan
Pearson Education Malaysia, Pte. Ltd.
Pearson Education, Upper Saddle River, New Jersey

10 9 8 7 6 5 4 3 2 1
ISBN 0-13-027016-4

Contents

❖

Introduction   v

Acknowledgments   xi

About the Authors   xii

PART I
FOUNDATIONS FOR THE STUDY OF POLICE MISCONDUCT

Chapter 1   Ethical Police Behavior   1
Thomas Barker, Eastern Kentucky University

Chapter 2   Historical Perspectives of Police Misconduct   27
Kenneth Bolton, Jr., Southeastern Louisiana University

PART II
VARIETIES OF POLICE MISCONDUCT

Chapter 3   All Is Fair in Love and War   55
Kim Michelle Lersch, University of South Florida

Chapter 4   The Use and Abuse of Force by Police   85
Robert E. Worden and Shelagh E. Catlin, State University of New York at Albany

Chapter 5   Media Accounts of Police Sexual Violence: Rotten Apples or State-Supported Violence?   121
Danielle McGurrin, University of South Florida, and Victor E. Kappeler, Eastern Kentucky University

Chapter 6   The Looking-Glass World of Policing: The Ethics and Integrity of Women Police   143
Donna C. Hale, Shippensburg University

PART III
PREVENTION AND CONTROL OF POLICE MISCONDUCT

Chapter 7   Drug Abuse, Corruption, and Officer Drug Testing: An Overview   157
              Tom Mieczkowski, University of South Florida

Chapter 8   Community Policing and Police Corruption   193
              Joseph A. Schafer, Southern Illinois University at Carbondale

Chapter 9   Early Warning Systems as Risk Management for Police   219
              Samuel Walker, University of Nebraska at Omaha, and
              Geoffrey P. Alpert, University of South Carolina

Chapter 10   The Existence of Police Misconduct: Forever Present?   231
              M. L. Dantzker, University of Texas Pan American, and
              Kenneth Bolton, Jr. , Southeastern Louisiana University

Introduction

❖

If you asked a relatively young student of policing to describe an incident of police misconduct, you would probably get a summary of a highly publicized act of police brutality. Perhaps the student would describe the incident involving Rodney King, the African American motorist who was beaten dozens of times by a group of Los Angeles officers. Or maybe the student would describe the incident involving Abner Louima, a Haitian immigrant who was tortured with a toilet plunger while in a New York City Police Department precinct house. Others may bring up the Amadou Diallo case, in which a Guinean immigrant was shot forty-one times in the doorway of his apartment building in New York City.

For many people, the King, Louima, and Diallo incidents now define police misconduct. However, it is important to recognize that these cases, while tragic and deplorable, are also extremely rare events. On any given day, there are literally tens of thousands of police–citizen interactions. While not all of these interactions may end on a pleasant note for the citizen (I know I wasn't thrilled when I received my last speeding ticket!), many do. Acts of serious police misconduct, and especially violent police misconduct, are the exception and not the rule. While the dark side of policing is intriguing to many, it is important to keep the level of police misconduct in perspective.

When I introduce myself to a new class of undergraduates or to any group of people who may have a rather limited understanding of police practices, I never tell them that my primary area of research interest is police misconduct. Instead, I describe myself as someone interested in police behavior. It is amazing how much baggage immediately gets assigned to someone studying police misconduct. "You must hate the police." "Oh great, now I've got to sit through sixteen weeks of cop bashing." "She must really have an ax to grind." However, none of these stereotypes are accurate. I have a great deal of respect for the police, as do others who study the phenomenon of police deviance. My husband was a police officer for twenty years, as was his father before him. The vast majority of people who go into police work are honorable, decent men and women who deserve our respect. However, the everyday actions of these officers are not the ones that grab headlines.

When an almost unbelievable incident of police misconduct occurs and receives worldwide publicity, a number of things happen. Public attention turns to the behavior of the police in general, not just the officers involved in the particular incident. Police officers working in agencies thousands of miles away from the location of the publicized incident feel the effects. Citizens question the actions of all officers. The levels of fear and mistrust grow. At a time when more and more agencies are turning to community policing as their primary philosophy, incidents like the tragedy involving Abner Louima can undo months and even years of community relations progress, especially among minority citizens.

Therefore, it is under the following assumptions that I introduce this volume. First, incidents of police misconduct are very real but very rare events. Second, most officers are not involved in serious forms of misconduct. Third, when serious incidents do occur, the effects are detrimental not only to the individual officers and the agency involved in the case, but to all police officers. If we can better understand the phenomenon of police misconduct, we can then develop plans to prevent acts of future misconduct. If police misconduct can be controlled, then perhaps the jobs of police officers can be a bit easier to perform. Studying police misconduct ultimately helps policing and is not undertaken to somehow taint or draw attention to the worst that policing has to offer.

There is one last assumption: In spite of our best efforts, we will never be able to completely eliminate acts of police misconduct. Emile Durkheim is often credited with being the father of the discipline of sociology. Writing in the late 1800s, Durkheim made the rather astounding claim that it was impossible to have a society that did not have crime. He argued that even among a society of saints, someone would do something that would eventually be defined as deviant (for a discussion of Durkheim's contributions, see Vold et al., 1998). For Durkheim, crime was necessary and served a function for the health of the society as a whole. While most people in any given society are not criminals, it is normal to have a small group of people who do violate the rules. A society of police officers, like a society of saints, will always have a few individuals who engage in rule violation. It is when rule violation becomes the norm as opposed to the exception that problems occur. I believe our ultimate goal, in the language of Durkheim, is to try to maintain a normal level of police misconduct as opposed to one that is pathological.

WHAT IS POLICE MISCONDUCT?

One of the things that I have found really fascinating about police misconduct is our lack of basic knowledge in this area. What is police misconduct? How a person answers this question will vary based on the person's age, race, gender, social class, place of residence, and prior experiences with the police. For example, some research suggests that racial differences exist in the definition of what sort of behaviors constitute police misconduct, especially with respect to the use of force. In a poll conducted by *Time* magazine in the wake of the Rodney King incident, while 92 percent of the African Americans surveyed felt that excessive force had been used against King, only 72 percent of the Caucasians voiced a similar belief (Lacayo, 1992). As phrased by Flanagan and Vaughn (1995:125), "White residents in the suburbs have a different idea of police use of force than inner city African Americans." The use of racial slurs, profane or abusive language, and other forms of verbal abuse have also been defined as "police brutality" by many citizens, especially among minority citizens (Adams, 1995; Locke, 1995; President's Commission on Law Enforcement and Administration of Justice, 1967; Worden, 1995).

While it is difficult to provide a clear, unambiguous definition of excessive force, things get even muddier when you try to develop a definition of nonviolent acts of misconduct. When does aggressive, proactive policing become harassment? When does a professional, somewhat terse demeanor become rude? While studies of deadly force are relatively plentiful, very few studies have been conducted that focus on police–citizen interactions in which no criminal offense was committed, no arrest was made, and no acts of violence were recorded (Browning et al., 1994). Again, part of the problem is the lack of a clear operationalization of what, exactly, police misconduct is. One citizen may perceive an officer's actions as totally acceptable, while another may view the same behaviors as threatening and obnoxious.

As an example, in a previous research study, I analyzed the citizen allegations of misconduct that had been filed with the internal affairs office in a large police agency (Lersch, 1998). Complaints of nonviolent harassment were the most common type of allegation, accounting for almost half of the citizen complaints (49.7 percent). In one of the complaints included in this category, a citizen had alleged that, during the course of a routine traffic stop, an officer had rested his hand on his service revolver. The citizen filing the complaint of misconduct felt that this action was extremely intimidating and involved an unnecessary display of force. There was no indication that the officer had spoken in a threatening manner, nor had he been disrespectful to the citizen in any way. However, this behavior resulted in an official report of police misconduct against the officer, for which he received counseling. While in this case the particular citizen was very upset by the behavior of the officer, another citizen may not have even noticed the resting hand on the revolver.

What Is the Level of Police Misconduct? The Counting of the Undefined

How common is police misconduct? We really do not know. The lack of a clear operationalization of the term *police misconduct* clouds the interpretation of empirical studies of the phenomenon. No one knows exactly how many incidents of police misconduct occur. This issue is further complicated when researchers attempt to use various research methodologies to count incidents of police misconduct. A number of indicators, including observational studies, analyses of citizen complaints, citizen surveys, and official records, have been used.

While the use of multiple indicators is an advancement, each data source has its own unique measurement problems. Observers may differ on the definition of what behaviors constitute violent police conduct, citizens may file frivolous complaints, and survey results may be affected by recent highly publicized events. The use of offical records (such as use of force reports) poses validity concerns as well. The problems with this particular measurement technique are roughly analogous to critiques associated with the use of the Federal Bureau of Investigation's *Uniform Crime Reports* as a measure of the crime problem in the United States. Just as citizens may not call the police to report a crime, officers may not report each use-of-force incident.

PURPOSE OF THIS VOLUME

Recognizing the importance of the topic as well as our need to advance our knowledge in this area, I present this collection of essays on police misconduct. Contributors were carefully selected because of their unique perspective. The purpose of the volume is to provide the reader with information and theoretical orientations that are different from what might be presented in other forums. I do hope that you enjoy the contributions as much as I have.

This volume is divided into three parts: "Foundations for the Study of Police Misconduct," "Varieties of Police Misconduct," and the "Prevention and Control of Police Misconduct." In Chapter 1, Thomas Barker provides a historically grounded overview of the variety of forms of police misconduct. Police misconduct is not limited to incidents of excessive force. Unethical behavior can take many forms, and in some cases, such as accepting gratuities, there is some debate whether or not the behavior is in fact wrong. Barker provides descriptions of organizational/rule violations such as sexual misconduct, corruption, and abuses of authority as well as a variety of methods that have been employed for the control of police misconduct.

In Chapter 2, Kenneth Bolton, Jr. provides a critically oriented history of the growth, development, and changing role of the police in the United States. It is important to recognize that police misconduct is not a new phenomenon, nor can one address the problem of police misconduct without first taking its history into account. As Bolton illustrates, the history behind the misdeeds of police officers not only affects the causes of police misconduct but has implications for the success for various control mechanisms.

Part II provides the reader with materials that describe a diverse range of acts of police deviance with special emphasis on areas that have not received a great deal of attention by researchers over the years. In Chapter 3, I explore the issue of drug-related police corruption. While the number of incidents involving traditional forms of corruption such as bribery and kickbacks has declined over the years, drug-related police corruption is on the rise. Many scholars have attributed this increase to the "no holds barred" mentality associated with waging a war against crime and drugs. The War on Drugs has had great implications not only for how we as a society define drugs and drug dealers but for how far we are willing to tolerate (and, in some cases encourage) questionable practices by the police in their fight to win the war.

In Chapter 4, Robert E. Worden and Shelagh E. Catlin provide an excellent overview of the state of our knowledge concerning the use and abuse of force by the police. Incidents of excessive force are the most highly publicized and potentially the most serious form of police misconduct. Worden and Catlin begin their contribution with an overview of a few recent examples of excessive force: Rodney King, Malice Green, Abner Louima, and Amadou Diallo. For many citizens, these incidents define the pattern of police abuse of force: white officers targeting racial minorities for physical abuse. However, Worden and Catlin go beyond the anecdotal evidence and explore the theoretical and empirical literature to present what is known about police use of force.

In Chapter 5, Danielle McGurrin and Victor E. Kappeler discuss the phenomenon of police sexual violence. This form of police misconduct, while obviously very serious, has not received a great deal of attention from researchers. Using media accounts of police sexual deviance as a database, the authors present the types of sexual offenses committed by police officers, characteristics of the incident such as officer and victim demographics, location of the incident, and institutional response. McGurrin and Kappeler then explore the linkages between the phenomenon of police sexual violence and state power against women.

Donna C. Hale explores the issue of police misconduct and female officers in Chapter 6. Traditionally, women entering police work have been viewed as outsiders working in a male-dominated profession. Because women are marginalized, their socialization within the subculture of policing is different from their male peers. Hale provides an overview of the literature concerning female police officers, with special attention paid to the divergent role and policing styles of male and female officers.

In Part III, issues related to the prevention and control of police misconduct are discussed. In Chapter 7, Tom Mieczkowski presents an overview of drug-related issues, such as officer drug abuse, drug-related corruption, and drug testing for employees. For a variety of reasons, academicians and practitioners have largely ignored the level of drug use by current and prospective police officers. Mieczkowski adds to our knowledge in this area by providing data from a variety of sources regarding drug use by employees. The reader is also presented with a discussion of various legal issues surrounding drug testing for applicants and current employees. While urine testing is the more common screening method used by police agencies to detect drug use by applicants, Mieczkowski describes the relative strengths and weaknesses of this test relative to hair testing and other drug detection techniques. The chapter ends with a presentation of drug screening data for police applicants obtained from a large agency. The results may surprise you.

In Chapter 8, the implications of community policing on incidents of police misconduct are explored. Community policing is a very popular strategy, employed by many agencies in a variety of forms. While community policing has been hailed as the future of policing in the United States, this technique provides special concerns for the identification and control of incidents of police misconduct. Joseph A. Schafer begins the chapter with a historical overview of the growth and development of community policing. It has been argued that community policing may increase the probability of police misconduct. Schafer explores this debate and provides suggestions for the management of police officers in a community policing context.

In Chapter 9, Samuel Walker and Geoffrey P. Alpert explore the use of Early Warning systems as a risk management tool for police agencies. The basic assumption behind Early Warning systems is that a small pocket of officers account for a disproportionate number of problems. If this small group of officers could be systematically identified and controlled, intervention strategies could be developed and implemented before serious problems occur. Walker and Alpert provide an overview of the history of the development of Early Warning systems, as well as practical issues related to their implementation and use.

Finally, in Chapter 10, series editor M. L. Dantzker and Kenneth Bolton, Jr., synthesize the contributions of the authors and discuss the proposed solutions to police misconduct. Some of the most frequently proposed solutions include aggressive minority recruitment, the use of community relations units, better psychological screening of applicants, and the use of police review boards. Other reforms involve greater internal accountability and legal remedies. Dantzker and Bolton discuss the relative success and failures of these reforms, citing the influence of broader historical and societal influences on the attempts to control police misconduct.

Taken together, I hope that you, the reader, will find that these chapters have met their goal: to add to the body of knowledge on police misconduct in a reader-friendly format.

REFERENCES

ADAMS, K. (1995). Measuring the prevalence of police abuse of force. In Geller, W. A., & Toch, H., eds. *And Justice for All: Understanding and Controlling Police Abuse of Force* (pp. 61–98). Washington, D.C.: Police Executive Research Forum.

BROWNING, S. L., CULLEN, F. T., CAO, L., KAPACHE, R. & STEVENSON, T. J. (1994). Race and getting hassled by the police: A research note. *Police Studies* 17 (1): 1–12.

FLANAGAN, T. J., & VAUGHN, M. S. (1995). Public opinion about police abuse of force. In Geller, W. A., & Toch, H., eds. *And Justice for All: Understanding and Controlling Police Abuse of Force* (pp. 113–32). Washington, D.C.: Police Executive Research Forum.

LACAYO, R. (1992, May). Anatomy of an acquittal. *Time* 30–2.

LERSCH, K. M. (1998). Predicting citizen race in allegations of misconduct against the police. *Journal of Criminal Justice* 26 (2): 87–97.

LOCKE, H. G. (1995). The color of law and the issue of color: Race and the abuse of police power. In Geller, W. A., & Toch, H., eds. *And Justice for All: Understanding and Controlling Police Abuse of Force* (pp. 133–50). Washington, D.C.: Police Executive Research Forum.

PRESIDENT'S COMMISSION ON LAW ENFORCEMENT AND ADMINISTRATION OF JUSTICE. (1967). *A National Survey of Police–Community Relations: Field Surveys V*. Washington, D.C.: U.S. Government Printing Office.

VOLD, G. B., BERNARD, T. J, & SNIPES, J. B. (1998). *Theoretical Criminology*. 4th ed. New York: Oxford University Press.

WORDEN, R. E. (1995). The "causes" of police brutality: Theory and evidence on police use of force. In Geller, W. A., & Toch, H., eds. *And Justice for All: Understanding and Controlling Police Abuse of Force* (pp. 31–60). Washington, D.C.: Police Executive Research Forum.

Acknowledgments

—————————————————— ❖ ——————————————————

Many people contributed to this volume, both directly and indirectly. First and foremost, I thank the contributors. Without their efforts, this volume could not have become a reality. I truly appreciate their willingness to contribute to the collection.

M. L. Dantzker, series editor, and Kim Davies of Prentice Hall deserve my undying gratitude for their support and patience throughout the planning and preparation of this volume. They took a chance in awarding a contract to a relatively inexperienced assistant professor and, as a thanks, were forced to wade through a seemingly endless barrage of questions and e-mail messages throughout the project. Thank you for all your assistance.

Beyond the direct contributions, a number of people should also be acknowledged. As a first-generation college student, sometimes I still feel very intimidated by my colleagues. I am often revisited by the nightmare where the "Ph.D. Police" enter my office, discover my fraudulent representation as a faculty member, and snatch my sheepskin off the wall. Despite my perceived shortcomings, a number of individuals, through their kindness and support, have had a great influence on my professional career path. Tom Mieczkowski, who was an undergraduate instructor of mine, continues to be a positive influence on my career. My dissertation chair, Joe Feagin, took a chance on working with a rather bumbling student who was high on interest but low on academic sophistication. I also had the honor of being encouraged early on by Ron Akers, who truly is one of the nicest people I have ever met. Sam Walker and Geoff Alpert have always provided a kind word and patient advice when I have asked for it, and I am sure that it meant more than they realized. My colleagues at the University of South Florida have always been and continue to be a source of motivation and encouragement. Thanks to all.

A thank you also goes out to my parents, who sacrificed early on to ensure that I received a quality education. Finally, I thank my husband, John "Buzz" Lersch III, for all of his patience and support. Without his encouragement and belief in my abilities, I'd still be making pizzas on Fourth Street.

This work is dedicated to the memory of my mother, Eva Germain, and my in-laws, John P. Lersch, Jr., and Francis Jane Lersch. You were all so proud when I received my degree. I wish you could have lived to see this day.

About the Authors

❖

Geoffrey P. Alpert.   Dr. Alpert is Professor of Criminal Justice and Director of Research for the College of Criminal Justice at the University of South Carolina. For the past twenty years, Dr. Alpert has concentrated his research and training on the evaluation of high-risk police activities, including the use of force, deadly force, pursuit driving, and accountability systems including Early Warning systems. Dr. Alpert is currently working on a two-year study concerning police use of force to control suspects, funded by the National Institute of Justice. He has authored numerous books and monographs including *The Force Factor: Measuring Police Use of Force Relative to Suspect Resistance* (with R. Dunham), *Police Vehicles and Firearms: Instruments of Deadly Force* (with L. Fridell), and *Police Pursuit Driving: Controlling Responses to Emergency Situations* (with D. Kenney, R. Dunham, and W. Smith). Dr. Alpert has also written more than 100 articles on topics including the use of force, pursuit driving, and accountability systems.

Thomas Barker.   Dr. Thomas Barker is a Professor in the Department of Police Studies at the College of Justice and Safety at Eastern Kentucky University. Dr. Barker is a former police officer in Birmingham and has held various academic appointments, including Dean of the College of Criminal Justice at Jacksonville State University—Jacksonville. He has written extensively in the areas of police misconduct and corruption as well as serving as an advisor to various law enforcement agencies on matters relating to police deviance. In addition, Dr. Barker has done extensive work related to police pursuits and police policy issues.

Kenneth Bolton, Jr.   Dr. Kenneth Bolton, Jr., is Assistant Professor in the Department of Sociology and Criminal Justice at Southeastern Louisiana University. He holds a doctorate from the University of Florida. He is from Philippi, West Virginia.

Shelagh E. Catlin.   Shelagh E. Catlin is a doctoral student in criminal justice at the State University of New York at Albany. A former member of the Brunswick, Maine, Police Department, her research interests include complaint review processes, law and social control, environmental law, and police behavior. As a research assistant for the Hindelang Criminal Justice Center, she is currently working on the ADAM (Arrestee Drug Abuse Monitoring) Program.

Donna C. Hale. Dr. Donna C. Hale is Professor of Criminal Justice at Shippensburg University of Pennsylvania. She is Past President of the Academy of Criminal Justice Sciences (1997), and Editor of *Women & Criminal Justice*. Dr. Hale is the author/co-author of numerous articles on women in policing. She received the Academy of Criminal Justice Sciences Minorities and Women's Section Excellence Award in 2000 and the Academy of Criminal Justice Sciences Founder's Award in 1999; Professor Hale was a recipient of the "Breaking the Glass Ceiling" Award in 2000 from the National Center for Women and Policing. Dr. Hale is the author with Frankie Y. Bailey (State University of New York at Albany) of *Blood on Her Hands: The Social Construction of the Woman Murderer*, West/Wadsworth Publishing Co. (2000).

Victor E. Kappeler. Victor Kappeler is Professor in the Department of Police Studies at the College of Justice and Safety at Eastern Kentucky University. He is the author of numerous works on the topic of police deviance.

Kim Michelle Lersch. Dr. Kim Michelle Lersch is an Associate Professor in the Department of Criminology at the University of South Florida. Her research interests include police misconduct and race relations. Recent publications have appeared in *Policing: An International Journal of Police Strategies & Management, American Journal of Criminal Justice*, and the *Journal of Criminal Justice*.

Danielle McGurrin. Danielle McGurrin received a master's degree in criminal justice at Eastern Kentucky University in 1998 and is currently pursuing a doctorate in criminology at the University of South Florida. Her research interests include the intersections of race, class, gender, and sexuality, corporate and state crime, environmental crime, and activist scholarship.

Tom Mieczkowski. Dr. Tom Mieczkowski is Professor of Criminology at the University of South Florida. His research interests have included drug smuggling, theories of syndicated crime organizations, drug distribution organizations and methods, drug epidemiology, the validation of various drug detection technologies with an emphasis on ion mobility spectrometry and radioimmunoassay of hair, and the estimation of drug prevalence and incidence using bioassays and survey methods. Dr. Mieczkowski has published numerous scholarly articles, book chapters, and two books.

Joseph A. Schafer. Dr. Joseph A. Schafer is an Assistant Professor with the Center for the Study of Crime, Delinquency, and Corrections, Southern Illinois University at Carbondale. He holds degrees from the University of Northern Iowa (bachelor's in criminology) and Michigan State University (master's and doctorate in criminal justice). Dr. Schafer is currently conducting research in the areas of police behavior, police organizations, criminal justice management, citizen perceptions of the police, fear of crime/victimization, and extremist organizations. His research has appeared in *Justice System Journal, Journal of Criminal Justice,* and *Police Quarterly*; he has written several book chapters and is the author of *Community Policing: The Challenges of Successful Organizational Change* (2001, LFB Scholarly Publishing).

Samuel Walker.   Dr. Samuel Walker is Isaacson Professor of Criminal Justice at the University of Nebraska at Omaha. He is the author of eleven books on policing, criminal justice policy, and civil liberties. His most recent book is *Police Accountability: The Role of Citizen Oversight* (2001, published by Wadsworth). With Professors Geoffrey Alpert and Dennis Kenney, he completed a national evaluation of Early Warning systems. He recently completed a national study of mediating citizen complaints against police officers.

Robert E. Worden.   Dr. Robert E. Worden is an Associate Professor of criminal justice and public policy at the State University of New York at Albany. He holds a doctorate in political science from the University of North Carolina at Chapel Hill. Worden's research interests revolve around the accountability and responsiveness of public agencies—and particularly the police—to the public. Thus, his work includes basic research on the forces that influence the behavior of police officers and evaluative research on the implementation and outcomes of police strategies, policies, and operations. His previous research has appeared in *Law & Society Review, Criminology, Justice Quarterly*, and in other journals and edited volumes, and he is the co-author (with Timothy S. Bynum) of *Police Drug Crackdowns: An Evaluation of Implementation and Effects*, Michigan State University, 1996.

1

Ethical Police Behavior

Thomas Barker

❖

INTRODUCTION

Ethical police behavior has been a topic of discussion throughout the history of policing. In the late 1700s, the English began to examine two questions that would determine the evolution of modern-day policing in Great Britain and the United States: (1) Should the guardians of that time (watchman and police) be private or public employees? (2) Should they be amateurs (volunteers) or professionals (paid)? These considerations led to The Middlesex Justice Act of 1792 and the appointment of twenty-two Justices and the swearing in of forty-two constables—Bow Street System (Lee, 1971: 173). They became the first organized and paid police force established in England.

In addition to publicly paid watchmen in many English parishes (Reynolds, 1998), at the end of the eighteenth century, five distinct classes of peace officers existed in England: (1) elected parochial constables serving without pay; (2) parochial constables' substitutes or deputies paid by the constables; (3) salaried Bow Street officers and patrols; (4) stipendiary (paid by fees) police constables attached to public offices established under "The Middlesex Justices Act"; and (5) stipendiary water-police attached to the Thames Office—Thames River police (Lee, 1971: 176). The first two classes of peace officers were common throughout England. Publicly paid watchmen and the other three classes of peace officers were unique to London and the surrounding metropolitan area.

The behavioral standards for these watchmen and police were under constant consideration and scrutiny almost immediately. Minimum qualifications and background checks for watchmen were in place in many English parishes (Reynolds, 1998: 65). Complaint procedures and review systems were also in place in some watch systems. In fact, citizens were encouraged to register complaints against the early watchmen and police. Early records reveal that the watchmen and police were punished and disciplined for a variety of offenses including sleeping on duty, consorting with prostitutes, and drinking in pubs while on duty (Reynolds, 1998: 54). Some were even disciplined for not preventing crime. Corruption scandals involving bribe taking and extortion also occurred in these early police forces (Reynolds, 1998: 125). Nevertheless, professional (paid) policing became the norm in London by the 1820s (Reynolds, 1998: 5)

The New Occupation

In 1829 with the Metropolitan London Police Act, the publicly paid watchmen, voluntary watches, and paid police in the London area were centralized under the national government and became members of a new occupation that would spread throughout England and Wales and reach the shores of the colonies that were to become America. It was immediately recognized that the new police should be held to a higher standard of integrity than the average citizen. However, the original London Metropolitan Police were not of high moral caliber. Many were often accused of being drunk on duty and associating in public houses with prostitutes and suspicious characters. In the first two years, more than 3,200 constables had left the new police; more than two thirds of them were dismissed for drunkenness (Ascoli, 1979: 89). There is evidence that some metropolitan police officers accepted payoffs from illegal gambling dens and brothels (Miller, 1997: 28–29; Reynolds, 1998: 153).

The new model of policing was a morally dangerous occupation. This became painfully clear when the new model of policing was transported to America, where local control of police agencies was constitutionally mandated (Lane, 1971; Miller, 1997). The early American experience demonstrated that the police can become not only corrupt but the instruments and servants of local politicians. Community control run amok is an apt description of the American police at that time (Walker, 1977). The early American police became a greater threat to a free society than corrupt police officers and led to a series of reform attempts that continues today (Fogelson, 1977).

Blessing or Curse

The early framers of what were to become the modern-day police organizations also knew that a professional (paid) public police agency could become a blessing or a curse in a democracy (Lee, 1971: xxxi). That is, they could be the defenders of liberty or the oppressors of a free people. The early framers recognized the possibility of noble cause injustice (discussed below). Prevention of crime (noble end) by oppressive and undemocratic means could become more intolerable than the effects of crime. Whatever justice is applied in a free society begins with the first decision makers—the police. Lee stated that the ideal police force is one that grants the maximum protection with the minimum interference in the lives of the people (Lee, 1971: xxx):

> Government cannot be exercised without coercion, but the coercion employed ought to be reduced to the lowest possible limit consistent with safety, the ideal police force being the one which affords the maximum of protection at the cost of a minimum of interference with the lawful liberty of the subject.

The constitutional and legal restraints on American police officers exist to limit the coercive intrusions of the police into the personal lives of American citizens. The Common Law, courts decisions, and acts of Parliament exist to limit the coercive intrusions of police into the personal lives of British citizens (Robilliard & McEwan, 1986). However, the modern-day police forces in Great Britain and the United States are expanding their coercive "interference" into the lives of their citizens under the evangelistic rhetoric of community policing. Ultimately, the complex questions involved in police discretionary decisions, particularly extralegal practices, as they deal with "quality-of-life" crimes/problems of disorder will be decided in the courts of both countries (Livingstone, 1997). Brogden (1999: 181) states that "community policing is only possible when the constitutional rights of citizens are vague rather than distinct, and especially where the police mandate is permissive rather than restrictive—conditions that do not exist in Great Britain or the United States. Whether or not this "expansion of coercive interference" will be a revolutionary new police reform or another politically motivated police management fad that passes into history remains to be seen.

The American police as individuals, groups, and organizations have been both a blessing and a curse. Admittedly, the list of blessings is voluminous. However, the litany of horrors and abuse in the 1990s include Rodney King, Malice Green, Abner Louima, Amadou Diallo, Michael Dowd, Waco, Ruby Ridge, Mark Furhman, Antoinette Frank, and Len Davis. One hears terms associated with the police like racial profiling, positional asphyxia deaths, choke-holds, whoops raids, hog tying, stun belts, pepper spray, and "testilying." In the 1990s, corruption scandals occurred in New York City, Philadelphia, Chicago, Cleveland, Los Angeles, New Orleans, Miami, Detroit, and Atlanta. Police officers have been convicted of murder, rape, robbery, drug dealing, and auto theft. Cases and convictions have been dismissed in Los Angeles, New York, Philadelphia, and Chicago because officers planted evidence or lied in reports, warrants, and in court. The unethical behavior receives more attention and is easier to measure than the good, or ethical behavior, or at least that is the way it appears from examining the media and the literature, particularly the scholarly literature. This is inevitable because of the basic nature of policing.

The ethical behavior of police officers in any democracy (Great Britain, the United States, or any free state) is central to police work because of the basic nature of policing. Policing is forceful, or potentially forceful, social control; it has been and always will be. The use of force, or potential use of force, has been used by every community in history as a means to secure the effective observance of laws (Reith, 1952). Given the inherent coercive nature of police work, a commitment to ethical conduct is a prerequisite to policing a free society. Ethical police conduct is ultimately what protects the citizens of a free society from the police.

PROFESSIONAL/OCCUPATIONAL ETHICS

Morality refers to the standards of behavior that should be followed by everyone. *Ethics* is concerned with how individuals should conduct themselves (Heffernan, 1996: 25). Dan Carlson, Associate Director of the Southwestern Law Enforcement Institute, states that one way of defining ethics is "Doing the right thing, when nobody will know if you do the wrong thing" (*http://web2airmail.net/slf/summer95/tick.html*). *Professional/occupational ethics* deals with behavior that all members of a professional/occupational group should adhere to because they are members of the group (Davis, 1997: 37). This is practical ethics, concerned with how members of the affected group solve practical problems (Kamm, 1997: 123).

Professional/occupational ethical standards are contained in the codes of ethics adopted by the occupational group. Codes of Ethics are put forward as public evidence of a "determination, on the part of the providers themselves, to serve in ways that are predictable and acceptable" (Kleinig, 1996: 242). Codes are no substitute for good character and wisdom; however, they can serve as a general guideline for the groups' behavior (Delattre, 1989: 32). The ethical principles are in effect the occupation's recognition of guidelines for action.

A Code of Ethics was embedded in the standards for the London Metropolitan Police in 1829. However, it was not until 1928 that a Code of Ethics was developed for the U.S. police (Kleinig, 1996: 235). The current version follows:

Law Enforcement Code of Ethics

As a law enforcement officer, my fundamental duty is to serve the community; to safeguard lives and property; to protect the innocent against deception, the weak against oppression or intimidation and the peaceful against violence or disorder; and to respect the constitutional rights of all to liberty, equality, and justice.

I will keep my private life unsullied as an example to all and will behave in a manner that does not bring discredit to me or to my agency. I will maintain courageous calm in the face of danger, scorn or ridicule; develop self-restraint; and be constantly mindful of the welfare of others. Honest in thought and deed both in my personal and official life, I will be exemplary in obeying the law and the regulations of my department. Whatever I hear of a confidential nature or that is confided to me in my official capacity will be kept ever secret unless revelation is necessary in the performance of my duty.

I will never act officiously or permit personal feelings, prejudices, political beliefs, aspirations, animosities or friendships to influence my decisions. With no compromise for crime and with relentless prosecution of criminals, I will enforce the law courteously and appropriately without fear or favor, malice or ill will, never employing unnecessary force or violence and never accepting gratuities.

I recognize the badge of my office as a symbol of public faith, and I accept it as a public trust to be held so long as I am true to the ethics of police service. I will never engage in acts of corruption or bribery, nor will I condone such acts by other police officers. I will cooperate with all legally authorized agencies and their representatives in the pursuit of justice.

I know that I alone am responsible for my own standard of professional performance and will take every reasonable opportunity to enhance and improve my level of knowledge and competence.

I will constantly strive to achieve these objectives and ideals, dedicating myself before God to my chosen profession . . . law enforcement.

The International Association of Chiefs of Police

Source: www.theiacp.org/pubinfo/Pubs/CodofEthic.htm (accessed March 1, 2000)

In addition, the International Association of Chiefs of Police (IACP) is considering a Law Enforcement Oath of Honor to be sworn to by all police officers.

Law Enforcement Oath of Honor

On my honor, I will never betray my badge, my integrity, my character, or the public trust. I will always have the courage to hold myself and others accountable for our actions. I will always uphold the constitution and community I serve.

Source: www.theiacp.org/pubinfo/Pubs/ethicTrain.htm (accessed March 1, 2000).

The Oath of Honor was recommended by the Ethics Training Subcommittee of the IACP Ad Hoc Committee on Police Image and Ethics.

There is also a Statement of Ethical Principles for police officers in England, Wales, and Northern Ireland (Haggard, 1994: 2–3):

Statement of Ethical Principles
(England, Wales, and Northern Ireland)

I will act with fairness, carrying out responsibilities with integrity and impartiality;

Perform duties with diligence and the proper use of discretion;

In dealings with all individuals, both outside and inside the police service, display self control, tolerance, understanding and courtesy appropriate to the circumstances;

Uphold fundamental human rights, treating every person as an individual and display respect and compassion towards them;

Support all colleagues in the performance of their lawful duties and in doing so, actively oppose and draw attention to any malpractice by any person;

Respect the fact that much of the information I receive is confidential and may only be divulged when my duty requires me to do so;

Exercise force when justified and use only the minimum amount of force to affect my lawful purpose and restore the peace;

Use resources entrusted to me to the maximum benefit of the public;

Act only within the law, in the understanding that I have no authority to depart from due legal process and that no one may place a requirement on me to do so;

Continually accept responsibility for self-development, continually seeking to improve the way in which I serve the community;

Accept personal accountability for my own acts and omissions.

The interest in codes of ethics governing police behavior is growing worldwide. The second principle of democratic policing drafted for the United Nations Police Task Force in Sarajevo-Herzegovina stated that the police as recipients of public trust should be governed by a code of professional conduct (Travis, 1998: 3). Furthermore, this code should reflect the highest ethical values that could provide the basis for identifying acts of misconduct. On June 10 and 11, 1996, the Council of Europe, a thirty-nine–member organization, met in Strasbourg, France. The topics of their meeting were police ethics and developing a code of conduct for European police officers (McDonald et al., 1997: 81).

The ethical violations that transgress these established and proposed codes of ethics can be categorized as organizational/rule violations, money corruption, and abuse of authority.

ORGANIZATIONAL/RULE VIOLATIONS

Technically speaking, all ethical violations involve a violation of an organizational rule or established police standard. However, money corruption and abuse of authority will be discussed separately because they are serious breaches of established police standards, laws, and often constitutional guarantees. They are usually acted on externally—*external reaction*. The penalty for these acts (money corruption and abuse of authority) can be either criminal or civil or both in some cases. Most, but not all (see the following section entitled "Sexual Misconduct"), of the ethical violations included under the category of organizational/rule violations involve departmental discipline or termination—*internal reaction*. The most common organizational/rule violations that involve ethical issues are drinking on duty, use of drugs, accepting gratuities, and sexual misconduct.

Gratuities

One can argue that accepting gratuities should be included in money corruption or considered as a nonthreatening fringe benefit. One could also view it as an ethicist would define immoral acts: "immoral acts negatively affect the welfare of the person who commits the acts, either because they diminish moral character or because they form a 'slippery slope' that leads to even worse actions" (Welfel, 1997: 135). Furthermore, if any services (more protection, faster response, etc.) are provided in return, it "takes time and unjustly deprives other members of the public of the attention they deserve" (Delattre, 1989: 10).

Kania (1988) argues that accepting gratuities does not lead officers into corrupt acts. That may be the case for most officers. However, many officers have been "sucked" into the corruption habit through "freebees." What became known as the Dowd Test, after New York City Police Officer Michael Dowd (convicted of drug trafficking), involved getting officers to accept small gratuities and then move them into more serious acts (*http://web2. airmail.net/slf/spring94/dowd.html*). Kania says that the Dowd Test was successful "because the rules [departmental] define otherwise normally motivated behavior as corrupt. It is normal behavior to accept minor gifts from people who wish to maintain good social relations with us" (*http://web2.airmail.net/slf/winter94/test.html*). Kania ignores that many of those "normal" people wishing to maintain good relations with police officers have a great deal to gain by good relations with cops. One must also wonder how, and who, will define "minor" gifts.

Michael Josephenson of the Josephenson Institute for Ethics (*http://web2. airmail.net/slf/spring94/dowd.html*) poses two questions for officers concerning gratuities: (1) Why take it? and (2) If you were not a police officer, would that person still be offering you that freebie? Furthermore, one must consider the impropriety of uniformed police officers accepting free and discounted meals and other services. Citizens observing this behavior do not join in philosophical debates. To them, the officers are freeloaders. At least, that is what numerous citizens have told this author.

All gifts to the 1829 London Metropolitan Police had to be reported and approved (Reynolds, 1998: 153). However, gratuities, still forbidden, are also common among the British police, where some shops are known to be "GTP" (good to the police) (Holdaway, 1984: 43).

Delattre (1989) states that the prevailing view, myself included, is that all gratuities should be prohibited by police. There is always the danger of creating an environment of tolerance. The IACP's *Model Policy: Standards of Conduct* ("Section 8: Abuse of Law Enforcement Powers or Position") states:

> a. Officers shall report any unsolicited gifts, gratuities, or other items of value that they are offered and shall provide a full report of the circumstances of their receipt. (IACP, 1997)

Such mandatory reporting practices would make public the offering and accepting of gratuities and provide a check on any abuse of power or position by the police officer. It would serve as a chilling effect on any person, business, or group who had an ulterior motive in the offer. It would also provide protection for the officer against any allegations of misuse of authority. Now we turn to more serious organizational/rule violations that involve no debate.

Sexual Misconduct

Police sexual misconduct while on duty has occurred since the creation of the London Metropolitan Police and before them in the Watch and Ward. Some acts have been police initiated, others citizen initiated. Sapp (1994) identified seven categories of sexually motivated or sexual harassment behaviors by police officers:

Sapp's Categories of Police Sexual Misconduct

1. Non-sexual contacts that are sexually motivated. A category of sexual harassment. Example—non-valid traffic stops to check out the female driver.
2. Voyeuristic contacts. Example—seeking out sexual activities in "lovers lane."
3. Contacts with crime victims. Sexual harassment of crime victims. Example—unnecessary callbacks to crime victims.
4. Contacts with offenders. Examples—sexual demands on offenders, or inappropriate body searches, frisks, and pat downs.
5. Contacts with juvenile offenders. Sexual harassment and sexual contact.
6. Sexual shakedowns. Demanding sexual services from prostitutes, homosexuals or other citizens involved in illicit or illegal activities.
7. Citizen-initiated sexual contacts.

Some of the behaviors that Sapp cited may involve criminal violations. Those identified by Kraska and Kappeler (1995) definitely are crimes. In their study of 124 cases of police sexual violence, Kraska and Kappeler found 37 cases of sexual assault and rape committed by on-duty police officers against female citizens.

Money Corruption

Money corruption is defined as any proscribed (law, rule, regulation, ethical standards) act involving the misuse of the officer's official position for money or money's worth. Three elements distinguish money corruption: (1) The behavior must be forbidden. (2) The behavior must involve the misuse of the officer's official position. (3) The reward, or expected reward, must be money or money's worth (T. Barker & Roebuck, 1973). Corruption began with the Watch and Ward and regulation over morals. From the earliest times of policing, there have been incidents of police corruption and efforts at reform, primarily efforts to professionalize (see Reynolds, 1998).

I (T. Barker, 1977) have previously identified the following types of police money corruption:

Barker's Typology

Kickbacks—money, goods and services from "legitimate" businesses that service the clients of the police (examples include—garages, lawyers, bondsmen, service stations, etc.)

Opportunistic Thefts—stealing money or other valuables from suspects and crime victims, crime scenes and unprotected property.

Shakedowns—extorting money or valuables from criminals or traffic offenders.

Protection of Illegal Activities—receiving money or valuables from vice operators or legitimate businesses operating illegally.

Fixes—the quashing of misdemeanor or felony cases and the disposal of traffic tickets.

Direct Criminal Activities—Police officers directly involved in crimes such as robberies, burglaries, and trafficking in drugs.

Internal Payoffs—officers prerogatives are bought, bartered or sold to each other.

Thirty years ago when I first began my research on police corruption, there were no national data sources on its nature and extent. There still are none (U.S. Government Accounting Office, 1998: 1). Nevertheless, the corruption scandals of the 1990s demonstrate that the nature of police corruption has changed.

Rotten Apples Revisited.   The traditional view of police corruption by police management in the 1960s, 1970s, and 1980s was that the acts were the result of a few "rotten apples" that slipped through the screening processes and succumbed to the temptation of the occupation. The police corruption scandals of the 1970s and 1980s provided little support for this view, as systemic corruption was found in department after department (T. Barker & Carter, 1994). However, many writers and researchers on this topic, myself included, may have gone too far in dismissing rotten apples as an explanation of some corrupt police behavior. It is now apparent that rotten apples do occur in many police departments.

A true rotten apple is a corrupt officer in a police department where systemic corruption is truly rare (T. Barker, 1996: 39). The rotten-apple argument has been confirmed in many police departments (Delattre, 1989). For example, Delattre (1989) is correct in pointing out that the River Cops involved in the drug corruption scandal in Miami, Florida, in the late 1980s were rotten apples in a department without evidence of systematic corruption. The River Cops were hired during a period of accelerated hiring and relaxed standards for employment (more on this later).

The Mollen Commission's investigation (the sixth commission to investigate corruption in New York since 1890) of drug corruption in the New York City Police Department in the early 1990s arrived at the same conclusion: The corrupt acts were the result of small groups of rotten apples and not systemic corruption within the department (Mollen Commission, 1994). I am not aware of any evidence to discredit this conclusion. However, as in Miami, management and supervisory deficiencies, including the failure to support a sergeant who reported the corrupt acts, contributed to the problem (McAlary, 1994).

The current investigation into the Los Angeles Rampart Area corruption incident appears to be the result of rotten apples and not corruption throughout the department (Los Angeles Police Department, 2000). Although numerous management and supervisory deficiencies contributed to the corrupt acts and the abuses of authority, it appears that the corruption was limited to members of a Rampart CRASH (specialized gang) unit. The unit had a "gunfighter attitude" and a siege. mentality. One could also argue that the unit's name, CRASH, is confrontational.

LAPD Board of Inquiry

After careful consideration of the information developed during the Board of Inquiry's work, it is the Board's view that the Rampart corruption incident occurred because a few individuals decided to engage in blatant misconduct and, in some cases, criminal behavior. Published assertions by former Rampart CRASH Officer Rafael Perez that the pressure to produce arrests caused him to become corrupt, simply ignores the fact that he was convicted of stealing narcotics so he could sell them and live the life style of a "high roller." Even the finest corruption prevention system will not stop an individual from committing a crime if he or she has the will to do so. However, had the Department and the Rampart management team exercised more vigorous and coordinated oversight of Area operations, and its CRASH unit in particular, the crimes and misconduct that occurred may have been prevented, discouraged, or discovered much earlier.

(Los Angeles Police Department, 2000: 311)

The recent Chicago drug corruption scandal also was confined to specialized units. The ten Chicago officers indicted were tactical unit officers whose primary function was narcotics enforcement. They were assigned to the two districts with the highest incidence of narcotics arrest (Commission on Police Integrity, 1997).

From all accounts, the 1999 charge of police corruption in the Seattle Police Department was limited to one police detective accused of stealing $10,000 from the home of a man who died in a police shoot-out (SPD Citizens Review Panel, 1999: 1). Significantly, a Seattle Homicide Detective reported the incident to a county deputy prosecutor, even though the original detective returned the money at the urging of his colleagues on the scene. The single allegation in a department with a national reputation for being corruption free led the mayor to convene a citizens panel to investigate the incident.

Relaxed Hiring Standards.   Particularly troubling about the Los Angeles Police Department's (LAPD's) Rampart investigation is that 4 of the 14 officers (12 men and 2 women) involved were hired during periods of accelerated hiring and were disqualified by the police department only to be hired by the personnel department (LAPD, 2000: 332). During the background checks, the police department learned that the 4 officers had criminal records, inability to manage personal finances, histories of violent behavior, or narcotics involvement. One had sold narcotics as a juvenile. Nevertheless, the personnel department, which has the final say on employment, overruled the police department.

During the 1989–90 hiring drive in Washington, D.C., numerous officers who were to become problem officers were hired under relaxed standards and background checks. In 1997, one hundred of the officers hired under the relaxed standards had been charged with criminal offenses ranging from shoplifting to rape and murder. One quarter of the total number had been charged with crimes involving domestic abuse (Human Rights Watch, 1998). The special committee appointed to examine the allegations of misconduct recommended that the Metropolitan Police Department be prohibited from hiring an applicant without a full background check, including a review of juvenile criminal records (*www.dcwatch. com/police/981006a.htm#introduction: 6&7*).

A most disturbing example of the consequences of hiring the wrong person occurred in New Orleans in 1995. On-duty Officer Antoinette Frank and an accomplice entered a Vietnamese restaurant, killed an off-duty police officer moonlighting as a security guard, and then executed a brother and sister who worked in the family business. She later answered the call to the restaurant as if nothing had happened. Officer Frank received the death penalty for the murders. In 1993 Officer Frank had failed the civil service psychiatric evaluation and hired her own psychiatrist, who found her fit. A second civil service psychiatrist evaluated the contradictory evaluations and declared her suitable for employment as a New Orleans police officer (Human Rights Watch, 1998).

The failure of the internal discipline system may result in identified rotten apples staying in a police department. Carter (1990) reports the case of a police officer who was confiscating drugs for his own use. To avoid bad press, the department charged the officer with a departmental rule violation instead of a crime. The department hoped to fire the officer. The officer's due process rights were violated during the process, and a labor arbitrator put the officer back to work with most of his back pay. This same officer was later promoted to sergeant. It is not uncommon for arbitrators or civil service commissions to overturn departmental disciplinary decisions (Coulson, 1993).

Change in Nature.   The nature of money corruption has apparently changed over the last fifteen to twenty years, partly as the result of changes in departmental control systems. Hugo Masini, former chief and the first director of the Institute for Criminal Justice Ethics, states that, before the administration of New York City Police Commissioner Patrick Murphy, there had never been a "clear-cut" message in the department that corruption would not be tolerated and that officers and supervisors would be held accountable for it (Masini, 1985: iv). The systematic corruption scandals of the 1970s and 1980s led to administrative changes in most major police departments. However, the biggest change in the nature of money corruption is directly related to drugs.

Drug-related corruption has changed the nature of police money corruption. Police officers involved in drug-related corruption are more likely to operate on their own or in small groups and to be involved in a variety of crimes such as stealing drugs and money from drug dealers, selling drugs, and lying under oath about illegal searches (U.S. Government Accounting Office, 1998: 3). Rotten apples have come together in corrupt groups (T. Barker, 1996). The crimes of these corrupt groups are more likely to involve shakedowns of drug users or dealers, or robberies of dealers and crackhouses. They are real, badge-packing criminals. New York City's former Police Commissioner William Bratton, commenting on the Mollen Commission's findings, stated "we have criminals in blue uniforms who are more vicious than some of the criminals they are supposedly policing" (Bratton, 1995: 39).

Carter (1990) reports that his subjects (involved in drug corruption) had an interesting rationalization for their acts. They would not take bribes; that was corruption. However, stealing from and robbing drug users and dealers did not "hurt anyone except the criminals" (p. 91). I have heard this same rationalization on several occasions, sometimes during ethics training sessions, "It's not corruption when you're taking from the dirt bags." This has implications for noble cause injustice, discussed further.

ABUSE OF AUTHORITY

Police abuse of authority is "any action by a police officer without regard to motive, intent or malice that tends to injure, insult, trespass upon human dignity, manifest feelings of inferiority, and/or violate an inherent legal right of a member of the police constituency in the course of performing 'police work'" (T. Barker & Carter 1994: 7). There are three forms of abuse of authority. First is physical abuse, which incorporates brutality and police violence: that is, the officer's use of more than necessary force to effect an arrest or search and/or the wanton use of any force under the color of the officer's authority. Second is psychological abuse, which occurs when an officer verbally assaults, harasses, or ridicules a citizen. The third type of abuse, legal abuse, occurs when police officers violate a citizen's constitutional, federal, or state rights. The latter will be discussed under noble cause injustice.

The first two forms of abuse of authority, physical and psychological abuse, can occur in any police–citizen encounter. However, they are most likely to occur in proactive police–citizen encounters because of aggressive police tactics. The effect of the professional model (reform model) of policing to control corruption and inefficiency resulted in the crime-fighter image, which increased the abuse of authority (Brown, 1981: 288). The professional model's primary objective was crime fighting. The principal method of crime fighting was/is aggressive patrol. The primary tactic of aggressive proactive patrol was/is the field stop. The result of field stops often was, and is, abuse of power and citizen resentment. A field stop is an exercise in pure power, and nobody likes to feel powerless (Rubinstein, 1973: 233). In most criminal cases, the result comes about without judicial control. In most citizen–police encounters, there is no review or control by the judiciary, supervisors, or the department. This in itself increases the likelihood of excessive use of physical and psychological abuse.

Use of Force

As stated, the use, or potential use, of force is at the core of the police role. The police have it within their power to use any number of instruments/techniques that can lead to injury or death: handcuffs, batons and nightsticks, flashlights, knives, stun and Taser guns, physical techniques (choke-holds, hog tying), tear gases and pepper sprays, dogs, vehicles, and a variety of other weapons. Any of these instruments/techniques can, and have been used excessively. They have been used in making arrests and while the subjects were in custody. Exact information of the police use of force is not known; however, there have been efforts to obtain the data.

Section 210402 of the 1994 Violent Crime Control and Law Enforcement Act requires the Attorney General to gather data and make an annual report to Congress on the use of excessive force by police officers. The second annual report estimated that 0.2 percent of the population over age 12 had been "hit, held, pushed, choked, threatened with a flashlight, restrained by a police dog, threatened or actually sprayed with chemical or pepper spray, threatened with a gun, or experienced some other form of force" in 1996 (Greenfield et al., 1997: iv). The report concluded that the use of force is rare in police–citizen contacts and is usually provoked. However, police use of force against certain minority groups in some U.S. cities may be a problem.

One author, writing just after the Rodney King incident, states that African American, Latino, and other minority males in Los Angeles are singled out by the Los Angeles Police Department and the Los Angeles Sheriffs Department for "special attention, harassment, detention, physical abuse, brutality, and sometimes death" (Hoffman, 1993: 1471). Hoffman attributes this abuse to the patterns and practices of the two departments and their use of military tactics in the War on Drugs, gangs, and crime (Hoffman, 1993: 1472). Both departments are well-known for their hardnose, aggressive crime-fighter style of policing.

Many civil rights groups, such as the American Civil Liberties Union (ACLU), the National Association for the Advancement of Colored People, and Amnesty International, have complained that the present aggressive police strategies and zero-tolerance policing have led to increased use of force. Whether or not such complaints are true is a matter of controversy. However, the ACLU has reported that, since police departments have instituted restrictive policies on the use of deadly force, the number of incidents has dropped—as much as 35–40 percent in the fifty largest cities (ACLU, 1997: 15). This drop has been accompanied by a drop in the racial disparity in the use of deadly force use. However, most of this drop might be a direct result of the 1985 U.S. Supreme Court's decision in *Tennessee* v. *Garner*. This landmark decision limited the use of deadly force to only those instances where the suspect posed a threat of serious injury or death to the public or the police officer. Prior to this decision, deadly force could be used to prevent the escape of all felony suspects.

The crime-fighter model, with its aggressive police tactic, is alive and well in American policing, particulary in the War on Drugs, specialized paramilitary units, zero-tolerance and quality of life policing. The war mentality, with its emphasis on crime fighting and preoccupation with the coercive use of force, has licensed the use of force in many police organizations (Kleinig, 1996: 96).

The crime-fighter image also predominates among the police in Great Britain, even though crime fighting is a minor part of their work duties (Holdaway, 1984). The use of force against citizens in Britain occurs for the same reasons as in America (see T. Barker & Carter, 1994): when police authority is challenged, when officers are assaulted, when danger is present, and as punishment, such as at the end of police chases (Holdaway, 1984). The constables' working rules allow for force under these circumstances. It is summary justice. " 'Just desserts' are adjudicated and administered by Hilton's officers" (Holdaway 1984: 130).

Noble Cause Injustice

The first U.S. presidential commission to examine the American criminal justice system, the 1931 Wickersham Commission, devoted two of its fourteen volumes to the unlawful enforcement of the law by American police officers. The reformer, Ernest Jerome Hopkins, in one of those volumes, said that the American police operated under what he called the "War Theory of Crime-Control" and used unlawful means, primarily third-degree interrogation techniques to control crime (Hopkins, 1972: 314–47). Hopkins pointed out that the police, after using the third-degree techniques, had to perjure themselves to conceal their unlawful acts and sway the court. The police frequently perjured themselves to obtain convictions. All the police activities were justified by the phrase "This is war." Hopkins summed up the philosophy:

> The criminal is the enemy; he is to be defeated by being quelled. Being the enemy, he has no rights worthy of the name. He is to be met by the weapons of war. Individual rights, including those of non-combatants, are subject to invasion like the rights of non-combatants in wartime. The policeman is a peacetime soldier. If bullets go astray, if civil rights are suspended, those are accidents inherent in warfare that is waged in crowded cities. (Hopkins, 1972: 319)

Nevertheless, the Wickersham Commission declared "The fight against lawless men, if waged by forbidden means, is degraded almost to the level of a struggle between two law-breaking gangs" (Hopkins, 1972: 13). Hopkins and the Wickersham Commission were railing against noble cause injustice.

Noble cause injustice involves the idea "yes, I did something wrong, but justice demanded it, not tolerated it but demanded it, because I could put the guy away who otherwise wouldn't be successfully prosecuted" (Moore, 1997: 63). Heffernan, in his Typology of Disinterested Rules Violations, identifies two types related to noble cause misconduct (noble cause injustice): (1) meting out justice via violations of the constitution and (2) promotion of social order via violations of the constitution (Heffernan, 1985: 7–8). Heffernan opines that the first type occurs because officers, through illegal searches and arrests, seek to punish those systematically involved in crime who are believed to be relatively immune from prosecution. Known criminals are getting their due. The second type occurs because officers believe that the courts do not understand the value of preventive police actions. According to many officers, restrictive concepts such as probable cause and articulable suspicion unfairly "handcuff" the police in maintaining public order.

Feeling that one is right to do what one does is not always the right thing to do. Nevertheless, Brown (1981: 285) stated that a good pinch even at the expense of legality was an occupational norm for the police he studied. Herbert (1997: 52) reports that the "creative use of probable cause" in the Los Angeles police in their "pooping and snooping" activities (field stops) was encouraged and praised by the department.

If the officer's behavior is discovered, the state will suffer via the exclusionary rule; however, in most instances, nothing happens to the officer administratively or in the courts. There is the possibility of discovery, but the probability is low. Nevertheless, if it is discovered or raised, the officer will have to lie. Once engaged in lying, perjury is a possibility. Whatever the rationale, lying by police officers under these circumstances is an especially egregious violation in a free society with the traditions of liberty and openness, governmental accountability, and fear of central authority (Marx, 1985: 94). Heffernan states that if an officer feels that the aims of criminal justice are being subverted by the current rules of his office, the officer has two choices: (1) resign or (2) protest the rules while still honoring them (Heffernan, 1985: 14). Nevertheless, documented incidents have occurred.

In an incident reported to the Florida Criminal Justice Standards and Training Commission (certifies and decertifies Florida police officers) in 1995, a Metro-Dade police officer lied on a police report and again in sworn testimony (*www.sun-sentinel.com/news/copd2b.htm*). She said she saw the suspect drop a bag of cocaine. Another police officer and witnesses contradicted this. She said that she arrested the suspect in his car, also contradicted, and found a pistol under the driver's seat. Testimony revealed that another police officer found the pistol in the trunk. The policewoman, instead of being terminated, received a twenty-day suspension. Decertification is automatic for felony convictions or misdemeanor convictions involving perjury. In addition, for forty-five crimes ranging from stalking to engaging in sex on duty, officers can receive penalties ranging from probation to revocation.

According to Holdaway (1984), British police officers sometimes "construct or adjust the evidence" in court to ensure a conviction. They adjust, refine, and correct evidence to render the suspect's guilt more obvious. However, not all British officers engage in this behavior.

> Two of Hilton's [subdivision] officers had arrested suspects for attempting to take a motor vehicle. Their colleagues discussed the arresting officers' unwillingness to construct the evidence in order to gain a conviction: "And it is a foreign [another subdivision] court anyway, so there we are. You see, he doesn't believe in that sort of thing." (Holdaway, 1984: 74)

Holdaway reports that procedural rules are often considered irrelevant by the British police as they go about their daily duties. The occupational culture of the British police condones the use of "verbals" or "working the oracle." A verbal is an oral statement of admission or incrimination invented by the arresting or interviewing officer and attributed to the suspect (Holdaway, 1984: 109). They, like their American counterparts, feel that they have privileged information knowing that the suspect is guilty and that they only help the evidence along.

> [Police Constable] When you have a legal system that allows people to get off and makes you break the law to get convictions, then you have to be slightly bent. (Holdaway, 1984: 113)

> [Police Constable] . . . It's part [verbals] of being a policeman. If you know their [sic] guilty, there's nothing wrong, and if you're not willing to do it, you shouldn't be in the job. (Holdaway, 1984: 113).

Noble Cause Injustice in the War on Drugs.   The result of the thirty-year War on Drugs has been an unwinnable war by police officers wearing black masks, dressed in fatigues with buzz haircuts, and trained in the use of submachine guns, explosives, and chemical weapons. These police "ninjas" are the street warriors in the ultimate "us against them" mentality (see Kraska, 1996).

The current War on Drugs is not this country's first drug war. August Vollmer, writing in 1936, stated:

> The deteriorating effects of drugs upon the victims, and the intimate associations of the drug habit with the commission of crimes, are so inescapably evident that the police are encouraged to employ every means known to them to eliminate the supply agent and the peddler. (Vollmer, 1971: 108)

Vollmer said that drug addiction is not a police problem and not to be solved by policemen. He said it was first and last a medical problem that could only be solved by "scientific and competently trained medical experts" (Vollmer, 1971: 118).

The police historian James Richardson (1974: 103) also pointed out that the police cannot serve the dual purposes of enforcing the drug laws and observing the constitutional protections of individual rights. He stated that full enforcement of the drug laws would be possible only in a police state "where the police would be allowed to stop and search at will and where there could be no question of police infringement of constitutional guarantees since there would be no guarantees" (Richardson, 1974: 103). Richardson stated that if society asks the police to serve both purposes, they will be tempted to bypass the legal structure. They have done so, resulting in many instances of noble cause injustice.

During police drug activities, lying as a means to an end is an acceptable practice for many officers, the "good that comes from an end, such as protection from serious crime, will outweigh the bad that comes from lying" during undercover operations (Marx, 1985: 105).

The popular anticrime-punish-the-criminal rhetoric leads many citizens to agree with the police that the guilty, particularly drug offenders, deserve less than strict constitutional protection. There is public support for the officers who violate civil rights and lie to make a case stick against the "dirt bags." Witness the popularity of the television show *NYPD Blue*, where constitutional violations of the guilty, as determined by the detectives, especially Andy Sipowitz, is an art form. However, the police are the guardians of our civil liberties. The "avenging angel syndrome" to which some officers fall prey can be very dangerous—to the officers and citizens.

Carter states that the officers he studied rationalized their actions as "perhaps a form of 'winning' or 'revenge'" (1990: 90). Examples of this winning or revenge behavior included:

- False statements to obtain arrest or search warrants against "known" drug dealers/traffickers.
- Perjury during hearings and trials of drug dealers.
- "Planting" or creating evidence against "known" drug dealers.
- Overt and intentional entrapment.
- Falsely spreading rumors that a dealer is a police informant, thus placing that person's safety in jeopardy.

MECHANISMS FOR CONTROLLING POLICE UNETHICAL BEHAVIOR

Self-Control

The ideal control system of ethical behavior is inner control; however, the real-world control is external (Kleinig, 1996: 217). Individuals have, or should have, internal "moral compasses" that distinguish between right and wrong. This "moral compass" is the result of the socialization process that begins at birth. This socialization process continues on to the workplace.

The police occupation has traditionally tried to *screen out* candidates who possess bad qualities: arrest records, history of bad debts, drug use, violent behavior, untrustworthiness, and so on. At times this has worked, only to be defeated by other police occupational socialization practices (T. Barker, 1977).

The police occupation has not tried to *screen in* candidates who possess the good qualities for police work (Gaines & Kappeler, 1992). Part of the reason for this is that there is no general agreement, outside the possession of commonsense (whatever that is) of the good qualities for police work outside the absence of bad qualities. Research in the area could possibly lead to reliable predictors for ethical behavior. Experienced police officers can recognize differences between officers. Every police officer with at least five years' experience in the same department can name officers known for their unethical behavior. The British officers studied by Holdaway (himself, a police sergeant) were well aware of their colleagues who used verbals, adjusted the evidence, or used excessive force.

However, we might wish for inner-directed officers, it must be recognized that ethical conduct is assisted or made more difficult by situational factors that include the organizational structure and peer group culture.

Peer Group Control

Within the police occupation, there are three patterns of social interaction, two internal to the organization and one external: police to police, police to supervisors, and police to the public. The first, police to police, has often been described as a subculture with dominant values, one of which, loyalty, breeds a code of silence protecting miscreant officers. The socialization process of the police (academy and peer group) also emphasizes danger, mutual assistance, and loyalty as core values (Crank, 1998). The peer group can, and will, reinforce ethical behavior or provide the rationalizations for unethical behavior (T. Barker, 1977; T. Barker & Carter, 1994). The occupational culture of police organizations is where officers learn their working behavior.

There are indications that the Blue Wall of Silence may not be as solid as once thought. Joan Barker's (1999) twenty-year ethnographic study of the occupational subculture of the LAPD lead her to conclude that traditional solidarity is breaking down with the influx of new officers, particularly minorities and women. This is evidenced by a proliferation of complaints by officers against their colleagues. Coulson (1993) cites six cases (Claremont, Massachusetts; Cochella, California; Fort Lauderdale, Florida; Erie, Pennsylvania; and Denton, Texas) of officers filing complaints against their colleagues. Three of the complaints involved the use of excessive force. Whistleblowers among the police do exist.

The Board of Inquiry into the LAPD corruption scandal reports that in 1996, 1997, and 1998 there were thirty cases where LAPD personnel were the primary witness in charges of misconduct against other officers (LAPD, 2000). The charges ranged from excessive force to neglect of duty.

Traditionally, the Blue Wall of Silence breaks down when careers and pension benefits are mentioned. The wall crumbles when prison time is mentioned. Police officers, like most offenders, will blow the whistle under these conditions. However, one must distinguish between whistleblowers. There are two types of police whistleblowers: the informer (traitor among the participants) and the informant (in possession of knowledge). The New York City Police Department (NYPD) informers, such as Bob Leuci, William Phillips, and Michael Dowd, betrayed those who were involved with them in corrupt practices. They are Blue Rats, cooperating in their best interest. The NYPD informants, such as Frank Serpico and Joe Tromboli, provided information on corrupt activities, not their accomplices. These were essentially "good guys" reporting corrupt activities.

Shame attaches, as it should, to the status of informer, a participant who has "flipped" out of self-interest. Shame should not attach to the informant who has reported misconduct because of a sense of duty. There is a huge difference between the individual who blows the whistle because of the interests of the organization and the occupation and the cop who flips because he is trying to save himself. Often, the deals made with the police informers are like the deal made with the Mafia hitman Sammy "the Bull" Gravano—"shaking hands with the devil." Patrolman William Phillips (Knapp Commission) was a rogue cop engaged in far more serious behaviors than those he flipped on (Schecter & Phillips, 1973).

The current *Code of Law Enforcement Ethics* makes no mention of what a police officer should do if he discovers the corrupt behavior of another officer (Wren, 1985: 26). It should be clear that the discovering officer is the good cop betrayed by a bad cop and not the other way around. Wren (1985: 40) suggests the following addition to the code:

> The [police department] should safeguard the public and itself against [police officers] deficient in moral character of professional competence. [Police officers] should observe all laws, uphold the dignity and honor of the profession and accept its self imposed disciplines. They should expose without hesitation illegal or unethical conduct of a fellow member of the profession.

The Washington, D.C., Metropolitan Police Department has a general order (MPD General Order 201.260) requiring police officers to promptly report misconduct or any violation of MPD rules to a supervisor. However, testimony to the special committee investigating corruption revealed that this rarely happened, and if it did, the whistleblowers were retaliated against (*www.dcwatch.com/police/981006b.htm#Chapter3:4*). The committee stated that there was a culture of retaliation in the MPD. Following the report of the special committee, the Council of the District of Columbia enacted the Whistleblower Reinforcement Act of 1998, D.C. Act 12-239, to strengthen already existing legislation protecting government whistleblowers.

The problems faced by a police officer discovering the unethical behaviors of a fellow officer are virtually the same for all occupational groups. Welfel (1997) aptly describes the difficulties encountered by her fellow psychologists under the same circumstances (Welfel, 1997: 141). Both groups (police and psychologists) face competing values (ethical conduct and peer group culture) in moral decision making. Loyalty to colleagues is a desirable characteristic in both groups. The police occupation, however, clearly is more dangerous and often requires less time to reflect and deliberate about ethical dilemmas (Welfel, 1997).

Supervisory Control

Supervisory control, combined with quality leadership and training, is the manner in which the police occupation provides the external "moral compass" for officers to make ethical judgments in line with the police occupation and the organization. Proactive management oversight, particularly at the mid-level (sergeants and lieutenants), is the organization's first line of defense against unethical police behavior.

Ineffective field supervision and the fear of disclosing corruption because of its adverse effect on the supervisor were cited by the Mollen Commission as contributing factors to the scandal (Baer, 1995). Nevertheless, there is little chance that field supervision can keep all bad cops from doing bad things.

The nature of police work—individual or pairs of officers working alone under little supervision—works against close field supervision. For one, there are too many police officers and too few supervisors (Vicchio, 1997). The nature of police actions also works against close supervision. Reactive police work (calls for service) occurs primarily in private settings (homes), and proactive police work (officer initiated) occurs primarily in public places (usually public streets), unobserved by anyone but the citizens and the officers. At times, the supervisor can contribute to abuse. If the supervisor urges or demands that officers make arrests, "some of them will ignore the law and the truth to improve their performance" (Rubinstein, 1973: 58).

Field supervision is only one part of supervisory control; auditing the officer's behavior is also a part of the supervisor's responsibility. Included within these audits is closely monitoring the charges that are most often used in "cover-up" charges (resisting arrest, assaulting an officer, disorderly conduct, obstructing and interfering with an officer). Repeated findings of a small minority of officers being involved in multiple incidents of alleged ethical violations and civil actions has made Early Warning audit systems a necessity.

Early Warning Audit Systems

Two hundred and thirty Chicago police officers with repeated complaints against them accounted for 46 percent of the $16 million in judgments against the city from 1991 to 1994 (Nelson, 1995). The Chicago Commission on Police Integrity, appointed after the latest corruption scandal in two precincts, recommended an Early Warning system to alert command when an officer may be involved in a pattern of misconduct (Commission on Police Integrity, 1997).

The Christopher Commission, convened after the King incident, found that 183 Los Angeles police officers had four or more allegations of excessive force or improper tactics, 44 had 6 or more, and 16 had 8 or more (Christopher, 1991). One officer had 16 allegations. The New Orleans police officer convicted in 1996 of having a woman killed for filing a complaint against him had been the recipient of 20 complaints between 1987 and 1992 (ACLU, 1997: 18). Most of the allegations involved brutality. The officer had previously been suspended for 51 days for hitting a woman in the head with a flashlight. The ACLU has advocated Early Warning systems to identify officers who have an inordinate number of physical force incidents.

The U.S. GAO in its report to Congressman Rangel recommended an Early Warning system to identify potential problem officers (U.S. Government Accounting Office, 1998: 5). The consent decree entered into by the Pittsburgh Police Department with the U.S. Department of Justice includes an Early Warning system to identify problem officers (Vera, 1998: 16). Amnesty International reports that, in an April 16, 1999 speech, before a national summit on police brutality, Attorney General Janet Reno endorsed Early Warning systems to identify officers who engage in misconduct (Amnesty International, 1999: 4).

In mid-1995, following the murder convictions of the police officer mentioned above, New Orleans instituted an Early Warning system called the Professional Performance Enhancement Program (PPEP). Officers are picked for this program based on complaints, use of force, and shooting incidents. The officers receive additional training, supervision, or counseling (Human Rights Watch, 1998). Portland, Oregon, has a "command review" that acts as an Early Warning system. The system reviews officers who receive 5 complaints within a year, 3 in 6 months, or 2 of the same type in 6 months (Human Rights Watch, 1998).

The institution of these Early Warning audit systems should act as a problem-solving approach to ethical violations. However, the administration's handling of the data generated is important. (See Chapter 9 for a discussion of Early Warning systems.)

Administrative Reaction

An indifferent attitude toward officer misconduct by the organization can quickly erode the confidence of the public and the police officers (Delattre, 1989: 51). The organization must create an atmosphere that reinforces the good character and motivations of a carefully selected and trained workforce. The atmosphere must, to some sense, be punishment oriented for those who commit unethical acts and be supportive of those who do not and who report the unethical actions of others. A purely punishment-oriented approach is counterproductive.

Videotaping high-risk encounters (pursuits, interrogations, booking, protests and riots, raids, warrant servings) can serve as an administrative check on use-of-force incidents; failing this, it could provide evidence for disciplinary actions. The new NYPD management tool Compstats is being used as an administrative weapon against police misconduct (Silverman, 1999: 187). Compstats involves the diagnosing, analyzing, crime, and quality-of-life problems to discover their commonalities and patterns. The technique is also used to monitor and address civilian complaints of misconduct. Included within the analysis are FADO (force, abuse, discourtesy, and obscene language) citizen complaints citywide—by borough, precinct, and hour and time of day.

Often, the police organization does a poor job of investigating corruption/misconduct when it comes to its attention. This conclusion was reached by the Mollen Commission investigating corruption in the NYPD:

> The shock is not that there are corrupt police officers but that too often police departments are incompetent when it comes to investigating corruption.
>
> Judge Milton Mollen

Judge Mollen said on a number of occasions that the NYPD was incompetent and inept in their dealing with corruption. Therefore, an administrative reaction must include a fair, timely, and competent investigation of all complaints.

External Accountability

All democratic police forces are subject to monitoring and accountability by outsiders (Bayley, 1997: 5). These outsiders include elected politicians; civil, criminal, and administrative courts; the media and civilian complaint-review boards.

The Department of Justice's Civil Rights Division was created by Congress in 1957 and has had criminal enforcement powers over civil rights violations by police officers since its inception. Police officers, acting under the color of law, can, and have, been prosecuted for civil rights violations, particularly for violations of excessive force and unwarranted seizures and false arrests. A new weapon has been added to their arsenal.

Since 1994, Congress has authorized the Civil Rights Division of the Department of Justice to bring pattern-or-practice civil suits for declaratory or injunctive relief against entire police departments instead of individual police officers. The pattern or practice of behavior has to be conduct by police officers that deprives persons of rights, privileges, or immunities secured or protected by the Constitution of the United States (42 U.S.C. 14141). These pattern-or-practice suits can include excessive force, discriminatory stops, harassment, false arrests, coercive sexual conduct, and unlawful stops, searches, and arrests and supervisory failures (Vera, 1998: 15). The Pittsburgh, Pennsylvania, Police Department was the first to be sued under the pattern-or-practice concept. As mentioned, the Pittsburgh Police Department entered into a consent decree that established comprehensive and specific measures to end systematic police misconduct.

Soon after the Pittsburgh case, the Civil Rights Division entered into a consent decree with the City of Steubenville, Ohio. Its police department was accused of engaging in a pattern or practice of excessive use of force, false arrests, charges and reports, and improper stops, searches, and seizures. Steubenville police officers were alleged to have beaten witnesses of misconduct, falsified reports, and tampered with official police records in order to cover up misconduct (Vera, 1989: 16).

In April 1999, a report from the New Jersey Attorney General's Office concluded that New Jersey State Troopers were engaging in racial profiling when stopping motorists for possible drug arrest. Amnesty International reports that the U.S. Department of Justice announced the same month that they had enough evidence of discriminatory treatment by the N.J. State Troopers to bring a pattern-or-practice civil suit (Amnesty International, 1999: 3). Now, the Civil Rights Division can bring criminal prosecutions against officers, as in the Rodney King incident, or civil actions against entire police departments in pattern-or-practice suits.

External Review Boards.   Civilian review boards have been a contentious issue for the American police since first brought up in the 1950s. However, civilian review of police organizations in some form may be becoming the norm. According to the ACLU (1997), civilian review boards are the norm in more than 75 percent of the nation's largest cities. Eighty cities have them.

External review boards need not be confined to the traditionally understood civilian review boards. However, some outside entity should audit the police department's control of corruption and misconduct and Early Warning systems. The external board does not, and probably should not, conduct the investigations.

CONCLUSION

The ethical violations discussed (rule violations, money corruption, and abuse of authority) have existed in the police occupation since its inception in England. The various forms have continually surfaced in British and American forces/departments throughout the short history of policing. Police reformers have always recognized that their work was a morally dangerous occupation. They recognized this in Codes of Ethics and numerous reform efforts. Nevertheless, the police occupational culture in many forces/departments has traditionally provided its members with ready-made rationalizations for many of these ethical violations (Ahern, 1972; Banton, 1964; T. Barker, 1977; T. Barker & Carter, 1994; Chevigny, 1969, Crank, 1998, Kappeler et al., 1994, Manning, 1977, Reiss, 1971, Skolnick, 1966; Rubinstein, 1973; Westley, 1970). Nevertheless, peer pressure, weakness in others, impulses, opportunity, and personal rationalizations (blaming the system—noble cause injustice) do not excuse lapses of character by the police (Kleinig, 1996: 65). Democratic societies have the right to expect ethical behavior among their police forces. Therefore, the profession and the citizens of a free society must continue their efforts to control the ethical violations.

There must be a two-pronged approach to controlling ethical violations: avoiding rotten apples and avoiding rotten structures (Delattre, 1989: 88). Avoiding rotten apples involves establishing higher standards for recruitment and selection and good educational programs for newcomers and experienced personnel. Rotten structures should be dealt with through a nontoleration policy by police leadership, institutional audit procedures to ensure accountability, systematic investigations of complaints and suspicious circumstances, and external review.

Any efforts to control the ethical violations of the American police are constrained by a lack of data on several issues. There is a need to know the nature and extent of ethics training in American police agencies. The IACP, the world's oldest and largest police professional association, in their first and only attempt to learn this information from its members received a dismal 18 percent return rate on their survey (*www.theiacp.org/pubinfo/ Pubs/ethicTrain.htm*). If the police establishment is not serious about the *Law Enforcement Code of Ethics* and ethical training for all officers (academy and in service), then the code could be perceived as a compilation of useless homilies put forward by an occupational work group calling itself a profession (T. Barker, 1996).

A 1993 Texas survey of training academies conducted under the auspices of the Law Enforcement Ethics Center of the Southwestern Law Enforcement Institute (response rate of 32.7 percent) revealed that an average of 6.73 hours of ethics training comprised only 1.6 percent of the total recruits' time (*http://web2.airmail.net/slf/oct93/training.html*). The study also found that ethics training was less than 1 percent of the total in-class time. The center has been training police ethics trainers since May of 1994.

Anecdotal evidence suggests that some departments that have experienced scandals are improving their ethics training. The Chicago Police Department's Education and Training Center will soon be instituting an ethics training concept, Ethics Across the Curriculum, based on the ethics training used at the U. S. Naval Academy. Integrity issues will be a part of the entire curriculum of the center (Commission on Police Integrity, 1997).

Following the Rampart Scandal, the LAPD began distributing the *Law Enforcement Code of Ethics* to every recruit class, directing officers to abide by the standards (Los Angeles Police Department, 2000: 304). Recruit officers are now required to sign for the code. All six of the existing LAPD's recruit and in-service courses (Recruit O, Detective Supervisors, Sergeant/Civilian Supervisors, Captains, and West Point Leadership) have a section on the *Law Enforcement Code of Ethics* (Los Angeles Police Department, 2000: 306). The Board of Inquiry also recommended that every police officer receive from two to four hours of ethics and integrity every two years.

Ethics training is important; however, there is a need to know what effect, if any, the training (ethics, academy, in-service) has on officers. Longitudinal studies are needed on the existing training programs and any created in response to scandals. Baer (1995: 8) states that it was at the New York Police Academy that "some recruits first learned about being corrupt." It was also at the academy that the recruits were introduced into the "we against them" mentality and the Blue Wall of Silence value for officers.

Finally, research is needed into the circumstances under which some officers report their fellow officers' misconduct. Researchers, myself included, have said for too long that police officers will not report fellow officers. The anecdotal evidence cited here seems to contradict this in some departments and for some officers. Why? If we knew the answer to that question, the profession would be in a better position to ensure ethical police behavior.

REFERENCES

AHERN, J. (1972). *Police in Trouble: Our Frightening Crisis in Law Enforcement*. New York: Hawthorne Books.

AMERICAN CIVIL LIBERTIES UNION. (1997). *Fighting Police Abuse: A Community Action Manual*. New York, N.Y.: American Civil Liberties Union.

AMNESTY INTERNATIONAL. (1999, September). *United States of America: Race, Rights and Police Brutality*. Amnesty International-Report-AMR 51/147/99. Amnesty International, New York, N.Y.

ASCOLI, D. (1979). *The Queen's Peace: The Origins and Development of the Metropolitan Police 1829–1979*. London: Hamish Hamilton.

BAER, H. (1995). Speech—The Mollen Commission and beyond. *New York Law School Law Review* 40 (1–2): 5–11.

BANTON, M. (1964). *The Policeman in the Community*. London: Travistock.

BARKER, J. (1999). *Danger, Duty, and Disillusion: The Worldview of the Los Angeles Police Officers*. Prospect Heights, Ill.: Waveland Press.

BARKER, T. (1977). Peer group support for police occupational deviance. *Criminology* 15 (3):353–66.

BARKER, T. (1996). *Police Ethics: Crisis in Law Enforcement*. Springfield, Ill.: Charles C. Thomas.

BARKER, T., & CARTER, D. L. (1994). *Police Deviance*. 3d ed. Cincinnati, Ohio: Anderson Publishing.

BAYLEY, D. H. (1997). The contemporary practices of policing: A comparative view. In *Civilian Police and Multinational Peacekeeping—A Workshop Series: A Role for Democratic Policing*. NIJ Research Forum, Washington, D.C., October 6, 1997, U.S. Department of Justice.

BRATTON, W. J. (1995). Fighting crime as crime itself. *New York Law School Law Review* 40 (1–2): 35–43.

BROGDEN, M. (1999). Community policing as cherry pie. In Mawby, R. I., ed. *Policing Across the World: Issues for the Twenty-first Century* (pp. 167–186). New York: Garland Press.

BROWN, M. K. (1981). *Working the Street: Police Discretion and Dilemmas of Reform*. New York: Russell Sage.

CARTER, D. L. (1990). Drug related corruption of police officers: A typology. *Journal of Criminal Justice* 18 (2): 85–89.

CHEVIGNY, P. (1969). *Police Power: Police Abuses in New York City*. New York: Panthenon Books.

CHRISTOPHER, W. (1991). The Independent Commission on the Los Angeles Police Department. *Report of the Independent Commission on the Los Angeles Police Department*. Los Angeles: City of Los Angeles.

COMMISSION ON POLICE INTEGRITY. (1997, November). *Report of the Commission on Police Integrity*. Presented to the City of Chicago Richard M. Daley Mayor. Chicago: City of Chicago.

COULSON, R. (1993). *Police Under Pressure: Resolving Disputes*. Westport, Conn.: Greenwood Press.

CRANK, J. P. (1998). *Understanding Police Culture*. Cincinnati, Ohio: Anderson Publishing.

DAVIS, M. (1997). Teaching police ethics: What to aim at? In Kleing, J., & Smith, M. L., eds. *Teaching Criminal Justice Ethics: Strategic Issues* (pp. 35–58). Cincinnati, Ohio: Anderson Publishing.

DELATTRE, E. (1989). *Character and Cops: Ethics In Policing*. Washington, D.C.: American Enterprise Institute for Public Policy Research.

FOGELSON, R. M. (1977). *Big-City Police*. Cambridge, Mass.: Harvard University Press.

GAINES, L. K., & KAPPELER, V. E. (1992). The police selection process: What works? In Cordner, G., & Hale, D., eds. *What Works in Policing? Operations and Administration Examined* (pp. 107–124) Cincinnati, Ohio: Anderson Publishing.

GREENFIELD, L. A., LANAGEN, P. A., & SMITH, S. K. (1997). *Police Use of Force: Collection of National Data*. Washington, D.C.: U.S. Government Printing Office, U.S. Department of Justice.

HAGGARD, P. (1994). *Police Ethics*. Lewiston, N.Y.: Edwin Mellen Press.

HEFFERNAN, W. C. (1985). The police and their rules of office: an ethical analysis. In Heffernan, W. C., & Stroup, T., eds. *Police Ethics: Hard Choices in Law Enforcement* (pp. 3–24). New York: John Jay Press.

HEFFERNAN, W. C. (1996). Rejoinders: William C. Heffernan and John Kleing. In Kleing, J., & Smith, M. L., eds. *Teaching Criminal Justice Ethics: Strategic Issues* (pp. 25–34). Cincinnati, Ohio: Anderson Publishing.

HERBERT, S. (1997). *Policing Space: Territoriality and the Los Angeles Police Department*. Minneapolis: University of Minnesota Press.

HOFFMAN, P. (1993). The feds, lies, and videotape: The need for an effective federal role in controlling police abuse in urban America. *Southern California Law Review*. 66 (4): 1455–1531.

HOLDAWAY, S. (1984). *Inside the British Police: A Force at Work*. New York: Basil Blackwell.

HOPKINS, E. J. (1972). *Our Lawless Police: A Study in the Unlawful Enforcement of the Laws*. New York: DaCapo Press. (First published in 1931.)

HUMAN RIGHTS WATCH. (1998, June). *Shielded from Justice*. New York: Human Rights Watch.

INTERNATIONAL ASSOCIATION OF CHIEFS OF POLICE. (1997). *Model Policy: Standards of Conduct*. Alexandria, Va.: IACP National Law Enforcement Policy Center.

KAMM, F. M. (1997). Response to Callahan and Whitbeck: Practical ethics, moral theories, and deliberation. In Kleinig J., & Smith, M. L., eds. *Teaching Criminal Justice Ethics: Strategic Issues* (pp. 123–130). Cincinnati, Ohio: Anderson Publishing.

KANIA, R. E. (1988). Should we tell police to say "Yes" to Gratuities? *Criminal Justice Ethics* 7(2): 37–49.

KAPPELER, V. E., SLUDER, R. D., & ALPERT, G. P. (1994). *Forces of Deviance: The Dark Side of Policing*. Prospect Heights, Ill.: Waveland Press.

KLEINIG, J. (1996). *The Ethics of Policing*. Cambridge: Cambridge University Press.

KRASKA, P. B. (1996). Enjoying militarism: Political/personal dilemmas in studying U.S. police paramilitary units. *Justice Quarterly* 13(3): 405–29.

KRASKSA, P. B., & KAPPELER, V. E., (1995). To serve and pursue: Exploring police violence against women. *Justice Quarterly* 12 (1): 85–111.

LANE, R. (1971). *Policing the City: Boston 1822–1885*. New York: Atheneum.

LEE, M. W. L. (1971). *A History of Police in England*. Montclair, N.J.: Patterson Smith Reprint. (First published in 1901.)

LIVINGSTONE, D. (1977). Police discretion and the quality of life in public places: Courts, communities, and the new policing. *Columbia Law Review* 97 (3): 551–672.

LOS ANGELES POLICE DEPARTMENT. (2000, March 1). *Board of Inquiry into the Rampart Area Corruption Incident: Public Report*. Los Angeles: LAPD.

MANNING, P. K. (1977). *Police Work: The Social Organization of Policing*. Cambridge, Mass.: M.I.T. Press.

MARX, G. T. (1985). Police undercover work: Ethical deception or deceptive ethics. In Heffernan, W. C., & Stroup, T., eds. *Police Ethics: Hard Choices in Law Enforcement* (pp. 83–115). New York: John Jay Press.

MASINI, H. J. (1985). Preface. In Heffernan, W. C., & Stroup, T., eds. *Police Ethics: Hard Choices in Law Enforcement* (pp. i–ix). New York: John Jay Press.

MCALARY, M. (1994). *Good Cop, Bad Cop*. New York: Pocket Books.

MCDONALD, P. P., GAFFIGAN, S. J., & GREENBERG, S. J. (1997). Police Integrity: Definition and historical significance. In Gaffigan, S. J., & McDonald, P. P. (project managers). *Police Integrity: Public Service with Honor* (pp. 81–91). Washington, D.C.: U.S. Government Printing Office, U.S. Department of Justice.

MILLER, W. R. (1997). *Cops and Bobbies: Police Authority in New York and London, 1830–1870*. 2d ed. Columbus: Ohio State University Press.

MOLLEN COMMISSION. (1994). *The City of New York Commission to Investigate Allegations of Police Corruption and the Anti-Corruption Procedures of the Police Department: Commission Report*. New York: City of New York.

MOORE, M. (1997, January). Epilogue. In Gaffigan, S. J., & McDonald, P. P. (project managers). *Police Integrity: Public Service with Honor* (pp. 59–70). Washington, D.C.: U.S. Government Printing Office, U.S. Department of Justice.

NELSON, D. (1995). Cops' free rein costs city millions. *Chicago Tribune*, January 10.

RICHARDSON, J. F. (1974). *Urban Police in the United States*. Port Washington, New York: Kennikat Press.

REISS, A. J. (1971). *The Police and the Public*. New Haven: Yale University Press.

REITH, C. (1952). *The Blind Eye of History: A Study of the Origins of the Present Police Era*. Montclair, N.J.: Patterson Smith.

REYNOLDS, E. A. (1998). *Before the Bobbies: The Night Watch and Police Reform in Metropolitan London, 1720–1830*. Stanford, Calif.: Stanford University Press.

ROBILLIARD, ST. J., & MCEWAN, J. (1986). *Police Powers and the Individual*. New York: Basil Blackwell.

RUBINSTEIN, J. (1973). *City Police*. New York: Farrar, Strauss & Giroux.

SAPP, A. (1994). Sexual misconduct by police officers. In Barker, T., & Carter, D. L., eds. *Police Deviance*. 3d ed. (pp. 187–200). Cincinnati, Ohio: Anderson Publishing.

SCHECTER, L., & PHILLIPS, W. (1973). *On the Pad*. New York: Putnam.

SILVERMAN, E. B. (1999). *NYPD Battles Crime: Innovative Strategies in Policing*. Boston: Northeastern University Press.

SKOLNICK, J. (1966). *Justice without Trial*. New York: John Wiley.

SPD CITIZENS REVIEW PANEL. (1999). *Seattle Police Department: Citizens Review Panel Final Report*. Seattle: City of Seattle.

Tennessee v. *Garner*, 471 US1 (1985).

TRAVIS, J. (1998, June 12). *Plenary Address at the Fourth Biennial Conference: International Perspectives on Crime, Justice and Public Order*. Budapest, Hungary.

U.S. GOVERNMENT ACCOUNTING OFFICE. (1998, May). *Law Enforcement: Information on Drug-Related Police Corruption*. Report to the Honorable Charles B. Rangel, House of Representatives. Washington, D.C.: U.S. Government Printing Office, Government Accounting Office.

VERA. (1998). *Prosecuting Police Misconduct: Reflections on the Role of the U.S. Civil Rights Division*. New York: Vera Institute of Justice.

VICCHIO, S. J. (1997). *Ethics and Police Integrity: Some Definitions and Questions for Study*. Key Note Address, Police Integrity: Police Service with Honor, January, 1997, National Institute of Justice and the Office of Community Oriented Police Service.

VOLLMER, A. (1971). *The Police and Modern Society*. Montclair, N.J.: Patterson Smith. (First published in 1936.)

WALKER, S. (1977). *A Critical History of Policing: The Emergence of Professionalism*. Lexington, Mass.: Lexington Books.

WELFEL, E. J. (1997). Psychology's contribution to effective models of ethics education in criminal justice. In Kleinig, J., & Smith, M. L., eds. *Teaching Criminal Justice Ethics: Strategic Issues* (pp. 131–152). Cincinnati, Ohio: Anderson Publishing.

WESTLEY, W. A. (1970). *Violence and the police: A sociological study of law, custom, and morality*. Cambridge, Mass.: M.I.T. Press.

WREN, T. E. (1985). Whistle-blowing and loyalty to one's friends. In Heffernan, W. C., & Stroup, T., eds. *Police Ethics: Hard Choices in Law Enforcement* (pp. 25–43). New York: John Jay Press.

2

Historical Perspectives of Police Misconduct

Kenneth Bolton, Jr.

❖

INTRODUCTION

Serious studies of policing began only a generation ago or, so spurred on, in part, by the civil unrest of the 1960s and violent encounters between police and groups of citizens voicing their concerns over the direction of American society. Scholars have used various techniques of research and analysis, explored differing perspectives and dimensions of policing, and drawn insightful, yet often contradictory, conclusions about the origins and continuing development of policing in America. Much of this work has addressed police misconduct in some fashion, but little attempt has been made to provide students of policing with a focused, in-depth historical and analytical perspective on police misconduct.

From the late 1970s to the early 1990s, studies of policing waned, and many who wrote about policing focused only on the daily administration of policing. Events of the early 1990s, such as the Rodney King beating and the O.J. Simpson case, have inspired renewed public and scholarly focus on the behavior of police officers, yet we still lack the analytical ability to understand and adequately explain continuing acts of police misconduct.

There are many reasons for this lack of a clear theoretical focus of police misconduct. The first, discussed in Chapter 1, is the problem of defining what constitutes police misconduct. Clearly, this is a political and cultural as well as a research problem: Behavior that some consider misconduct constitutes acceptable behavior to others, and what many now consider to be misconduct may have been acceptable behavior in the past. Second, methodological problems impede study. Historical records of policing and police practices are poor and, where available, are not uniform. This makes sifting through these records a timely and exhaustive process, and information about misconduct frequently is nonexistent or not clearly spelled out. Therefore, third, scholars often draw inferences about policing and create narratives about past police behavior from present experiences. This renders much of what we think we know about the development of policing problematically transhistorical—more of a descriptive narrative than a useful theoretical construct that could guide our understanding of police misconduct and help us begin to think about adequate solutions.

The task of this chapter is to recognize these problems and still illustrate, somehow, that an appreciation of the historical context of questionable police practices can be useful to catalyze, in all of us, the initiative and ability to develop effective policies to prevent and/or control police misconduct. This chapter first outlines those social processes and factors identified by scholars as influencing both the normative and non-normative behavior of police officers and, from them, form an analytical model of the dimensions of police misconduct that focuses on the relationship between these dimensions.

This model can be used to guide our understanding of the persistence of police misconduct as well as the practical and theoretical complexities and contradictions of the topic. However, because the ideas are drawn from existing literature, it should not be considered a complete model. Rather, it should be regarded as a flexible starting point in understanding police misconduct that can be further developed as our theoretical sophistication grows. This chapter concludes by considering past and currently proposed solutions to police misconduct in light of this model, emphasizing how solutions have dialectically seemed to create new problems.

WHAT SHAPES POLICE MISCONDUCT

This section categorizes and discusses the social processes and factors identified by scholars as important in shaping the behavior of police officers—that which must be considered to historically contextualize and understand police misconduct. The diverse, often conflicting, findings of scholarly work suggest that police misconduct is a multidimensional phenomenon resulting from a complex intertwining of social processes that belie easy answers and solutions.

Structural Economic Conditions

The economic organization of American society is the starting point of scholars who have argued that the development and transitions of industrial capitalism has shaped all institutions including policing. For example, in his analysis of deviant behavior, Steven Spitzer maintains that the "superstructure [institutions] of society emerges from and reflects the ongoing development of economic forces . . . [and] preserves the hegemony of the ruling class through a system of class controls" (1996: 29–30).

Those groups that have been able to control the economic system have been disproportionately able to use police power to maintain their control to the disadvantage of those groups that come to be defined as "problem populations." Members of these "problem" groups are both subjected to direct forms of police misconduct as well as denied protection of their constitutional and human rights by the police. Although this relationship is generally treated as unidirectional—one in which policing is shaped by the demands of the economically powerful—dialectically, the efforts of subordinate groups to free themselves from oppression have been shown to have a tremendous impact on shaping policing. What constitutes policing at any point in time results from the struggle of groups vying to determine their place in the social world and to define how they should be regarded and treated.

Historically, in relatively homogeneous agrarian societies, police power is carried out by the members of the community themselves. However, as societies become more economically differentiated and more socially heterogeneous, policing gradually emerges as the paid activity of a selected number of members of the community. Beyond the night watch system, which is an antecedent of policing, Walker (1992) and Barlow (1994) argue that modern policing can be traced to attempts to control the black population in eighteenth-century America. Both demonstrate that the first modern-style American police department was established in the 1740s in Charleston, South Carolina, and then soon after in other southern cities as part of a general approach to the control of the enslaved population.

Modern policing, therefore, is related to seventeenth- and eighteenth-century slave codes (Genovese, 1974; Higginbotham, 1978), which were economically motivated laws passed by those who controlled the economic and political systems to make enormous profits through the exploitation of enslaved African labor. However, these codes could not have had their desired effect without a means of enforcement. Very early on, landowners who composed and/or controlled state legislatures created militias, formed slave patrols, and employed bounty hunters to enforce their will. These "enforcers" are viewed by many scholars as the precursors of modern policing.

Higginbotham (1978), for example, describes in rich detail the origins of slave patrols that were required by legislators or authorized to be used at the community level in many states from South Carolina to New York in the early 1700s. His work illustrates how the economic imperatives that led to the creation of policing simultaneously fostered the emergence of police brutality, which quickly emerged as an integral part of slave patrols. Genovese (1974) similarly discusses how the brutality of the patrols, made up of poor whites, drew widespread protests from both the enslaved who experienced excessive violence and the masters who were unsettled by witnessing it and its aftermath. Although difficult to identify an exact reason for the emergence of this brutality, landowners who had an economic interest in maintaining control over the enslaved population clearly set the context in which brutality thrived. Legislators in Georgia and South Carolina, for example, paid rewards to bounty hunters who brought back the scalp and ears of runaway slaves (Higginbotham, 1978).

People of African descent continually resisted attempts to control them (Genovese, 1974) and were crucial to the defeat of the southern military in the Civil War and integral to the attempt to economically and politically reconstruct the South after the war (Du Bois, 1962). However, from the time that reconstruction efforts were dismantled around 1876 to the successes of the Civil Rights movement in the 1950s and 1960s, the black population was subjected to a horrendous display of force designed to maintain them in a subjugated status. To uphold postreconstruction "black codes" and the twentieth century's Jim Crow laws, police were actively involved in both terrorizing black communities and allowing them to be terrorized by others without offering any substantial protection.

This historical record clearly and unambiguously demonstrates that policing and the unequal treatment of people of African descent by police has developed hand in hand as a legitimated means of protecting the interests of those with economic and political power. However, it must be remembered that responses by members of African American communities to this treatment and to their relationship with police agencies have set the context for much of policing in the mid to late twentieth century. From the early struggle of the National Association for the Advancement of Colored People (NAACP) against lynching (Zangrando, 1980) to the civil rights struggles of the 1950s and the massive urban unrest of the 1960s, a specific focus of the organized political movement of African Americans has historically been the redefinition of American policing.

Other scholars have demonstrated how police have similarly been created and employed to control members of other non-European ethnic groups to ensure the economic benefit of a few. Coramae Mann (1993), for example, provides the most complete analysis illustrating how state and private power have historically been used to control, not only African Americans, but the Native American population, Asian Americans, and Latinos to suppress their opposition to white economic and ideological hegemony.

Barlow (1994), for example, explains how the government's increasing frustration with the prolonged military effort to control the Native American populations led to the formation of tribal police in the 1870s. This strategy, he argues, proved very effective in undermining Native self-government and the power of the traditional chiefs and in establishing a new form of social control from which the economic potential of the land and its resources could be exploited by economically powerful groups. That the effort was driven by economic interest is clear: "the process of privatizing the land meant breaking the Indians' communal monopolistic control over the land within the reservation and creating new opportunities for land acquisition by white Americans" (1994: 144). Without discussing overt forms of misconduct, this work demonstrates how powerful groups set the context for misconduct by creating police to break traditional social institutions and further a group's exploitation for profit.

The formation of police agencies in primarily northern urban areas has also been shown to be shaped by the struggle between economically powerful groups and those who migrate to these areas for jobs. Many historians of policing argue that the development of modern-style policing occurred in the mid-1800s in northern cities in response to urban unrest. Race and ethnicity played a vital role, but, again, the driving force was economic. Lane (1992), for example, discusses how the transition from a local to a national marketing system associated with the early development of industrialism was crucial to the development of police departments in northern cities as tensions among the settled population, various immigrant groups from Europe, and the free black population were exacerbated, resulting in constant urban violence, mostly in the form of riots. These riots led for some to call for the creation of an objective, paid police force that would control the unrest through any available means—including violence.

In his examination of mining towns in Pennsylvania, McDonough (1997) shows how economic conditions translated into political and judicial power in the early 20th-century boom time for industrial capitalism as America transformed from an agricultural economy. "The coal companies had political and economic power and they could manipulate the powers of the state, particularly the judiciary and the police, to their advantage" (1997: 384). McDonough details how companies built towns around their mines and exercised absolute authority to control all aspects of the workers' daily lives. When miners went on strike for better living and working conditions, the companies refused to deal with them and instead used the courts and the police to harass, intimidate, and force them back to work.

Lane (1992) and others, however, demonstrate that although police were founded as instruments of social control, they never fully operated as agents of oppression. While the police were created to protect the interests of economic and political elites, members of subjugated immigrant groups attempted to control and use the police to help them better their economic and political positions. For example, scholars who discuss the importance of urban unrest in the formation of police illustrate how officers recruited from ethnic groups increasingly served the interests of those members of their ethnic and/or religious groups and not merely the interests of the economic elites. Similarly, scholars who concentrate on the formation of police to control labor illustrate how many local officers had strong community ties with striking workers and often sympathized with their struggle and sought to protect them from violence.

This work promotes a more complex understanding of how police are not formed merely as a result of the interests of economic elites but as a product of the conflict between groups with conflicting economic interests. Although police forces were initially formed to protect the economic interests of the powerful, subjugated groups realized the importance of the police to their economic interests and attempted to form relations with and/or control agencies.

The economically powerful groups responded to this problematic relationship between immigrant and labor groups and local police agencies by subverting the authority of local police, placing authority, at first, in private police and, later, centralizing it at the state and federal levels. By breaking local ties between communities and police and by making the function of police more objectively tied to employers and/or legislatures, those with economic power sought to create conditions in which they could more freely exercise their will over subjugated groups.

Scholars have demonstrated that the economic elite (1) used local judges, often members of elite groups to rule in such a way that local officers were forced to act against their personal wishes; (2) hired deputies and gave them legal sanction to act in the company's interest; (3) formed private police, such as Pennsylvania's coal and iron police, commissioned by the governor and manned by members of detective agencies. "In 1914, there were 275 detective agencies in the United States whose prime source of income came from providing assistance to management in labor disputes" (McDonough, 1997: 397); and (4) used their political power to form the state police, beginning in many states in 1905. Ten years after their creation, the state police were described by the 1915 Commission on Industrial Relations as an extremely efficient force for crushing strikes.

This historic struggle demonstrates that, the more insulated officers are from the populations they police, the more efficiently policing protects the economic interests of elite groups. Although close ties between officers and members of communities have often been blamed for fostering various forms of police corruption, it is seemingly easier for police to be brutal and engage in misconduct if they are not intimately familiar with those they police. Similarly, if it can be assumed that familiarity of community members with police decreases the likelihood of police violence, the economically powerful, intentionally or otherwise, have historically promoted brutality by mandating that the police objectively act in their interests regardless of the needs of the local populations.

Women, too, have a historic relationship with policing that promotes various forms of misconduct; however, this relationship has only begun to be examined since the 1980s. Although different scholars focus on different causes for the secondary status of women in American society, it is clear that one of the major reasons is economics and the exploitation and control of women's labor. Women have historically been exploited for their labor in general and, in particular, their reproductive and domestic labor while perpetually denied economic and political power. Catherine MacKinnon argues that "male dominance is probably the most pervasive and tenacious system of power in history and is organized so that men may dominate and women must submit" (MacKinnon quoted in Harris 1995: 257), and this domination is promoted by all societal institutions, including the police.

The control and treatment of women has historically been the purview of their spouses with the state refusing to intervene even in instances of domestic violence. For example, examining historical accounts of battering, Joanne Belknap concludes "that men were more likely to be punished for not dominating their wives than for beating them" (1996: 185). The realization that force against women has been historically mandated allows a greater understanding of the relationship between gender oppression and policing. First, women rarely receive police protection from the violence of their "loved ones," and the freedom of women to move outside of their homes has been greatly restricted as rape and sexual harassment are trivialized and police refuse to protect women, thus ensuring greater control of women by the men in their household.

Even as we enter a new millennium, domestic violence calls are often viewed as frustrating and unimportant by officers, and women who have been raped and women who are harassed are often regarded with disdain or hostility. Further, racial and gender oppression interact, making the relationship between African American women and police even more problematic. Angela Harris, for example, concludes that rape for black women includes not only a vulnerability to rape but a lack of legal protection radically different from that experienced by white women (1993: 263).

Women who work or travel outside of their homes face the possibility of encountering overt forms of police misconduct or more subtle forms such as being denied protection. The control of women's sexuality extends beyond the household to include those women who engage in commercial sex, making these women particularly vulnerable to police misconduct. As women engage in this form of economic activity, they encounter police who manipulate, harass, arrest, and exploit them through various forms of corrupt behavior.

Finally, economic productivity is strongly related to technological innovation, which in turn shapes policing through both intended and unintended consequences. During the twentieth century, technological innovations such as cars, radios, investigative tools, weapons, and more recently computers have set the daily context in which officers work. Policing today is dramatically different from policing at the turn of the century, in large part because of the technological transitions of American industrialism. However, it is not technology, in and of itself, that determines police behavior, but the social administrative organization that emerges to control the implementation of new technology.

Reiss, for example, illustrates how the desired separation of the relationship between community members and police was furthered by early twentieth-century technological innovations.

> Perhaps the major impact that technological inventions had was to solidify the bureaucratic centralization of command and control. The separation of the working police from the communities was organizationally complete. The era of the dial-a-radio-active-rapid-response-cop was by the seventies the dominant model of American policing. (1992: 52)

Technological advances served to increase the level of separation between the police and citizens that they had sworn to protect and to serve. The insulation of the police from the community members they policed came at a high price.

> The patrol officer in his air-conditioned and heated car no longer got out of the police vehicle to do preventive patrol or to learn more about the community being policed. . . . No longer did the public have confidence that the police were handling, or could handle, their problems, and many, particularly minority groups, felt alienated from the police. (Reiss, 1992: 53)

As we look at the behavior of the police in the present time of rapid economic transformation, we must continually remind ourselves how the two are inextricably linked. Policing matured as industrialism drew millions of people to the cities who hoped to share in its prosperity. As the American economy begins to be reorganized around new technologies and as businesses become global, what will become of the millions of poor people left in the inner cities and scattered rural areas whose economic hopes were never realized? As the new millennium begins, there is an unprecedented gap between rich and poor. Assuming that the police represent the economically powerful, intentionally or otherwise, relations between police and the economically and politically powerless are entering a new age of struggle.

In conclusion,

> the data suggest that police actions such as arrest, use of deadly force, [corruption] and verbal abuse reflect the broader patterns of social and economic inequality in American society. . . . the injustices suffered by racial and ethnic minorities at the hands of the police are a result of both discrimination against people of color and the disproportionate representation of minorities among the poor. (Walker et al., 1996: 115–6)

Although policing and the daily conduct of officers clearly are influenced by economic structural conditions, that these conditions should not be looked at as a final, causative factor of police misconduct should also be clear. Despite the development of capitalism and the consequent stratification system, groups of people continually struggle to define and control police forces in their local communities and make them more responsive to their needs. The crux of these struggles is where much misconduct occurs.

Politics

In smaller communities and rural areas today, local political leaders still exert tremendous influence on policing and the relationship between local departments and members of the community. However, throughout the twentieth century, power struggles between political leaders at the varying levels of government, legislatures, and appointed commissions over the control of policing have been responsible for setting the tone for police activities.

Historians of policing in the northern U.S. cities have concluded that, faced with growing unrest, local leaders explored the necessity of having a paid, objective police force similar to the London Metropolitan police model to protect the interests of the community and business. As it proved to be an effective strategy, the willingness to have a permanent police force grew. However, unlike the London model, control of police in the United States became political rather than judicial. As Monkkonen points out, "increasing functional differentiation in revised city governments located the police under the executive rather than the judicial branch. . . . The shift also ensured a structural antagonism between the courts, prosecuting attorneys, and the police" (1992, 550–1).

Although it was still unclear what communities' expectations of officers entailed and what the full responsibilities of police agencies would be, the trend to establish police agencies took off. Between 1845 and 1875, nearly every major city developed an organized police department, and what many now consider to be misconduct was accepted behavior. Force, for example, was permitted because, "fear of street violence prompted politicians, judges, and the middle classes generally to encourage cops . . . to use extralegal personal authority, muscle and hickory in putting down the poor, the criminal, and the riotous" (Lane, 1992: 18).

As structural conditions set the stage for the emergence of policing, political concerns sought to define its initial development. Some scholars maintain that control over police soon became one of the most important political problems of the mid-nineteenth century. It was realized that the police could be used and were, in fact, already being used to benefit different groups in different ways. In his insightful study of police history, for example, Walker (1977) illustrates the early link between partisan community politics and the use of police as a means of ensuring one group's power over less powerful opposition groups.

Many social historians similarly illustrate how, "the battle for control of the police was the symbolic focus of a wider conflict between an entrenched native elite and a largely immigrant majority in the nation's great cities" (Lane, 1992: 19). Many European ethnic groups that were at first objects of social control efforts by elite political and economic groups came to see local political machinery and the police as a way to exert influence over their lives by gaining some authority over decisions that impacted their communities on a daily basis.

Paying officers regular salaries made positions in departments more desirable and simultaneously furthered misconduct. Monkkonen argues that police jobs became "political plums to be handed out by the political party gaining the mayor's position. From this then developed the use of police in political control, police officers sometimes deterring voters and generally working for a partisan control of the ballot boxes" (1992: 552). This relationship benefited the police officers as well as the political machinery in power, since they were able to have a steady income and, importantly, cultural and ethnic group identification added legitimacy and respect to officers' self-worth after years of being treated by the general public with disrespect and hostility.

However, as others point out, in both northern and southern communities, the attempt of African Americans to gain similar influence through electing leaders and appointing supportive officers from their communities was violently rejected. Political leaders continued to use policing as a method of controlling African Americans and fought against all attempts at political and economic equality. Hawkins and Thomas (1991) discuss how white leaders conceptualized policing as the first line of defense against the black "hordes" through the socially demanded use of force and brutality. While European immigrants were able to gain some measure of control over life in their communities, white groups continued to exercise a monopoly on power over African Americans in economics, politics, and raw physical force through the authority of law.

Where ethnic groups were able to exert influence and control over police in their communities, officers became central figures in partisan politics, racketeering, and corruption. Frequently denied legitimate economic and political opportunities by the economic elite, many local political machines depended on vice districts and the money they generated through bribes and fines to fund the operations of the political machinery (Monkkonen, 1992).

After the turn of the century, the control of police came to be viewed as a strategy to break the power of local political machines. As the political machinery of local communities benefited from their ability to shape local policing in their interests, political groups at state and federal levels continually fought to diminish the influence of local political machinery and to exert greater control over local politics and police agencies. Often, these political leaders aligned themselves with groups of moral entrepreneurs and attacked local politicians and police as corrupt and immoral and sought to enforce moral legislation, such as the control of alcohol consumption and prostitution, as a means of gaining political power while limiting the power of local political machines.

Morn (1990), for example, illustrates the dynamic nature of political conflict between leaders at the national and local levels in his analysis of commercial sex in the midwest. At various times in the twentieth century, national campaigns to stop prostitution were launched at the national level, although prostitution was accepted in local communities and benefited local politicians and police officers. In spite of their initial resistance, as public pressure mounted, local political leaders told police chiefs—who Morn refers to as "frequently puppets of politics, reflecting the will of the political elites of their towns" (1990: 153)—to more tightly control prostitution. As public pressure faded, prostitution would reemerge in, perhaps, a different location or a slightly different form, supported, once again, by the local political machinery and the police.

Political patronage and police corruption were further circumvented by the promotion of a civil service system and the growing influence of a business model of management in cities and towns. Increasingly, the old city aldermen style of government was replaced with a mayor, an elected council and, more importantly, a professional city manager whose function was to handle the day-to-day administration of the affairs of the city. This new system had the effect of limiting corruption and cronyism and made the police more accountable to the city administration instead of a political boss.

The increased control of police from the national political level continued as exemplified by the crime commissions of the period from 1919 to 1931, which became the primary vehicle for police reform. Many of these commissions were ostensibly formed to investigate the role police played in virtually all racial riots of the period. However, although their effect in limiting racially inspired violence by police is debatable, these commissions took an active role in attempting to limit the local political machinery's control of police. Commissions investigated, evaluated, and made recommendations that shaped policing at the local community level from the early to mid-twentieth century.

Local political influence in shaping policing persists in varying degrees. Studies have shown, for example, how in small towns and rural areas, political groups exert a continually tremendous impact on local police forces. Further, recent analyses have shown how elected officials in larger cities have the ability to set the tone for police departments and officer behavior through, among other means, their stated expectations and political rhetoric. Similarly, national political bodies continue to exert influence over policing at all levels of government through funding decisions, appointing investigative commissions and, perhaps most importantly, making law. Recent examples of legislators' ability to shape police practices that impact the relationship between police officers and members of communities include forfeiture laws, which have been widely assaulted as promoting police misconduct, and disparate penalties governing crack versus powder cocaine, which have been widely critiqued as examples of racism.

Although scholars like Cohen argue that "pervasive and systematic abuse lowers trust in the government and ruins what hope there is for cooperation between the government and the people" (1996: 183), it is clear that politically powerful leaders and groups have, historically, used their positions of authority to shape policing and the conduct of officers—for good or bad—depending on their perceived interests. In fact, history demonstrates that if political leaders convince enough of the public that police abuse is in their interest, the public will cooperate and allow disadvantaged groups to be subjected to police force. The operation of ideology that culminates in various forms of police misconduct against the economically and politically powerless also needs to be addressed.

Ideology

Several analyses in the last twenty-five years or so have sought to demonstrate the relationship of social control and its ideological justification. In terms of continuing economic and political control of disadvantaged groups using police agencies, increased surveillance of the population in general goes hand in hand with the process of defining some segment of the population as objects of control, thereby permitting police to act on them. This increased control is then ideologically justified as being in the general public's best interest. This process of ideological construction has historically been the purview of economic and political leaders using their power to influence the content of the media; however, recent studies illustrate the ability of police agencies to similarly employ the media to their advantage. Consumers of information, including the public and police officers, are swayed by the media reports, and the treatment of members of oppressed populations is generally accepted.

In one of the most complete works on this topic, Mann (1992) develops an in-depth analysis of ideological construction throughout American history. Her work illustrates how the members of powerful groups, politicians, and the media have historically interacted with each other to create and perpetuate racial beliefs and stereotypes for political gain, allowing the maintenance of economic control over exploited minority groups. However, others have discussed how labeling a particular group as a problem to be monitored and controlled is only one aspect of the constructive process. The creation of a general social atmosphere in which increased control seems desirable is equally important.

Scholars have shown how the terminology of *war* has emerged throughout the twentieth century and served to shape public perceptions. First, the War on Crime, popularized in the mid-1920s, and currently the War on Drugs serve to transform the public's idea of policing from a community-service orientation and from the acceptable social control of criminal behavior to a state of emergency. "We no longer face losses of one kind or another from the depredations of criminals; we are in imminent danger of losing everything . . . this war mentality legitimizes the police methods necessary to win the war developing 'a will to ruthlessness'" (Lasswell, quoted in Bittner, 1970: 48–9).

Forms of police misconduct, therefore, are generally accepted against members of disadvantaged groups if the general public accepts that society is at war with these groups that are perceived as engaging in behavior that will ultimately destroy society. For example, Keith (1991) examines how structural forces of society in the 1980s and 1990s have interacted with the construction of a discourse that promotes the idea that black communities are more "criminal" than others, in order to legitimize the selective oppression of these communities. Bell (1992) maintains that this creates and reinforces stereotypes in the minds of the public, providing both a moral and a legal justification for the mistreatment of black people by the criminal justice system.

The print media has historically been used for ideological purposes, however, the mass media emerged in the late twentieth century as a more diverse means for shaping the public's view of reality, including shaping public perceptions of crime and its control. Oliver (1992) looked at one aspect of the media by conducting a content analysis of "reality-based" police shows and concluded that the entertainment media portrays black people as "bad guys" and white officers as the restorers of justice. How this portrayal ultimately affects the public is not completely understood, yet it serves as an illustration of how ideological messages are part of what all members of the society view for entertainment.

Consequently, one reason that members of oppressed groups encounter police misconduct is that officers, like other members of society, have learned to accept sexist and racist ideology as correct. Officers learn how to think about groups that are different from themselves through their association with all societal institutions on a daily basis. The media, however, has proven particularly potent in shaping the stereotypical images that influence how officers perceive and deal with members of these groups who they come to believe as more likely to engage in criminal behavior and who, therefore, warrant tougher treatment.

Other studies have also shown that police agencies have become actively involved in shaping ideology to further their perceived interests. Martin concludes that:

> few modern institutions are as successful as the police at shaping the discourse concerning them. . . . policing discourse shapes public understanding of social order, resisting outside, non-police control and criticism through the use of press releases, "tips" to favored reporters (and punishment of critical reporters through denial of information), and staged media events. (1993: 159)

Illustrating this process, Stuart Hall (1978) demonstrated how the police and media tapped into popular common sense images about race in the inner cities to construct a crime model predicated on the notion that black communities were social problems. Similarly, Cashmore and McLaughlin (1991) argue that police promote the idea of crisis and relate social disorder with black people to extend their political and legal powers while justifying increases in their resources. Chambliss (1994) further details how a coalition of political, law enforcement, and media interests has created a moral panic over crime to create growth in the crime industry.

Finally, Beyer (1993) suggests that the repeated exposure in the media of the shocking brutality of the Rodney King case may actually be detrimental to our understanding and treatment of police misconduct cases, as it serves to set an exaggerated standard by which all other claims of misconduct are judged. As members of the public come to understand police misconduct through constant media exposure, do they come to believe that if the conduct of officers does not involve repeatedly pummeling a defenseless person that they really are not behaving so badly?

The economic and political control over some groups is furthered by the ideas used to justify their treatment. Structural, political, and cultural processes, therefore, interact in such a way that police misconduct can emerge and even be regarded as acceptable. The ideological justification for social control is particularly powerful in times of economic uncertainty and political crisis. That economic and political leaders have the power to control the media is clear; however, the preceding discussion included the emergence of police agencies as increasingly influential in shaping the media, public perceptions of their activities, and, therefore, their own course. The following discussion examines the transformation of police agencies from a political "puppet" to a self-conscious, independently powerful social force responsible, therefore, in part, for officer misconduct.

THE ADMINISTRATION OF POLICING

Although the origins of policing are rooted in economic concerns and its early development is tied to political expediencies, police officers have become increasingly involved over the years in defining their role in society and creating a workplace environment best suited to their perceived self-interest. This process of emerging self-definition in relation to other institutions is important in understanding current police agencies and the behavior of officers. Many scholars argue that an understanding of the administration of policing is central to explaining police misconduct. Martin, for example, maintains that "all police misconduct is systemic, the product of institutionalized policies and practices, both officially and unofficially sanctioned" (1993: 144).

As previously discussed, officers in the nineteenth century were often the tools of local political machinery; however, it is important to understand that officers also performed a variety of welfare functions and that their general orientation tended to be community service. This orientation began to change beginning in the early 1890s and culminating in the 1920s, as policing began to adopt a crime-control model.

Scholars discuss the period from 1887 to 1890 as the dawning of organizational self-consciousness among American police. Cincinnati developed the first professionalized department in 1886 that, in its efforts to control and discipline its officers to reduce brutality and corruption, employed a military model of command. Other departments followed suit and adopted a quasi-military form of organization to promote internal control and discipline. Monkkonen (1992) points out that this model allowed a superior ability to communicate and issue commands, which gave police an organizational efficiency lacking in previous systems and in other governmental organizations.

According to Samuel Walker, reform of policing was, in part, an attempt by business and professional interests to break the power of the working-class–based political machines that dominated the police, "professionalism was itself a movement that served partisan ends" (1977: 31). However, the police themselves were vitally important to this process of defining themselves as a profession. In fact, most scholars agree that growing occupational identity and the search for professional autonomy by local police agencies is the primary story of twentieth-century policing. Around the turn of the century, policing became more of a career instead of labor, and by the 1920s, the community-service orientation had faded and the crime-control model had taken hold. Officers increasingly perceived themselves to be professionals whose area of expertise was crime.

Police reform continued to be an uneven process at best, with some agencies achieving a measure of professionalization long before others and with others claiming to be more professional when, in fact, they operated as usual. The Great Depression of the 1930s and the resulting financial crisis forced many reluctant departments to initiate long-delayed reform programs. This so-called "second generation" of reformers undertook scientific studies of policing that represented considerable advances in sophistication (Walker, 1977). These studies analyzed police work and developed a scientific basis for assignments and promoting the crime-fighting model. The simultaneous creation of the Federal Bureau of Investigation (FBI) and its emergence as the primary vehicle for promoting police reform solidified the focus of police administrators on moving in the direction of increased professionalism.

By the end of the 1930s, the dominant features of modern American police administration had taken shape. Police agencies conformed to a single model of large bureaucratic structures organized along hierarchical, semi-military lines, which promoted the accumulation and use of knowledge, professional autonomy, and a public-service ideal. Enhancing the power of police executives, installing centralized, rational administrative procedures, and improving the quality of officers were the three most important goals of efficiency-minded reformers who were often police professionals and police chiefs rather than rank-and-file officers. By the 1960s, Bittner (1970) found that police reform had become an internal goal of police departments actively pursued by leading institutional officials.

Despite the activities of the professionally minded reformers during the first half of the twentieth century, police misconduct persisted. Reasons for continued misconduct range from the economic and political, discussed previously, to administrative problems in agencies that have yet to be fined-tuned. Many point to the fact that policing is, inherently, unlike any other profession.

First, officers are authorized to use force when they deem it necessary. Bittner, for example, describes police procedure as "non-negotiably coercive" and suggests that it is "defined by the feature that it may not be opposed in its course, and that force can be used if it is opposed" (1970: 39–41).

Second, and inextricably related to the first, officers have the discretion to judge a situation and determine how to respond:

> It is hard to think of any hierarchical organization in which the lowest-level employees routinely exercise such great discretion with such little opportunity for objective review. . . .
> Hard and fast rules are viable in mechanical work situations, but they are of little assistance in dealing with the fluid discretionary situations that are the core of police work. (Skolnick & Fyfe, 1993: 120)

Due to these two aspects of modern policing, scholars debate whether misconduct results from institutionalized malpractice or is the responsibility of an individual officer.

Many argue that the tone of any police agency and the actions of the officers are set by the chief. "He must take and interpret what he conceives to be the political and public will and translate them into police operations and behaviors" (Morn, 1990: 164). Brutality in general and shooting in particular have more to do with individual police chiefs' personal philosophies and policies than with rates of crime; this is supported by examinations of the role of black urban political power and community-sensitive police chiefs since the early 1970s in the declining rates of police brutality (Skolnick & Fyfe: 1993).

Others dismiss the focus on the chief's style and personality and focus instead on an agency's development of administrative guidelines to shape the behaviors of officers. For example, Barker and Carter maintain that "a written directive system is the cornerstone for administrative guidance and control" (1991: 25). However, they report survey data from 1982, which found that 24 percent of agencies had no written policies pertaining to sixteen types of police deviance. The percentage was higher for smaller departments (40 percent). Further, even when agencies had developed clear written policies, many failed to fully communicate those rules to all members of the department.

The importance of administrative guidelines is further essential for agencies to govern the behavior of officers through a disciplinary system that clearly relates forms of inappropriate behavior to specific penalties. Carter maintains that "it is important that a department have a well-planned, objective, structured, and equitable disciplinary system which is clearly articulated by formal policy and procedures" (1991: 351). This system is necessary to promote the notion of accountability in which officers are held responsible for their behavior.

Alison Patton (1993) found that police departments lack internal accountability systems that are preventative or that contain corrective disciplinary actions. A big part of the problem is the lack of will to institute an effective system of accountability or administrative indifference. She concluded that, unless a case of sufficient brutality occurs that gains media attention and costs taxpayers a lot of money, departments will not move forward to address issues such as training, promotion, supervisor accountability, discipline, and oversight—all of which could actually impact police misconduct.

Officers have enormous discretionary powers to perform their jobs, creating the opportunity for misconduct. It is difficult for agency leaders to hold officers accountable for their decisions because "discretionary decisions can be reviewed only when they are directly supervised or a matter of record" (Cohen, 1996: 193). Professionalism as a solution to misconduct has yet to escape the administrative conundrum it has created, and the misconduct it was supposed to diminish persists.

Further, the military model that police agencies have chosen to follow in order to effectively fight crime seems to create conditions for misconduct. This model and the ideological justification of a "war" combine to encourage police violence and misconduct. Some groups are treated as more adversarial than others, and their communities are more frequently patrolled and their members more arrest prone. As an example, Tonry suggests that the tactical emphasis of police departments on disadvantaged minority neighborhoods "produces racial proportions in arrests that do not mirror racial proportions in drug use" (1995: 107). A white officer was quoted as saying that "even for minor violations, there was an open-season on Negroes (Cray, 1967: 185).

The view of police officers as soldiers engaged in a War on Crime further diverts attention and resources from more effective strategies for crime control while creating tension between the police and citizens and the police and other societal institutions. More recently, police agencies have gone beyond merely employing a military model of administrative organization to the actual militarization of their agencies. The use of the equipment, training, and tactics of warfare by police agencies is on the rise nationwide, exemplified by the fact that the number of militarily trained police quadrupled from 1980 to 1995. Agencies increasingly receive funding from drug-war budgets and use material donated from the Department of Defense.

In conclusion, the tension between professional expertise and public control over the police and their activities continues to form one of the fundamental problems of policing. Professional agencies have become increasingly isolated from the communities they police, and the military model fosters the treatment of some segments of the public as enemies of the state. Most agencies still have not determined how to best control the use of officer discretion and implement adequate systems of accountability. Further, the hierarchical style employed by police agencies fosters conflict between the administrators and rank and file officers, which promotes the development of police subcultures and a working atmosphere in which misconduct thrives.

The Police Subculture

Officer misconduct is fostered by the organization and administration of police agencies; however, as the organization gives rise to a subculture, that group further promotes misconduct. Subcultures have been defined as problem-solving devices that arise as people in specific groups attempt to solve the structural and organizational problems they encounter. Where circumstances block aspirations, alternative values develop as a way of coping with the frustrations of exclusion from legitimate routes to success. Most observers of policing maintain, therefore, that the police subculture forms in response to the unique structural conditions of the occupation. "Isolation, cops against bosses, hostile clientele—all help to account for the rare degree of camaraderie and group loyalty among police officers" (Skolnick & Fyfe, 1993: 122). The following discussion outlines the various parameters of the development and persistence of police subcultures and explores their role in promoting misconduct.

The conditions under which the subculture emerged in American policing began as early as the formation of policing. In the nineteenth century, officers had no training and little real instruction, and they were basically sent on patrol with little supervision and little real understanding of how to perform their tasks. To survive life on the job, officers had to develop strategies that included communicating with, supporting, and learning from each other. At some point, like members of other working-class groups, officers began to realize that their new occupational interests needed political action to be protected, beyond the support given by local political machinery, which was increasingly under attack by reformers. Officers began to form fraternal and benefit societies as an expression of their collective will.

To promote greater solidarity among officers, job security, and greater control over the daily workplace environment, officers saw collectivities as essential. However, opposition was as fierce to their efforts as it was to the efforts of other working-class groups, and their efforts were repeatedly defeated. It is difficult to remember that officers once exhibited greater solidarity with workers than they appear to do currently. However, Monkkonen emphasizes that "until the defeat of striking police officers in Boston in 1919 ended police unionization efforts for almost a half century, police themselves were often part of the American labor movement" (1992: 561), and the historical record is full of incidents in which local police sided with striking workers.

Efforts to unionize did not end even as the primary path of police development became "professionalism," pushed by experts and implemented by the heads of the departments. Officers again fought for unions in the period of 1943–47 and were again defeated. Provoked by the social crisis of the 1960s and feeling a lack of public support, police officers once again turned to unionism and finally gained the right to unionize in 1966 (Walker, 1977). Police unions have since become a crucial factor in shaping the attitudes and conduct of officers. Carter (1991) concluded that unions are the most significant factor affecting the structure of a department's disciplinary system through the enormous pressure on chiefs to avoid scrutiny of police behavior. Unions further support officers accused of misconduct financially and legally.

However, without a high degree of job security and frustrated by their lack of collective bargaining ability, the police subculture began to emerge early on as a collective strategy of officers to exert some control over their daily work lives. Subcultural development was also furthered by officers' isolation from the public. Walker (1977) argues that earlier generations of police officers had to be brutal in order to establish their personal authority in the community. Skolnick (1969) adds that, because of this antagonism with members of communities, the police occupation has become increasingly isolated and based on internal solidarity and secrecy. Most scholars agree that because the police had an often antagonistic relationship to the public and low status vis-à-vis other professionals with whom they worked, they tended to develop an isolated and defensive perspective and came to feel that they could rely only on themselves for support and respect. Cohen agrees that isolation created an adversarial relation between the police and the public and adds that the "rhetoric of war also [fostered a] siege mentality that alienated the officer from the community" (1996: 178).

Interestingly, professionalization and the military model promoted by agency leaders also had the unanticipated consequence of furthering subcultural development. Among rank-and-file officers, the difficulty of communicating up and down the rigid chain of the military-style command hierarchy exacerbated their isolation and promoted the inclination to devalue rules and find shortcuts around them (Skolnick & Fyfe, 1993). As agency bureaucracies form rules to structure and regulate the daily behavior of its officers, these officers reflect on and interpret these rules in particular ways that guide how they actually perform their jobs. For officers who cooperate with those who operate the system of punishment, the subcultural price is absolute exclusion from the informal life of officers and a refusal by all officers to work with them (Reiss, 1971).

The subculture actively holds officers together by a process of occupational socialization: reinforcing, rewarding, and punishing the behavior of its members. Understanding how it operates to teach behavior and values that deviate from formal legal and organizational rules is crucial to understanding the persistence of misconduct. Barker provides a succinct discussion of the relationship between police subcultural socialization and misconduct:

> the peer group indoctrinates and socializes the rookie into patterns of acceptable corrupt activities, sanctions deviations outside these boundaries, and sanctions officers who do not en-

gage in any corrupt acts. The peer group can also discipline officers who report or attempt to report fellow officers. (1991: 53)

The unique context of policing furthers this learning process. In the closed society of policing, "views are constantly reinforced during idle-hour conversations and after-hour socializing, they come to form a sort of 'groupthink'; a common set of lenses through which all members of the department view and interpret the world around them" (Skolnick & Fyfe, 1993: 241). Beyond learning to operate in the institutional setting, officers are influenced by other officers in the meaning they derive from their experiences in the everyday world. This includes how officers learn to perceive members of minority groups. Studies have shown, for example, that, rather than police officers merely being overtly racist, police behavior manifests itself as racist to the extent that the subculture expresses racism and condones brutality and to the extent that organizational controls are weak.

The formation of distinct values that guide behavior is a characteristic of all subcultures; however, it is important to understand that all subcultures take dominant cultural values and exaggerate those that are important within the institutional and group context of the subcultural group. Consequently, scholars have attempted to delineate the societal norms that form the core of police subcultures in order to better understand misconduct. Herbert (1998), for example, concludes that there are six normative orders that shape police subcultures: law, bureaucratic control, adventure/machismo, safety, competence, and morality. He maintains that these orders provide different sets of rules and practices that officers use to define situations and to determine their response. They also "imbue police work with meaning, as an opportunity, for example, to uphold the legal order, to demonstrate courage, to preserve the good in the face of unflinching evil" (Herbert, 1998: 361).

Bittner agrees that "their attitude is basically American. Like all of us, the police have a love–hate affair with the administration of justice; they distrust lawyers, including judges, profoundly and they have an indomitable faith in 'The Law.'" (1970: 27). Skolnick (1969) deviates a little from emphasizing the norm of *law*, concluding that officers generally value the familiar, the ordinary, the status quo rather than social change and are more likely to focus on order than on legality. Police, he argued, tend to view themselves as society's experts in the determination of guilt and the apprehension of guilty persons and are particularly sensitive to what they see as challenges to "their" system of criminal justice—whether by unruly Black Panthers or "misguided" judges.

Police subculture consists, Reiss (1971) argues, in part, of developing standards of doing justice. Justice becomes necessary in the eyes of the police when deference is violated, when outcomes violate their sense of justice, when they are degraded in status, and when their efforts to control are subverted. Skolnick and Fyfe similarly conclude that there is a causal connection between the traditional culture of policing and brutality. Officers believe in a code they consider to be moral: "cops protect other cops, no matter what and . . . cops of higher rank back up working street cops no matter what" (1993: 7). In departments where subcultures condone brutality, the belief prevails that officers, in their interactions with suspect members of the community, should "teach them a lesson."

Other scholars focus on machismo as a norm characteristic of the police subculture. America has long been a patriarchal society that stresses male dominance, and the police subculture correspondingly rewards those who develop a reputation for personal toughness, including an intolerance of "deviant" behavior. The police subculture further promotes the idea that "law enforcement is a man's job, and it is feared that its image of masculinity can be tarnished by the presence of women wearing police uniforms and carrying guns" (Van Wormer & Bartollas, 1999: 175). Women officers, therefore, experience an almost unbelievable amount of hostility in departments.

Some evidence indicates that the subculture may not be so isolated but is also tied to other institutional and organizational processes. Herbert (1998) examines internal and departmental variations in the strength of subcultural norms and concludes that the link between informal processes and formal bureaucracies shapes the form that subcultures take in particular departments. Further, Morn (1990) shows how police subcultures may be generationally influenced as well in many towns and cities as the police occupation runs in the family. This may blur lines between occupational and familial socialization. However, police organizations clearly are sites of ongoing political struggles over how to define and act on different normative orders, struggles that fundamentally shape the daily practices of officers—especially those that are perceived as misconduct, the overall orientations of departments, and the state of police–community relations (Walker, 1977).

The Individual Officer

Whether the focus is on the structural conditions of society, politics, the administration of policing, or police subcultures, it should be clearer that understanding police misconduct is not a simple task. Officers are social beings who live lives full of contradictions facing uncertain futures guided by confusing messages. Looking at an instance of misconduct, it is often difficult to comprehend that officers are more similar to us than they are given credit for being. Like all Americans, they deal with role conflict and strain as they struggle to interpret society's expectations of their behavior. In this section, the discussion posits that understanding an officer's background and struggle for fulfillment in a difficult occupational setting is essential to developing a complete understanding of the persistence of police misconduct.

The rotten-apple theory of one crooked cop acting independently of the police administration and other officers is a large part of public discourse on police misconduct. However, much of this discourse is uncritical and makes the assumption that if the criminal justice system is good, then any misconduct must be individually motivated. In fact, little real attention has been paid to understanding officer's motivations, aspirations, emotions, and general sense of self-worth. Of all the examinations of policing since the 1960s, very few employ in-depth qualitative studies in an attempt to understand how officers see themselves.

Some scholars focus on the background characteristics of officers to understand how their subjective perceptions of the various subgroups in society shape their treatment of them as problems arise (Young & Matthews, 1992). Many maintain that it is surely impossible for police who work in cities where social class and race make so much difference in everybody's life to claim that they can perform their work uninfluenced by such considerations. However, this does not necessarily mean that officers make conscious decisions to act on the basis of class, race, and/or gender. Martin (1993), for example, argues that officers, more often than not, do not engage in willful misconduct, but rather, their behavior reflects systemic biases and assumptions about class, race, and gender.

In 1969 Bayley and Mendelsohn concluded that racial segregation of communities promotes conditions in which officers lack an ability to understand the behavior of minority group members and that anxiety levels among officers are likely to be higher in minority areas than in other parts of the city. David Smith (1984), Michael Banton (1964), and Michael K. Brown (1981: 56) similarly describe the major influences on police behavior as an officer's knowledge of the community and the officer's interpretation of the community's expectations of how the police should act.

Further, as policing is a dangerous occupation, an officer's fear for his or her life shapes his or her conduct. Van der Wolf, 1992 argues that the probability of threat and the formulation of a response to it place an officer at a disadvantage in a citizen encounter. Similarly, Robinson (1987) argues that, in part, brutality is the result of fear and consequent overreaction based on perceptions to potentially dangerous situations. Lack of knowledge of a community or its citizens can heighten these perceptions. Others support this conclusion and delineate the important situational variables that influence an officer's behavior. Donahue and Horvath (1991) and Son et al. (1996) emphasize the location of an encounter, the officer's perception of the criminal involvement of the citizen, and the citizen's general demeanor; Walker et al. (1996) concur, adding the importance of the citizen's social class.

Others concentrate on examining the interaction between an officer's background and the occupational socialization of policing. Bayley and Mendelsohn (1968), for example, suggest that there seems to be something about being a police officer that either selects more conservative individuals or encourages them to become conservative. Focusing on the occupational socialization, Bayley and Mendelsohn maintain that the act of belonging to an occupation serves to impose meaning on an individual's behavior. Riksheim and Chermak (1993) similarly suggest that the origins of police misconduct lie in organizational factors rather than merely in officer characteristics and personality traits, which have been shown through extensive quantitative analysis not to be significant predictors of the use of police force.

Understanding that officers are workers who face structural and occupational barriers and respond creatively to define and shape their world, it becomes clear that organizational factors often have contradictory, unintended effects on officers' behavior. Police historians have shown how policing created an atmosphere ripe for corruption under the old political patronage systems because officers generally received tips to supplement their often meager incomes. In 1969 Skolnick found that one major problem facing the police is a decline in pay relative to comparable occupations, implying that misconduct could result as the quality of police recruits declined. The relationship between pay and behavior is still a concern to current scholars of policing who argue that underpaid officers can be easily tempted by the vast sums of money produced by the drug trade they are supposed to police (Glazer, 1995).

The lack of pay is compounded by the absence of occupational mobility. Workers dream of advancing and improving their lot in life; however, in policing it has been historically difficult for officers to move to other departments, and movement within is very competitive. Reiss (1971) argues that this structural feature of American police departments renders them vulnerable to many forms of internal subversion.

Officers, viewing their job as essential to the maintenance of order in society, find little real recognition of their efforts. While attacked and criticized from all sides, "police want first of all to be regarded as people who do a difficult job well" (Bayley & Mendelsohn, 1969: 168). Observers of police behavior find, similarly, that criticism can create an oppositional mentality in officers that results in forms of misconduct. "The cops who head down the road to misconduct are frequently those who perceive themselves as victims. "The courts let criminals go, nobody cares, we put our life on the line" (Glazer, 1995: 1046).

Importantly, though officers have tremendous authority to shape the lives of the citizens they encounter, they increasingly have less control over both their public and private lives. Doss (1990), for example, illustrates how the courts have allowed the government greater justification for regulating the private lives of police officers than of any other type of public employee, including their sexual identities and behaviors. Officers are expected to be held to a high level of accountability to ensure that they do not engage in misconduct; however, this raises the crucial question of officers' rights to have private lives as well as job security. Jurisdictions, for example, can define a behavior, such as adultery or homosexuality, as a form of misconduct and, through court rulings, grant agencies the legitimacy to impose moral standards of conduct on their employees both on and off the job. Agencies further have the authority to investigate officers' private lives, determine the moral and legal extent of their private behavior, and sanction them accordingly.

This high level of scrutiny is a problem for officers who, like all workers, feel the need to have as much control of their workplace as possible, not the other way around. Officers correspondingly feel the need to insulate their activities from scrutiny, seemingly creating a veil of untruths. One consequence could be the tightening of subcultural bonds. The more the courts allow the private lives of officers to be scrutinized, the greater the levels of stress, isolation, and strengthening of subcultural influence. Another consequence could be a detrimental impact of diversity in departments by limiting the number of officers from other sexual orientations, for example.

To develop a fuller understanding of misconduct, it will be necessary for scholars to more completely examine how individual officers are shaped by both their backgrounds and their occupational environments. Although not completely explored, how individual officers are shaped by their place in a complexly stratified society and how they respond to occupational barriers and stress most assuredly have an impact on shaping their behavior.

The Courts

While historians have generally focused on economic, political, and ideological processes that shape policing and police scholars focus on administration, subcultures, and police interaction with members of the community, legal scholars have developed an analysis of the ability of the courts to influence police practices. This section briefly examines the importance of Fourth-Amendment rights and the later recognition that members of minority populations need specific protection for their rights to be respected. Next, key decisions composing the court's response to civil rights concerns since the 1960s are discussed, particularly, the strategies of individual, and later municipal, liability as solutions to police misconduct.

Although not active in shaping police behavior until the late twentieth century, the courts have historically defined individual rights by which police behavior can be interpreted. Claims of misconduct against officers historically have fallen under the Fourth

Amendment's prohibition against unreasonable searches and seizures. Treated as tort cases involving professional negligence claims, in cases of misconduct, the plaintiff must show that the officer was "deliberately indifferent" to his or her constitutional rights (Beyer, 1993). Since 1914 the Supreme Court has issued a series of rulings requiring the police to observe certain legal restrictions in questioning, detention, and search and seizure (Bittner, 1970).

In the 1960–61 term of the U.S. Supreme Court, the justices issued landmark opinions that signaled a significant change in the Court's direction concerning remedies for police misconduct. Many scholars argue that during this time the court was the most influential shaper of police behavior. The Court ruled on search and seizure practices in *Mapp* v. *Ohio*, requiring the exclusion of improperly seized evidence. In 1963 the Supreme Court expanded this protection by holding that under the Fourth Amendment police are required to announce their presence before entry—the "knock and announce rule." Both decisions were designed to protect individual rights while limiting police authority.

In the same term, the U.S. Supreme Court also ruled, for the first time in the *Monroe* v. *Pape* decision, that victims of police brutality could seek damages under 42 U.S.C. Section 1983 of the Ku Klux Act of 1871, which Congress passed to grant federal rights to those whose Fourteenth-Amendment rights were denied by state agencies. This ruling was looked on favorably as a significant change in the approach to controlling misconduct, as it allowed victims of misconduct to sue individual officers who had violated their rights. Officers were finally required to be financially accountable for their conduct.

The notion that the only effective way to influence police practices is to hold the city liable gained influence with the 1978 *Monell* v. *Department of Social Services of New York* decision, in which the U.S. Supreme Court held for the first time that a municipality could be considered a person under Section 1983 and not immune from liability. However, this ruling applied only where a policy, practice, or custom established by a single act of a municipal official who was, as a matter of state law, the final policymaker for the act in question, caused a constitutional violation.

The trend continued in *Osborne* v. *Lyles* (1992) when the Ohio Supreme Court became one of a growing number of states that have allowed municipalities to be held vicariously liable for police officer behavior using the "respondeat superior" theory. This doctrine holds that an employer is liable for injury to person or property of another proximately resulting from acts of an employee done within the scope of his or her employment in the employer's service (*Black's Law Dictionary* quoted in Marcus, 1994: 656). This is broader than other civil remedies, such as *Monell*, because one must show only that the officer was acting within the scope of his or her employment, not that a specific official policy or custom approved by a specific agency head allowed the misconduct to occur. The court must determine only the parameters of an officer's scope of employment.

Despite much promise of remedy, after nearly forty years of the courts' attempts to curb police misconduct, abuses continue. In fact, early on it became clear that these rulings would have little effect on police misconduct. In 1970 Bittner argued that the series of U.S. Supreme Court decisions concerning admissibility of evidence had influenced police practices but reminded readers of the tremendous difference between influence and control. The courts lack the ability to supervise officers and agencies, and any court review is dependent on the records kept by the agency being scrutinized.

While setting the standard by which police behavior has been understood, the courts have contradictorily allowed police misconduct to persist. Ed Cray (1967) observed that the judgment and discretion of the police officer are important factors precisely because the law of arrest has been deliberately left flexible by courts and legislatures as an aid to the police.

Legal scholars illustrate that all Fourth-Amendment claims have been assessed by a standard of reasonableness that balances the nature and the quality of the intrusion on the individual's rights' against governmental interests. "An officer's decision to use force must be viewed from the perspective of a reasonable officer at the scene, rather than with the 20/20 vision of hindsight" (van der Wolf, 1992: 385–6). Misconduct persists, in part, because the courts have permitted officers' subjective interpretations and explanations of incidents to carry more weight than those of citizens who claim to be the victims of misconduct.

Therefore, most claims of misconduct are not clear-cut violations of civil rights. They tend to be ambiguous because they generally involve the word of the officer(s) against the word of the citizen(s) with no third-party witnesses. Importantly, these types of cases are almost never sustained. As a consequence, only the prosecution of extraordinarily sensational crimes is successful, while most police misconduct goes unpunished (Cohen, 1996).

Other scholars have labeled this the "good cop" assumption of the courts, which holds that, as long as officers demonstrate "good faith," their actions are justified to the courts, and they escape either criminal or civil prosecution (Hess, 1993). Developing this critique, Magee (1994) maintains that the "myth of the good cop" promoted by the courts grants undue deference to police judgment and illustrates a misplaced confidence that police will use discretion appropriately.

Further placing great faith in police officers, in the case of the "knock and announce rule" for example, exceptions to the rule have always been permitted. Currently, because, in part, of the War on Drugs, some jurisdictions allow unannounced entries in all drug cases because the evidence is easy to destroy, and other courts apply this exception where the officer's belief is based on facts specific to each situation (Driscoll, 1995).

Civil liability has also failed to be a successful deterrent to police misconduct for a variety of reasons. Hess (1993) concludes that, as criminal convictions against officers are exceptionally rare, there is no certainty of punishment and consequently little deterrent effect. Municipalities have relied on sovereign immunity to protect them against civil suit and consequently rarely settle cases. Therefore, they can force prolonged prosecution in which the victim of misconduct has limited discovery and limited funds to pursue a just solution. Taylor (1999) agrees that liability cases are very costly, particularly for members of poorer communities, who tend to be the victims of police misconduct. He further argues that judges are often hostile to such case because they are very time-consuming. Patton (1993) and Marcus (1994) further argue that *Monell* created such a strict standard for municipal liability that these cases are generally dismissed as a matter of summary judgment.

Many scholars note that the courts have historically favored police officers despite tension between the two. Supreme Court guidelines are sufficiently ambiguous that officers engaged in misconduct face no serious prosecution, if any prosecution at all. Further, since the District Attorney's Office relies on the investigative function of police officers, it often fosters police misconduct by failing to investigate or charge officers or rules that conduct was within legal bounds.

The American court system has played an important role in shaping the behavior of officers, particularly since the early 1960s. However, despite aspirations to the contrary, the courts have little real control over police behavior. "Since the judge is not the policeman's superior there is nothing that prevents the latter from doing as he pleases while forwarding cases on a take it or leave it basis (Bittner, 1970: 25). However, it is difficult to prove that court decisions have no ability to shape the agency guidelines and the behavior of officers. Many legal scholars maintain that remedies to misconduct do lie within the purview of the courts but disagree as to which would be more effective and how they should be implemented without ambiguity and realistically enforced.

The Public

Members of the public, as implied throughout the previous discussion, are involved in a dynamic relationship with policing that is far more complicated than merely being served or victimized by officers. Members of the communities in the United States have historically shaped policing through their actions or their indifference. Police officials frankly refer to public opinion as one source of their authority (Bittner, 1970). Every police encounter with a citizen carries a sizeable amount of history with it. This "includes the institutional history of the police, the entire history of race and power relations in this country, and the past and present use of excessive force and the various attempts to curb it" (Cohen, 1996: 173). This brief discussion examines how the public plays a role in the persistence of police misconduct and consequently must actively participate in developing solutions.

Enforcement of criminal law in preindustrial societies, including early America, "was largely the responsibility either of the community as a whole or of the individual victim of some offense, rather than delegated to specialized agents of the state" (Lane, 1992: 5). As policing emerged and officers gained the power of social control, members of the community became less active in formal control functions, although they did not do so uniformly or without resistance.

Albert Reiss (1972) concluded that the capacity of police officers to maintain legality in their relations with citizens depends to an important degree on their ability to establish and maintain the legitimacy of their legal authority. Officers had to establish their legitimate right to intervene without challenge to their authority. It is crucial to understand that policing is always an interactive, interdependent relationship between agents of social control and members of the public. This relationship, which is of course variable across social and temporal context, allows misconduct to occur or can control its occurrence.

To illustrate the public's role in the control of police misconduct, many scholars examine the efforts of disadvantaged groups to overcome their oppression by combating the activities of the police. The voice of black political power critiquing police conduct during the Civil Rights movement helped to shape it as a social problem worthy of national attention. This crisis focused public attention on the police as never before, particularly the limitations of police professionalization as tactics such as aggressive preventive patrol, designed by professional experts to suppress crime efficiently, exacerbated racial tensions. This focus and growing group power helped to elect black leaders and led to the appointment of police chiefs who projected values that promoted behavior more sensitive to the needs and wishes of minority communities (Skolnick & Fyfe, 1993).

A further strategy to eliminate misconduct was to hire black officers, to create diversity in historically white police departments. Dulaney (1996) illustrates how black citizens began to demand political power, which translated into greater numbers of black officers; the integration of black officers in police agencies was promoted as a solution to community tension. Many felt that black officers would be more sensitive to members of black communities, be less brutal, be less likely to harass, and would, therefore, inspire community trust and reduce tension. Button (1989) similarly concluded that black community leaders worked hard to maintain close relationships with the officers once they were hired.

The Civil Rights movement set the stage for the emergence of wide-scale social protest in the 1960s, including the Chicano movement in Los Angeles. However, Escobar (1993) describes that, as members of the Chicano movement began to organize and demonstrate for their civil rights, a planned process of infiltration, intimidation, arrest, harassment, and brutality by the police department and the FBI was designed to destroy the movement. Importantly, he argues, the brutality of the police became an increasing rallying point of the Chicano movement and strengthened its resolve to fight for its rights and allowed it to broaden its base to attract those more politically conservative members of the community outraged by the brutality. "Police repression not only invigorated the Chicano movement but also helped politicize and empower the Mexican-American community" (Escobar, 1993: 1488).

CONCLUSION

The police and the public are engaged in an ongoing constructive process in which the actions of one spurs a response from the other. Scholars illustrate how the result can be positive as minority groups achieve greater participation in local political processes and diversity in police departments, thereby impacting levels of police misconduct, particularly brutality. However, more recently, some analyses have demonstrated how members of the public also play a role in promoting police misconduct.

Historically, the public's frustration with crime and disorder led to the formation of police in northern urban areas and their general acceptance of police practices even when these practices fell outside of constitutional guidelines. Recent examinations of ideology further develop the notion that the power of economic and political leaders, the police, and the media influence how the public perceives crime and its prevention, promoting a "war mentality," in which citizens feel that bad people get what they deserve.

Many citizens, scared of crime and becoming victimized, begin to feel that police excesses are necessary to fight crime, and since these excesses most frequently occur against members of the lower classes and minority groups, the public tends to ignore their complaints against police practices (Currie, 1998), only becoming concerned during extreme acts of brutality or corruption or when innocent people suffer from some form of misconduct. Martin (1993) concurs that the public often gives the police the ambiguous message that order is more important than justice. Therefore, the troublesome problem of police brutality lies at the heart of the contradiction that we expect the police to use force but refuse to state clearly what we mean by force.

The work of these scholars forces members of the public to realize their role in the persistence of police misconduct. Members of the public can collectively act to reduce unacceptable police behavior or allow it to continue. Clearly the conduct of police will not be acceptable to all members of the public until an agreement of how the police can best protect and serve is reached by the public and agencies working together toward the realization of common goals.

REFERENCES

BANTON, M. (1964). *The policeman in the Community*. New York: Basic Books.

BARKER, T. (1991). Peer group support for police occupational deviance. In Barker, T., & Carter, D. L., eds., *Police Deviance* (pp. 45–57). Cincinnati, Ohio: Anderson Publishing.

BARKER, T., & CARTER, D. L. (1991). A typology of police deviance. In Barker, T., & Carter, D. L., eds., *Police Deviance* (pp. 3–12). Cincinnati, Ohio: Anderson Publishing.

BARLOW, D. E. (1994). Minorities policing minorities as a strategy of social control: A historical analysis of tribal police in the United States. *Criminal Justice History* 15:141–163.

BAYLEY, D. H., & MENDELSOHN, H. (1969). *Minorities and the Police: Confrontation in America*. New York: The Free Press.

BELKNAP, J. (1996). *The Invisible Woman: Gender, Crime, and Justice*. Belmont, Calif.: Wadsworth Publishing.

BELL, D. (1992). *Race, racism and American law*. 3d ed. Boston: Little, Brown.

BEYER, W. C. (1993). Screening, evaluating, and settling police misconduct cases. *Trial* 29 (7): 36–40.

BITTNER, E. (1970). *The Function of the Police in Modern Society: A Review of Background Factors, Current Practices, and Possible Role Models*. Chevy Chase, Md.: National Institute of Mental Health.

BROWN, M. (1981). *Working the Street: Police Discretion and the Dilemmas of Reform*. New York: Russell Sage Foundation.

BUTTON, J. W. (1989). *Blacks and Social Change: Impact of the Civil Rights Movement in Southern Communities*. Princeton, N.J.: Princeton University Press.

CARTER, D. L. (1991). Police disciplinary procedures: A review of selected police departments. In Barker, T., & Carter, D. L., eds., *Police Deviance* (pp. 351–372). Cincinnati, Ohio: Anderson Publishing.

CASHMORE, E., & McLAUGHLIN, E., eds. (1991). *Out of Order?: Policing Black People*. London: Routledge.

CHAMBLISS, W. J. (1994). Policing the ghetto underclass: The politics of law and law enforcement." *Social Problems* 41 (2): 177–94.

COHEN, D. S. (1996). Official oppression: A historical analysis of low-level police abuse and a modern attempt at reform. *Columbia Human Rights Law Review* 28 (1): 165–201.

CRAY, E. (1967). *The Big Blue Line: Police Power vs. Human Rights*. New York: Coward-McCann.

CURRIE, E. (1998). Crime and punishment in the United States: Myths, realities, and possibilities. In Kairys, D., ed. *The Politics of Law: A Progressive Critique* (pp. 381–409). New York: Basic Books.

DONAHUE, M. E., & HORVATH, F. S. (1991). Police shooting outcomes: Suspect criminal history and incident behaviors. *American Journal of Police* 10 (3): 17–34.

DOSS, M. T., JR. (1990). Police management: Sexual misconduct and the right to privacy. *Journal of Police Science and Administration* 17 (4): 194–206.

DRISCOLL, R. J. (1995). Unannounced police entries and destruction of evidence after Wilson v. Arkansas. *Columbia Journal of Law and Social Problems* 29 (1): 1–38.

DUBOIS, W. E. B. (1962). *Black Reconstruction in America*. New York: Russell & Russell.

DULANEY, W. M. (1996). *Black Police in America*. Bloomington: Indiana University Press.

ESCOBAR, E. J. (1993). The dialectics of repression: The Los Angeles police department and the Chicano movement, 1968–1971. *The Journal of American History* 79 (4): 1483–1514.

GENOVESE, E. D. (1974). *Roll, Jordan, Roll: The World the Slaves Made*. New York: Vintage Books.

GLAZER, S. (1995). Police corruption. *CQ Researcher* 5 (44): 1041–64.

HALL, S. (1978). *Policing the Crisis*. London: Macmillan.

HARRIS, A. (1995). Race and essentialism in feminist legal theory. In Delgado, R., ed. *Critical Race Theory: The Cutting Edge* (pp. 253–266). Philadelphia: Temple University Press.

HAWKINS, H., & THOMAS, R. (1991). White policing of black populations: A history of race and social control in America. In Cashmore, E., & McLaughlin, E., eds. *Out of Order: Policing Black People* (pp. 65–86). London: Routledge.

HERBERT, S. (1998). Police subculture reconsidered. *Criminology* 36 (2): 343–369.

HESS, M. V. (1993) Good cop–bad cop: Reassessing the legal remedies for police misconduct. *Utah Law Review* (1): 149–203.

HIGGINBOTHAM, A. L. (1978). *In the Matter of Color. Race and the American Legal Process: The Colonial Period*. Oxford: Oxford University Press.

KEITH, M. (1991). Policing a perplexed society? No-go areas and the mystification of police–black conflict. In Cashmore, E., & McLaughlin, E., eds. *Out of Order: Policing Black People* (pp. 189–214). London: Routledge.

LANE, R. (1992). Urban police and crime in nineteenth-century America. In Tonry, M., & Morris, N., eds. *Modern Policing* (pp. 1–50). Chicago: University of Chicago Press.

MAGEE, R. (1994). The myth of the good cop and the inadequacy of Fourth Amendment remedies for black men: Contrasting presumptions of innocence and guilt. *Capital University Law Review* 23: 151–219.

MANN, C. R. (1993). *Unequal Justice: A Question of Color*. Bloomington: Indiana University Press.

Mapp v. *Ohio*, 368 U.S. 871 (1961).

MARCUS, J. M. (1994). Up against the wall: Municipal liability for police brutality under respon-deat superior. *Osborne* v. *Lyles*, N.E.2D. 825 (Ohio 1992). *Southern Illinois University Law Journal* 18: 655–84.

MARTIN, D. L. (1993). Organizing for change: A community law response to police misconduct. *Hastings Women's Law Journal* 4 (1): 131–74.

MCDONOUGH, J. (1997). Worker solidarity, judicial oppression, and police repression in the West-moreland County, Pennsylvania coal miner's strike, 1910–11. *Pennsylvania History* 64 (3): 385–406.

Monell v. *Department of Social Services of New York*, 436 U.S. 658 (1978).

MONKKONEN, E. H. (1992). History of urban police. In Tonry, M., & Morris, N., eds. *Modern Policing* (pp. 547–80). Chicago: University of Chicago Press.

Monroe v. *Pape*, 365 U.S. 806 (1961).

MORN, F. (1990). Prostitution, police and city culture in a small Midwestern city: A history, 1900–1960. *Journal of Crime and Justice* 13 (2): 149–73.

OLIVER, M. B. (1992). Portrayals of crime, race, and aggression in "reality-based" police shows: A content analysis. *Journal of Broadcasting and Electronic Media* Spring: 179–191.

Osborne v. *Lyles*, Supreme Court of Ohio, 587 N.E. 2d 825 (1992).

PATTON, A. (1993). The endless cycle of abuse: Why 42 U.S.C. 1983 is ineffective in deterring po-lice brutality. *Hastings Law Journal* 44 (3): 753–809.

REISS, A. J., JR. (1971). *The Police and the Public*. New Haven: Yale University Press.

REISS, A. J., JR. (1992). Police organization in the twentieth century. In Tonry, M., & Morris, N., eds. *Modern Policing* (pp. 51–97). Chicago: University of Chicago Press.

RIKSHEIM, E. C., & CHERMAK, S. M. (1993). Causes of police behavior revisited. *Journal of Criminal Justice* 21 (4): 353–82.

ROBINSON, C. D. (1987). Community relations through community history. *Social Justice* 15 (3/4): 179–96.

SKOLNICK, J. (1969). *The Politics of Protest.* New York: Simon & Schuster.

SKOLNICK, J., & FYFE, J. J. (1993). *Above the Law: Police and the Excessive Use of Force.* New York: The Free Press.

SMITH, D. (1984). The organizational context of legal control. *Criminology* 22: 19–38.

SON, I. S., ET AL. (1996). Race and its effect on police officers' perceptions of misconduct. *Journal of Criminal Justice* 26 (1): 23–8.

SPITZER, S. (1996). The production of deviance in capitalist society. In Delos H. K., ed. *Deviant Behavior: A Text-Reader in the Sociology of Deviance* (pp. 29–36). New York: St Martin's Press.

TAYLOR, G. F. (1999). A litigator's view of discovery and proof in police misconduct policy and practice cases. *DePaul Law Review* 48:747.

TONRY, M. (1995). *Malign Neglect: Race, Crime and Punishment in America.* New York: Oxford University Press.

WALKER, S. (1977). *A Critical History of Police Reform.* Lexington, Mass.: D. C. Heath and Company.

WALKER, S. (1992). *The Police in America: An Introduction.* New York: McGraw-Hill.

WALKER, S., SPOHN, C., & DELONE, M. (1996). *The Color of Justice: Race, Ethnicity, and Crime in America.* Belmont, Calif.: Wadsworth Publishing.

WOLF, W.-J., VAN DER (1992). The legal aspects of police misconduct in the United States, part 1: The use of force by law enforcement officers. *Tilburg Foreign Law Review* 1 (4): 381–96.

VAN WORMER, K. S., & BARTOLLAS, C. (1999). *Women and the Criminal Justice System.* Boston: Allyn & Bacon.

YOUNG, J., & MATTHEWS, R. (1992). *Rethinking Criminology: The Realist Debate.* London: Sage Publications.

ZANGRANDO, R. L. (1980). *The NAACP Crusade against Lynching, 1909–1950.* Philadelphia, Pa.: Temple University Press.

3

All Is Fair in Love and War

Kim Michelle Lersch

❖

INTRODUCTION

Misconduct in the form of corruption within our police departments is not a new phenomenon; in fact, the earliest police departments experienced problems related to extortion and other acts of misconduct in which personal gain were placed ahead of the obligations associated with duties of the officer. However, the nature of police corruption has changed over the past 150 years. While other forms of police corruption, which include such behaviors as accepting bribes, protecting illegal activities for profit, or receiving kickbacks, have decreased over the years, drug-related police corruption is on the rise. Is this increase in drug-related acts of misconduct an unintended consequence of the War on Drugs? This chapter explores this question. To do so, we begin by examining a contemporary drug scandal in the Los Angeles Police Department (LAPD) and the history of the drug problem in the United States.

MISCONDUCT OVERDOSE: AN LAPD STORY

On March 2, 1998, six pounds of cocaine were checked out from the property room at the headquarters of the LAPD. Supposedly, the cocaine was to be used as evidence in a drug trial. By the end of the month when the drugs had not been returned, an internal investigation was launched. In August 1998, Officer Rafael A. Perez, a nine-year veteran of the

LAPD, was arrested on suspicion of stealing the cocaine. Unknown to investigators at the time, this incident would ultimately lead to the discovery of what has become the biggest scandal in the history of the LAPD.

At the time of his arrest, Officer Perez was assigned to a special anti-gang unit in the Rampart Division. The precinct served one of Los Angeles's poorest minority communities. Nearly 80 percent of the Rampart residents were Latino, and another 15 percent were of Asian descent. The crime rate in this rather small densely populated area was quite high, and there were thirty known youth gangs with thousands of members. Violence between the various gangs was common, as were the open sales of crack cocaine and other drugs on the neighborhood street corners. Because of the high level of criminal activity, the LAPD established the Community Resources Against Street Hoodlums (CRASH) unit.

The CRASH unit engaged in an aggressive, confrontational style of policing. To enhance their efforts to clean up the streets, officers were assisted with special legal injunctions that allowed them to target suspected gang members. Blocking sidewalks and carrying pagers became reason enough for the officers to stop, question, and harass local residents suspected of gang-related activities. Numerous allegations of misconduct were filed against Rampart officers, including charges of planting evidence and stealing drugs. However, since suspected or known gang members filed most of the complaints, the allegations were ignored. The feeling among many of the CRASH officers was that the law-abiding residents were supportive of their actions, no matter what these actions were. As long as the targets of the abuse were gang members, the perception was that no one cared. The end justified the means.

The arrest of Rafael Perez thrust the CRASH unit within the Rampart Division into the national spotlight. After his first trial ended in a hung jury, Perez entered into a plea agreement. In exchange for his testimony against his fellow officers, Perez received five years in prison for the cocaine theft and immunity for any additional crimes he admitted to. Perez began an almost unbelievable tale that centered on the activities of the Rampart CRASH unit, which itself had come to resemble a gang. Describing an organized criminal subculture of more than thirty street officers and supervisors within the anti-gang unit, Perez testified that brutality and the fabrication of evidence had become routine activities (Cohen, 2000).

In his sworn testimony, Perez identified 57 different cases involving nearly 100 defendants in which Perez and his former partner, Nino Durden, regularly planted drugs and weapons on suspected gang members. Perez also detailed how he and his former partners perjured themselves in court. The motivation given for these acts was to impress LAPD supervisors and the public with arrests and convictions and to satisfy the officers' own personal greed.

Perez further described several cases in which unarmed suspects were shot and guns were planted. Perez and Durden were involved in the shooting of Javier Ovando, a nineteen-year-old gang member. The officers planted a gun on Ovando and testified in court that he had attacked them. Ovando, who was paralyzed as a result of the incident, was sentenced to twenty-three years in prison. As a result of Perez's testimony, Ovando was released after serving nearly three years in prison. Ovando is now suing the city of Los Angeles for damages.

Perez also stated that he and Durden regularly used a drug-addicted homeless woman as one of their key informants, trading crack cocaine for her information. Armed with the tips that she provided, the officers targeted drug dealers, stealing their drugs and money.

The repercussions of Perez's damning testimony were wide reaching. Several hundred lawsuits have been filed against the LAPD alleging harassment, brutality, and evidence tampering. A number of allegations also charge that arresting officers tried to recruit Rampart residents to sell drugs for the officers' personal gain. While the investigation continues to unfold, to date, 28 officers and 3 sergeants have been suspended, have been fired, or have quit as a result of Perez's statements. Another 70 officers are currently under investigation for their illegal conduct or for failure to report such acts. Nearly 100 criminal cases, mostly involving false drug or weapons charges, have been thrown out of court due to questionable evidence, and scores of convictions have been overturned. Public defenders estimate that thousands of cases could ultimately be affected.

Perez testified that he and his partners engaged in regular patterns of misdeeds over a period of several years. The American public has been shocked by the unfolding events of the LAPD and demands answers: How can such acts of misconduct develop and prosper among those sworn to protect and serve? Given the intense pressure that is put on our police officers to win the War on Crime and especially the War on Drugs, patterns of drug-related police misconduct, including such acts as corruption and abuse of authority, become more understandable. This pressure to make arrests and get convictions combined with an occupation marked by minimal supervision, low pay, and the perception of isolation and hostility from the general public all contribute to an environment that is ripe for misdeeds to occur.

THE CONSTRUCTION OF A DRUG PROBLEM IN THE UNITED STATES

Before the enactment of the Harrison Act of 1914, no drugs were defined as "illegal." If one chose to use such substances as marijuana, opium, or cocaine, no laws defined the act as criminal. Any limitations placed on the use or abuse of such substances were culturally based, not legally defined. If an individual overindulged in a substance, he or she was met with displeasure and negative feedback from the peer group, not an arrest (Duke & Gross, 1993).

The passage of the Harrison Act marked the first major attempt by the federal government to make the use of drugs, especially opiates and cocaine, a criminal act. The Harrison Act was intended to be a regulatory law that required physicians, dentists, pharmacists, and others who dispensed the drugs to be licensed and pay a fee. The act did not completely eliminate the distribution of cocaine and opiates and provided for a number of exceptions. For example, the products containing opiates and cocaine were still allowed to be sold over the counter and by mail order if the concentration of the drugs fell below the legally prescribed limit (Akers, 1992; Duke & Gross, 1993). The use of marijuana remained legal for nearly another quarter century, until its use was criminalized by the Marihuana Tax Act of 1937 (Dunlap & Johnson, 1992).

We have come a long way over the past eight and a half decades in how we view drugs, the drug problem, and its control. The popularity of some drugs has waxed and waned over time, and other new drugs have emerged. The use of heroin grew after World War II, but demand decreased in the 1960s, only to increase in the 1970s again. In the 1960s, marijuana became the drug of choice for many college students and inner-city residents. While the popularity of powder cocaine grew from 1975 to 1985, its hefty price made the drug difficult to obtain for many poorer users. However, the crack cocaine epidemic, which began in the mid-1980s, dramatically altered the patterns of use, abuse, and distribution, especially in large urban centers.

Rock, or crack cocaine, is made by heating a mixture of regular cocaine, water, and baking soda in a pot. The resulting product is dried and broken into small chunks or rocks. These rocks can be placed in small vials and sold at a relatively inexpensive price: $3–$10, depending on the local market conditions. The popularity of crack cocaine was not only driven by the cheap cost (Dunlap & Johnson, 1992): The "high" from smoking the drug can be quite intense and short-lived. Depending on the preparation, crack cocaine can be up to ten times more potent than regular powdered cocaine. The euphoria the user experiences will last only a few minutes, after which time more of the drug is sought.

The short-lived high associated with crack cocaine results in many repeat uses on a daily basis. While heroin and cocaine users may have comparatively low need for repeat consumption, crack cocaine users may consume a rock from five to fifteen times per day (Dunlap & Johnson, 1992). The heightened demand for the drug changed the market, bringing in more and more buyers and more opportunities for sellers. The result was a new highly competitive and explosive drug market located on street corners.

The scenes for such open-air drug sales have become almost immortalized due to their portrayal in popular movies and reality-based television shows like *Cops*. A buyer drives up to a dealer, who is often waiting on a heavily trafficked street corner. The sales are quick and impersonal, allowing the buyer and seller to quickly return to their business. More complicated sales networks can develop, with sentries assigned to watch out for police intervention, a "bag man," whose duties are to hold the drugs, and the actual drug seller. The drug cache may be stored nearby in a vacant building, automobile, or overgrown lot. In more recent years, the utilization of electronic equipment may enhance the operation, which may include the use of cellular telephones, beepers, and police scanners (Hayeslip & Weisel, 1992).

The sale of drugs, even at the street level, can be a highly profitable enterprise (Dunlap & Johnson, 1992). For some inner-city youths growing up in our urban centers in the 1980s, the opportunities that drug sales opened for them may have been perceived as their only realistic alternative for gainful employment. It is no surprise that the popularity of crack cocaine coincided with a recession in our 1980s economy. The minority communities in our inner cities were especially hard hit by the depressed economic conditions. For urban residents in Boston, Newark, New York, Philadelphia, and Pittsburgh, the percentage of males ages 16–24 who were not working increased from 19 percent in 1968–70 to 44 percent in 1986–88 (Kasarda, 1992). Virtually no legitimate employment opportunities existed in the inner-city communities, and the drug trade became an attractive source of income for many urban residents (Dunlap & Johnson, 1992).

Setting the Stage for War: The Need for Action

As the use of crack cocaine grew, media reports sensationalized images of violent street gangs and heavily armed dealers taking over inner cities, leaving a trail of random shootings of innocent bystanders. Crack cocaine was viewed as the drug that would threaten the lives of an entire generation of youths. No one was safe from the crack epidemic. Even babies were not immune: In 1988, media sources reported that approximately 375,000 crack babies had been born to addicted mothers. According to media reports, these infants would suffer permanent damage due to their "addiction" and would ultimately pose a perpetual drain on society's resources (Brownstein, 1997; Walker, 1998).

Politicians fueled the mass hysteria over crack cocaine. In January 1987, the governor of New York State, Mario Cuomo, made the following statements in his annual address to the legislators:

> This year, we must intensify our efforts as never before in the face of the emergence of crack—the extraordinarily potent, highly addictive, and relatively inexpensive cocaine derivative. The lightning speed with which this lethal drug has spread through society is evident in substantial increases in drug-related deaths and demands for treatment by drug users. Crack has also been accompanied by rising incidents of violent crime, including robberies and murders. We must attack this new menace by enacting stiffer penalties for its sale and possession. (cited in Brownstein, 1997: 69)

Violent, heavily armed, and well-organized gangs were quickly associated with street-level drug dealing. It was argued that street gangs, with their hierarchical, cohesive, and highly controlled group structure, were especially suited for drug distribution. The propensity of gang members to engage in violent acts to protect their territories would be especially useful in the drug trade (Klein & Maxson, 1994). An especially charged report by the California Council on Criminal Justice (1989), stated:

> Today's gangs are urban terrorists. Heavily armed and more violent than ever before, they are quick to use terror and intimidation to seize and protect their share of the lucrative drug market. Gang members are turning our streets and neighborhoods into war zones, where it takes an act of courage simply to walk to the corner store. (California Council, 1989, p.viii; cited in Klein & Maxson, 1994: 44).

However, as was the case with most of the reports surrounding the hysteria of crack cocaine, the assumptions that were made about the organization of gangs and the domination of the drug trade was largely inflammatory and not based on empirical evidence.

In an examination of 1,889 cocaine arrests that occurred in the most notorious areas in Los Angeles in 1983–85, Klein et al. (1988; 1991) reported that at its highest level, gang-related crack sales accounted for 25 percent of all the crack sales arrests. This would imply that the majority of the arrests for crack cocaine sales were not gang related (which was defined as one or more gang members present at the time of arrest). Furthermore, Klein et al. did not find any increase in the level of drug-related violence associated with gang involvement in crack sales. In fact, it was the category of non–gang-related homicides that experienced an increase during the period of analysis.

Racism also entered into the images of the "typical" crack dealer. Poor urban minorities, especially blacks, were viewed as the primary distributors of crack cocaine. The media, especially television news, provided regular and frequent images of black men as criminals who were pushing drugs on America's youths (Klein & Maxson, 1994; Russell, 1998). As phrased by Lusane (1997: 35), "The racist myth is that most inner-city, young black males are gun-toting, crack-smoking criminals-in-waiting." White middle-class Americans were painted as especially vulnerable to the violence perpetuated by minorities in their quest for the sale and use of crack cocaine (Brownstein, 1997).

The Time Had Come: Declaring a War on Drugs

Because of both the exaggerated and very real concerns voiced by many Americans, a call to arms was made to draw an end to the sale, manufacture, and use of drugs. In 1971, President Richard Nixon became the first politician to declare a "War on Drugs" (Weisheit, 1990). While other elected officials similarly carried the battle slogan, Ronald Reagan and George Bush added even greater momentum to the cause. War was redeclared in 1982 by President Reagan with an even greater emphasis on drug trafficking. In 1986, then-President Reagan pushed for the passage of the Anti-Drug Abuse Act. The goal of this act was to reduce both the demand and supply of illegal drugs. Most of the funds earmarked for this project went to the construction of new prisons, as well as for radar, aircraft, and the financial support of foreign nations in the combined interdiction efforts (Akers, 1992; Miller & Selva, 1997).

In 1988, the Anti-Drug Abuse Bill passed, which brought even more resources to deal with the issues presented by crack cocaine and gang-related violence. The Anti-Drug Abuse Bill included resources for the purchase of new equipment and additional policing efforts, and it provided elevated penalties for those convicted of drug-related offenses (Miller & Selva, 1997). Additionally, the bill reinvigorated the practice of asset seizures through the creation of the Asset Forfeiture Fund. Forfeiture of assets may include any cash profits made by the operation of a criminal enterprise, items purchased with the ill-gotten gains (including homes, boats, cars), and all instruments associated with the crimes (Greek, 1992).

During his inaugural address, President George Bush vowed that the drug problem would be eliminated from our society. On September 5, 1989, President Bush created the office of National Drug Control Policy (which marked the birth of a drug "czar") and announced a number of policy initiatives. These policies, as discussed by Walker (1998: 249) included the following initiatives:

- Intensive street-level drug enforcement
- Joint federal, state, and local enforcement efforts
- Cooperative arrangements with other countries to interdict the flow of drugs into the country and eradicate the cultivation of drugs in the field
- Tougher sentencing policies for drug offenders
- A renewed attack on the use of "soft" drugs such as marijuana on the grounds that they are the "gateway" to the use of harder drugs
- More anti-drug public education

The War on Drugs had been effectively declared, and the repercussions of the policy were quickly felt. In 1990, the federal government allotted 9.5 billion dollars to the war efforts (Miller & Selva, 1997). Traditionally, the policies for addressing the crime problem have fallen into two categories: education and treatment; and the use of force through the application of the law. As phrased by Weishet (1990: 4), "the language of war is the language of force, and force has been the primary strategy for fighting the War on Drugs." The emphasis has fallen on incapacitation and deterrence strategies of certain, swift, and severe punishment. To win the war, the government must catch drug offenders, and they must face imprisonment.

To this end, dramatic changes have taken place in our judicial and correctional facilities. The number of arrests for drug offenses has increased from 601,000 in 1975 to 1.3 million in 1994 (Walker, 1998). Our court systems have become overwhelmed with drug-related offenders. Plea bargains or outright dismissals are forced due to the shear volume of cases moving through the judicial system (Duke & Gross, 1993). Over half of the inmates in federal institutions have been convicted of drug-related offenses, while the number of prisoners in state facilities charged with drug-related offenses has swelled as well (Walker, 1998; Weisheit, 1990).

African Americans have been especially hard hit by the War on Drugs. About half of all crack cocaine users are Caucasian, but whites account for only 4 percent of all the defendants charged and convicted under the federal crack law. Conversely, African Americans, who account for 38 percent of crack users, are disproportionately tried and convicted under the federal statutes. In 1995, fully 88 percent of those convicted under federal cocaine laws were African Americans. Furthermore, the sentences provided for crack cocaine are much harsher than those for regular power cocaine. It takes possession of only 5 grams of crack cocaine to qualify for a punishment of 5 years in federal prison, whereas possession of 500 grams of powder cocaine is necessary to receive a prison sentence of equal term (Russell, 1998).

THE PRESSURE COOKER OF NARCOTICS ENFORCEMENT

In most larger police agencies, the bulk of the responsibility for the enforcement of drug laws has fallen on specialized narcotics units, which are often organizationally housed within vice sections (Hayeslip & Weisel, 1992). Other units, such as juvenile or gang units, violent traffickers' units, and specialized strike forces, may also be involved in drug-interdiction efforts. While the patrol division is also involved in the enforcement efforts against drug trafficking and use, the narcotics units play a key role in collecting information and launching the more sophisticated investigations against traffickers.

Narcotics units are characteristically composed of a small, cohesive group of individuals that is under a great deal of pressure, both external and internal, to produce results. Individuals assigned to the narcotics unit are often socially and professionally isolated from other officers, especially when working undercover. Narcotics officers are immersed in a world marked by large amounts of cash, drugs that are tempting both for use and easy sale, and the deviant lifestyles of informants as well as users and dealers targeted for arrest and prosecution.

As described by Manning and Redlinger (1986), the demands that are placed on these officers to produce hard evidence of their activities and achievements can be quite intense. Internal pressures may be driven from a number of sources including the motivations of the individual officer as well as directives from superior officers. The individual officers may place pressure on themselves with their aspirations for promotion, salary enhancement, recognition, and overall success as measured by the number of arrests, field interviews, or drug buys that they make. These motivations may be enhanced if supervisory personnel base the internal reward structure primarily on these visible, easily counted markers for success.

Furthermore, to enhance their level of productivity, officers may feel the need to protect the criminal activities of their informants. As discussed later in this chapter, the use of informants in the War on Drugs poses special concerns. To maintain the flow of information from a key informant, officers may intervene on behalf of their informants when under investigation from other divisions or agencies. An officer's stable of informants may be increased with threats of prosecution for the prospective informant's criminal activities or, in some cases, with intimidation techniques marked by the "throwing down" of evidence.

Beyond the need for recognition among one's peers, officers may place pressure on themselves in other ways. Described by Radelet and Carter (1994) as drug-related corruption that is driven by a search for legitimate goals, "bending the rules" may be something that officers may feel the need to do to feed their own need for psychological gain. Some officers may enhance their self-esteem by achieving success through a high number of arrests and drug buys. Others may feel a sense of moral righteousness when they have locked up another drug dealer, thereby protecting society's children and winning another fight in the War on Drugs.

Manning and Redlinger (1986) further described external pressures such as the media, elected officials, neighborhood associations and watch groups, and even funding agencies that provide monies for overtime, additional hiring of officers, and equipment. With respect to requests for additional funds targeted for drug-interdiction efforts, statistics concerning the number of drug-related arrests, homicides, and calls for service are often requested to justify the enhanced funds.

The public can exert intense, and often constitutionally illegal, expectations for performance. Law-abiding residents living in a neighborhood with high levels of street-level drug activity demand action from their local police without accurate knowledge of rules of evidence and arrest. For example, during the evaluation of a small agency's problem-solving effort to reduce street-level drug dealing in a residential community, I attended a number of meetings between local residents and the police. The residents were frustrated and angry that drug dealers had taken over their neighborhood, and voiced equally charged dissatisfaction with the efforts of the police to take care of the problem. The officers in attendance tried to explain to the residents the legal limitations placed on their investigations by the Constitution, but the residents only voiced their dissatisfaction with the agency to take their concerns seriously. The residents knew who the drug dealers were (as did the local police), but the basic issue boiled down to difficulties in legally obtaining evidence that would ultimately lead to convictions.

The charges of incompetence that were leveled against this one agency were scathing. Local political leaders who were in attendance at the meeting supported the discontent expressed by their constituents, making further demands that the police take action against the dealers. The local media picked up the story, and the area radio stations and newspapers came down against the police. While the goal of this project was to involve the community in developing new, innovative responses to reduce the level of street dealing, ultimately, the agency returned to its traditional mode of intervention: street-level drug sweeps, in which both buyers and sellers were targeted for arrest. In this sort of climate of hostility and disrespect toward the police officers, one could easily imagine how the officers might feel not only pressure but also justification to overstep the legal bounds of their authority.

While the arrests of drug dealers and their customers may appease the public, the front-line officers in this war know one fact all too well: Arrests are largely ineffective in reducing the flow of drugs. Given the high demand for drugs, if a dealer is arrested, then his vacancy is quickly filled by another dealer, who may be even more violent and successful than the dealer who was taken off the streets. Furthermore, given the overburdened nature of our criminal justice system, the likelihood of certain, swift, and severe punishment is highly unlikely. As argued by Moore and Kleiman (1997: 239):

> If the practical value and moral vindication of arrests for drug offenses only come with successful prosecutions and suitable punishment, then street-level enforcement is undermined from the beginning, for there is no reasonable prospect for such results. The outcome of most street-level arrests is several weeks in jail prior to trial, a bargained guilty plea, a sentence to time served, and a long period of inadequately supervised probation.

Ultimately, the internal and external pressure to produce results coupled with a growing dissatisfaction with the criminal justice system to effectively follow through on the arrest with punishment and incapacitation can lead the officer down a couple of paths. The officer may continue to make arrests under the realization that the most probable punishment is the process itself; the officer may refuse to make arrests; or finally, the officer may turn to more deviant means. These alternative actions may involve taking steps to ensure that a drug offender is punished, or in some cases, adopting the ideology that "if you can't beat 'em, join 'em." In the next section, a number of types of drug-related police deviance are explored.

MAJOR ISSUES: SPECIAL CONSIDERATIONS FOR POLICING

The War on Drugs has resulted in many unintentional consequences for policing, especially in the areas of drug-related corruption and abuse of authority. This section examines a few of the various types of misconduct that can occur as a result of narcotics enforcement.

Drug-Related Corruption

There is a great deal of disagreement among scholars and policing experts as to what sort of behaviors are included under the term *corruption*. Some definitions of *police corruption* are very broad and include a variety of behaviors, such as taking bribes or gratuities, verbal abuse on citizens, acts of brutality, and even homicide (Kappeler et.al., 1994; U.S. General Accounting Office, 1998). "Traditional" police corruption was typically marked by a relationship that was mutually beneficial for both the officer and the citizen involved. A motorist may offer an officer a bribe in exchange for the officer ignoring his traffic violation, or a prostitute may trade cash for immunity from arrest. Barker and Carter (1994) define acts of corruption as follows: The act is forbidden by some law, rule, regulation or ethical standard; the act involves the misuse of the officer's position; and the act involves some actual or expected material reward or gain. While Barker and Carter define the gain in terms of money, goods, services, and/or discount, others have broadened the definition to include psychological gains in the form of vindication, recognition, or commendations (see, e.g., Radelet & Carter, 1994).

In the special cases of drug-related police corruption, the acts in question can become more serious. In his analysis of a number of police agencies, Carter (1990) identified the following behaviors as "typical" of drug-related corruption:

- Accepting bribes from drug dealers/traffickers in exchange for "tip" information regarding drug investigations, undercover officers, drug strategies, names of informants and so on.
- Accepting bribes from drug dealers/traffickers in exchange for interference in the justice process such as non-arrest, evidence tampering, and perjury.
- Theft of drugs by the officer from property rooms or laboratory for personal consumption of the drug or for sale of the drug.
- Street seizure of drugs from users/traffickers without an accompanying arrest with the intent of converting the drug to personal use.
- Robbery of drug dealers of profits from drug sales and/or the drugs for resale.
- Extorting drug traffickers for money (and sometimes property such as stereos, televisions, etc.) in exchange for nonarrest or nonseizure of drugs (Carter, 1990:90–1).

While in some agencies, acts of drug-related police corruption may be confined to a few officers, in other cases, the corruption may become systematic within the agency. Take, for example, the case of the Miami Police Department (MPD), especially among the notorious River Cops, whose misdeeds clouded the name of the MPD in the mid-1980s. The criminal actions of these officers related to their corrupt drug activities included all of the above-described behaviors and even a few others including witness tampering, conspiracy to commit murder, and murder.

The Miami River Cops.   The Miami case begins with a valuable lesson in the effects of relaxed hiring standards. From 1981 to 1982, there was a virtual hiring frenzy in the MPD. A total of 714 officers were hired, more than doubling the size of the agency in a very short time. The new hires were made under an Affirmative Action Consent Degree that required that the majority of the new officers had to be minorities or women. Furthermore, the Miami City Commission restricted the pool of potential applicants first to residents of the city of Miami, and when these potential candidates were exhausted, the pool was extended to residents of Dade County.

The control for the screening of applicants was removed from the MPD and placed with the city personnel office. Standards for employment were relaxed, and as a result, individuals who would previously have been denied employment were now welcomed into the police department. Individuals with poor work histories, credit problems, poor driving records, and criminal records were now offered positions with the MPD. The relaxed screening mechanisms were especially troublesome in the area of drug use. A failed polygraph examination could no longer be used as a sole disqualifying factor. It is difficult to ask an applicant about his or her prior drug use without the use of a polygraph examination. However, if an applicant denied using drugs and the polygraph detected a falsehood, this incident could not automatically eliminate the candidate from consideration.

Furthermore, while disclosure of any prior use of cocaine, heroin, or other drug would have automatically eliminated a candidate from consideration before the hiring blitz, these standards were also relaxed. While any heroin use still would eliminate a candidate from consideration (assuming, of course, that this information was revealed without the use of a polygraph), cocaine use was dependent on the level of use.

With the dramatic increase in the number of officers came the inevitable promotion of inexperienced individuals to supervisory level positions. Especially troublesome was the lack of seasoning among the field training officers. A field training officer assumes an important role in the socialization of a new recruit into the culture of the police department, guiding the inexperienced through their fragile first months of employment. Unfortunately, officers with less than a year's experience became field training officers and were responsible for making recommendations as to whether or not a recruit should be retained beyond the probationary period.

Among the new officers recruited by the MPD during the hiring blitz under the lax standards was a group of nineteen Hispanic officers who became known as the "River Cops." These officers were accused of a variety of state and federal crimes, including using the MPD as a racketeering enterprise to commit acts of felony murder, threats involving murder, civil rights violations, robbery, possession of narcotics, and various conspiracy charges. Ultimately, the officers were convicted of varying charges from murder to conspiracy and were given prison sentences that averaged twenty-three years.

The criminal careers of the River Cops began by stealing drugs and cash from motorists stopped for traffic violations and culminated in major drug rip-offs (Dombrink, 1988). At the time, the salary for a patrol officer in the city of Miami was approximately $27,000 annually. However, the take home pay for the River Cops was obviously much higher. One officer who was present at two major drug heists was able to purchase three Corvettes, a Cadillac, a new home worth a quarter of a million dollars, and vacationed in Europe. Several other River Cops had purchased expensive cars such as Porsches and Lotuses, boats, expensive homes, businesses, Rolex watches, jewelry, and other symbols of wealth. The officers did not try to hide their purchases from the MPD. Given the virtually nonexistent supervision and oversight, the extravagances seemed to go unnoticed. Furthermore, the Internal Affairs Unit had other problems to worry about than just the River Cops. From January 1985 to November 1987, no less than 72 MPD officers were suspended, fired, or asked to resign due to acts of misconduct. By 1988, this number had risen to 100 officers (Mancini, 1996).

The decade of the 1990s did not bring much relief in the area of drug-related corruption. Police agencies from a number of large cities came under federal scrutiny, including Atlanta, Chicago, Cleveland, Los Angeles, New Orleans, Savannah, and Washington, D.C. These sorts of deviant acts were not confined to large metropolitan police departments. Members of the Delta squad, an elite drug-interdiction team at the Manatee County Sheriff's Office in Florida, pled guilty to a number of federal charges including conspiracy to distribute crack cocaine and conspiracy to violate civil rights (Caldwell, 2000). Nationwide, from fiscal years 1993 to 1997, a total of 640 officers were convicted as a result of corruption investigations led by the Federal Bureau of Investigation (FBI). Of those officers convicted, nearly half were involved in drug-related offenses (U.S. General Accounting Office, 1998).

Abuse of Authority

With respect to the War on Drugs and its effect on police behavior, the abuse of authority by police officers may take a number of forms. In this section, special emphasis will be placed on asset forfeiture, racial profiling, and other enforcement issues.

Asset Forfeiture

In the past 30 years, a "new" tool has been introduced in the war against drugs: asset forfeiture. It is not uncommon in some areas of the country to see an expensive automobile, such as a Mercedes Benz, BMW, or Porsche, serving as a special police car. Often, these cars are painted with a striking DARE (Drug Abuse Resistance Education) logo with a conspicuous notation that the automobile was seized from a drug dealer. Because of the highly profitable nature of drug distribution, the practice or asset forfeiture is gaining popularity. In 1998, the U.S. Customs Service reported nearly 14,000 seizures with a domestic value of $94 million. That same year, the Drug Enforcement Administration (DEA) reported asset seizures in excess of $500 million. In addition to cash, the seizures may include vehicles, aircraft, boats, real estate, guns, jewelry, art, and even intellectual property rights.

The practice of seizing assets associated with the commission of a crime is not new. The origins of this form of punishment may be traced back to the English feudal system. Acts of treason against the crown were often met with capital punishment as well as the forfeiture of all land and property to the King (for an outstanding review of the history of asset seizures, see Greek, 1992). However, the use of forfeiture was not popular among the early American colonists, who strongly objected to this practice. One of the primary reasons for the revolution centered on the Colonists' disdain for the policy. By the late 1700s, the first U.S. Congress had virtually eliminated the policy of criminal forfeiture of assets.

In 1970, the practice of criminal forfeiture was reintroduced as part of a number of initiatives, including the Racketeer Influenced and Corrupt Organizations Act (RICO) and the Continuing Criminal Enterprises Act. Drug dealers were specifically targeted under the Comprehensive Drug Abuse Prevention and Control Act of 1970. The forfeiture of assets may include any monies made as a result of the operation of the criminal enterprise, anything purchased with these monies (including homes, cars, boats, etc.), as well as any assets used to further the enterprise, like airplanes.

Coinciding with the declaration of War on Drugs, the popularity of asset seizure became more prevalent in the early 1980s. In 1982, the DEA developed the Model Forfeiture of Drug Profits Act and published a training manual for other police agencies to follow in their own efforts to seize tainted monies and property. The DEA also encouraged states to allocate the revenues generated through this practice to further drug enforcement efforts. Three years after the bill was introduced, 47 states had passed legislation incorporating the ideas and suggestions of the DEA (Miller & Selva, 1997).

The growth of asset forfeiture was further assisted by the 1988 Anti-Drug Abuse Bill, which created the Asset Forfeiture Fund. The fund had two important characteristics. First, it allowed for the creation of special units within federal agencies who would then be responsible for conducting seizures. Second, while the Treasury Department retained some of the proceeds of the fund, a percentage was returned to local police agencies to supplement their budgets. It is this provision that poses special concerns for potential abuse of authority, especially when the proceeds from the seizure of assets are seen as a reliable source of income. For example, in the late 1980s, the city of Los Angeles required then-Police Chief Darrell Gates to include revenues from asset forfeiture seizures into the annual budget for the LAPD (Greek, 1992). In many financially strapped cities, narcotics enforcement has evolved into a highly profitable business.

The potential for abuse in the area of forfeiture is high, especially with civil forfeiture of assets. There is a difference between criminal and civil forfeiture. Currently, civil seizures, which are sometimes referred to as *in rem seizures*, are much more common than criminal. It was the use of civil forfeiture that was encouraged in the DEA's training manual. With civil forfeitures, it is much easier for the agency to successfully seize an alleged dealer's property. Due process protections do not apply in the arena of civil forfeitures. Properties may be seized without notice or hearing, based on an officer having probable cause to believe that the property had somehow been involved in criminal activity. Civil seizures may be upheld even if the crime in question was discovered through the use of an illegal search, or if a Miranda warning was not given prior to questioning. Furthermore, the standard of evidence is lower in civil proceedings: in civil law, attorneys must only meet the standard of "preponderance of the evidence," as opposed to "beyond a reasonable doubt" (Greek, 1992; Miller & Selva, 1997; "Horror Stories," 1997: 7A).

Other defenses that are commonplace in the criminal arena do not apply in civil seizures, such as dismissal or acquittal of the criminal charges. In some cases, the owner of the seized property may not even be charged with a crime. If an officer happens upon a suspected drug dealer with a large sum of cash, the cash may be seized without an arrest. The drug dealer is given a choice: be arrested and have the money seized anyway, or go free and sign a disclaimer stating that he or she was not the owner of the money, had no knowledge of where it came from, and would not attempt to recover it (Miller & Silva, 1997; "Horror Stories,"1997: 7A).

Once property is seized, it is very difficult for the property owner to recover his or her assets. For years, seizures were upheld even if the owner of the property was not the one involved in the alleged crime and had no knowledge that someone else was using their property in the commission of the crime. Regardless of whether or not it was the actual owner of the property or someone "borrowing" the asset during the commission of the alleged crime, it is the burden of the former owner to prove the innocence of the seized property. This policy was especially troublesome during the 1980s when, under "zero tolerance" legislation, rented luxury yachts could be seized upon the discovery of even a single marijuana seed (Greek, 1992). In one case in Florida, a homeowner was out of the country when federal agents received a tip that drug dealers were unloading cocaine from his dock of his waterfront home. Apparently, a friend was using the dock without the knowledge or consent of the homeowner. Federal agents seized the $300,000 house. After three years and $40,000 in legal fees, the homeowner was able to recover his home. This case was rare both for the challenge to the seizure and the homeowner's success. In 1995, of 33,000 contested seizures only 48 resulted in judgments against the government ("Horror Stories,"1997: 7A).

Police agencies that rely heavily on assets from narcotics-related seizures are setting themselves up for problems. As described by Miller and Selva (1997), it is the asset and its potential value that become the primary concerns, and not the criminal activity of the property holder. Individuals with expensive homes, cars, and other properties but are only peripherally involved in the drug trade may be targeted not because of their criminal involvement, but because of their assets. The goal becomes the seizing of the asset, and not the criminal prosecution of the drug dealer. If one can seize large sums of cash from a dealer based on suspicion and without a legal search, then why bother with an arrest? In this chapter, I have previously discussed issues related to the use of easily countable events such as number of arrests, field interview reports, and drug buys as measuring sticks for the performance of narcotics officers. Clearly, the use of the amount of money seized as a barometer for success brings even more problems.

Racial Profiling: Driving while Black

The War on Drugs has also been blamed for encouraging the discriminatory police practice of stopping minority motorists who fit a drug courier or gang member profile. A traffic stop may be used as a pretext for the officer to find evidence linking the individual to drug trafficking or other criminal activities. While the targeting of racial minorities for suspicion and differential enforcement is, unfortunately, not a new charge against police agencies, the practice of racial profiling has gained national media attention in the past few years. Hearings on the issue were recently held in the state of Pennsylvania, where minorities who felt that they had been targeted for harassment based solely on their race were encouraged to contact their state representatives. Angry protests were held in New Jersey and in Austin, Texas. The American Civil Liberties Union filed a number of lawsuits against state and local police agencies that challenged the practice of racial profiling. The national push to end the policy culminated in an executive order issued by President Clinton in June 1999 ordering that federal law enforcement officials collect data on the race and gender of the individuals stopped for questioning and arrest.

The use of profiling can be traced back to the late 1970s, when DEA agent Paul Markonni was assigned to surveillance duty at the Detroit Metropolitan Airport. Agent Markonni developed a behavioral profile of drug couriers that was soon adopted in over twenty airports across the country. The profile included such behavioral attributes as nervousness; paying for the airline ticket in cash and in large bills; traveling under an assumed name; and going to or arriving from a travel destination considered to be a place of origin of cocaine, heroin, or marijuana. Race did not enter into Markonni's profile of a drug courier; it was not until the crack cocaine epidemic that race became a major component of drug profiles (Harris, 1999).

What sorts of characteristics are used in a drug profile? In 1985, Florida was under great pressure to curb the flow of drugs in the South Florida area. The Florida Department of Highway Safety and Motor Vehicles issued a number of guidelines to assist the police in the identification and apprehension of motorists carrying drugs. These characteristics included motorists who were driving rental cars, maintaining strict adherence to traffic laws, wearing excessive amounts of gold jewelry, drivers who did not appear to belong in the vehicle, and motorists who were members of ethnic groups that were tied to the drug trade (Harris, 1999). Russell (1998) described a number of situations in which African American men may find themselves subject to vehicle stops by the police. These may include driving in a car with other black men; driving too fast, driving too slow, driving in a low-income neighborhood known for its drug traffic, and driving a luxury automobile.

While a great deal of anecdotal evidence supports the allegations of racial profiling against many police agencies, an emerging body of statistical data supports the charge as well. In the pending class action lawsuit *Chavez* v. *Illinois State Police* which was filed by the ACLU, databases maintained by the Illinois State Police were analyzed for racial disparities in traffic stops and vehicle searches. According to the report prepared for the ACLU case, minority motorists were targeted for enforcement of the traffic code. This pattern was especially evident in the drug-interdiction program called "Operation Valkyrie." Hispanic citizens comprise less than 8 percent of the population of the state of Illinois. However, 30 percent of the motorists stopped by the drug-interdiction officers for discretionary offenses were Hispanic. Discretionary offenses included minor violations such as failure to signal a lane change or driving one to four miles over the speed limit.

With respect to vehicle searches requested by the troopers, Hispanic motorists were again disproportionately targeted. In one of the districts surrounding East St. Louis, Hispanics account for less than 1 percent of the local driving age population. However, Hispanics drove 41 percent of the vehicles searched in this district. African Americans were similarly overrepresented among those searched. In one district, African Americans account for nearly 25 percent of the local driving age population but accounted for 63 percent of the vehicle searches (for a discussion of the ACLU lawsuits, see Harris, 1999).

In 1993, the ACLU brought a class action lawsuit on behalf of Robert Wilkins against the Maryland State Police (MSP). Wilkins, an African American attorney, claimed that he was stopped, detained, and searched by the MSP for no apparent reason. On the way home from a funeral in Chicago, Wilkins and his family were ordered out of their car after Wilkins was stopped for speeding. When Wilkins questioned the officer about the basis for probable cause, the officer told Wilkins that he and his family would be detained until they got out of the vehicle. Eventually, the family did get out of the car, and a drug dog was brought to the scene to search their car. No drugs were found, and the family was released with a $105 speeding ticket.

In their investigation, the ACLU found evidence of a race-based policy that was designed to curb the flow of drugs in the state. A confidential police memorandum stated that the dealers and couriers were predominantly black men and women; no other race was mentioned specifically (Russell, 1998). Furthermore, for this lawsuit, the MSP was required to maintain computer records of motorist searches. According to an analysis conducted by the ACLU, between January 1995 and September 1996, a total of 823 motorists were searched by the MSP on I-95, north of the city of Baltimore. Only 19.7 percent of those searched in this area were Caucasian; the majority of those searched (80.3 percent) were black, Hispanic, or other racial minorities.

Similar results have been found in analyses of other cities as well. In the state of North Carolina in 1995, twelve state troopers comprised the Special Emphasis Team (SET), a special drug unit. Forty-five percent of all of the individuals stopped by the SET troopers were black men. This was nearly twice the level of black men stopped by troopers who were not assigned to the special drug unit (Russell, 1998). An analysis of vehicle stops on the New Jersey turnpike found that African Americans with out-of-state plates drove 4.7 percent of the cars. However, fully 80 percent of the drug arrests were of such individuals. In Memphis, Tennessee, while only 4 percent of the flying public is African American, nearly 75 percent of the air travelers stopped by drug police in 1989 were African American (Duke & Gross, 1993).

The tendency for allegations of racial profiling to be concentrated within narcotics enforcement units should not go unnoticed. One need only look to our prison system to see the effects of selective suspicion and enforcement of our drug laws. If one suspects only minority involvement in drug use and dealing, and if minorities are stopped and searched at a higher rate than are white citizens, it is no surprise that the police will find drugs at a higher rate among minority citizens. Further, with every minority citizen that an officer finds with drug-related contraband, the image of the dangerous minority drug dealer is reinforced. The cycle becomes a self-fulfilling prophecy and will ultimately lead to further targeting of minority citizens. For many analysts, the War on Drugs has become a war on minorities, who have borne the brunt of our enforcement policies.

OTHER ENFORCEMENT ISSUES: THE TACTICS OF WAR

When then-President George Bush presented his battle plan for the War on Drugs, the formula included demand reduction strategies related to education and treatment. However, the primary strategy adopted by police agencies falls under the category of "expressive law enforcement." This plan involves such tactics as increasing the level of funding, number of personnel, and other resources devoted to drug enforcement efforts, creation and/or expansion of specialized units devoted to narcotics enforcement, and providing explicit and implicit encouragement to all officers, even those assigned to patrol, to pursue drug-related stops and arrests.

The emphasis on winning the battle against a domestic enemy raises special concerns for policing and for society. In the United States, certain values are held steadfast, such as the support for extensive liberties, privacy, freedoms, and protections for all citizens. As argued by Weisheit (1990), it would be a shallow victory indeed if the War on Drugs was won at the price of democracy. However, a number of actions taken by misguided police officers, such as the use of illegal searches and seizures and the planting of evidence, gnaw away at the core of our belief system.

The Fourth Amendment guards against unreasonable searches and seizures. However, there is a fine line between a legal and an illegal search. The application of the exclusionary rule, which holds that evidence obtained in violation of the Fourth Amendment cannot be used against a defendant, is largely confined to cases involving drugs, gambling, and weapons (Walker, 1999). In these types of cases, there are often serious questions as to how the evidence was discovered by the police. What, exactly, makes a search unreasonable in the eyes of the court? What sorts of behaviors constitute probable cause? In the game of cat and mouse played between drug dealers and the police, officers will always push the envelope with respect to the legality of a search. In 1988, newspaper reporter David Simon was given access to the Baltimore City's homicide unit. Consider the following statements of one of the officers, reflecting on drug enforcement and the Fourth Amendment:

> For narcotics or vice detectives in particular it's become a ridiculous game, this business of establishing the correct legal prerequisites for a search or arrest. Not surprisingly, it isn't enough to say that the suspect was a squirrel who'd been out on that corner about ten minutes too long. No, the law of the land requires that the arresting officer had the opportunity to observe the defendant operating in a suspicious manner on a corner known for drug trafficking and that upon closer inspection, the officer noticed a glassine envelope sticking out of a sweatshirt pocket as well as a bulge in the front waistband indicative of a weapon. Yeah. Right. *Probable cause on a street search is and always will be a cosmic joke, a systematic deceit.* In some parts of Baltimore, PC means looking at a passing radio car for two seconds longer than an innocent man would. The courts can't acknowledge it, but in the real world you watch a guy until you're sure he's dirty, then you jack him up, find the dope or the gun and then create a legal justification for the arrest. (Simon, 1991: 462, emphasis added)

Given the questionable nature of how evidence may be gathered in drug-related arrests, it is no surprise that in an analysis of felony arrests filed in the state of California from 1976 to 1979, the majority of the cases rejected for Fourth-Amendment reasons involved drug-related offenses (Livingston, 1996). More recently, the Rampart case in Los Angeles involved allegations of illegal searches as well as planted evidence and perjury. It is not unheard of for officers involved in narcotics enforcement to claim a quantity of drugs was in plain sight, therefore allowing for the search of the house, apartment, or vehicle of the suspected individual. Another tactic is for the officer to claim that the suspect was seen throwing drugs or other contraband as the officer approached, thereby allowing the suspect to be searched.

The planting of evidence is another enforcement-related issue. Officers may plant drugs on suspects to uphold the necessity for a search or may engage in the practice of "padding." This involves an officer adding drugs to the quantity legitimately recovered from a suspect. The officer may pad the evidence to increase the quality of the evidence or to increase the quantity, which would result in a felony rather than a misdemeanor arrest (Manning & Redlinger, 1986).

The threat of planting evidence on a suspect is another useful tool. While conducting research for my dissertation, I uncovered an internal affairs complaint that was made against two narcotics officers for a large police agency in the southeastern United States. The allegation, which was upheld by internal affairs investigators, charged that the officers had threatened to plant a large quantity of crack cocaine on the suspect if he did not cooperate. Apparently, the officers had previously stopped a suspected drug dealer who was attempting to sell a substance that resembled crack cocaine but was not. For the "dealer's" own protection, the officers confiscated the phony drugs and put them in the trunk of their car. Later, the officers picked up another individual and threatened to plant the "drugs" on him and charge him with attempting to distribute. Internal affairs investigators sustained the allegation, in part because when the investigators searched the trunk of the narcotics officers' vehicle, the "crack" was found just as the complainant had described.

While illegal searches and the planting of drugs are obviously illegal practices, other tactics of war sometimes dance on the fringe of acceptable police practices. The heavy reliance on informants, while a perfectly legal and widely used tool in the War on Drugs, has been criticized. Recall the sworn testimony of Officer Perez of the LAPD CRASH unit, who described how he and his partner regularly used a drug-addicted homeless woman as one of their key informants, trading crack cocaine for her information. While the information provided by this woman did lead to the arrest of drug dealers, is it acceptable for the police to become involved in the furthering of the drug trade by providing drugs to users?

Not all agencies broker drugs for information. However, all major federal enforcement agencies provide cash payment for information, as do most major police agencies. One estimate puts the payments from state and federal agencies to informants at over $100 million per year (Duke & Gross, 1993). Billboards encourage citizens to anonymously "Turn in a Pusher" for possible cash rewards, as do bumper stickers on marked police vehicles. As additional encouragement for citizens to get involved in the War on Drugs, in 1989 Congressman Dick Schultze proposed H.R. 3346, which became known as the Bounty Hunter Act. If a citizen turned in a drug dealer, then he or she would be eligible to receive 50 percent of the value of all assets seized by the government as a result of the tip. Do these monetary incentives encourage vigilante justice? As described by Greek (1992), several communities have experienced problems with angry community groups taking the law into their own hands, burning down suspected crack houses, and harassing suspected drug dealers on the streets.

While the lure of a monetary payment may entice the non–drug-using community to become an informant, many informants are themselves drug users. By providing payments to these individuals, it could be argued that the police have become a link in the drug trade. Furthermore, as informants become more sophisticated and knowledgeable in the value of their information to agencies, they may "shop" their tips to various agencies for the best deal. As mentioned previously, informants may also exchange their information for lenient treatment for their own criminal activities. When agencies do protect their informants from criminal prosecution, it could be argued that the police are trading one form of criminal behavior for another.

Another legal police tactic that deserves some attention is the use of crackdowns. Crackdowns, which are often used in lower-income minority communities, raise civil liberties issues. Crackdowns involve the saturation of a targeted neighborhood with an aggressive, intense police effort. It is important to note that the term *crackdown* does not imply a single-standard enforcement strategy. Crackdowns may vary in the tactics employed by the individual agency, the intensity of the effort, and duration of the emphasis (Worden et al., 1994). The actual plan selected for a crackdown effort will be based on the nature and severity of the drug problem, the resources allotted, the tenacity of the criminal element, and the talents of the agency.

One of the best-known crackdown efforts was dubbed Operation Pressure Point by the New York City Police. In 1984, during the height of the crack cocaine epidemic, over 240 additional officers were assigned to a predominantly Hispanic neighborhood in the Lower East Side. Officers worked the area on foot, on horseback, and in helicopters. The Organized Crime Control Bureau conducted hidden surveillance operations and posed as drug dealers in buy and bust operations. Canine units were dispatched to vacant buildings in the area, which had been used to hide the caches of the dealers. After 17 months of intensive enforcement, over 14,000 arrests had been made and 62,000 traffic summonses issued (Zimmer, 1997).

The overall effectiveness of Operation Pressure Point has been debated. The local media reported the effort to be a success; new businesses opened up in the area, property values experienced an increase, and urban gentrification was facilitated. While it was reported that open sales of narcotics decreased in the targeted area, displacement of the criminal activity was not measured. Furthermore, the reduction was not uniform throughout the area. While drug activity decreased in the area occupied by middle-class Caucasians, the intensive efforts were least successful in the areas inhabited by poor and working-class minorities.

With respect to police misconduct issues and crackdowns, the real issue may not be so much with the actual behavior of the officers, but the perception of the heightened level of intrusive enforcement. The potential for abuse is an ever-present temptation for police when targeting drug dealers and may be stronger when the officer knows that many of his or her peers are nearby if a situation should escalate. Unfortunately, not a great deal of research has been done to explore the effects of crackdown efforts on public attitudes. In a review of the research conducted on the effectiveness of crackdowns, Worden et al. (1994) noted that conventional wisdom would lead one to conclude that more intrusive and aggressive police procedures may not be popular among all residents. In a description of a recent crackdown effort in the city of Philadelphia, Worden et al. (1994: 99) stated, "The public was critical of what it saw (probably justifiably) as indiscriminate enforcement activity."

This effect may be even more pronounced among minority residents, whose communities are often the targets of crackdown efforts. Operation Invincible in Memphis, Operation Clean Sweep in Chicago, Operation Hammer in Los Angeles, and the Red Dog Squad in Atlanta were all crackdown efforts targeted at lower-income minority neighborhoods. The relationship between the police and minority citizens has not had a proud past, and in many communities, the relationship continues to be strained at best. When officers enter a community en masse, stopping and questioning all residents, emphasizing zero tolerance enforcement, making numerous arrests, and maintaining a highly visible presence, the crackdown may be viewed as a hostile takeover by an army of occupation.

To put things in perspective, consider the Fear Reduction Experiment in Houston, Texas. This was not a crackdown, but a community policing effort designed to reduce the level of fear expressed by local citizens. The program included a number of initiatives, including the establishment of local storefront ministations that would be more accessible to the area residents, the distribution of community newsletters, and a victim recontact program. In this program, police officers contacted recent victims of crime, expressed their sympathies and concerns to the victim, and checked to see if any further assistance was needed. The program was designed to reduce citizen complaints that, once the initial investigation had concluded, the victim was forgotten. Interestingly, this program seemed to backfire among victims with poor English skills who were primarily of Hispanic descent. While the recontact program had no effect on reducing crime for most citizens, for the residents with poor English skills, the fear of crime actually increased. It was hypothesized that these individuals were fearful and confused when they received the follow-up call from the police department (discussed in Walker, 1999:161–2). If a kind-natured phone call from the police can distress some citizens, imagine the effect of having several hundred uniformed officers swarming the neighborhood streets.

A THEORETICAL FRAMEWORK FOR UNDERSTANDING THE CAUSES OF DRUG-RELATED POLICE MISCONDUCT

While a number of causes for drug-related police misconduct have already been discussed, such as internal and external demands for performance, monetary temptations, and lower hiring standards, in this section, I examine the various roots within a theoretical framework. The application of a theoretical framework will not only assist in furthering understanding of the phenomenon but will also suggest practical steps that administrators can take to reduce the occurrence of drug-related police misconduct.

A Social Learning Approach to Drug-Related Police Misconduct

Social learning theory is a social psychological theory of deviance developed from a behavioral revision of Sutherland's differential association theory (Sutherland, 1947). Proponents of social learning theory view norm-violating actions as learned behaviors acquired and maintained by the same process as conforming behavior. Although the theory refers to the whole range of learning mechanisms, in empirical tests of the theory, researchers have

concentrated on four main concepts or sets of explanatory variables: differential association, definitions favorable or unfavorable to the act in question, differential reinforcement,
and imitation.

Differential association refers to both behavioral and normative dimensions of social
interaction. Behaviors, both good and bad, are learned through our communications with
other people. The greatest amount of learning occurs through our interactions within intimate groups—family, close friends, and peers—basically, those individuals with whom we
have the most contact. These primary groups have the most influence over our actions because they have the ability to reinforce or to punish our behavior the most. While social
learning theorists focus on communication and interactions within intimate groups, the influence of other forces, such as the media, co-workers and employers, are also recognized
as having the ability to sway our behavior.

Through the social process of differential association, individuals are exposed to social norms that approve or disapprove of various acts. To the extent individuals learn these
and take them in as their own attitudes, they will hold definitions favorable or unfavorable
to the act in question. If a definition is favorable to a deviant act, the action becomes an acceptable and approved form of behavior. In terms of police misconduct, if an officer has
been exposed to definitions favorable to shaking down drug dealers and defines this type of
behavior as acceptable, then the officer is more likely to engage in this type of behavior.
However, if, through interactions with others, the officer comes to define this type of behavior as morally unacceptable, then the officer will refrain. Other definitions may be favorable to police misconduct because they serve to neutralize the undesirability of the act
and thereby make the act appear to be more justified or excusable in the eyes of the officer
(Akers, 1985).

Deviant behavior is acquired and sustained through differential reinforcement. In this
process, given two separate acts, if an action produces a greater amount of rewards for the
individual with higher frequency and greater certainty than costs, the act is likely to be repeated (Akers, 1985). Therefore, regardless if the act is labeled deviant or conforming in
nature, the act that results in greater reinforcement for the individual is the act that is likely
to be repeated. This type of learning is a form of instrumental conditioning, in which a behavior is learned as a result of its outcome. Behaviors that are met with reinforcement or rewards are strengthened; behaviors that are met with punishment or negative outcomes are
likely to be extinguished. In addition to the influence of direct rewards and punishments,
differential reinforcement also recognizes the influence of anticipated positive or negative
responses. The rewards and costs that may be anticipated from the act may be balanced
against the chance of discovery and the possible negative sanctions that could result.

In addition to the learning that occurs as a result of direct instrumental conditioning,
modeling and imitation may also occur. According to Akers (1985), models may be real or
fictitious (such as actors in television shows or movies). An individual may imitate the behavior of others if the observer sees that the model has been reinforced. This influence is
stronger if the observer likes or respects the model and especially if, once the observer actually performs the act, he or she then receives similar reinforcement for performing the act.
However, if the observer does not like the model, if the model has received negative feedback or punishment for performing the act, or if the observer receives punishment once he
or she performs the act, then the likelihood that the act will be repeated is reduced (Curran
& Renzetti, 1994).

Differential Association and the Police Subculture

Differential association and the resulting exposure to definitions favorable or unfavorable to deviance must be analyzed within the distinct occupational characteristics of the police role. The behavior of the individual officer is not only affected by the influence of others but also by the attributes of the job itself. Given the socially isolated nature of police work and the cohesive bonds that are formed between the officers, the influence of an officer's co-workers becomes even more powerful than what would be expected among co-workers in other occupations.

An oft-cited sociological explanation that has been proposed for police misconduct involves the subculture of policing. Proponents of this perspective (Skolnick, 1966; Stark, 1972; Westley, 1970) discuss the police officer as being affected by the norms, values, expectations, and regulatory principles of their occupations. While the term *subculture* is usually applied to lower-class youth gangs, a subculture may be defined as a group that maintains a distinctive set of values, norms, and lifestyles that sometimes differs from the overall culture of society. For a variety of reasons, the distinct occupational characteristics of the police officer tend to be in conflict with and isolated from the community in which they are employed to protect and to serve.

From the beginning of their employment as officers, young recruits find themselves in a different lifestyle from most of their nondepartmental friends. Because they are low in seniority, many rookies must work the night shift. At a time when most young couples or individuals are developing friendships and socializing, the pool of available people declines due to the odd hours that the police officer works. Officers are forced to rely heavily on their co-workers for companionship, which further serves to isolate them from society. In Skolnick's analysis (1966), 35 percent of the 700 friends listed by 250 police officers were officers as well. Further, 54 percent of the officers had attended 3 or more police banquets or dinners in the past year. Skolnick contrasted this figure to that given by a sample of printers in a similar study, in which 54 percent of the printers had not attended any sort of organized social function with their co-workers in the past 5 years.

Further, the dangerous nature of police work fosters an environment based on friendship and trust. Danger is always present, and the authority of the officer is always being challenged (Skolnick & Currie, 1970). Officers must rely on each other for protection; norms that stress the importance of teamwork, cooperation, and mutual responsibility are extremely high among officers (Stark, 1972; Westley, 1970). Officers turn to each other for support and understanding. Mainstream society is viewed as unsympathetic and hostile toward officers, and the officers must have someone to turn to in order to alleviate the stress of their occupation (Stark, 1972).

Police officers develop a distinctive way of looking at the world that sets them off from normal citizens and further contributes to their social isolation. Officers tend to become cynical and hardened, and the conversations among officers tend to focus on violence, crime, and murder (Van Maanen, 1980). Further, since officers must enforce laws that control social and leisure activities of the community (such as public drinking, parties, etc.), and since many officers sometimes engage in some of these same activities and behaviors, the officers tend to segregate their social lives from ordinary citizens. Police clubs, sporting teams, and organizations whose memberships are exclusive to officers are common (Stark, 1972).

The Importance of Positive Role Models: Field Training Officers and Clean Barrels

As a result of the combined forces of isolation, either real or perceived, the officers become a distinctive group from mainstream society (Skolnick, 1966). As a result of this isolation, the influence of the behaviors, attitudes, and beliefs of an officer's co-workers become a powerful force. For the moment, imagine yourself as new recruit hired in the early 1980s by the Miami Police Department (MPD). As a result of your occupation, you find yourself more and more isolated from your old friends. When people find out that you are a police officer, they tend to avoid you or bombard you with complaints about the effectiveness of the police, a recent ticket that was "wrongfully" received, and so on. As a result, you find yourself relying to a greater extent on your co-workers for friendship and support. You want to please them and elevate your status among them.

Further, imagine that your assigned field training officer (FTO) is Arturo De la Vega, an officer who was ultimately convicted and sentenced to thirty years in prison for his part in the Miami River Cops scandal. Arguably, FTOs have the greatest influence over the future actions of inexperienced recruits. Constant feedback and evaluations are provided, based on both the departmental and individual expectations of the FTO. The FTO is called on to recommend whether the new recruit is to be retained beyond the probationary period, whether the individual needs further training, or whether the new recruit should be terminated. It is essential that the new recruit gain respect and receive positive feedback from their assigned FTOs.

Ideally, FTOs should be carefully screened to ensure impeccable character, and they should undergo extensive training. Unfortunately, this is not always the case. Standards for the selection and training of FTOs vary with the individual agency, and, in some agencies, the FTO program is virtually nonexistent. During periods of rapid expansion of agencies with binge hiring, individuals selected to serve in the important role as FTOs may not have the level of experience or flawless ethical character that an agency would prefer. In the case of the MPD of the 1980s, FTOs were assigned after only months of service with the MPD, and in some cases provided the models for misconduct. Miami River Cop De la Vega worked as an FTO and claimed his own FTO would often come to work "high on something." Other River Cops stated that they had been taught to deviate by their FTOs (Mancini, 1986). The influence of these early models on the future behaviors of young recruits cannot be underestimated.

Beyond the careful selection of FTOs, agencies are also particularly vulnerable to misconduct when hiring standards are lowered. Given the strong influence that the peer group exerts over its members, it is essential that the agency maintain the highest standards in their hiring process. While the hiring of individuals demonstrating exemplary character does not guarantee that these same individuals will not be later tempted by misconduct, the agency needs to take steps to ensure that the barrel is not tainted by the hiring of individuals with questionable backgrounds. If an agency hires individuals who have already demonstrated their susceptibility to definitions favorable to law violation by prior arrest histories, drug use, or associations with known felons and drug dealers, then the agency is encouraging the growth and development of a culture of misconduct within the department.

The hiring frenzy of the MPD has already been addressed, where it was not uncommon for recruits of the 1980s to be called out of their academy classes only to be arrested for outstanding criminal warrants. In the case of the River Cops, the background investigations of several of the officers indicated that they had been terminated for on-the-job thefts, a violation that in previous times would have automatically eliminated them from employment consideration (Mancini, 1986). In the case of the LAPD Rampart CRASH unit, four of the officers under administrative leave as a result of the allegations of misconduct should never have been hired as police officers in the first place. Prior arrests, criminal convictions, and poor credit histories should have eliminated the officers from employment consideration. However, given the intense pressure on the LAPD to fill vacancies, these individuals were given the go-ahead. Similarly, in the early 1990s, Washington, D.C., hired nearly 1,000 new officers under political pressure. To date, nearly a quarter of these new hires have been fired from the agency for their involvement in various acts of misconduct or have been indicted for their criminal activities (Cohen, 2000). The New York City Police Department and the Chicago Police Department have also experienced cases of drug-related police misconduct involving individuals who were hired under relaxed standards.

Clearly, when an agency invites troubled individuals to join the department, the agency should not be surprised when misconduct becomes the standard for behavior. In the case where deviant behavior becomes the norm in an agency, then those individuals involved in acts of misconduct are no longer labeled as deviant. Officers who perjure themselves or plant evidence on suspects are not seen by others as engaging in wrongdoing, nor do they define themselves as being "bad" for performing the misdeeds. Definitions favorable to violating the criminal law and the ethical standards of policing become dominant. In this type of situation, it is much easier and more rewarding for the young recruit to become deviant than to try to maintain high standards for behavior. Furthermore, as corruption and misconduct become entrenched in an agency, the risk of detection, exposure, and sanction become minimal.

Differential Reinforcement: Powerful Rewards Coupled with Limited Detection, Few Costs

Perhaps one of the more distinguishing features of policing as an occupation is the relative lack of supervision. Officers generally work alone or in pairs and are basically free to roam large geographic areas with little or no direct contact with their supervisors (Kappeler et al., 1994; Walker, 1999). Further, the majority of police–citizen interactions occur outside of the eye of the public in alleys, deserted streets, private residences, or other isolated locations. The end result is that an officer's everyday behavior and decision making is free from scrutiny from both the officer's direct supervisor and the general public.

Furthermore, in the special case of drug-related police misconduct, the risk of punishment that an individual officer faces for engaging in questionable behaviors is minimal. Street dealers who have had their drugs or cash stolen are not likely to report the theft to internal affairs investigators. When drugs are planted or evidence rules subverted, the complainant is, after all, someone of questionable character. These types of activities are likely to occur outside of the eye of the general public, leaving only the accused drug offender and the police as witnesses. In this type of situation, police officers are viewed as providing credible statements, and the drug offender is presumed to be guilty.

And, lest we forget, there is a war being waged. However, as Weisheit (1990) argues, the war is really not against drugs, but against people—bad people who use drugs, and are then in violation of the standards and values of society. If a drug dealer or a user's rights are stepped on, there is not a great deal of moral outrage from the general public. The perception among many Americans is that drug offenders are not like other citizens or even other law violators. In effect, drug offenders have become "less than human" and are undeserving of many of the legal protections enjoyed by the rest of the law-abiding public (Weisheit, 1990: 2).

The culture of policing also provides officers with the perception of impunity for misdeeds. "The Blue Curtain" of policing is a code of silence in which nothing is held more sacred than the loyalty of officers to each other, no matter what. While there is some controversy surrounding the incident, the most highly publicized example of what can happen to an officer who violates this code of silence is illustrated by the case of Frank Serpico. Serpico was shot during a heroin buy-and-bust operation that went sour after his fellow officers did not back him up. Allegedly, his fellow detectives did not assist Serpico because of Serpico's violation of the Code of Silence—he had attempted to inform officials of widespread corruption within the New York Police Department (NYPD).

As discussed by Skolnick and Fyfe (1993), the fear that other officers will not back up a Blue Curtain violator is exaggerated. Arguing that "the police code of silence is not a mafia-style life-or-death pact with the devil (1993: 110)," Skolnick and Fyfe point to a very real code that is enforced by two punishments: the shunning of the violator from his or her peers, and the exposure and ultimate sanction of one's own misdeeds. Officers who violate the code of silence are isolated from their peers. This segregation may be psychologically crippling, especially given the high perception of isolation that many officers feel with respect to the general public. Few officers are without sin; by drawing attention to the misdeeds of others, an officer opens up his or her own behavior to scrutiny.

While the actual punishments associated with violations against the code of silence are open to debate, the code does exist. Police fraternities are not the only bearers of a fierce code of loyalty. Other professionals—including doctors, lawyers, even academic researchers—protect the misdeeds and indiscretions of its members. However, in terms of social learning theory, the code of silence can further encourage acts of deviance due to the perception that the misdeeds will go unreported and therefore will not be met with negative sanctions.

SOLUTIONS TO THE PROBLEM

Unfortunately, police agencies can do little to dissuade politicians and the media from their focus on winning the War on Drugs. Nor can the police lobby for the legalization of drugs. An individual police administrator can do little to change the culture of the general public toward narcotics enforcement. As long as narcotics are an illegal and highly profitable substance, the possibility for drug-related police misconduct will persist. Given the parameters within which the police must operate, this section explores some of the solutions to reduce drug-related police misconduct.

Differential Association: Recruiting and Maintaining a Clear Barrel

It is essential that police agencies make integrity a priority. This commitment needs to be made by officers at every level—from top administrators to patrol officers. Furthermore, the commitment needs to be woven throughout the agency, from hiring decisions, to account-ability measures, to reward structures. A new recruit needs to be brought up into a culture in which honest and ethical behavior is the norm, not the exception. To do so, both formal and informal rewards for ethical behavior need to be cultivated and reinforced. The police subculture, a powerful influence on the behavior of officers, must promote integrity, not corruption. Officers must be socialized into a culture in which deviant acts will be met with negative consequences, both formally by the administration and informally among his or her peers.

In its report on drug-related police corruption, the U.S. General Accounting Office (U.S. GAO) (1998) recommended a number of practices to prevent and reduce police cor-ruption. At the hiring and recruitment phase, the following steps were recommended (U.S. GAO, 1998: 21–2):

- Better candidate screening
- Raising the age of recruits
- Raising educational standards
- Incorporating integrity training into police academy curricula
- Reviewing police officers' integrity as part of probationary period evaluations
- Extending the probationary period

Unfortunately, given the current employment conditions, many police agencies are experiencing great difficulty in recruiting perspective officers. The number of qualified can-didates applying to agencies is down. Further, due to the time lag between the application for employment and hiring, many qualified individuals find employment elsewhere. It is difficult for agencies to raise standards given the low supply of interested applicants. Con-sider, for example, the area of educational standards. In 1967 the President's Crime Com-mission recommended that the bachelor's degree should be the minimum requirement for the hiring of police personnel. However, in the state of Florida, while several state-level law enforcement agencies require a bachelor's degree for employment consideration, only one police department requires a four-year degree. Because of the high number of vacancies coupled with few interested recruits, this agency is now reconsidering this requirement. In the state of Florida, as is the case in many states, a 19-year-old with a general equivalency diploma (GED) may be hired as a sworn police officer.

Beyond the recruitment and initial training phase, it is essential that agencies maintain the high level of integrity that has been instilled at the academy. The U.S. GAO (1998: 22) sug-gested the following techniques to prevent the occurrence of drug-related police corruption:

- Integrity training as part of the continuing education of officers
- The inclusion of integrity assessments in in-service evaluations
- A consideration of integrity assessments when determining promotion
- Rotational assignments, to reduce pressures from personal ties that may lead to opportunities for corruption

The general notion is to promote and reinforce norms that advocate ethical behavior. It is not enough that an agency include a brief statement of the importance of integrity in its mission statement; officers must be keenly aware of the departmental stance on corrupt activities and truly adopt this high standard of behavior as part of their own Code of Ethics.

Differential Reinforcement: Detection and Discipline

Promoting ethical standards by thorough selection and continuous reinforcement will only go so far. When administrators know that an act of corruption has occurred, it is essential that an appropriate action be taken. The National Advisory Commission on Criminal Justice Standards and Goals (1973) recognized the importance of agencies taking acts of police misconduct seriously. According to the commission report (1973: 72), "Once a finding sustains the allegations of wrongdoing, disciplinary sanctions commensurate with the seriousness of the offense that are imposed fairly, swiftly, and consistently will most clearly reflect the commitment of the department to oppose police misconduct." The report then discusses various penalties that could be assigned to officers, based on the nature of the charge. Verbal reprimands, suspensions, demotions, reassignment, and permanent removal from duty were suggested. The report further stated that "departments that are serious about preventing police misconduct can do something about it" (p. 93).

Beyond taking a reactive stance to acts of corruption, agencies can also utilize their expertise in the area of narcotics investigations in their own internal investigations. The U.S. GAO recommended the following proactive and somewhat controversial stances that an agency may use to enforce standards of ethical behavior (1998: 23):

- Place officers suspected of involvement in illicit drug-related activities under surveillance.
- Get drug dealers and corrupt officers to testify against other dealers or other corrupt officers.
- Debrief arrested drug dealers to obtain information on police corruption.

The U.S. GAO described the investigations conducted by the NYPD in its effort to detect corrupt activities. The NYPD has, for example, used undercover officers posing as a married couple involved in local drug dealing. When these "dealers" interacted with police officers, the encounters were videotaped to see if the officers engaged in corrupt activities, such as attempting to buy drugs from the couple. This sting operation was used against specific officers who were suspected of being involved in corrupt activities or randomly as a tool for identifying problem officers.

While this technique has been criticized, the NYPD defended the practice, stating that officers who had been identified as corrupt through this technique often assisted in the identification of other corrupt officers. Additionally, the practice was justified by the belief that patrol officer training needs could be identified and met. Because patrol officers were keenly aware of the integrity tests, the NYPD felt that the program was providing a useful deterrent effect on drug-related corruption.

A second proactive measure concerns the implementation and use of Early Warning systems. Kappeler et al. (1994) discussed the increasing trend of departments to use various Early Warning (EW) systems, in which citizen and departmental complaints are tracked and monitored. Data concerning the number of civilian complaints filed against the officer, the outcome of departmental investigations, and demographic variables of the citizens filing the complaints should be recorded to investigate for possible patterns. Similarly, Geller and Toch (1995) discussed the supplemental use of other data sources, such as peer nominations, to supplement complaint data in the identification of problem-prone officers. Regardless of the type, properly used EW systems may assist a department in identifying problem-prone officers before the situation gets out of control. (For a further discussion of EW systems, see Chapter 9.)

A third proactive measure concerns the detection of illicit drug use by both perspective and currently employed officers. The use of drugs by an officer does not automatically imply that he or she is engaging in other serious forms of police corruption discussed in this chapter. However, by virtue of the fact that the officer is using drugs, the officer no longer defines drugs as a harmful and potentially corrupting substance. Individuals holding definitions favorable to drug use need to be identified and dealt with before their beliefs are adopted by other officers. While officers testing positive for drugs do not necessarily need to be terminated, their problem needs to be addressed (see Chapter 7, for a discussion of police and drug-testing issues).

The goal of these various strategies is to reduce the potential for introducing and maintaining norms favorable to corrupt activities. The process of instilling norms that promote integrity never really ends. Just because an agency has impeccable standards for hiring does not guarantee that the officers will not become involved in corruption. Norms promoting acceptable behavior need to be constantly reiterated and reinforced, and violators need to be met with an appropriate level of punishment. Agencies need to do more than just adopt a reactive stance to acts of corruption after the event has occurred. Proactive investigations and preventative measures must be taken to reduce drug-related police misconduct.

CONCLUSION

This chapter explored the effects of the War on Drugs on drug-related police corruption. Clearly, the impact of the "all is fair in war" mentality has had a great impact on policing over the past several decades. The lure of substantial amounts of untraceable cash coupled with societal norms that demand action against the enemy have combined to form a powerful temptation for many officers charged with narcotics enforcement. However, it is important to stress that corruption does not have to be an inevitable result of this pressure. If one views the actions associated with drug-related misconduct as just another learned behavior, steps can be taken to extinguish this behavior. While the internal and external pressure to deviant may be extreme and, in some cases easily rationalized, police agencies can do a great deal to discourage the incidence and prevalence of drug-related police misconduct.

REFERENCES

AKERS, R. (1985). *Deviant Behavior*. 2d ed. Belmont, Calif.: Wadsworth.

AKERS, R. (1992). *Drugs, Alcohol, and Society*. Belmont, Calif.: Wadsworth.

BARKER, T., & CARTER, D. L. (1994). *Police Deviance*. 3d ed. Cincinnati, Ohio: Anderson Publishing.

BROWNSTEIN, H. H. (1997). The media and the construction of random drug violence. In Gaines, L. K., & Kraska, P. B., eds., *Drugs, Crime, and Justice: Contemporary Perspectives* (pp. 67–86). Prospect Heights, Ill.: Waveland Press.

CALDWELL, A. (2000, June 18). Crime, in the name of the law. *St. Petersburg Times*, pp. 1A, 10A.

CALIFORNIA COUNCIL ON CRIMINAL JUSTICE. (1989). *State Task Force on Gangs and Drugs: Final Report*. Sacramento, Calif: California Council on Criminal Justice.

CARTER, D. L. (1990). Drug-related corruption of police officers: A contemporary typology. *Journal of Criminal Justice* 18 (2): 85–98.

Chavez v. *Illinois State Police* 94 C 5307 (2000).

COHEN, A. (2000, March 6). Gangsta cops. *Time*, pp. 30–34.

CURRAN, D. J., & RENZETTI, C. M. (1994). *Theories of Crime*. Needham Heights, Mass.: Allyn & Bacon.

DOMBRINK, J. (1988). The Touchables: Vice and police corruption in the 1980's. *Law and Contemporary Problems* 51: 201–32.

DUKE, S. B., & GROSS, A. C. (1993). *America's Longest War: Rethinking Our Tragic Crusade against Drugs*. New York: Putnam.

DUNLAP, E., & JOHNSON, B. D. (1992). The setting for the crack era: Macro forces, micro consequences (1960–1992). *Journal of Psychoactive Drugs* 24 (4): 307–21.

GELLER, W. A., & TOCH, H. (1995). Improving our understanding and control of police abuse of force: Recommendations for research and action. In Geller, W., & Toch, H., eds., *And Justice for All: Understanding and Controlling Police Abuse of Force* (pp. 277–337). Washington, D.C.: Police Executive Research Forum.

GREEK, C. (1992). Drug control and asset seizures: A review of the history of forfeiture in England and colonial America. In Mieczkowski, T., ed., *Drugs, Crime, and Social Policy* (pp. 109–37). Boston: Allyn & Bacon.

HARRIS, D. A. (1999, June). *Driving While Black: Racial Profiling on our Nation's Highways*. New York: American Civil Liberties Union.

HAYESLIP, D. W., & WEISEL, D. L. (1992). Local level drug enforcement. In Cordner, G. W., & Hale, D. C.. eds., *What Works in Policing? Operations and Administration Examined* (pp. 35–48). Cincinnati, Ohio: Anderson Publishing.

Horror stories prompt House to review asset-seizure laws. (1997, June 22). *Pensacola News Journal*, p. 7A.

KAPPELER, V. E., SLUDER, R. D., & ALPERT, G. P. (1994). *Forces of Deviance: Understanding the Dark Side of Policing*. Prospect Heights, Ill.: Waveland Press.

KASARDA, J. E. (1992). The severely distressed in economically transforming cities. In Harrell, A., & Peterson, G., eds., *Drugs, Crime and Social Isolation: Barriers to Urban Opportunity*. Washington, D.C.: Urban Institute Press.

KLEIN, M. W., & MAXSON, C. L. (1994). Gangs and crack cocaine trafficking. In Mackenzie, D. L., & Uchida, C. D., eds., *Drugs and Crime: Evaluating Public Policy Initiatives* (pp. 42–60). Thousand Oaks, Calif.: Sage Publications.

KLEIN, M. W., MAXSON, C. L., & CUNNINGHAM, L. C. (1988). *Gang Involvement in Cocaine "Rock" Trafficking. Final Report to the National Institute of Justice*. Los Angeles: University of Southern California.

LIVINGSTON, J. (1996). *Crime and Criminology*. 2d ed. Upper Saddle River, N.J.: Prentice Hall.

LUSANE, C. (1997). Racism and the drug crisis. In Gaines, L. K., & Kraska, P. B., eds., *Drugs, Crime, and Justice: Contemporary Perspectives* (pp. 35–66). Prospect Heights, Ill.: Waveland Press.

MANCINI, C. (1996). *Pirates in Blue*. Miami, Fla.: National Association of Chiefs of Police.

MANNING, P. K., & REDLINGER, L. J. (1986). Invitational edges of corruption: Some consequences of narcotic law enforcement. In Barker, T., & Carter, D. L.. eds., *Police Deviance*. Cincinnati, Ohio: Pilgrimage.

MILLER, J. M., & SELVA, L. H. (1997). Drug enforcement's double-edged sword: An assessment of asset forfeiture programs. In Gaines, L. K., & Kraska, P. B., eds., *Drugs, Crime, and Justice: Contemporary Perspectives* (pp. 275–96). Prospect Heights, Ill.: Waveland Press.

MOORE., M. H., & KLEIMAN, M. (1997). Police and drugs. In Gaines, L. K., & Kraska, P. B., eds., *Drugs, Crime and Justice: Contemporary Perspectives* (pp. 227–48). Prospect Heights, Ill.: Waveland Press.

NATIONAL ADVISORY COMMISSION ON CRIMINAL JUSTICE STANDARDS AND GOALS. (1973). *Police*. Washington, D.C.: U.S. Government Printing Office.

RADELET, L. A., & CARTER, D. L. (1994). *The Police and the Community*. 5th ed. Upper Saddle River, N.J.: Prentice Hall.

RUSSELL, K. (1998). *The Color of Crime*. New York: New York University Press.

SIMON, D. (1991). *Homicide: A Year on the Killing Streets*. Boston: Houghton Mifflin.

SKOLNICK, J. (1966). *Justice Without Trial: Law Enforcement in Democratic Society*. New York: Wiley.

SKOLNICK, J. H., & CURRIE, E. (1970). *Crisis in American Institutions*. Boston: Little Brown.

SKOLNICK, J. H., & FYFE, J. J. (1993). *Above the Law*. New York: The Free Press.

STARK, R. (1972). *Police Riots: Collective Violence and Law Enforcement*. Belmont, Calif.: Wadsworth Publishing.

SUTHERLAND, E. H. (1947). *Criminology*. 4th ed. Philadelphia: Lippincott.

U.S. GENERAL ACCOUNTING OFFICE. (1998, May). *Law enforcement: Information of Drug-Related Police Corruption*. Washington, D.C.: U.S. General Accounting Office.

VAN MAANEN, J. (1980). Beyond account: The personal impact of police strategies. *Annals of the Academy of Political and Social Science* 452: 145–56.

WALKER, S. (1998). *Sense and Nonsense about Crime and Drugs*. 4th ed. Belmont, Calif.: Wadsworth Publishing.

WALKER, S. (1999). *The Police in America: An Introduction*. 3d ed. Boston, Mass.: McGraw-Hill College.

WEISHEIT, R., ed. (1990). *Drugs, Crime and the Criminal Justice System*. Cincinnati, Ohio: Anderson Publishing.

WESTLEY, W. A. (1970). *Violence and the Police: A Sociological Study of Law, Custom, and Morality*. Cambridge, Mass.: MIT Press.

WORDEN, R. E., BYNUM, T. S., & FRANK, J. (1994). Police crackdowns on drug abuse and trafficking. In Mackenzie, D. L.. & Uchida, C. D., eds., *Drugs and Crime: Evaluating Public Policy Initiatives* (pp. 95–113). Thousand Oaks, Calif.: Sage Publications.

ZIMMER, L. (1997). Proactive policing against street-level drug trafficking. In Gaines, L. K., & Kraska, P. B., eds., *Drugs, Crime, and Justice: Contemporary Perspectives* (pp. 249–74). Prospect Heights, Ill.: Waveland Press.

4

The Use and Abuse of Force by Police

Robert E. Worden and Shelagh E. Catlin

❖

INTRODUCTION

On March 3, 1991, in Los Angeles, Rodney King refused to stop his vehicle on the freeway for a routine traffic stop. The ensuing pursuit, which took place through residential sections of the city at high rates of speed, attracted a number of police units. When King, a black man, finally pulled over, his two passengers were arrested without incident. King, however, was belligerent and seemingly uncooperative during the arrest, although bystander accounts of his resistance differ enormously: One bystander noted that King was kicking and fighting the officers as they attempted to subdue him, while another stated that King was passive and did not provoke the officers. But one civilian bystander recorded much of the incident on videotape. The tape showed that King was struck between 53 and 56 times by police officers wielding side-handle batons, kicking and hitting him after he did not succumb to a reportedly 50,000-volt Taser electric dart gun or respond to officer commands. Following the arrest, in which King suffered cuts, bruises, and broken bones (the bones holding his eye in its right socket were broken, and he suffered 11 broken bones at the base of his skull), officers downplayed details of the beating in their reports. At least 27 uniformed officers were at the scene: 21 from the Los Angeles Police Department (LAPD), 4 from the California Highway Patrol (CHP), and 2 from the Los Angeles Unified School District. Following the arrest, CHP officers were apparently so shocked at the brutality that they specifically took note of officers' names. Officers Lawrence Powell, Timothy Wind, and Theodore Briseno, and Sergeant

Stacy Koon, all of the LAPD, were indicted on felony charges of assault with a deadly weapon and unnecessarily beating a suspect under color of authority. All four were found not guilty, sparking widespread rioting in Los Angeles.

On November 5, 1992, Malice Green was questioned by Detroit police officers Larry Nevers and Walter Budzyn, who suspected Green of possessing drugs, as he sat in a parked car. Green allegedly failed to comply with the officers' order to drop something in his hand (which, although disputed, may have been drugs). Budzyn reportedly hit Green's fist and wrestled with him in the front seat of the car. Nevers allegedly hit Green in the head repeatedly with his flashlight during the incident. Another officer placed him on the ground and allegedly kicked him. An Emergency Medical Service (EMS) worker arrived on the scene and sent a computer message to his superiors asking, "[W]hat should I do, if I witness police brutality/murder?" Other officers and a supervisor arrived but did not intervene to stop the beating. Green had a seizure and died en route to the hospital. After the beating, officers reportedly washed blood from their hands with peroxide and wiped blood from their flashlights and Green's car. Then-Police Chief Stanley Knox quickly labeled Green's death a murder and dismissed seven officers who were involved in the incident because of their actions or inaction (Human Rights Watch, 1998).

On August 9, 1997, at approximately 4 A.M., outside a Brooklyn, New York, nightclub, while he was attempting to disperse an unruly crowd, Police Officer Justin Volpe was struck in the head by a black man, who fled the scene. Abner Louima was subsequently apprehended by Police Officer Charles Schwarz; Louima punched Schwartz, according to their patrol supervisor's report, and he was thought to be the man who struck Volpe. Volpe assaulted Louima in the back seat of the patrol car, while the arrestee's hands were cuffed behind his back, and after escorting Louima into the bathroom at the precinct station, Volpe then inserted a stick into his rectum. Another officer was present and did not attempt to prevent the assault or report it. Louima suffered a punctured rectum, among other injuries. Five police officers were charged in the incident. Volpe eventually pled guilty, admitting his role in the circumstances. Two of the officers were sentenced to lengthy prison terms. One of the two, plus two others, were convicted of conspiracy to conceal the details of the crime.

On February 4, 1999, around midnight, four on-duty members of the New York City Police Department's Street Crime Unit were driving an unmarked police car down Wheeler Avenue in the Bronx when they saw twenty-two-year-old Amadou Diallo standing at the vestibule of an apartment building. The four plainclothes officers were searching for a serial rape suspect and believed that Diallo resembled the man for whom they had been searching. The four officers told the young man to "freeze" and identified themselves as police officers. He allegedly did not respond and reached into his pants pocket and pulled out a shiny object, which at least one of the officers believed was a gun. One of the officers fired the first round through the doorway, investigators said. Then the other officers, apparently believing that Diallo was shooting at them, fired into the vestibule. In less than four seconds, forty-one shots were fired. Nineteen bullets struck the victim, who died in the doorway of his apartment building. Police speculated that Diallo might have reached for his wallet to show the officers his identity. It was in his pocket at the time of the shooting, along with his keys and a beeper. All four officers, who expressed remorse about the shooting, were acquitted of manslaughter charges (Gotthelf, 1999).

These four incidents of the use of force by police, all of which were well-publicized and intensively scrutinized, illustrate several themes that run through portrayals of the abuse of force that appear in the popular media. First, all of the citizens against whom force was used were racial minorities, and the officers white. One might readily conclude not only that improper force is used more often against African Americans and other racial or ethnic minorities than against whites, but also that brutality is prompted by the racial prejudices and biases of (white) police officers. Second, each of the incidents involved a citizen who did not meet police expectations for compliance, and at least two of them involved citizens whom police took to be disrespectful: King, who defied police authority in fleeing, and who by some accounts failed to follow police directions after he got out of his car; and Louima, who was believed to have punched the officer earlier in the evening. Third, in these cases and others like them, questions were raised about the involved officers' histories of the use of force and civilian complaints. Fourth, each of the incidents involved what appeared to some observers to be efforts by police to protect and even cover up for one another. Finally, some of the incidents have been attributed not only to the judgments or motives of the individual officers but also, at least in part, to the policies and practices of the police departments.

Whether these incidents are representative of day-to-day policing—visible tips of an iceberg of routine police violence—is a question that cannot be answered with anecdotal evidence. Furthermore, whether the use of force, and particularly improper force, by the police is influenced by racial prejudices of officers, the perceived compliance and respect that citizens offer to (or withhold from) the police, individual officers' proclivities to use and abuse their authority, the police "code of silence," police culture more generally, and the policies and practices of police departments, are all empirical questions that are properly subject to empirical confirmation or refutation. They are questions about broad patterns of police behavior and the social, psychological, and organizational influences on officers' performance. In this chapter we draw on theory and empirical evidence to go beyond the anecdotes. We discuss what is known about the use of force by police, in general, and the abuse of force, in particular, based on social science. We also present some speculation, informed by theory, with respect to propositions on which little or no empirical evidence has accumulated.

POLICE AND COERCIVE AUTHORITY

The police are entitled to use force in performing their duties. They are called on to address problems, ranging from the apprehension of armed criminals to the quieting of noise disturbances, whose resolution may require the use of force. This, as Bittner (1974) has observed, is their "unique competence." Their function is to handle urgent problems—"something-that-ought-not-to-be-happening-and-about-which-someone-had-better-do-something-now" (1974: 30). They are endowed with coercive authority by the law; their coercive authority empowers them to resolve these problems, and in doing so, to overcome resistance that they may confront.

The coercive authority of the police need not take the form of physical force. Their mere presence is sometimes sufficient by itself to restore order to a disorderly situation (Bayley & Garofalo, 1989). When their presence does not suffice, police may direct or command people to perform or refrain from certain acts. As this chapter shows, police can handle many problems with no use of force greater than verbal commands. Skilled police officers are frequently successful in resolving even potentially violent incidents by persuading, cajoling, negotiating, or "bullshitting" angry, distraught, or irrational people to effect a peaceful resolution of the problem. Police may under some circumstances detain people, and they may take people into custody for the purpose of charging them with violations of the law; but people who are detained or arrested may submit to police authority without resistance. Thus, the application of police authority in any of these forms need not involve physical force. In fact, the police use force beyond verbal commands in only a small fraction of their encounters with the public. The typical police tour of duty involves no arrests. Many police officers work their entire careers without ever discharging their firearms.

But if police confront resistance in the application of their legal authority, they may use physical force. The statutes in which the authority of state and local police originates vary in their provisions for the use of force by police, although they generally include the "reasonableness" standard. Police may use the amount of force that is required to accomplish a legitimate police purpose, and no more than the amount necessary, based on what is "reasonable" given the circumstances. For example, Oregon law provides that "a peace officer is justified in using physical force upon another person only when and to the extent that the peace officer reasonably believes it necessary to make arrest or prevent the escape from custody of an arrested person unless the peace officer knows the arrest is unlawful" (Section 161.235 quoted in International Association of Chiefs of Police [IACP], 2001), although it also provides that "[a peace officer is justified in using physical force] for self defense or to defend a third person from what the peace officer reasonably believes to be the use or imminent use of physical force" (IACP, 2001), and also that "a peace officer making a stop may use the degree of force reasonably necessary to make the stop and ensure the safety of the peace officer, the person stopped or other persons who are present." Minnesota law provides that "reasonable force may be used upon or toward the person of another without the other's consent when the following circumstances exist or the actor reasonably believes them to exist: When used by a public officer of one assisting a public officer under the public officer's direction: (a) In effecting a lawful arrest; or (b) In the execution of legal process; or (c) In enforcing an order of the court; or (d) In executing any other duty imposed upon the public officer by law." The term *reasonable* is quite ambiguous, of course, and this ambiguity in the law mirrors the complexity and uncertainty of the situations with which police must deal; thus the law grants considerable discretion to police in determining whether and how much force is required to perform their functions.

The police may use deadly force, but only when the "officer has probable cause to believe that the suspect poses a threat of some physical harm, either to the officer or others" (*Tennessee* v. *Garner*, 1985: 11). Before the Supreme Court's *Garner* ruling, police in Tennessee and many other states were permitted to use deadly force against any fleeing felony suspect. As Fyfe (1988a) points out, the fleeing felon rule dates back to the English Middle Ages, when most felony offenders were executed for their crimes, and criminal trials bore little resemblance to contemporary American trials in felony courts. "Thus, for all practical purposes," Fyfe writes, "it made little difference whether the felon died during pretrial flight or at the hands of the executioner" (1988a: 171). The *Garner* ruling changed that, in Tennessee and every other state, limiting the use of deadly force to those fleeing felons whose offenses involved the infliction or threatened infliction of serious physical harm.

The police can abuse their coercive authority in two general ways: They can use a higher degree of coercion than that which is necessary (including some when none is required), or they can use less coercive authority than the situation requires (Muir, 1977). It is the former with which journalists, the courts, and the general public are normally con-cerned. The injuries and fatalities that may be caused by the use of unjustified force are con-sequences that bear immediate and indisputable connections to the abuse of authority; the crime, disorder, and other social costs that may stem from the use of too little authority are consequences that bear indirect and uncertain connections to the abuse of authority.

The police are empowered by their authority, but it also makes them vulnerable. Their work environment includes a potential for violence directed toward them. It is, as they see it, a hostile environment, and one in which they can count on only their co-workers for sup-port and assistance (Van Maanen, 1978; Westley, 1970). Their authority and the responsi-bilities that it entail estrange them from the public (Skolnick, 1975). They are expected—and they themselves expect—to prevail in the situations to which they are summoned, but nevertheless they are sometimes the targets of coercion by citizens. They are subject to be-ing shoved, punched, attacked with blunt objects, and even shot. While the statistical risk is fairly low, the risk is unpredictable, and police perceive their work environment as a dan-gerous one. They adapt and cope by becoming very attentive to harbingers of danger, and they value loyalty to one another. We will return to these elements of the police culture later.

Forms of Force

Police training and policy manuals often distinguish among various forms or levels of force and (roughly) corresponding forms or levels of suspect resistance (see Desmedt, 1984). The Phoenix Police Department, for example, specifies a six-step force continuum, which in-cludes police presence, verbal commands, control and restraint (i.e., cuffs), chemical agents, "tactics and weapons," and firearms (Garner et al., 1996). "Tactics" include a vari-ety of actions: holding, grabbing, twisting, pushing, punching, kicking, wrestling, and so forth (Garner et al., 1995). Weapons (other than firearms) include batons, flashlights, dogs, and electrical devices (e.g., Tasers, i.e., electric dart guns). "Higher" levels of force have a greater potential to do harm—or to do more serious harm—to the person against whom the force is used. The level of force that officers are justified in using depends on the kind and level of resistance that the person offers or on the threat that the person's actions represent. Police may escalate their use of force as needed to overcome the resistance; police are also expected to deescalate their use of force as the situation is diffused.

In many treatments of the use of force by police, however, only simple dichotomous distinctions are made: between physical force and no physical force; between lethal and nonlethal force; or between proper and improper force. Physical force is often considered to include any force greater than verbal commands or threats, although at least one study (Garner et al., 1995, 1996) followed the practice of research on violence generically to in-clude threats in the category of physical force. As Reiss (1968) comments, it is the abuse of physical force that inspires the greatest concerns under the rubric of "brutality." The use of verbal commands could be more than necessary force under some circumstances, but it does not do bodily harm, and it does not give rise to comparable media attention or public concern.

Lethal force is force that has a high probability of resulting in the death of the person against whom it is used, and it typically involves the use of a firearm. Lethal force is dis-tinguished, for practical, legal, and analytical purposes, because of its grave consequences, and despite the fact that it is rarely used. The use of lethal force is subject to greater regulation and monitoring by police departments (Pate & Fridell, 1993) and the judiciary. Textbooks on criminal procedure and on patrol operations tend to dwell largely or even exclusively on the use of deadly force, with little or no attention given to less-than-lethal force.

Improper force is force that is not required to overcome the resistance that police confront. Depending on the context and circumstances, any form of physical force can be either reasonable, necessary, and proper, or excessive, unnecessary, and improper. The law authorizes the police to use force as it is necessary to achieve police goals, but the law is ambiguous, and it must be interpreted as it is applied to concrete cases. If, for example, police are called to a tavern to break up a fistfight between two intoxicated patrons in the parking lot, the officers are authorized to use several means to take control of the situation if their verbal commands to desist are ignored. The officers may elect to wade into the fight and physically separate the combatants. They could use pepper spray, or mace, to incapacitate one or both of the individuals. Some officers might believe that it is necessary to use their batons to subdue the fighters. Depending on the mental and physical states of the combatants, the police could arrest one or both individuals, handcuffing the suspects in their custody; either or both of the participants might instead be detained until they are sober enough to drive or until relatives or friends arrive to provide a safe ride home. Thus, the force that is "required" in any situation is a matter of judgment.

The law is only one standard against which police judgment might be assessed. It is the standard that is used in litigation: when citizens sue the police for having used excessive force, the suit is resolved with reference to this legal standard. Within police departments, a bureaucratic standard—which may be higher or more demanding than the legal standard—is applied: when citizens or police supervisors allege that an officer used improper force, the allegation is resolved with reference to bureaucratic policy and procedures that govern the use of force. But as Klockars (1996) observes, one could also (or instead) apply a different standard, one that is based on neither the law nor bureaucratic procedures, but rather a craft standard: Uses of force could be compared with what a skilled police officer would have done and not with what the law or procedures permit. Skilled police officers take all possible measures to structure the situation into which they intervene in such a way that either resistance will not be offered or the resistance can be overcome with a minimum of force. Thus, for example, skilled officers wait for backup before entering a potentially violent situation. Skilled officers become familiar with the social and physical features of their beats—the people, the streets and alleys, the buildings, the parks, and so forth—which enables them to better plan their entry into situations.

This craft standard highlights an important consideration: that steps that police take early in—or even before—their encounter with a citizen may have an important bearing on whether and how much force must be used. An officer who (intentionally or unwittingly) escalates a potentially hostile interaction, rather than defusing it, may help to create (or at least fail to prevent) a situation in which the use of force is legally and bureaucratically justified. Even the use of deadly force may sometimes be forestalled if police take steps to avert a situation in which subjects resist their authority.

In some instances, police use force when none is required or justified. For example, a police officer might assault someone who is in their custody and properly restrained, and who is at the time offering no resistance, as a means of retaliation for an earlier assault on police (as in the Abner Louima case). Or an officer might use force against a suspect who surrenders at the conclusion of a vehicle pursuit but who offers no further resistance (as it appeared that LAPD and other officers did in the Rodney King case). We might call this a use of unnecessary force.

Sometimes police use more force than is required or justified in instances when some force is necessary. Impatient and ill-trained officers might, for example, use undue force in arresting a mentally ill person who is slow to obey their commands. Or officers might strike a person with their batons or flashlights, when grabbing or holding the person would suffice. We might call this excessive force—the use of too much force. Both unnecessary force and excessive force are improper. Unnecessary force can be distinguished from excessive force by whether any force is justified.

Another distinction is based on the motives of the officers. Sometimes officers misjudge when force is required or how much force is required, even while they make a good-faith effort to use their authority appropriately. Sometimes, their misjudgments stem from a lack of adequate training and preparation; at other times, their judgments might be affected by the emotional intensity of the situation, the level of illumination, or other factors. But sometimes officers use force wantonly and maliciously. Often, we might suppose, they do so when no force at all is required—when the person against whom force is used is not resisting the officer's direction and may even be securely in police custody. These are not misjudgments, but rather calculated brutality prompted by malevolence or corruption (Fyfe, 1988a).

SOCIAL RESEARCH ON POLICE USE OF FORCE

Empirical evidence about the use of force by police has been based on several sources or kinds of information. None of this information has been collected in laboratory settings, because of course police use force on the street, not in petri dishes; consequently, none of the information on which social science has relied is without shortcomings. But different kinds of information are subject to different shortcomings, so social scientists compare findings based on one kind of information with those based on other kinds of information. When the different sources of data yield congruent results, we have greater confidence in what they tell us. We will refer to this research as we discuss what is known about the use and abuse of force by police, so we will first describe the ways in which this research has been conducted.

Some research is based on the records produced by the police. Many police departments require that their officers complete reports whenever they discharge their firearms, including information about the purpose and circumstances under which the shots were fired. Some police departments require that their officers complete reports whenever physical force is used. Citizen complaints about the police also contain some information about the use of force by police.

Some research is based on direct, systematic observation of police at work in the field. The first such study was conducted in 1966, under the auspices of the President's Commission on Law Enforcement and the Administration of Justice (Black & Reiss, 1967); several large- and smaller-scale studies have been conducted since then. Trained observers are assigned to officers working in selected beats on selected work shifts, and the observers take brief field notes about the police–citizen encounters that they observe. They later record information about their observations according to a standardized protocol that provides for systematic information about the characteristics of citizens involved in each encounter (including their race, sex, and sobriety), the actions of the citizens, and the actions of the police.

Some research is based on surveys of the public. Survey respondents may be asked about their contacts with the police, the nature of any contact (e.g., calling for assistance, or being stopped by police), and whether they were mistreated by police (and, if so, in what way). For one recent survey, the Police–Public Contact Survey, the Census Bureau interviewed a nationally representative sample of more than 6,000 U.S. residents, of whom 21 percent had a face-to-face contact with the police during 1996 (Greenfeld et al., 1997). These respondents were asked about the nature of their contacts with the police and about whether the police used or threatened to use force against them.

Finally, some research is based on surveys of police. For one study (Garner et al., 1996), Phoenix police officers were asked, after completing their paperwork on arrests, to complete a questionnaire about the force (if any) that they had used in making the arrest, and the resistance (if any) that the arrestee had offered; this study was later replicated in several other police departments (Garner & Maxwell, 1999). For another recent study (Weisburd & Greenspan, 2000), responding officers were asked about the frequency with which officers in their departments use improper force and the frequency with which officers respond to verbal abuse with physical force. Commissions such as the Independent Commission on the Los Angeles Police Department (the Christopher Commission) and the Commission to Investigate Allegations of Corruption and the Anti-Corruption Procedures of the Police Department (the Mollen Commission) also rely to some extent on interviews with police—patrol officers, supervisors, and managers—although the selection of interviewees does not normally conform with the principles of scientific research.

Different kinds of information have different advantages and disadvantages. With police records, social scientists have been able to analyze events that occur infrequently and at unpredictable times. Studies of the use of deadly force have relied predominantly on police records about the discharge of firearms, which (fortunately) occurs so infrequently that neither direct observation of the police nor surveys of the public could feasibly produce sufficient cases for analysis (and of course some of the people at whom the police shoot could not be contacted for a survey even if they could be identified). The principal drawbacks to police records are that they may omit an unknown number of incidents that police choose not to record—presumably more of a problem with respect to the use of nonlethal force than the use of deadly force—and much or all of the information on recorded incidents is provided by the officer who used force. We might suppose that the information contained in a police report tends to be recorded with a view toward justifying the action that the officer has taken and is likely to favor the officer's interpretation of the event. As a corollary, we might assume that police reports would form a weak basis for the analysis of improper force, because few officers will write reports from which one could reliably surmise that the force used by police was improper.

Citizen complaints about excessive or improper force have some similar drawbacks and others in addition. Aggregate numbers of complaints are nearly impossible to interpret, because they reflect not only the behavior of police officers but also the behavior of complainants, the behavior of (would-be) complainants, and the characteristics and operation of complaint review mechanisms. We might suppose that the information provided by complainants represents one perspective on what transpired in a police–citizen interaction—one that contains a bias opposite to that contained in police reports. More specifically, citizen complaints may contain allegations that are either fabricated or mistaken, with claims that improper force was used when it was not, as complainants may seek retribution or legal advantage, or complainants may be uninformed about police policy and practice. Furthermore, in a significant proportion of incidents involving improper force, no one files a complaint. Walker and Bumphus (1992) estimate that "official complaints received by police departments represent about one-third of all incidents of alleged police misconduct." Finally, as Walker and Bumphus note, the "number of complaints may reflect administrative procedures rather than police performance." A high complaint rate, relative to that in other police departments, is not necessarily indicative of poor policing or high rates of excessive force by officers; instead, it may be indicative of the success of the complaint process, signaling the ease that citizens feel in filing complaints. Conversely, a low complaint rate might be related to the difficulties that citizens have in navigating the system when attempting to file complaints, or it might reflect the efforts of a professional police agency that does not condone the abuse of force. One can identify no specific baseline for the number of incidents of police misconduct; estimated rates of citizen complaints for "undue force" range from 5.9 per 1,000 white citizens and 2.8 per 1,000 black citizens to between 1 and 5 per 10,000 citizens. Terminology is a problem, for often the very different phrases of "undue force," "citizen complaints," and "mistreatment by police" are used interchangeably.

Direct observation enables researchers to examine incidents of the sort that may never or seldom appear in official records and to construct measures of key variables based on information that is recorded systematically (i.e., with respect to every incident, using the same criteria) by a neutral party. One of the principal drawbacks to direct observation is that even when observation is conducted on a large scale, with thousands of hours of in-person observation in the field, only a modest number of incidents in which police use force are observed. Furthermore, observational data are subject to an unknown degree of reactivity: Officers may not act the way that they normally act when they are in the presence of an observer. Finally, judgments that observers might be asked to make about whether the force used by the police was excessive would be of unknown reliability.[1]

Surveys of the public are, like direct observation, a net in which we may capture information on incidents that police would not routinely record, although the net must be a very wide one to catch a sufficiently large number of incidents for analysis of the characteristics of incidents or citizens with which the use of force is associated. For example, the Police–Public Contact survey in 1996 found among its 6,421 respondents only 14 (two-tenths of 1 percent) who indicated that they had a contact with the police that involved a threatened or actual use of force (Greenfeld et al., 1997). Furthermore, like police reports, surveys provide information from the perspective of one of the participants, and the information might not reflect an impartial interpretation of events.

---

[1] Albert J. Reiss, Jr. (1968), and Robert Freidrich (1980) analyzed the same set of 1,565 encounters between police and suspected offenders in Boston, Chicago, and Washington in 1966. Freidrich's analysis rests on the characterizations of coders, who "examined pertinent passages of the observation reports to determine if physical force had been used and if it was justified in terms of self-defense or the need to make an arrest," while Reiss "had an expert panel decide whether or not force on the order of an aggravated assault was used" (1980: fn. 12; also see Reiss, 1968). These different procedures yielded somewhat different numbers of encounters in which the force used was considered improper: Freidrich identified twenty-nine cases of improper force, while Reiss (1968) identified thirty-seven cases.

Surveys of police are the most direct approach to collecting information about officers' use of force, but they nevertheless have important limitations, especially since the use and abuse of force is a sensitive subject. Survey items might ask officers about general patterns of the use of force; such items would normally be couched in terms of what officers in the respondent's department do, rather than what the respondent individually has done, in order to elicit more candid responses. For example, in a recent survey conducted by the Police Foundation (Weisburd & Greenspan, 2000), respondents were asked how often "police officers in your department respond to verbal abuse with physical force?" Such measures are very imprecise, however, as respondents are asked to make general characterizations, with response categories such as "seldom," "sometimes," or "often." Alternatively, survey methodology was recently used to collect information about the use of force by police in specific instances—arrests made by the responding officers—although respondents were not asked to characterize the force that they had used as proper or improper (Garner et al., 1995; Garner & Maxwell, 1999). Since neither kind of survey information is used for the organizational purposes of monitoring, investigating, and sanctioning officers for their use of force, we might suppose that respondents are more forthcoming than the officers are when they complete police reports. However, insofar as respondents are skeptical about the confidentiality of the survey, or wish to present themselves in a favorable light, then such surveys will underestimate the use of force. Moreover, like surveys of the public, surveys of police provide information from a single perspective.

The Incidence of Police Use of Force

Social research on police use of force shows that officers use force in a small fraction of their contacts with the public, and that when they use force, it is typically a low level of force—nothing more than gripping or holding. For example, Elizabeth Croft (1985) analyzed use-of-force reports completed by officers in the Rochester, New York, Police Department. Between 1973 and 1979, Rochester police completed 2,397 use-of-force reports; during the same period, officers made 123,491 arrests. Thus, the ratio of arrests to incidents in which police used force was 52 to 1.

Based on a nationwide survey of police departments concerning the use of force during 1991, Anthony Pate and Lorie Fridell (1993) found that the most commonly used forms of force—handcuffing and leg restraints, bodily force, and "come-alongs"—were infrequently used. Among city police departments, they estimated that handcuffs and leg restraints were used at a rate of 490 per 1,000 sworn officers; bodily force and come-alongs were used at rates of 272 and 227 per 1,000 officers, respectively. The rates in other types of agencies (sheriff's departments and state and county police agencies) were lower still. More serious forms of force—the use of batons, flashlights, and chemical agents—were seldom used (at rates between 20 and 40 per 1,000 sworn officers). The use of deadly force was quite rare: Including all incidents in which civilians were shot at (and missed, wounded, or killed), deadly force was used in city police departments at a rate no greater than 4 per 1,000 sworn officers, and at lower rates in other types of agencies.

Although one might suspect that use-of-force reports would understate the frequency with which police officers use nonlethal force, as well as the level of force that they use, observational studies of police lead to a similar conclusion. Analyzing data collected through observations in Boston, Chicago, and Washington in 1966, Robert Freidrich (1980) found that police used force in approximately 5 percent of their encounters with suspected offenders. Observations conducted in other places and at other times corroborate these findings. Observations in three New York City precincts in 1986 focused on 467 "potentially violent mobilizations," that is, "police–citizen encounters that had at least some possibility of resulting in violence," which were observed over the course of approximately 350 eight-hour patrol shifts. Analysis of these incidents showed that police used force against citizens in only 37, or 8 percent, and that the force "consisted almost exclusively of grabbing and restraining" (Bayley & Garofalo, 1989: 7). Observations of almost 900 patrol shifts in the Metro-Dade Police Department in 1985–86 showed that in one sample of incidents, police used physical force in 17 percent, and in almost 60 percent of those, the only force used was a "firm grip" (Klinger, 1995). Finally, observations of 900 patrol shifts in 1977 for the Police Services Study, which examined 24 police departments that served large, medium, and small municipalities, showed that police used physical force in less than 5 percent of their encounters with suspected offenders (Worden, 1995a). The Police Services Study data are especially valuable, compared with those collected for other observational studies, in that the study was not limited to a single large city; thus, we can with greater confidence extrapolate the findings based on these data to urban policing more generally, and not only to big-city policing.

A few studies based on observation have sought to examine the use of *improper* force. Albert Reiss, Jr. (1968), and Robert Freidrich (1980), using somewhat different procedures to discriminate proper from improper force (see footnote 1, earlier), found that the Boston, Chicago, and Washington, D.C., police observed in 1966 used improper force in no more than 2.5 percent of their encounters with suspected offenders. Worden (1995a) found that improper force was used in 1.3 percent of the police encounters with suspects that were observed for the Police Services Study in 1977.

A similar conclusion may be drawn from an analysis of police use-of-force reports. Geoffrey Alpert and Roger Dunham (1997, 1999) analyzed such reports completed in the Metro-Dade, Florida, Police Department and the Eugene and Springfield, Oregon, Police Departments. They measured the levels of suspects' resistance and the force used by officers, each on a four-point scale. Suspects' resistance was characterized as (1) no resistance, (2) passive resistance, (3) active resistance, and (4) assaultive, while officers' use of force was characterized as (1) no force, (2) minimal force, (3) forcibly subdued with hands, and (4) forcibly subdued with methods other than hands. The "force factor" was computed as the difference between officers' use of force and suspects' resistance. In each department, Alpert and Dunham found that in most cases the level of force used by police matched that of the suspect's resistance and also that officers tended to follow the force continuum. They further found that officers' force was rarely more than one level greater or less than that of suspects' resistance, and that the differences tended to reflect the department's training: In Metro-Dade, where officers are trained to use a level of force somewhat less than the level of resistance, the distribution of the force factor was skewed somewhat toward the negative side of the scale (where the level of force was less than the level of resistance), while in Eugene and Springfield, where officers are trained to use a level of force that is somewhat higher than the level of resistance, the distribution of the force factor was skewed somewhat toward the positive side of the scale.

Surveys of the public also suggest that police use force in a small proportion of police–citizen interactions, but it also suggests that large numbers of people have such experiences. Extrapolating the results of the Police–Public Contact survey (described earlier) to the population of the United States, an estimated 45 million Americans aged twelve or older had a face-to-face encounter with police in 1996; of that number, an estimated 500,000 people were threatened with or experienced some form of force. The type of force reported by the fourteen respondents in this survey included being hit, held, pushed, subjected to a choke-hold, threatened with a flashlight, restrained by a police dog, threatened or sprayed with chemical or pepper spray, threatened with a gun, or some other form of force. (None of the respondents reported being kicked, hit with a flashlight, shot at by police, or attacked by a police dog.) Thus, while the use of force is rare as a proportion of police–citizen encounters—even as a proportion of police encounters with suspected offenders—police have so large a volume of contacts with the public that a large number of people have experience on the receiving end of (justifiable or unjustifiable) police force.

Ten of the fourteen people who reported some threat or use of force also admitted that their own actions may have provoked the use of force. For example, respondents admitted resisting arrest, threatening or assaulting the police officer, attempting to escape, possessing a weapon, inciting others to become involved in the situation, or drinking or using drugs during the incident. Unfortunately, such a small number of cases cannot be used to draw firm conclusions about the role of citizens in provoking police use of force. The results can, however, suggest areas for future research, including the role of citizens in prompting police use of force as well as the dynamics of situations in which force is used notwithstanding the passivity of the subjects.

Surveys of police also indicate that police do not frequently use force and that, when they do use force, it is normally a form of force at the lower end of the force continuum. For a recent study based on self-completed questionnaires, Phoenix police officers reported that they used some form of physical force in 349 (22 percent) of 1,585 arrests. Physical force was defined for this study as including the threatened use of force and not only the actual use of physical force, and it appears that the use of force encompassed "hold only" as a weaponless tactic. The confidential nature of the questionnaire might have elicited more complete reporting by officers than one finds in departmental use-of-force reports, like those analyzed by Croft (1985), which subject the officers to the possibility of supervisory oversight and sanction.

Weisburd and Greenspan (2000) conducted a study more to the point of concerns about the abuse of force. In their nationwide survey of police officers conducted by the Police Foundation, Weisburd and Greenspan found that 22 percent of respondents indicated that police officers in their department sometimes, often, or always use more force than necessary to make an arrest; 62 percent said that officers seldom use more force than necessary, and 16 percent said that officers never use unnecessary force.

Race, Disrespect, and the Use of Force

Police have contact disproportionately with people who are on the social margin, as they either request police intervention or attract police attention as suspected offenders. So it should come as no surprise that police use force against the same categories of people with a frequency that is disproportionate to their representation in the population. But it is sometimes claimed that this disparity stems not only from different levels of contact but also from differential treatment; that is, police are more likely to use force against the racial or ethnic minorities with whom they have contact than they are to use it against whites. According to this view, the race of the citizen affects whether police use force, and perhaps how much force police use, with all other things being equal.

Research on police behavior in general, and the use of force in particular, has yielded mixed results on the question of racial bias. Some of the earliest studies of police reported disparities in the treatment of white and African American suspects, to the (expected) disadvantage of the latter: African American suspects who encountered police were arrested at higher rates than white suspects. But these disparities were attributed to causal factors other than race itself: to the more frequently disrespectful demeanor of African American (or other minority) suspects (Black, 1971; Lundman, 1974), or to the more frequently proarrest preferences of African American complainants (Black & Reiss, 1967). Some later, more technically sophisticated analysis (Smith & Visher, 1981) showed that race has an effect independent of these other factors, while other equally sophisticated analysis has indicated that race has no effect (Mastrofski, Worden, & Snipes, 1995).

Analyses of the use of force have produced similarly mixed results. Analyzing data collected through the observations of police in Boston, Chicago, and Washington, D.C., Albert Reiss, Jr. (1968), found that white and African American suspects were subjected to improper force at comparable rates, suggesting that "the application of force by the police operates without respect to the race of the offender." This finding is all the more noteworthy in view of the racially prejudiced attitudes expressed by three fourths of the officers assigned to predominately African American precincts. Reiss explains: "As sociologists and social psychologists have often shown, prejudice and attitudes do not necessarily carry over into discriminatory actions" (1968). Robert Freidrich's (1980) analysis of the same data, using more sophisticated statistical techniques, confirms the finding that the suspect's race has no effect on an officer's use of force. But a later analysis of Police Services Study data showed that when other factors are statistically controlled, the race of the suspect does have an effect on officers' use of force (Worden, 1995a).

Research on the use of deadly force has also produced mixed results. The empirical evidence confirms that minorities are overrepresented among the people at whom police shoot, relative to their numbers in city populations. A number of studies, however, also indicate that minorities are overrepresented among those whose actions precipitate the use of deadly force by police (Alpert, 1989; Blumberg, 1982; Fyfe, 1980, 1981a; Geller & Karales, 1981; Milton et al., 1977), that is, the commission of violent offenses (such as robberies) and the possession of a gun or knife. The hypothesis that minorities are more likely to be the objects of police deadly force merely because of their race has received support in only a few analyses (Fyfe, 1982; Geller & Karales, 1981: 123–5; Meyer, 1980). We might make sense of these mixed findings by inferring that, like other decisions by criminal justice officials, the use of force by police is affected by race only under some circumstances (Walker et al., 1996), that is, in some places at some times, although research does not enable us at this time to specify the circumstances with confidence. The issue of racial disparities has not been resolved by social research.

One consistent finding is that police are more likely to use force against suspects who are disrespectful. One of the first systematic studies of the police suggested that police treat citizens punitively when the citizens fail to act with deference toward the police. Based on surveys of police in one city in 1949–50, William Westley (1953, 1970) found that the main-tenance of respect is an important norm among police. Disrespect for the police, he ex-plained, is symbolized by "the 'wise guy,' the fellow who thinks he knows more than they do, the fellow who talks back, the fellow who insults the policeman" (1970: 123). Further-more, Westley learned, police considered it appropriate to use force against disrespectful citizens in order to compel deference.

A similar phenomenon was detected by John Van Maanen in his study of the "Union City" police. Van Maanen discovered a different label—"asshole" rather than "wise-guy"—applied to the same categories of people. He describes the way in which officers per-ceive and assess displays of disrespect, or "affronts." An affront, he writes,

> is a challenge to the policeman's authority, control, and definition of the immediate situation. As seen by the police, an affront is simply a response on the part of the other which indicates to them that their position and authority in the interaction are not being taken seriously. . . . [Affronts] push the encounter to a new level wherein any further slight to an officer, however subtle, provides sufficient evidence to a patrolman that he may indeed be dealing with a cer-tifiable asshole. (1978: 229)

An affront is the first stage of the process by which "the tag asshole arises, sticks, and guides police action during a street encounter" (1978: 228). The second stage is "clarification," when officers determine whether the citizen should be held responsible for the affront. Af-fronts are excusable, provided that the affronting citizen is not responsible for his or her ac-tions; an asshole is someone who could be expected to have acted differently under the cir-cumstances, and who was aware of the offensive nature of his or her actions and the possible consequences. According to Van Maanen, the cultural norms of police permit or encourage the application of street justice to an asshole, in the form of a beating or "thumping," with charges of disorderly conduct or resisting arrest filed in order to construct a legally justified account of the interaction.

Richard Sykes and Edward Brent (1980: 60–8), who analyzed the ways in which of-ficers "regulate" or maintain control in their interactions with citizens, echo Van Maanen's observations. They report that:

> The most common technique of regulation of interaction is that of repetition. The officer asks a question. The citizen refuses to answer. The officer asks the question again, perhaps in a slightly different way. Then the citizen answers. A common alternative strategy is to ask a question, and then, after the citizen responds, make an accusation of a violation, which the citizen then denies. Then the accusation is repeated and the citizen admits to it. . . . In the great majority of cases this [repetition] is sufficient. (1980: 67)

We might speculate that when repetition fails to elicit compliance, an officer perceives an affront and treats the citizen as an "asshole."

Michael Brown's description of the "attitude test" (1981: 196) extends and refines our understanding of how officers evaluate suspects' demeanor. He writes,

> A rough but accurate definition of the attitude test is that the person confronted by police au-thority must exhibit acceptance of that authority and deference to the officer and his admon-ishments. . . . The attitude test is a way of maintaining police authority and punishing those who would defy it. . . . This is the most common understanding of the attitude test, but it is not the only one. A person's "attitude" toward the law and, in particular, his feelings about

the violation he may have committed become rough criteria for deciding whether a citation should be written or a warning given. In this sense, the attitude test is an indirect way of determining whether an informal action will sufficiently deter future behavior rather than a formal action. (1981: 196)

According to Brown, disrespect includes not only overt hostility but also a failure to accept and defer to officers' authority, as well as a failure to show deference to the law that the police believe that they symbolize.

Police expectations for deference, and the imposition of sanctions on "assholes," are not anachronisms. Systematic observational studies of police have repeatedly found that the demeanor of suspects affects their treatment by police. Suspects who display what police take to be disrespect, through even passive noncompliance or active but only verbal resistance, are more likely to be subjected to punitive action by the police: arrest or the use of physical force (see Worden & Shepard, 1996, and the studies cited there). Furthermore, in the nationwide survey of police officers conducted by the Police Foundation, Weisburd and Greenspan (2000) found that almost 15 percent of the respondents said that officers in their departments sometimes, often, or always respond to verbal abuse with physical force, and 54 percent said that officers "seldom" do so; 32 percent said that officers in their department never respond to verbal abuse with physical force.

Officers' expectations for deference and respect, in the context of racial inequity in society at large, can make adversarial and potentially hostile interactions with suspected offenders still more explosive. Sykes and Clark (1975: 586) observe that police–citizen encounters, like other interactions between parties of unequal status, are governed by an "asymmetical status norm" that structures the "flow of deference." Police officers generally hold higher status in their encounters with citizens, by virtue of their authority and also, in many instances, by virtue of their social class. The asymmetry is still greater, Sykes and Clark point out, when the citizen is an alleged violator. However, the operation of this norm is complicated in police encounters with minorities or other subordinate groups, if the subordination is disputed and displays of deference are therefore withheld. As Sykes and Clark explain,

> An entirely unprejudiced officer, in expecting general deference, may be interpreted by a minority civilian as indicating the officer's own ethnic group's superordination. On the other hand, the minority citizen's refusal to express deference may be viewed by the officer as refusal to acknowledge normal social obligations of all citizens and the officer's symbolic status. Thus, it is in encounters between the formerly subordinate and the symbolic representatives of the authority which subordinated them that both tend unintentionally to discredit the other. (1975: 590)

This means that we might expect that police will be more likely to encounter behavior that they interpret as affronts when they interact with minorities. Moreover, officers might (wittingly or unwittingly) evoke disrespect from citizens as the interaction plays out over time; as Sykes and Clark point out, this may be more likely in encounters with minority citizens than in encounters with whites.

Problem Officers

Force is used disproportionately by some officers. One might expect that force would be used more often by some officers than others, if only because officers who are assigned to high-crime, high-activity beats, or to special, tactical units, will be involved more frequently in situations in which the use of force is necessary. So, over a specified period of time, say, one year, some officers may not use force at all, and some might use it once or twice, while some justifiably use force multiple times. But we might find such a skewed distribution of use-of-force incidents across officers not only because of their assignments, but also because of variation among officers in their proclivity to use force. Thus, one might say that some officers use force excessively, that is, with a frequency that would not appear to be attributable to the conditions under which they work, even without making judgments about whether the force used in any particular incident was "excessive" or improper.

Elizabeth Croft found that some Rochester police officers were much more likely to use force than others were, even after controlling for officers' "hazard status" or the risk of "being exposed to police–citizen incidents having a potential for use of force" (1985: 160); 119 of 430 officers included in her analysis were classified as high-force officers, who used force in 6 percent or more of the arrests that they made. Similarly, in its investigation into the Los Angeles Police Department, the Christopher Commission (Independent Commission on the Los Angeles Police Department, 1991) used police records to identify a small group of forty-four officers who were disproportionately involved in incidents in which force was either used or allegedly misused. Moreover, the commission dismissed the possibility that officers' assignments produced the skewed distribution of use-of-force involvement. Instead, the commission suggested that the involvement of these "problem" officers in use-of-force incidents could be attributed to their outlooks or personalities. The commission found, in a survey of LAPD officers, that "a significant percentage . . . agreed with the statement that 'an officer is justified in administering physical punishment to a suspect who has committed a heinous crime' (4.9 percent) or 'to a suspect with a bad or uncooperative attitude' (4.6 percent)" (1991: 34). However, because individual officers' survey responses could not be linked with departmental data on the same officers' uses of force or personnel complaints, the commission could not establish that the officers who espoused these views were disproportionately represented among the "problem" officers.

One might suppose, more generally, that officers who have "authoritarian" personalities are predisposed to use force (Balch, 1972, and more generally, Adorno et al., 1950). Authoritarianism is a cluster of beliefs that includes a strong adherence to conventional, middle-class values, a tendency to think in terms of rigid categories, an identification with powerful figures, and a concern with displays of strength and "toughness." Unfortunately, research on the police has little to say about the extent to which these personality traits vary among officers, because it has been concerned primarily with whether officers, as an occupational group, are different from the citizenry. This research has turned on the question of a modal (and pathological) "police personality" that has all the earmarks of an authoritarian personality. Results have been inconclusive (Balch, 1972, cf. Lefkowitz, 1975). Moreover, such analysis is not designed to account for variation in the use of force (or any other behavior) among officers. Unless research examines officers' authoritarianism or other personality traits as characteristics that vary among officers, then these concepts will be of no value in explaining the disproportionate use of force by some officers.

In a recent survey of police psychologists, Ellen Scrivner (1994) found some traces of such a relationship: Her respondents reported that among the officers referred to them because of their use of excessive force, one group had personality disorders that placed them at chronic risk. These personality characteristics may not be detected during the pre-employment psychological screening. The behavioral characteristics associated with these personality traits include a general lack of empathy for others, antisocial and paranoid tendencies, and a proclivity toward abusive behavior. Additionally, these officers do not seem to learn from their experiences and do not accept responsibility for their actions, which may increase the likelihood for repeated citizen complaints.

It remains to be seen whether such personality traits are disproportionately characteristic of officers who use force improperly or excessively, and as Scrivner pointed out, "the number who fit this profile is the smallest of all the high-risk groups" (1994). The other groups that Scrivner identified included officers whose job-related experiences (e.g., traumatic incidents such as police shootings) put the officers at risk for abusing force; young and inexperienced officers who were also "highly impressionable and impulsive"; officers who developed inappropriate patrol styles; and officers with personal problems.

Further insight into some of these differences among officers can be gleaned from studies that formulate typologies of police officers (Broderick, 1977; Brown, 1981; Muir, 1977; White, 1972). Each typology is based on two (or in one case, three) attitudinal dimensions. For example, Michael Brown (1981) classifies officers according to their aggressiveness—"a matter of taking the initiative on the street to control crime and the preoccupation with order that legitimizes the use of illegal tactics"—and their selectivity, which distinguished officers "who believe that all laws should be enforced insofar as possible, and those who consciously assign felonies a higher priority" (Brown, 1981: 223). Although these studies are based on field research conducted in different places and at different times, and although they use different attitudinal dimensions to define the types, their descriptions of the types suggest that five composite types can be identified (Worden, 1995b). These types appear to differ in their propensities to use force.

One type of officer, which might be called (following White, 1972) the "tough cop," is perhaps the most likely to use force improperly. Tough cops are cynical, in that they believe that people are motivated by narrow self-interest. They define the role of police in terms of only crime control, focusing especially on "serious" crime. They believe that the public is hostile toward and unsupportive of police, and they strongly identify with the police culture. They believe that experience and common sense are the best guides in dealing with the realities of the street and that "curbstone justice" is sometimes appropriate and effective.

By contrast, "problem solvers" have a deeper understanding of human motivation and behavior; they recognize that people's actions are influenced by complex sets of physical, economic, and social circumstances, and not narrowly conceived self-interest. They believe that the role of police is one of "offering assistance in solving whatever kind of problem… [their clientele] face" (White, 1972: 72). They are skeptical of traditional police methods and may even feel that the use of their coercive authority is difficult to justify under any but extreme circumstances. This type of officer is probably the least likely to use force improperly (or at all).

The descriptions of these and the other types of officers (Worden, 1995b) suggest that, if there are officers with pronounced propensities to use force, they share several outlooks that distinguish them from other officers.[2] Officers who are the most likely to use force could be expected to (1) define the role of the police in narrow terms, limited to crime fighting and law enforcement; (2) believe that this role is more effectively performed when officers may use their authority at their discretion; and (3) regard the public as unappreciative at best and hostile and abusive at worst.

Unfortunately, the empirical evidence that officers with different attitudes behave differently is impressionistic, based on limited and/or unsystematic observation of officers. The few efforts to systematically test such propositions have produced little or no support. Worden (1989, 1995a) conducted analyses that show that officers' attitudes are only weakly related to their patterns of behavior on the street, in general, and to their use of force, in particular. Likewise, Freidrich (1980) found that the use of force is unrelated to either officers' job satisfaction or (among white officers) their attitudes toward blacks. If, as Toch (1996) suggests, "violence-prone" officers resort to undue force only under some "catalytic" circumstances, then these null findings may stem from the failure of the analyses to capture the complexity of the causal dynamics. The results of this research are hardly definitive, and propositions that officers' outlooks or personality traits affect their use and abuse of force remain plausible but are not established scientific facts.

More evidence has accumulated on the relationship of officers' behavior to their background and characteristics: their race, sex, length of police service, and especially education. Officers' educational backgrounds have been the subject of numerous studies, and although this research has shown that education is only weakly related to officers' attitudes (Hudzik, 1978; Miller & Fry, 1976; Weiner, 1974; Worden, 1990) and unrelated to the use of deadly force (Sherman & Blumberg, 1981), it also indicates that college-educated officers generate fewer citizen complaints than less-educated officers do (Cascio, 1977; Cohen & Chaiken, 1972; Kappeler et al., 1992). The evidence is consistent with the hypotheses that college-educated officers "are more tolerant of citizens who are different from themselves, are better able to analyze problems, make decisions, and apply verbal skills in effecting solutions" (Worden, 1990: 588), but the evidence is only indirect, as the behavioral manifestations of these characteristics have not been directly measured for comparison.

Similarly, the most systematic comparison of male and female officers shows small or no differences in attitudes other than job satisfaction (Worden 1993). Other research reveals some behavioral differences between male and female officers—in the frequency with

---

[2]The other types are "professionals," "clean-beat crime-fighters," and "avoiders" (see Worden, 1995b):

"Professionals...are...willing to use coercive means to achieve desirable ends, but they use it with a keen sense of when, and in what proportion, it is necessary...[They] believe that...the application of the law should be tempered by a sensitive appreciation of its consequences, justifying the enforcement of the law in terms of helping people...[These] officers are neither overly aggressive on the street nor resentful of legal restrictions on their authority."

"Clean-beat crime-fighters...stress the law enforcement function of the police....[They] justify uniform (non-selective) enforcement in terms of its deterrent effect. They are very aggressive on the street, although they lack the street sense of the tough cop."

"Avoiders...[are] unable to cope with the characteristic exigencies of police work....They prefer to do as little police work as possible, only that amount of work necessary to meet the minimum expectations of supervisors; otherwise, they adopt what has elsewhere been called a 'lay-low-and-don't-make-waves' approach to policing."

which they initiate encounters and make arrests—but on most behavioral dimensions, no differences can be detected (Bloch & Anderson, 1974; Sherman, 1975; Grennan, 1987).

One study of the effects of officers' race on behavior (Friedrich, 1977: 307–19) found that black officers patrol more aggressively, initiate more contacts with citizens, are more likely to make arrests, and more frequently adopt a neutral "manner" toward citizens of either race; but he also found that officers' race is unrelated to the use of force (1980). Other research has found that black officers are more likely than white officers are to use deadly force, either on-duty (Fyfe, 1981b; Geller & Karales, 1981) or off-duty (Fyfe, 1981b); but these differences in the use of deadly force can be attributed to black officers' duty assignments and to where they choose to live (also see Blumberg, 1982). Finally, analyses of officers' length of service indicate that less-experienced officers are more active, in that they patrol more aggressively and initiate more contacts with citizens, and that they are more likely to make arrests, to write crime reports (Friedrich, 1977: 280–90; Worden, 1989), and to use deadly force (Blumberg, 1982; cf. Alpert, 1989). But Friedrich found that officers' length of service was unrelated to the use of force.

Organizational Factors

Many proposed measures to control the use of force by police focus on the characteristics of police organizations, because organizational factors (e.g., rules, selection practices, training, external oversight mechanisms) can be altered with a view toward affecting officers' behavior. The dynamics of police organizations are of interest also because the enforcement of rules and imposition of sanctions with respect to improper force is presumably thwarted by the police culture, or "code of silence," and because there is reason to believe that police crime-control strategies have a bearing on the incidence of police use of force. Unfortunately, the hypothesized effects of organizational factors have not been subjected to much empirical study, and so our knowledge about these relationships is based almost entirely on informed speculation rather than empirical evidence.

Rules and Regulations.   One mechanism by which police departments might influence the use of force by their officers is, of course, through rules and regulations that set limits on when police may use force and on how much force they may use. Research on the use of deadly force suggests that this mechanism can be effective, under some circumstances. In 1972, well in advance of the *Garner* ruling by the Supreme Court (in 1984), the New York City Police Department (NYPD) made its policy about the use of deadly force much more restrictive than it had been (and more restrictive than New York State statutes), providing that "every other reasonable means will be utilized for arresting, preventing, or terminating a felony or for the defense of oneself or another before a police officer resorts to the use of his firearm" (quoted in Fyfe, 1979). Furthermore, warning shots were prohibited, and so too (with limited exceptions) was shooting at or from a moving vehicle. A study of the effects of this policy change, conducted by James Fyfe (1979), showed that the policy had a substantial effect on officers' use of their firearms. Officers who reported discharging their firearms dropped from 18.4 per week during the 85 weeks immediately before the adoption of the policy, to 12.9 per week afterward. The policy had an especially pronounced effect on what Fyfe elsewhere (1988a: 185) called "elective" shootings, that is, situations in which officers could have chosen not to shoot at no risk to themselves or other parties. Furthermore, he reported that the reduction in shootings was achieved with no increase in officer injuries or deaths.

But as Fyfe (1979) points out, the effectiveness of this policy almost certainly depended to a significant degree on vigorous enforcement. The NYPD instituted a Firearms Discharge Review Board to investigate and, as necessary, adjudicate all firearm discharges. Thus, officers could anticipate that they would be held accountable for their use of firearms. Fyfe's inference is corroborated by other research that suggests that restrictive deadly force policies are effective only if they are vigorously enforced (Meyer 1980; Waegel, 1984). Following Pennsylvania's adoption of a more restrictive statute regarding the police use of firearms in 1973, William Waegel reviewed documented cases of shootings by the Philadephia Police Department, finding that 20 percent of shootings did not comply with the new law. The statute by itself, unaccompanied by the support of police management and an enforcement mechanism, failed to produce the desired change in the use of deadly force (also see Fyfe, 1988a).

The success that police departments may enjoy in regulating the use of deadly force through policy does not, in theory at least, extend readily to the regulation of nonlethal force. The circumstances under which nonlethal force is justified are arguably more varied and more ambiguous, and so policies cannot specify with equivalent clarity when nonlethal force of different kinds may or may not be used. Use-of-force continua and matrices specify different kinds and degrees of force, and the degrees of citizen resistance to which the use of force is to correspond, but the forms that resistance can take are widely varied, and the behavioral lines that conceptually demarcate different levels of resistance are far from clear in practice; ambiguity is inherent in the work of the police and the rules that govern the use of nonlethal force (Desmedt, 1984). Moreover, the use of nonlethal force is probably subject to more nonreporting by officers, and even if such force is infrequent as a proportion of police–citizen contacts, it happens with sufficient frequency that police superiors may not be able to routinely investigate every use of nonlethal force in order to determine whether it complied with policy prescriptions. In addition, even if the resources were sufficient to conduct such investigations, many would be inconclusive, as the evidence would be limited to the account of the event provided by the officer and the (potentially conflicting) account provided by the citizen against whom force was used. Thus, the enforcement of such policies would almost inevitably lack the teeth associated with the firearms discharge reviews of the NYPD (where, as Fyfe [1988] points out, the population density is so high that one might reasonably suppose that few firearms discharges could be safely concealed).

These observations might make us skeptical about the effectiveness of sanctions applied to officers whose improper use of nonlethal force is detected, investigated, and substantiated. Many occasions when officers use force improperly will be undetected by officers' superiors, because the citizens against whom force is used often do not report it. Furthermore, we might suppose that the code of silence among officers would undermine efforts not only to detect the improper use of force—as officers fail to report the misconduct of their peers—but also to investigate allegations when they are made—as officers cover up for one another. Taking these conditions as premises, we might surmise that the probability that an officer would be sanctioned for the improper use of force would be too low for the sanction to serve as an effective deterrent.

The *code of silence* refers to the unwritten expectation of group solidarity and support among "street cops" against not only outsiders, including "assholes," other offenders, "watchdog" groups that are critical of the police (such as the American Civil Liberties Union), and the general public, but also against police supervisors, managers, and internal affairs investigators. Fostered by the "us versus them" mentality to which work in a dangerous and hostile environment can give rise, and perhaps also by a punitive style of police management, cultural norms hold that officers should neither report on nor incriminate fellow officers who engage in misconduct (see Reuss-Ianni, 1983; Westley, 1970).

As Jerome Skolnick and James Fyfe (1993: 108–12) observe, officers who break the code of silence by informing on their workmates are socially shunned for their breach of loyalty and ostracized as informants or "rats." While Skolnick and Fyfe do not conclude that officers are placed in physical danger by their peers as a result of their violation of group norms, the officers nevertheless suffer emotionally. Likewise, the Independent Commission on the Los Angeles Police Department, known as the Christopher Commission acknowledged that the enforcement of rules and regulations governing the use of force is limited, finding that "perhaps the greatest single barrier to the effective investigation and adjudication of complaints is the officers' unwritten 'code of silence'" (1991: 168), even in a department (the LAPD) that was criticized for its failure to investigate and sanction improper uses of force. The Police Foundation's survey of police attitudes toward abuse of authority suggests that "even though officers do not believe in protecting wrong-doers, they often do not turn them in" (Weisburd & Greenspan, 2000: 3). More than 80 percent of the survey's respondents did not accept the code of silence as "an essential part of the mutual trust necessary to good policing," but even so, two thirds indicated that "an officer who reports another officer's misconduct is likely to be given the cold shoulder by his or her fellow officers," and slightly more than half agreed that "it is not unusual for a police officer to turn a blind eye to improper conduct by other officers" (2000: 3–5). The fear of losing status and identity in the group results, it seems, in few breaches of the code of silence.

One recent study suggests that these characterizations may be overgeneralized. Carl Klockars and his colleagues surveyed officers in thirty U.S. police agencies, and they found considerable variation among agencies in officers' perceptions of the seriousness of various acts of misconduct (including improper force) and their willingness to report such acts of misconduct (Klockars et al., 2000). Given a hypothetical case of improper force,[3] respondents indicated their opinions about the seriousness of the behavior, on a scale from 1 (not at all serious) to 5 (very serious) and also whether they would report a fellow officer who engaged in the behavior, on a scale from 1 (definitely not) to 5 (definitely yes). The average rating of the seriousness of the improper force case was 4.05 on the 5-point scale, and the average willingness-to-report score was 3.39. But equally or more important, Klockars et al. found that officers in different agencies had different views. As an illustration, they contrasted two agencies, in one of which the code of silence was quite strong, because "there was *no* case [among the eleven studied] that the majority of officers indicated they

---

[3]"Two police officers on foot patrol surprise a man who is attempting to break into an automobile. The man flees. They chase him for about two blocks before apprehending him by tackling him and wrestling him to the ground. After he is under control, both officers punch him a couple of times in the stomach as punishment for fleeing and resisting" (Klockars et al., 2000).

would report," while in the other agency, a majority of officers indicated that they would report all but the least serious forms of misconduct. Thus, we might conclude that the degree to which the code of silence is a barrier to the enforcement of rules and regulations varies across police agencies.

Selection and Training.   Given the difficulties in sanctioning, and hence in deterring, police abuse of force, one might hope that in selecting police recruits from among applicants for the job, police departments would screen out those who would be prone to violence or to otherwise abuse their authority. When police applicants have a history of violent behavior, for example, thorough background checks could eliminate such candidates from further consideration. Unfortunately, research suggests that neither background investigations nor other screening devices, such as personality testing, are very successful in identifying applicants who will subsequently abuse their authority (see Grant & Grant, 1996). The effectiveness of this approach rests on an assumption: that information about police recruits, such as their scores on a psychological test (e.g., the Minnesota Multiphasic Personality Inventory), or the results of interviews or other selection mechanisms, can be used to predict their future behavior as police officers, with a high degree of certainty. But experience belies the assumption. Psychological tests and other selection devices do not permit one to make accurate predictions about the applicants' later abuse of force as police officers.

Training takes various forms: preservice training in an academy, field training, and specialized in-service training. Academy training is "by the book," and much of it is (with the exception of some training curricula) conducted in the classroom. Recruits are taught the legalities of using force as well as self-defense tactics and the use of police weapons. During their subsequent field training, new officers face the challenges of handling volatile situations, making judgments about what if any physical force to apply to flesh-and-blood people, with real consequences for both the civilians and the officer. Trainees are not left alone to meet these challenges; instead, they accompany their field training officers, from whose example and instruction they learn the police craft, in general, and their department's "way of doing things," in particular. In-service training is provided at regular and/or irregular times on a variety of subjects throughout officers' careers.

Although training is unlikely to have any effect on the wanton and malicious use of force, it is reasonable to hypothesize that officers would use force less often and would use force *improperly* less often, if their training has better prepared them to handle incidents without using physical force, and to make sound judgments about when and how much force is required to overcome citizen resistance. Such hypotheses have been rarely tested. But one study experimentally tested the effects of an in-service, violence-reduction training program. Street officers, training officers, and supervisors in the Metro-Dade Police Department reviewed and critiqued 100 reports of incidents in which officers used force or were injured, or that resulted in complaints, in an effort to determine what had gone wrong in these interactions. The task force was then assigned to create "Dos and Don'ts" lists for responding to the most common potentially violent situations: disputes, crimes, routine traffic stops and stops of suspicious vehicles. These lists formed the basis for a three-day violence-reduction training program. The program's effects were analyzed by James Fyfe (1988b). Selected officers were experimentally assigned either to undergo the training or to a "control" group, and all of the officers were observed both before and after the training.

Fyfe's comparison of the two groups' behavior showed that the training program had some detectable effects.

Other departments have provided training that includes role playing, outfitting officers with devices that modify their duty weapons to fire paint bullets. Officers then work through scenarios gleaned from their department's use-of-force reporting forms or from scenarios devised by training officers and designed to test officers' ability to handle potentially volatile situations in which they may be required to control suspects verbally or physically. An officer's responses result in the situation either improving, if officers take appropriate steps, or deteriorating, if they take inappropriate steps. These simulations of common situations reinforce department policies as well as provide opportunities to critique each officer's individual abilities to react appropriately in use-of-force scenarios. Such training allows the department to address the realities of their organizational strengths and weaknesses by providing continuous feedback, reinforcing the positives of verbal deescalation of situations while correcting negative behaviors.

In addition to the instructional benefits of training, field training normally coincides with the probationary term of an officer's employment, when the officer can be more readily dismissed from the police agency. Hence, field training is an opportunity to remove officers who may be violence prone. When a trainee demonstrates an inability or unwillingness to make appropriate decisions during field training, it is vitally important that supervisors and field training officers closely monitor the trainee for indications that the new officer is unprepared for or ill-suited to police work. But research has not, to our knowledge, shown the frequency with which probationary officers are terminated during field training, and for what reasons, and it has not demonstrated the efficacy of such practices in preventing the abuse of force.

Bureaucratization.   Police departments vary in their size and, relatedly, degree of bureaucratization. Larger agencies tend to be more bureaucratized, in that they (1) have a larger number of organizational levels or ranks between the top and the bottom of the organizational hierarchy; (2) provide for more functional specialization, with dedicated units for particular tasks, such as traffic enforcement, juvenile crime, vice enforcement, and so forth; and (3) rely on "objective," quantitative measures of performance. As the chief of one larger department (with 381 full-time patrol officers) acknowledged,

> a big problem in law enforcement was an overwhelming concern for statistical measures of performance, such as arrest rates, clearance rates, crime rates. [The chief] indicated that many of the statistics are misleading, but that nearly all professional departments use them, people come to expect their use, and it is difficult to come up with other more meaningful comparative measures of police performance. (quoted in Worden, 1995a)

Quantitative indicators of performance are useful primarily for measuring officers' productivity in enforcement, but they reveal little about officers' performance of other police tasks, or even about some aspects of their enforcement activities, such as the judiciousness with which they use force.

One might expect that in smaller police departments, which typically have fewer levels of hierarchy, administrators could more closely monitor and supervise street-level performance by taking advantage of the less-distorted information that flows through the shorter formal channels of communication, and of the greater information that flows through the wider informal channels of communication (Whitaker, 1983). In principle, managers in smaller agencies could more directly and hence effectively communicate their priorities and expectations to street-level personnel. In addition, since they need not rely so heavily on statistical summaries of individual performance, managers can base their evaluations of officers' performance on a richer and probably more accurate base of information; consequently, patterns of (problematic) behavior are likely to be more readily detectable, and the incentive system need not emphasize quantifiable, enforcement-related activities at the expense of the more qualitative aspects of police performance. Michael Brown's (1981) study, even while it led him to conclude that the police culture is more important than formal organizational structure in shaping the exercise of police discretion, also confirms the expectation that administrative controls are more palpable in smaller departments. Brown found that officers in smaller departments are more reluctant to take the risk of administrative sanction that they would run by practicing an aggressive style of patrol. Furthermore, insofar as work groups are more stable in smaller departments, immediate supervisors could be expected to more frequently and effectively play an instrumental role in the development of subordinate officers' judgment and moral outlooks (see Muir, 1977).

Organizational Climate.   The organizational whole may be greater than the sum of these structural parts: rules and regulations, selection and training, and even bureaucratization. Let us contrast two hypothetical police departments.

In one department, the chief executive espouses a conception of policing as professional law enforcement in the service of the War on Crime: professional in the sense that the law is applied consistently and impartially without political interference from the community and also that vigorous efforts are made to detect crime and apprehend offenders. Officers are rewarded—with promotions or assignments to specialized units—for high levels of documentable enforcement activity: arrests, citations, and field interrogations. Thus, officers are encouraged to practice an aggressive style of policing that entails frequent police-initiated contacts with the public for the purpose of detecting crime and apprehending offenders. These enforcement outputs can be easily counted, and officers' performance can be measured quantitatively. To avoid undermining officers' commitment to such a style by sanctioning them for the civilian complaints that such presumably adversarial contacts can be expected to generate, citizen complaints are discouraged at intake by police supervisors, few resources are allocated for the investigation of complaints (with the consequence that investigators do not have the time to probe deeply into alleged improprieties), and substantiated complaints are lightly punished.

In another department, the chief executive espouses a view of policing as community service. Community input about the priorities and practices of the department is solicited at many levels, including regular beat meetings of residents and officers. Thus, the police agenda includes not only (if at all) "serious" and suppressible crime such as robbery and auto theft but also "soft" crime and disorders such as vandalism, noise disturbances, loitering and panhandling, and harassment, and even conditions that are taken as "signs of crime" such as vacant buildings, abandoned cars, and litter. Officers are rewarded for working in collaboration with neighborhood associations, merchant groups, and other community organizations on community-defined problems, and for solving those problems through the creative use of police and other community resources, which may include but are not limited to enforcement actions. The role of supervisors is to facilitate such efforts and to coach officers in the performance of community-oriented problem solving. Because these activities cannot be readily quantified, appraisals of officers' performance depends on qualitative assessments by their supervisors. Like other forms of community input, civilian complaints are taken very seriously and investigated thoroughly, with appropriate sanctions for substantiated misconduct.

We might expect to find in both departments officers whose occupational attitudes and operational styles vary, that is, some officers who are "tough cops," some who are "problem solvers," and some of other types. But in the first department—with the War on Crime orientation—the written and unwritten rules validate the outlooks and practices of tough cops and other enforcement-oriented officers, particularly their "us versus them" outlook on citizens and their stress on crime fighting, and the bureaucratic system does little to regulate officers' use of coercive authority. While problem solvers in such a department might be no more likely to abuse their authority than they would be in other departmental contexts, we might expect that tough cops would more frequently use and misuse force. In the second department—with the community-service orientation—the written and unwritten rules validate the outlooks and practices of problem solvers and other community-oriented officers, and the organization regulates the use of authority as closely as possible. Tough cops in such a department, we might expect, would use their coercive authority more sparingly and carefully, and hence they would use improper force less often.

Furthermore, one might expect that the outlooks and practices of the officers whose styles are consonant with the stated mission, values, reward structure, and other properties of the organization would be established over time as the dominant ethos or culture of the police department, a culture into which each cohort of new recruits would be socialized. Formal and informal expectations about how police work is done, including the unwritten rules about what officers should do or may not do, are passed from one generation of officers to the next. Some officers whose individual styles are not compatible with the department's culture may leave to seek employment elsewhere. Other officers might choose—or be compelled—to modify their day-to-day performance so that they are not too far out of step with the organization's expectations. We would speculate that, like most organizations, most police departments have an identity that is shaped by the demands, support, and constraints of external constituencies, and the formal and informal elements of internal structure.

Social scientific evidence on such hypotheses is notably lacking. A similar approach to describing police organizations as constellations of structural properties, including their recruitment and selection, incentive systems, formalized rules and regulations, and the "ethos" or culture to which these properties give rise, was adopted by James Q. Wilson over thirty years ago. Wilson's (1968) exploratory research formed the basis for the delineation of three organizational styles of policing—the legalistic, watchman, and service styles—and organizational structures that supported these styles.

In legalistic departments, the police role is defined as one of law enforcement, and officers tend to treat situations as law enforcement matters, resolving them by making arrests or issuing citations, applying the law uniformly and without reference to citizens' social status or political connections. Officers are rewarded for being productive, in terms of enforcement outputs, and as a consequence, they act on their own initiative (e.g., by stopping cars, running license checks, and the like) with some frequency.

Watchman-style police departments put much less emphasis on enforcement productivity than legalistic departments do, and they therefore tend to be more reactive, intervening in situations when they are summoned by citizens or when the offense is a serious one. They also tend to rely less on the law, and correspondingly more on extralegal measures, to resolve the situations in which they become involved, and they tend to apply different standards of conduct for different social groups.

Service style policing is usually the hallmark of suburban communities. Residents expect their requests for assistance or service to be taken seriously and expect the police to aid them in their needs. Officers in service-style departments tend to intervene on their own initiative more often than do officers in watchman-style departments, but to invoke the law less often than do officers in legalistic departments. The misdeeds of community residents especially tend to be handled discreetly and with warnings rather than arrests.

Wilson's study has more to say about the use of the law than about the use of physical force; however, it suggests that improper force is more likely to be used by officers in watchman-style departments, usually in response to perceived disrespect for police authority. Only a few studies have empirically tested hypotheses derived from Wilson's framework (Gardiner, 1969; Smith, 1984; Wilson & Boland, 1978), with results that are generally supportive, but only Robert Friedrich (1980) tested hypotheses about the use of force. He found that the incidence of the use of force overall, and of improper force particularly, was somewhat lower in the legalistic department (Chicago) than in the watchman department (Boston), as he had hypothesized. The incidence of force, and especially of improper force, however, was (unexpectedly) lowest in the "transitional" department (Washington, which was thought to be undergoing an organizational transformation) (Friedrich, 1980).

The report of the Christopher Commission also makes use of such an analysis. The commission identified LAPD's "assertive style of law enforcement" as a reason for "aggressive confrontations with the public" (1991: 97). The commission traced this style of policing to a "'professional' organizational culture" that was cultivated by LAPD administration through training and the incentive structure. Officers in the LAPD were rewarded for proactive enforcement that is likely to (occasionally) produce arrests and (often) to bring police into conflict with citizens. The commission further found that the administration of LAPD failed to discourage the improper use of force, in that (1) the complaint-intake process discouraged citizens from filing complaints, (2) many complaints that were filed were not substantiated as a result of inadequate resources and procedures for investigating complaints, and (3) the sanctions imposed on officers against whom complaints were substantiated were too light, both as a deterrent and as a message that such behavior is inappropriate. Like Wilson (1968), then, the commission concluded that the LAPD's incentive structure influences officers' behavior directly and that there is a link between the (formal) administrative structure and the (informal) organizational culture.

These questions are not merely of historical interest, as the aggressive zero-tolerance strategy of the NYPD was widely celebrated by public officials for its apparent crime-control effectiveness and widely emulated by other police departments, until the Louima, Diallo, and other incidents called the strategy into question. *Zero tolerance* involved attending to and taking enforcement action against even less-serious offenses, including "quality-of-life" offenses—infractions, such as open container violations, that are individually of minor consequence, but which in the aggregate may detract from the quality of life in a neighborhood—and "fare beating" (failing to pay the fare for a subway ride). There is some reason to believe that if minor offenses and other "incivilities" are tolerated or ignored, they can contribute to a "spiral of decline" in social and economic conditions that includes higher rates of serious crime (Skogan, 1990). This is the "broken windows" theory (Wilson & Kelling, 1982), which seems to imply that the decline could be averted if preventive steps are taken; zero tolerance is intended to serve that purpose. In addition, the NYPD learned that when it arrested people for minor violations, they sometimes apprehended people who were wanted for more serious offenses, and in other cases, they recorded information on the arrestees (including fingerprints) that later proved instrumental in linking them to crimes that they subsequently committed (Silverman, 1999). It appeared that zero tolerance had several crime-control effects.

Furthermore, zero tolerance in the NYPD accompanied managerial changes that held precinct commanders accountable for crime reduction and applied intense pressure via Comp-Stat meetings, at which information on crimes was displayed on electronic pin maps and commanders were grilled on their awareness of crime "hot spots" and the measures that they were taking to address those crime problems. Commanders who could not rise to the challenge of meeting crime-reduction goals were thus threatened with public humiliation at CompStat meetings and with reassignment (see Silverman, 1999). This pressure, we might suppose, reverberated downward through precinct supervisors to officers on the street.

Such an aggressive policing strategy brings police into more frequent contact with the public, as police initiate enforcement action against violators and suspected violators; moreover, those contacts are of an intrinsically adversarial nature. While such police–citizen interactions can be conducted in an entirely civil manner, with neither verbal nor physical abuse perpetrated by the officer or perceived by the citizen, one might expect that a fraction of them will eventuate in some conflict, as the officer, the citizen, or both parties say or do something to which the other objects. As Sykes and Clark (1975) observe, with reference to the dynamics of deference exchange, the potential for such conflict might be greater still when the citizen is a racial or ethnic minority.

Furthermore, in striking the balance between crime control and due process (Packer, 1968), the weight of bureaucratic pressure in police departments tilts toward crime control, inasmuch as crimes can be enumerated—and displayed on large-screen, computerized maps in CompStat meetings—more readily than respect for civil liberties can be measured. The intensified pressure to address crime problems might be expected to tilt the balance even further. It was in this context that members of the NYPD's specialized Street Crimes Unit spotted Amadou Diallo, who, the officers later explained, resembled a rape suspect for whom they were on the lookout. The results were clearly tragic. Were they inevitable?

Robert Davis and Pedro Mateu-Gelabert (1999) dispute the hypothesis that the NYPD's aggressive policing strategies are necessarily and inextricably linked with higher levels of police misconduct and (presumably) correspondingly higher rates of complaints against the police. They analyze the 42nd and 44th precincts in the South Bronx, where decreases in crime rates coincided with *decreases* in complaint rates between 1996 and 1998. They conclude that demographic changes in those precincts, along with decreases in service calls, played a minor role in the reduction of complaints against the police and cannot account entirely for the decline. Instead, they point to comprehensive in-service training programs coupled with the strong management styles of the precincts' commanding officers.

The training included verbal judo, which was adopted by the NYPD training academy in 1995. Officers who are trained in verbal judo learn how to communicate in high-pressure situations in a way that effectively encourages voluntary compliance by citizens. In addition, the NYPD's CPR (Courtesy, Professionalism, Respect) Program, adopted in 1997, mandated training for all officers in dealing with the public, and it also provided for monitoring of problem officers and precinct rates of complaints, as well as a system of incentives and disincentives for officers who performed especially well or poorly with respect to civilian complaints.

Moreover, the commanding officers of the 42nd and 44th precincts were responsive to community concerns and created strong bonds between the community and the police. This strong and demonstrable ethic for police–community cooperation, along with a combination of internal training programs, intensive monitoring, and alternate assignments for recidivist officers, sent a clear message that complaints and abusive behavior would not be tolerated. The management styles of these two precinct commanders are not compared with the attitudes and practices of commanders in precincts with higher rates of citizen complaints, however, which weakens the conclusions that one can draw about the effects of management styles. These two precincts were exceptions, as complaint rates had risen in the city as a whole, but we cannot say whether the same management styles were practiced in other precincts with different outcomes.

We might cautiously conclude that police executives can influence the incidence of the abuse of force and that salutary effects on brutality require that managers send a definitive message—through their public pronouncements, internal communications, in-service training, and use of incentives and disincentives—that sets the tone of the department. As Skolnick and Fyfe (1993: 19) maintain, the "chief who is interested in reducing use of excessive force to a minimum must therefore make it absolutely clear that excessive use of force is unacceptable." This view is echoed in the findings of the Police Foundation's national survey of police (Worden, 1995), whose respondents agreed that "strong first-line supervision" guards against inappropriate uses of force, and that a chief's well-articulated beliefs about the inappropriateness of the unnecessary and excessive use of force will be emulated by department members. This is what appears to have happened in NYPD's 42nd and 44th precincts, where, despite the pressure from the department's executive echelon to produce impressive numbers, precinct executives maintained a tough stance against excesses and sent a clear message to patrol officers that complaints from the public would not be tolerated.

Civilian Review.   Civilian review of complaints against the police provides for an external check on the police, and it is frequently mentioned as a remedy for police abuse of force. It is based on assumptions that police will tend to be unreceptive to citizen complaints and to conduct investigations of misconduct by fellow officers that are not as thorough and probing as they should be and also that the punishment for misconduct that is applied to police by police will be insufficiently severe to deter such misconduct. Mechanisms of civilian review, it is thought, would more effectively detect abuses of authority by encouraging citizens to file complaints when they have suffered police abuses, generate evidence of abuse that is sufficient to establish the culpability of miscreant officers, and sanction officers with punishments that are proportional to their misdeeds. Creating a mechanism for civilian review, or strengthening it if one already exists, is commonly proposed in the aftermath of high-profile cases of police misconduct.

Most grievances by citizens about policing do not involve allegations of improper force. In an analysis of the composition of complaints that were formally filed, Douglas Perez (1994) found that 25 percent alleged unnecessary or excessive force, while in 35 percent, citizens complained that the police failed to take required or appropriate action, and in another 15 percent, citizens claimed that they were arrested illegally. In an analysis of survey data, which included incidents—whether or not a complaint was actually filed—about which citizens believed that they had some reason to complain about the police, less than 3 percent involved the use of physical force, while almost three fourths involved less serious forms of misconduct, such as "ineffective/incomplete police work" and unnecessary stops or no misconduct at all but rather a "request for more service, police presence, or visibility" (Walker & Graham, 1998: 73).

Citizens who believe they have been the victim of or witness to police abuse of force usually have several options. They may contact the police department, by calling the chief's office or a precinct station, for example, or by walking into police headquarters. They could contact an elected official, such as a city councillor or the mayor. They can complain to friends or family, representatives of neighborhood associations, other civic groups, the clergy, or the media. They can attempt to have civil or criminal charges filed against the officer(s). In some cities, they can approach a civilian review board with their concerns.

In police agencies across the United States, formal mechanisms are in place for receiving and processing citizens' complaints regarding police behavior. Civilian complaints about the abuse of force received minimal police attention until the 1960s, when several commissions studying violence and police uses of force called for the establishment of formalized internal review systems to satisfy communities' concerns about the handling of their complaints. Police departments responded by implementing internal complaint review systems, including specialized internal affairs divisions staffed with police investigators, to police themselves.

The structure and function of internal mechanisms can differ markedly, however. Internal processes might provide for the informal handling of "minor" cases, for example, and this category might even encompass some use-of-force complaints (as the Christopher Commission, 1991, discovered in its review of LAPD), with the consequence that the complaints are not included in reported tallies and, moreover, the handling of the complaints is not readily monitored.

Moreover, the impartiality of internal review systems is frequently questioned by the community. Doubtful that internal investigations are more than a front for the public, and presuming that few investigations will culminate in findings against the accused officers, citizens tend to have low levels of confidence in internal affairs divisions. Furthermore, details about the investigation and outcome of internal complaint review may be subject to statutory or other provisions for the confidentiality of personnel information, making the process effectively invisible to the public except in the most high-profile cases that attract media attention. Complainants in particular tend to be overwhelmingly negative about internal review systems, as they lack faith in the integrity of the process and thus do not differentiate the procedural fairness of the review system from the outcomes of their cases. Citizens' skepticism about internal review is thrown into sharp relief when formal complaint systems are modified to include civilian participation, as the public will respond by filing more complaints. This was true in Philadelphia, where the number of complaints dramatically rose from 200 per year to 100 per month following a substantial revamping of the police department's complaint system accompanied by the surrounding publicity (Littlejohn, 1981).

The first civilian review board was developed in Washington, D.C., in 1948. Philadelphia was the next to follow, in 1958. In the 1960s, several more cities fashioned civilian review procedures as a part of, or an alternate means of, reviewing complaints against the police. Large cities tend to have complaint review mechanisms that include civilians as participants in the process, while smaller municipalities and agencies tend to rely on exclusively internal investigations in handling complaints. In 1988, approximately 84 percent of departments across the United States had no civilian participation in complaint investigation or review (West, 1988). But larger cities have increasingly adopted some form of civilian participation in complaint review since the late 1980s; in 1994, thirty-six of the fifty largest cities in the United States had civilian review procedures (Walker & Kreisel, 1996).

The term *civilian review*, however, conceals a wide range of variation in the forms and degree of civilian participation. Essentially, a complaint review procedure is considered to provide for civilian review if citizens participate as legitimate members in any part of the review or oversight process. Samuel Walker and Vic Bumphus (1992) describe a three-part classification system to differentiate among civilian review mechanisms:

- Class I: The initial fact-finding investigations are conducted by nonsworn personnel (i.e., civilians). Their reports are forwarded to other nonsworn personnel for recommendations to a chief executive for action.
- Class II: The initial fact-finding investigations are done by sworn officers. Recommendations are made by nonsworn personnel to a chief executive for action.
- Class III: The initial fact-finding investigations are conducted by sworn officers, and sworn personnel also make recommendations. The complainant may appeal the outcome to a nonsworn person or group with nonsworn representation.

Thus in Class I systems, civilians participate in various ways: They investigate complaints, taking statements from victims, witnesses, and officers; they make recommendations for action; and they file reports. In Class II systems, civilians participate in making the recommendation for action, and they oversee what remains an essentially internal review of complaints. And in Class III systems, civilian review boards are appellate bodies whose involvement in a case begins only, if at all, after an initial outcome has been reached.

The participation of civilians in complaint review might be expected to make the system more accessible to those who wish to file complaints about misconduct, exert pressure for thorough investigations of alleged misconduct, increase the likelihood that substantiated complaints result in appropriate sanctions, and enhance the credibility and legitimacy of the system in the eyes of the public. Douglas Perez and William Ker Muir (1996) believe that the integrity of the complaint process is frequently compromised, due to the location (in police departments) and people (police) to which citizens must go in order to file complaints. Civilian intake workers and a location other than the police department are zones of increased neutrality and greater citizen comfort. Yet opponents of civilian review argue that civilians do not have an understanding of police procedures and operations that would enable them to properly evaluate officers' behavior. They claim that civilian review will discourage officers from taking appropriate and effective action because they anticipate that it would later be misjudged as unreasonable (Pate & Fridell, 1993). Police officers view the process with suspicion, assuming that external processes will be biased against them.

In any complaint review system, whether it is entirely internal or provides for some form of civilian participation, complaints normally eventuate in one of four outcomes. A complaint might be substantiated, meaning that the evidence is sufficient to establish the officer's misconduct. A complaint might be deemed "unfounded," which means that the evidence indicates that the alleged misconduct did not occur. An accused officer might be exonerated, meaning that the alleged actions were taken but were justified and proper under the circumstances. Finally, the complaint might be "not sustained," if the evidence is insufficient to establish that the accused officer engaged in misconduct and also insufficient to exonerate the officer or unfound the complaint.

The majority of complaints are "not sustained," regardless of the degree of civilian participation in the process, with relatively few cases (between 15 and 30 percent) resulting in an outcome of "substantiated" or "exonerated." It might surprise some to learn that "civilianized operations tend to develop even higher numbers of unsustained findings than do police-operated systems" (Perez & Muir, 1996: 223), as the former extend to accused officers procedural protections for which internal, administrative systems do not normally provide. Furthermore, Perez and Muir note, civilian review boards "never operate in a fashion that is more demanding than internal review. . . . Citizens in a position to review police behavior . . . invariably act liberally toward the individual police officer" (1996: 220). Where both internal and civilian review operate concurrently, one finds a high level of congruence in their outcomes. Thus, civilian review mechanisms appear to be neither as antipolice as many police officers fear nor as much an external check on police as its advocates might hope.

Wayne Kerstetter (1985) has identified four dilemmas that are inherent in the review of complaints about police misconduct:

1. The inability to articulate objective standards for police conduct
2. The inherent lack of credibility of internal review
3. The frequent inaccuracy of citizen perceptions regarding the fairness of the review process
4. The apparent costs of external review for substantive fairness

These four dilemmas lie at the heart of controversies about the appropriate form and level of participation by civilians in the review of complaints. It is difficult, if not impossible, to fashion a system that is responsive to the legitimate concerns of both citizens and the police.

Kerstetter (1985) concludes that the most effective complaint review is conducted by police officers but also that internal investigations should be subject to external civilian monitoring to ensure that they are complete, unbiased, and thorough. Investigations by police investigators, who are knowledgeable about police practices, are potentially more effective (Perez, 1994). Furthermore, the results of internal reviews might be expected to have more credibility with officers, as peer assessments of their performance (Perez, 1994) and might also be expected to have a greater bearing on promotions and assignments to specialized units; thus, internal review might be expected to have a greater effect on officers' performance. Civilian review, by contrast, might be seen by officers as an illegitimate disciplinary action based on a misunderstanding of police work, at best, or on a political agenda, at worst. Police officers who understand the structural basis of public cynicism about internal review agree that civilians should be included in some way. A compromise between internal and external review of complaints, the civilian monitor systems, provide optimal learning opportunities for the officer while simultaneously deterring police abuses. In such a system, discipline and quality control remain the prerogative of organizational management but subject to external accountability.

Empirical evidence on these questions is scant, indeed. Few studies have been conducted, and some of the research suffers from the limitations of small samples (e.g., of complainants surveyed about their experiences with the process). Police agencies are understandably guarded about—and may even be legally prohibited from—granting access to its complaint files, and even for their annual reports, they might only compile information about serious and less-serious events into a single category of "complaints." But aggregate data on overall complaint rates "fail to take into account relevant distinctions between incidents. . . . [The] unjustified use of physical force is far more serious than mere discourtesy" (Walker & Bumphus, 1992). The accumulation of evidence that would support firm conclusions is likely to take a considerable time, and until then, proposals for civilian review will probably be subject to intense controversy and symbolic conflict.

CONCLUSION

Social scientific evidence provides a sound basis for few firm generalizations about the use and abuse of force by police. But we can with some confidence answer the question that we posed at the outset: the King, Green, Diallo, and Louima incidents are by no means typical. We know that police use physical force in a small proportion of their encounters with the public and also that, when the police use force, it is normally a form of force at the lower end of a continuum of force. We are fairly sure that officers are more likely to use force when suspects are disrespectful toward police, although the dynamics of these interactions are not well-understood. We are also fairly sure that a small number of officers use force with disproportionate frequency, although we do not know why. We do not know whether the use of force, and particularly improper force, is affected by a citizen's race. We do not know with confidence how and to what extent police organizations or institutions of external review can affect the incidence of the abuse of force, although we have some basis for informed conjecture.

Aside from acknowledging the need for further research, we note that social scientific analyses of the use of force are useful even when the findings do not support firm conclusions, because they offer constructive ways of thinking about the issues. While we cannot say how often the use of improper force is prompted by misjudgments by police, rather than maliciousness, it is important to recognize that measures intended to curb the latter will not be equally effective in reducing the former. While we cannot specify all of the steps that exceptionally skilled officers would take to minimize the use of force, it is useful to understand that the proper use of force is not merely an instinctive response to exigent threats and, thus, that the use of force can be reduced if police learn from and emulate the practices of their skilled colleagues. While we cannot specify the characteristics, personality traits, or outlooks that shape the excessive use of force, it is useful to know that some officers may be especially prone to violence so that when the behavioral pattern begins to manifest itself, interventions can be undertaken. The application of these insights can improve the quality of police work, even as we learn more about the causes of and remedies for the abuse of force.

REFERENCES

ADORNO, T. W., FRENKEL-BRUNSWIK, E., LEVINSON, D. J., & NEVITT SANFORD, R. (1950). *The Authoritarian Personality.* New York: Harper & Row.

ALPERT, G. P. (1989). Police use of deadly force: The Miami experience. In Dunham, R. G., & Alpert, G. P., eds., *Critical Issues in Policing: Contemporary Readings* (pp. 480–97). Prospect Heights, Ill.: Waveland.

ALPERT, G. P. (1999). The force factor: Measuring and assessing police use of force and suspect resistance. In *Use of Force by Police: Overview of National and Local Data* (pp. 45–60). Washington, D.C.: National Institute of Justice.

ALPERT, G. P., & DUNHAM, R. G. (1997). *The Force Factor: Measuring Police Use of Force Relative to Suspect Resistance.* Washington, D.C.: Police Executive Research Forum.

BALCH, R. W. (1972). The police personality: Fact or fiction? *Journal of Criminal Law, Criminology, and Police Science* 63 (1): 106–19.

BAYLEY, D. H., & GAROFALO, J. (1989). The management of violence by police patrol officers. *Criminology* 27 (1): 1–25.

BITTNER, E. (1974). Florence Nightingale in pursuit of Willie Sutton: A theory of the police. In Jacob, H., ed., *The Potential for Reform of Criminal Justice* (pp. 1–25). Beverly Hills: Sage.

BLACK, D. (1971). The social organization of arrest. *Stanford Law Review* 23:1087–111.

BLACK, D., & REISS, A. J. JR., (1967). Patterns of behavior in police and citizen transactions. In *Studies of Crime and Law Enforcement in Major Metropolitan Areas*, Vol. 2. Report to the President's Commission on Law Enforcement and the Administration of Justice. Washington, D.C.: U.S. Government Printing Office.

BLOCH, P. B., & ANDERSON, D. (1974). *Policewomen on Patrol.* Washington, D.C.: Police Foundation.

BLUMBERG, M. (1982). *The Use of Firearms by Police: The Impact of Individuals, Communities, and Race.* Unpublished doctoral dissertation, State University of New York at Albany.

BRODERICK, J. J. (1977). *Police in a Time of Change.* Morristown, N.J.: General Learning Press.

BROWN, M. K. (1981). *Working the Street: Police Discretion and the Dilemmas of Reform.* New York: Russell Sage.

CASCIO, W. F. (1977). Formal education and police officer performance. *Journal of Police Science and Administration* 5 (1): 89–96.

COHEN, B., & CHAIKEN, J. M. (1972). *Police Background Characteristics and Performance.* New York: Rand.

CROFT, E. BENZ (1985). *Police Use of Force: An Empirical Analysis.* Unpublished doctoral dissertation, State University of New York at Albany.

DAVIS, R. C., & MATEU-GELABERT, P. (1999). *Respectful and Effective Policing: Two Examples in the South Bronx.* New York: Vera Institute of Justice.

DESMEDT, J. C. (1984). Use of force paradigm for law enforcement. *Journal of Police Science and Administration* 12 (2): 170–6.

FRIEDRICH, R. J. (1977). *The Impact of Organizational, Individual, and Situational Factors on Police Behavior.* Unpublished doctoral dissertation, University of Michigan.

FRIEDRICH, R. J. (1980). Police use of force: Individuals, situations, and organizations. *Annals of the American Academy of Political and Social Science* 452 (November): 82–97.

FYFE, J. J. (1979). Administrative interventions on police shooting discretion. *Journal of Criminal Justice* 7 (4): 309–23.

FYFE, J. J. (1980). Geographic correlates of police shooting: A microanalysis. *Journal of Research in Crime and Delinquency* 17 (1): 101–13.

FYFE, J. J. (1981a). Race and Extreme Police–Citizen Violence. In McNeely, R. L., & Pope, C. E., eds., *Race, Crime, and Criminal Justice* (pp. 89–108). Beverly Hills: Sage.

FYFE, J. J. (1981b). Who shoots? A look at officer race and police shooting. *Journal of Police Science and Administration* 9 (4): 367–82.

FYFE, J. J. (1982). Blind justice: Police shootings in Memphis. *Journal of Criminal Law and Criminology* 73(2): 707–22.

FYFE, J. J. (1988a). Police use of deadly force: Research and reform. *Justice Quarterly* 5 (2): 165–205.

FYFE, J. J. (1988b). *The Metro-Dade Police/Citizen Violence Reduction Project: Final Report.* Washington, D.C.: Police Foundation.

GARDINER, J. A. (1969). *Traffic and the Police.* Cambridge, Mass.: Harvard University Press.

GARNER, J. H., BUCHANAN, J., SCHADE, T., & HEPBURN, J. (1996). *Understanding the Use of Force by and against the Police.* Washington, D.C.: National Institute of Justice, Research in Brief.

GARNER, J. H., & MAXWELL, C. D. (1999). Measuring the amount of force used by and against the police in six jurisdictions. In *Use of Force by Police: Overview of National and Local Data* (pp. 25–44). Washington, D.C.: National Institute of Justice.

GARNER, J. H., SCHADE, T., HEPBURN, J., & BUCHANAN, J. (1995). Measuring the continuum of force used by and against the police. *Criminal Justice Review* 20 (2): 146–68.

GELLER, W. A., & KARALES, K. J. (1981). Shootings of and by Chicago Police: Uncommon Crises. Part I: Shootings by Chicago Police. *Journal of Criminal Law and Criminology* 72(4): 1813–66.

GOTTHELF, M. (1999). 41 shots heard around the world: Immigrants death sparks controversy. http://www.apbnews.com/newscenter/majorcases/diallo/background.html. March 31, 1999.

GRANT, J. D., & GRANT, J. (1996). Officer selection and the prevention of abuse of force. In Geller, W. A., & Toch . H., eds., *Police Violence: Understanding and Controlling Police Abuse of Force* (pp. 151–62) New Haven, Conn.: Yale University Press.

GREENFELD, L. A., LANGAN, P. A., & SMITH, S. K., with KAMINSKI, R. J. (1997). *Police Use of Force: Collection of National Data.* Wasington, D.C.: Bureau of Justice Statistics.

GRENNAN, S. A. (1987). Findings on the role of officer gender in violent encounters with citizens. *Journal of Police Science and Administration* 15 (1):78–85.

HUDZIK, J. (1978). College education for police: Problems in measuring component and extraneous variables. *Journal of Criminal Justice* 6 (1): 69–81.

HUMAN RIGHTS WATCH. (1998). *Shielded from Justice: Police Brutality and Accountability in the United States.* New York: Human Rights Watch.

INDEPENDENT COMMISSION ON THE LOS ANGELES POLICE DEPARTMENT (1991). *Report of the Independent Commission on the Los Angeles Police Department.* Los Angeles: Independent Commission on the Los Angeles Police Department.

INTERNATIONAL ASSOCIATION OF CHIEFS OF POLICE. (2001). *Model Statutes Project.* Available on-line: http://www.theiacp.org/pubinfo/Pubs/modelstatutesproj.htm.

KAPPELER, V. E., SAPP, A. D.. & CARTER, D. L. (1992). Police officer higher education, citizen complaints, and departmental rule violations. *American Journal of Police* 11 (2): 37–54.

KERSTETTER, W. A. (1985). Who disciplines the police? Who should? In Geller, W. A., ed., *Police Leadership in America: Crisis and Opportunity* (pp. 149–82). New York: Praeger.

KLINGER, D. A. (1995). The micro-structure of nonlethal force: Baseline data from an observational study. *Criminal Justice Review* 20 (2): 169–86.

KLOCKARS, C. B. (1996). A theory of excessive force and its control. In Geller, W. A., & Toch, H., eds., *Police Violence: Understanding and Controlling Police Abuse of Force* (pp. 11–30). New Haven, Conn.: Yale University Press.

KLOCKARS, C. B., IVKOVICH, S. K., HARVER, W. E., & HABERFELD, M. R. (2000). *The Measurement of Police Integrity.* Washington, D.C.: National Institute of Justice, Research in Brief.

LEFKOWITZ, J. (1975). Psychological attributes of policemen: A review of research and opinion. *Journal of Social Issues* 31 (1): 3–26.

LITTLEJOHN, E. (1981). The civilian police commission: A deterrent of police misconduct. *University of Detroit Journal of Urban Law* 59 (1): 5–62.

LUNDMAN, R. J. (1974). Routine police arrest practices: A commonwealth perspective. *Social Problems* 22 (1): 127–41.

MASTROFSKI, S. D., WORDEN, R. E., & SNIPES, J. B. (1995). Law enforcement in a time of community policing. *Criminology* 33 (4): 539–63.

MEYER, M. W. (1980, November). Police shootings of minorities: The case of Los Angeles. *Annals of the American Academy of Political and Social Science* 452: 98–110.

MILLER, J., & FRY, L. (1976). Reexamining assumptions about education and professionalism in law enforcement. *Journal of Police Science and Administration* 4 (2): 187–98.

MILTON, C. H., HALLECK, J. W., LARDNER, J., & ABRECHT, G. (1977). *Police Use of Deadly Force.* Washington, D.C.: Police Foundation.

MUIR, W. K., JR. (1977). *Police: Streetcorner Politicians.* Chicago: University of Chicago Press.

PACKER, H. L. (1968). *The Limits of the Criminal Sanction.* Stanford, Calif.: Stanford University Press.

PATE, A. M., & FRIDELL, L. A. (1993). *Police Use of Force: Official Reports, Citizen Complaints, and Legal Consequences.* Washington, D.C.: Police Foundation.

PEREZ, D. W. (1994). *Common Sense about Police Review.* Philadelphia: Temple University Press.

PEREZ, D. W., & MUIR, W. K. (1996). Administrative review of alleged police brutality. In Geller, W. A., & Toch, H., eds., *Police Violence: Understanding and Controlling Police Abuse of Force* (pp. 205–22). New Haven, Conn.: Yale University Press.

REISS, A. J., JR. (1968). Police brutality—Answers to key questions. *Trans action* 5: 10 19.

REUSS-IANNI, E. (1983). *Two Cultures of Policing: Street Cops and Management Cops.* New Brunswick, N.J.: Transaction Publishers.

SCRIVNER, E. M. (1994). *Controlling Police Use of Excessive Force: The Role of the Police Psychologist.* Washington, D.C.: National Institute of Justice, Research in Brief.

SHERMAN, L. J. (1975). An evaluation of policewomen on patrol in a suburban police department. *Journal of Police Science and Administration* 3 (4): 434–8.

SHERMAN, L., & BLUMBERG, M. (1981). Higher education and police use of deadly force. *Journal of Criminal Justice* 9 (4): 317–31.

SILVERMAN, E. B. (1999). *NYPD Battles Crime: Innovative Strategies in Policing* Boston: Northeastern University Press.

SKOGAN, W. G. (1990). *Disorder and Decline: Crime and the Spiral of Decay in American Neighborhoods.* Berkeley: University of California Press.

SKOLNICK, J. H. (1975). *Justice without Trial: Law Enforcement in Democratic Society.* 2d ed. New York: John Wiley.

SKOLNICK, J. H., & FYFE, J. J. (1993). *Above the Law: Police and the Excessive Use of Force.* New York: Free Press.

SMITH, D. A. (1984). The organizational context of legal control. *Criminology* 22 (1): 19–38.

SMITH, D. A., & VISHER, C. A. (1981). Street-level justice: Situational determinants of police arrest decisions. *Social Problems* 29 (2): 167–77.

SYKES, R. E., & BRENT, E. E. (1983). *Policing: A Social Behaviorist Perspective.* New Brunswick, N.J.: Rutgers University Press.

SYKES, R. E., & CLARK, J. P. (1975). A theory of deference exchange in police–civilian encounters. *American Journal of Sociology* 81 (3): 584–600.

Tennessee v. *Garner*, 471 U.S. 1 (1985).

Toch, H. (1978). The asshole. In Manning, P. K., & Van Maanen, J., eds., *Policing: A View from the Street* (pp. 221–38). Santa Monica, Calif.: Goodyear.

Van Maanen, J. (1978). The asshole. In Manning, P. K., & Van Maanen, J., eds., *Policing: A View from the Street* (pp. 221–38). Santa Monica, Calif.: Goodyear.

Waegel, W. B. (1984). The use of lethal force by police: The effect of statutory change. *Crime & Delinquency* 31 (1): 121–40.

Walker, S., & Bumphus, V. W. (1992). The effectiveness of civilian review: Observations on recent trends and new issues regarding the civilian review of the police. *American Journal of Police* 11 (1): 1–26.

Walker, S., & Graham, N. (1998). Citizen complaints in response to police misconduct: The results of a victimization survey. *Police Quarterly* 1 (1): 65–89.

Walker, S., & Kreisel, B. W. (1996). Varieties of citizen review: The implications of organizational features of complaint review procedures for accountability of the police. *American Journal of Police* 15 (3): 65–88.

Walker, S., Spohn, C., & DeLone, M. (1996). *The Color of Justice: Race, Ethnicity, and Crime in America*. Belmont, Calif.: Wadsworth Publishing.

Weiner, N. L. (1974). The effect of education on police attitudes. *Journal of Criminal Justice* 2 (4): 317–28.

Weisburd, D., & Greenspan, R., with Hamilton, E. E., Williams, H., & Bryant, K. A. (2000). *Police Attitudes toward Abuse of Authority: Findings from a National Study*. Washington, D.C.: National Institute of Justice, Research in Brief.

West, P. (1988). Investigation of complaints against the police: Summary report of a national survey. *American Journal of Police* 7 (2): 101–21.

Westley, W. A. (1953). Violence and the police. *American Journal of Sociology* 59: 34–41.

Westley, W. A. (1970). *Violence and the Police: A Sociological Study of Law, Custom, and Morality*. Cambridge, Mass.: M.I.T Press.

Whitaker, G. P. (1983). Police department size and the quality and cost of police services. In Nagel, S., Fairchild, E., & Champagne, A., eds., *The Political Science of Criminal Justice* (pp. 185–96). Springfield, Ill.: Charles C. Thomas.

White, S. O. (1972). A perspective on police professionalization. *Law & Society Review* 7 (1): 61–85.

Wilson, J. Q. (1968). *Varieties of Police Behavior: The Management of Law and Order in Eight Communities*. Cambridge, Mass.: Harvard University Press.

Wilson, J. Q., & Boland, B. (1978). The effect of the police on crime. *Law & Society Review* 12(3): 367–90.

Wilson, J. Q., & Kelling, G. L. (1982, March). Broken windows: The police and neighborhood safety. *The Atlantic Monthly* pp. 29–38.

Worden, A. P. (1993). The attitudes of women and men in policing: Testing conventional and contemporary wisdom. *Criminology* 31(2): 203–37.

Worden, R. E. (1989). Situational and attitudinal explanations of police behavior: A theoretical reappraisal and empirical assessment. *Law & Society Review* 23(4): 667–711.

Worden, R. E. (1990). A badge and a baccalaureate: Policies, hypotheses, and further evidence. *Justice Quarterly* 7(3): 565–92.

Worden, R. E. (1995a). The "causes" of police brutality: Theory and evidence on police use of force. In Geller, W. A., & Toch, H., eds., *And Justice for All: Understanding and Controlling Police Abuse of Force* (pp. 31–60). Washington, D.C.: Police Executive Research Forum.

Worden, R. E. (1995b). "Police officers' belief systems: A framework for analysis." *American Journal of Police* 14 (1): 49-81.

Worden, R. E., & Shepard, R. L. (1996). Demeanor, crime, and police behavior: A reexamination of police services study data. *Criminology* 34(1): 83–105.

5

Media Accounts of Police Sexual Violence

Rotten Apples or State-Supported Violence?

Danielle McGurrin and Victor E. Kappeler

❖

INTRODUCTION

Kathy was driving home to her apartment outside of Boston one evening. Alone on the Massachusetts Turnpike, Kathy saw flashing blue lights behind her. She was stopped and ordered by a state trooper to get into his car. What Kathy did not know was that State Trooper Robert Montero had a history of using his position as a law enforcement officer to prey on unsuspecting and unaccompanied female motorists along Massachusetts's highways. Kathy recalled that the trooper told the officers at the state police barracks not to tow her car. Before she realized what was happening, the trooper left the highway and headed into a cemetery. Terrified and in shock, Kathy could hardly believe that she was being raped by a police officer. After he raped her, the trooper took Kathy back to her car, told her he would call her sometime for a date, politely said good-bye, and drove off. Immediately following the rape, Kathy went home too horrified to report the assault and too fearful that no one would believe her. Kathy questioned, who was she to call—"someone wearing the same uniform?"

Two months later, the same trooper pulled over another victim, Deborah George, and viciously raped her. Not trusting police personnel to help her, Deborah George took

The authors express their sincerest thanks to Michael Vaughn for screening, collecting, and copying thousands of articles on police sexual violence as well as constructing the code sheet used for this study. We also thank book editor Kim Lersch and series editor M. L. Dantzker for providing helpful feedback in strengthening the final version of this chapter.

her case to the newspapers, hoping to stop the man she believed had raped before. Spotting the case in the local newspaper, Kathy recognized the trooper's name from his badge and decided along with Deborah to press charges against their attacker, State Trooper Robert Montero. When the case went to trial, six other people came forward, stating they too, had been victims of Montero. Some said they had complained about the trooper, but no disciplinary action had been taken. In the end, Trooper Montero was convicted of raping two women and was sentenced to thirty years in prison.

Cases like Montero's leave most people wondering how a sexually abusive officer was afforded the opportunity to abuse eight known victims before finally being exposed. And once the abuser is identified, many also wonder whether the appropriate departmental and criminal justice responses will follow. In the case of Officer Montero, many obvious warning signs were ignored before the beginning of his offending. Far from the aberrant, unforeseeable tragedy—which tends to characterize most descriptions of police officers who commit sexual offenses against their victims—Officer Montero's actions were rather unsurprising, given his previous record. According to an investigative report by the television show *20/20* (Jarriel, 1997), the first time Robert Montero applied to be a state trooper, he was denied admission because he had a history of criminal arrests. Montero persevered and was admitted to the Massachusetts police academy, though his training was tarnished by his attempts to solicit women while wearing his uniform. Despite the fact that all four of Montero's supervisors recommended against making him an officer, "on orders from above," Robert Montero became a Massachusetts state trooper in 1987.

Cases of law enforcement officials who betray the safety and trust afforded them by the state and depended upon them by the public occur much more commonly than most persons recognize. The Montero case is one of hundreds that involve law enforcement officials who breach the profound confidence supported by all of our major state, economic, social, and cultural institutions. The topic of police sexual violence is an important, albeit underresearched and underreported phenomenon that is telling of how state agents specifically and our society more broadly address the deeply rooted problem of violence against women and children. While many questions are raised in this chapter, perhaps the most significant is whether a hypermasculinist, exclusionary organization whose state-sanctioned decree grants it the authority to question, detain, arrest, and use deadly force can serve and protect marginalized and vulnerable citizens in the same manner that it serves and protects its own?

DEFINING POLICE SEXUAL VIOLENCE

Police sexual violence (PSV) takes many forms; it is not confined to a single definition or kind of victimization. Instead, PSV involves "those situations in which a . . . citizen experiences a sexually degrading, humiliating, violating, damaging or threatening act committed by a police officer, through the use of force or police authority" (Kraska & Kappeler, 1995: 93). More broadly, PSV is the abuse of state power to control women physically, emotionally, socially, economically, and politically (Wonders & Caulfield, 1993). Police sexual violence, with any significant or systemic frequency, could not be realized without the state's dictum and support. The state engages in political criminality "when it fails to define widespread and systemic harm against women as illegal, . . . neglects to enforce laws that do provide some measure of protection to women, and . . . provides structural support for institutional practices that clearly harm women" (Wonders & Caulfield, 1993: 80). Obviously, many forms of PSV are defined by state laws as criminal. Thus, the extent to which state officials neglect to enforce these laws and the extent to which the police institutions fail to respond to these incidents or provide structural support for these behaviors are the major linkages between PSV and political criminality.

As with many predominantly male institutions, policing maintains a strong culture and ideology that asserts male exclusivity (Hunt, 1990; Martin, 1980, 1990). Male exclusivity and a masculine culture, however, do not account for the varying means by which many institutions exercise control over women. It must also be recognized that the monopoly that police have on state-sanctioned violence lays the foundation for both personal and political sexual victimization. Although sexual violence occurs in many male-dominated organizations, those responsible for enforcing social control directives have the state-supported prerogative to search, detain, and use force against its citizens. As such, state institutions, whose duty it is to regulate societal norms, values, and mores, often do so at the expense of those who do not conform to normative standards—in short, the marginalized and disenfranchised, of which women are a part (Wonders & Caulfield, 1993). These observations are suggestive of at least a linkage between PSV and state power.

BACKGROUND OF POLICE SEXUAL VIOLENCE

The commission of sexual violence by male police personnel against citizens has only recently been explored outside the mainstream theories of deviance (Kelley, 1988; Kraska & Kappeler, 1995; Wonders & Caulfield, 1993). Although by no means a new or unusual phenomenon, attitudes surrounding the personal and private nature of sexual violence have similarly permeated the public sphere, preventing many scholars and criminal justice employees from seriously examining the problem of sexual violence by state officials (Wonders & Caulfield, 1993). When scholarly attention has focused on police as perpetrators of sexual violence, it has been traditionally seen as aberrational behavior and defined in terms of "sexual misconduct" (Sapp, 1986: 83). The basis for this description hinged on the conception that motivation and opportunity for "easy money, drugs, and sex" forced otherwise law-abiding officers into deviance. While opportunity certainly has a part to play in explaining PSV, the complexity and breadth of this behavior require a broader explanation.

Much of the earlier police deviance literature "implicitly presumed that police were a desired commodity willing to trade 'sexual favors' for leniency" (Kraska & Kappeler, 1995: 88). Sapp (1986: 88) reports a common theme in his interviews with hundreds of police officers from seven states:

> You bet I get sex once in a while by some broad who I arrest. Lots of times you can just hint that if you are taken care of, you could forget about what they did . . . some of the snooty broads will turn on real quick if they think their friends and the old man doesn't have to find out.

This presumption generates problematic inferences. First, this construction of police deviance leads to the inference that women criminals are the most likely victims of PSV. Second, it leads to the inference that police officers commit sex crimes based on naturally occurring occupational opportunities rather than intentionally seeking out sexual victims. Third, it implies that police officers are a wanted sexual commodity and that victims of PSV are willing participants when social forces are arranged to lessen social control on women's sexuality and provide for an exchange relationship. Fourth, the notion of the rogue officer engaging in consensual sex clearly ignores victim-based perceptions of coercion, fear, intimidation, and force (Kraska & Kappeler, 1995). Further, these conceptions trivialize female victimization, justify institutional sexism and discrimination, and implicitly reinforce male privilege. The rogue officer or "rotten-apple" construction coupled with the "willing women" hypothesis of this social problem has allowed theorizing of PSV to remain affixed to mainstream and conservative explanations of the problem. These explanations may obscure the systemic and state-power nature of PSV.

The possibility of victimization becomes of heightened concern when the already skewed power differential between officer and victim becomes even more exaggerated by the victim's involvement in illegal or illicit services. For example, in August 2000, an on-duty Nassau police officer was accused of pulling over an exotic dancer under the auspices of administering a Breathalyzer test. The plainclothes officer flashed his badge at the victim and then ordered her out of the car and onto the floor of his unmarked car. The officer then drove the woman to a secluded wooded area where he ordered her out of the car, told her to take off her clothes, and forced her to perform oral sex on him. The victim took her complaint to the department, but the case was not fully investigated. The internal affairs investigator failed to notify superiors of the complaint, and the precinct where the case was first filed misidentified it as a police impersonation case. The officer was finally arrested in February 2001 after Nassau police admitted mistakes and errors in judgment in handling her case. Since then, the officer has been rearrested for another charge of sodomy involving a different victim (Gearty, 2001).

In another case highlighting the victim's occupational vulnerability to PSV, a Gonzales, Louisiana, police officer was accused in February 1998 of kidnapping three prostitutes, forcing them at gunpoint to commit sexual acts, and shooting one victim in the arm when she attempted to escape from his car. The police officer was fired and later turned himself in for arrest ("Louisiana Cop Accused," 1998).

Women engaged in sex-industry services are not nearly the only vulnerable targets for PSV offenses. Female jail and prison inmates are also at risk as well. Recently, a Harris County (Texas) jury awarded $300,000 to a woman who had been raped twice by a sheriff's deputy while she was in county custody. The woman claimed that in 1993 a sheriff's deputy took her out of a hospital jail ward, raped her, and then returned her to custody. The jury found that Harris County violated her right to be free from cruel and unusual punishment by not protecting her from the threat of sexual assault and violence (Hanson, 1999).

As this discussion demonstrates, a person engaging in an illegal or illicit enterprise or a detained person has very little recourse to defend herself from sexual assault, let alone police sexual assault (Kappeler et al., 1994). As the following quote demonstrates, legislation that targets victimless crimes (specifically street prostitutes and deviant street workers), places women in much danger. By entrusting a predominantly male institution to regulate women's sexual behavior, legislators and administrators may inadvertently contribute to increased levels of victimization.

> I know several dozen guys who have worked vice in the ten years I've been assigned to the vice squad. I believe every one of them has gone beyond the rules on sex with prostitutes. When you are assigned to the prostitute detail, you have to get the female subject to offer

specific sexual acts and then state a price for those sex acts. Once you have that, you have a case and are supposed to identify and arrest; sometimes the officer goes ahead and has sex, then makes the arrest . . . if the whore claims otherwise, no one believes her anyway. (Sapp, 1986: 90–1).

Sapp's interviews were extremely significant as the first study by a police academic to research sexual violations by police officers. His research does not, however, examine more "overt forms of coercion through the use or threat of physical force, along with the authority of the uniform and the badge, to sexually harass, assault, or even rape female citizens" (Kraska & Kappeler, 1995: 89). While marginalized populations like women working in the sex industry, women who have been arrested or caught in criminality, and "snooty broads who turn on real quick" would seem to be at risk, one must question police constructions of PSV and whether criminal behavior on the part of victims accounts for a significant percentage of police sex crimes.

Recently, feminist criminologists have attempted to remedy some of the fallacies surrounding women and the police. With the advent of women's entry into policing in the mid-1970s, the problem of sexual harassment of police officers has been examined through occupational research (Hale & Wyland, 1993; Martin, 1980, 1990). Susan Martin (1992: 290) found that, of 70 female officers interviewed, two-thirds of the women identified at least one instance of sex discrimination, and 75 percent reported instances of sexual harassment on the job. Descriptions of harassment reported by the female officers included frequent occurrences of "blatant, widespread, and organized departmental and statutorial violations."

More recent evidence of such organizational discrimination is present in two 1997 reports from the Christopher Commission (formally known as Independent Commission on the Los Angeles Police Department) (1991) and the Los Angeles Police Commission. Both reports revealed that the Los Angeles Police Department (LAPD) Command had known for years about orchestrated sexual harassment and intimidation of female police officers and had done nothing to stop it. Internal Affairs reports secured by a reporter exposed that the LAPD had been regularly covering up serious problems of domestic violence, namely, wife beating, within its ranks (Spillar & Harrington, 1997). Legal documents of the department showed that more than sixty officers investigated by the department after having been accused of domestic abuse during a five-year period ending in 1992 were not arrested (Lait, 1997). According to the Christopher Commission and other reports, attempts by male police officers to rid the department of female officers only served to exacerbate the LAPD's brutality problem and cost the taxpayers millions in police brutality and sexual discrimination law suits.

Jennifer Hunt's (1990) field research in policing uncovered that police officers frequently utilized degradation and humiliation as a means to denigrate their female co-workers and to remind them that they did not belong in any substantive way to the male-dominated organization. She further found that police supervisors sanctioned these behaviors and reinforced these acts that were sometimes exacerbated by the values associated with the police occupational culture.

Indicative of these findings, a St. Louis Police Department major recently accepted a thirty-day suspension without pay and will undergo counseling for verbally abusing four women. The women's complaints include allegations that the major made sexual innuendos, verbally intimidated them, and made physically violent threats. One former departmental employee reported that the major pinned her against a wall and tried to kiss her in his office when he was an area commander. The Union President, who represents the department's 500 civilian employees, said it is quite possible that despite all of these allegations, the major may still keep his job (Bryan, 1997).

LINKING POLICE SEXUAL VIOLENCE TO STRUCTURAL AND CULTURAL FORMS OF GENDER DISCRIMINATION

The well-established links between institutional, organizational, and cultural male hegemony, coupled with the police authority to use force, establish a fertile environment for subordinating powerless groups and individuals. Although governments around the world do not limit their violence to females, some sexual violations are most often directed at women and girls as a means of coercion, humiliation, punishment, and control.

Kraska and Kappeler (1995: 94) illustrate this point through their PSV continuum; as the degree of intrusiveness increases, the offense moves from less severe, unobtrusive behavior, to extreme criminal conduct.

> Unobtrusive behavior can include viewing victims, photographs, and sexually explicit videos, invasions of privacy, and secondary victimization. Obtrusive acts may involve random "stop search and question," house raids, custodial strip searches, body cavity searches, warrant-based searches, illegal detentions, threat of sexual violence, deception to gain sexual favors, provision of services for sexual favors, and sexual harassment. Lastly, the most severe, criminal behavior, may comprise sexual harassment, sexual contact, sexual assault, rape, sodomy, and sexual homicide.

An exploratory analysis of 124 federal litigation cases published from 1978 to 1992, and media reports published from 1991 to 1993, was conducted by Kraska and Kappeler in 1995. Their study found that 37 rape and sexual assault cases were committed by on-duty police officers, and 69 were illegal strip searches, body cavity searches, illegal detentions, deceptions to gain sexual services, and sexual harassment. Their research contributed to the literature not only as one of the first studies of PSV but also as the first study to typologize the broad range of sexually violating behaviors. By their own admission, the authors state that their data include "only reported incidents of PSV that reached the media, or cases pursued by a plaintiff in the federal courts" (Kraska & Kappeler, 1995: 92). Thus, this use of secondary data analysis precludes the researchers from unveiling the actual frequency or "upper range" of PSV.

More recently the ABC news program *20/20* (Jarriel, 1997) filed over 1,000 requests for police records, under the Freedom of Information Act, "in an effort to determine the magnitude and the resolution of the problem of sexual assault among law enforcement officers" (Jarriel, 1997: 3). The ABC research examined officers who committed their crimes under color of law (i.e., "offenses occurring while on-duty, in uniform, while driving a marked patrol car, and conducting official business," *Battista* v. *Cannon*, 1996). Using official records from police agencies around the nation, their investigation uncovered "hundreds of cases of sexual assault, rape, and murder since 1990" (Jarriel, 1997: 3).

Specifically, ABC discovered cases of officers hired with criminal records, recidivist rapists, and officers who received "a slap on the wrist" for brutal assaults. The research also found rape cases resulting in convictions of a misdemeanor offense, "official oppression." Finally, they found officers who moved elsewhere and resumed their pattern of sexual victimization. In case after case, *20/20* found that officers with prior criminal records were hired by police departments as they continued their sexually violating behavior. Even when the officers were eventually fired, they were often rehired by a different agency, based on the recommendations afforded them, by the very department that forced their dismissal or resignation.

According to *20/20*'s Tom Jarriel (1997), sexual assault among police officers is a "systemic problem with chilling consequences" (1997: 2). Unfortunately, Jarriel (1997) is less substantive in the rest of his analysis. First, like the shortcomings of prior police deviance studies, Jarriel (1997: 10) attributes the PSV phenomenon to a few "bad apples." As Kraska and Kappeler (1995) state, this has been discredited in the best of police deviance literature over the past twenty years. Second, the study recognizes only those PSV incidents that were committed by on-duty police officers, the most obvious abuse under the color of law; off-duty officers commit many PSV incidents as well. Last, the conclusion focuses exclusively on myopic, "system tinkering" solutions to the exclusion of broader structural, cultural, and power factors that may encourage PSV. Jarriel's final reminder that the safety of society depends upon police officers reifies the necessity of broad sweeping police powers and superficially squelches alternative explanations that might contradict the rotten-apple assertion.

Conclusions and constructions of this sort, are of course, the product of the comfortable and symbiotic relationship between police and the media where a shared ideology serves both institutions' interests. Both the media and law enforcement present phenomenon in event-oriented, individualized terms. This functional perspective fixates upon problem individuals rather than problem social and power structures. Thus, to acknowledge PSV as a greater structural, power, and cultural problem could result in an assault, not only on the credibility of the police institution, but on the state that grants its power (Erikson, Baranek, & Chan, 1991).

To explore the possible linkages between PSV and state power as well as to examine various media constructions of PSV, we decided to collect newspaper accounts of PSV to provide a contrast and alternative source of information on this phenomena. Newspaper accounts of PSV have many limitations, but they do provide a contrast to research findings generated from interviews with police officers, official accounts of PSV, and court documents. Newspaper accounts provide easy accessibility, broad geographic representation, and high reliability. In the present study, these media accounts captured many of the cases for which charges were not filed or arrests made. Also, these newspaper reports contained a number of cases where final dispositions were not yet rendered. While media accounts of PSV are certainly not free from ideological and organizational influences, they may be more accurate than police officers' self-serving accounts of sexual deviance in that they provide a point of contrast that may complement or better inform existing research.

As with any research approach, there were some drawbacks to selecting PSV newspaper accounts. First, the newspapers ordinarily provided more general information, while the coding sheet was designed to capture a broad, albeit specific set of variables. Incomplete or nonexistent reporting in certain areas resulted in discarded variables; thus, not all variables in the coding sheet were measured. Second, this identical code sheet, if applied to court cases would have revealed a more detailed examination of PSV. The reason is that judicial documents provide primary data accounts, often unavailable to other sources. Unfortunately, neither newspaper articles nor court cases can encapsulate all victimizations. Both sources can only catalog reported sexual offenses, therefore underestimating the entirety of PSV incidents (see Kraska & Kappeler, 1995). Finally, the use of mediated data, and the employment of a quantitative content analysis, will reflect in part what these media sources deem significant. The ways in which news is constructed and presented lessen the possibilities of obtaining a richer understanding of both the victim's and officer's perceptions and beliefs.

Approach

We collected articles pertaining to PSV from 66 newspapers from 28 states, for the purpose of content analysis. We selected newspaper articles from three databases, *Newspaper Abstracts, Westlaw*, and *Dialog*, from the years 1989 to 1997. The collection of data began with newspaper articles published in 1989, because the majority of the newspapers indexed in these databases began indexing PSV incidents during this year. Although at least one major newspaper (*The Chicago Tribune*) began reporting PSV incidents in 1974, and a few more that began before 1989, this year was deemed the most appropriate cutoff, because only one major newspaper began reporting after 1989.

Key word searches of these 66 newspapers yielded 11,218 article abstracts. A manual reading of each abstract determined its relevance to PSV. The procedure produced a total of 1,255 newspaper abstracts related to sexual violence. Approximately 9,963 abstracts were excluded from collection because they pertained to police officers who were either investigating or reporting a rape, sexual assault, or other sex offense committed by someone other than a law enforcement official.

We paid careful attention to the duplication of articles across newspapers. We kept detailed lists of article citations then crossed checked across all three databases to exclude duplication. While coding the data, careful attention was given to each article, ensuring that news reports were separate acts of PSV. To avoid incidents of duplication, we flagged officers whose names appeared more than once in the database and checked against their corresponding articles, to ensure that the number of times their name appeared corresponded with the unique number of sexual violence incidents reported by the media. In several cases, an article or series of articles reported on multiple offenses. Consequently, the total number of PSV incidents (n = 747) exceeds the number of PSV articles in the study (n = 501). The data collection technique and coding strategy produced 501 unique articles on PSV from a total of 1,255 newspaper articles.

The coding instrument was designed to allow a content analysis of the newspaper articles and provide the greatest possible description of each incident of PSV. As a result, the instrument contained sixty-one variables pertaining to the form and severity of the sexual offense, the context of the crime, any organizational and media response, and the official disposition of the case.

The results of this study should be read with some caution. Because the data collected for this study are indirect accounts of PSV and are data collected, written, edited, and published in newspapers, caution should be used in generalizing to the actual population of

PSV cases. Media practices, what the media chooses or fails to report, certainly affect the results of this study. Given the difficulty of collecting primary data on this topic and the dearth of research on this topic, exploratory research seemed warranted.

Sexual Offense and Intrusiveness

Of the 501 newspaper articles on PSV, 469 (93.6 percent) reported the type of sexual offense. Sexual offense type was derived from the victims' allegations, the police agencies' description of the incident, or the legal classification used by the news reporters. Analysis of the type of sexual offense found that 31.3 percent (n = 147) of all alleged victimizations were rapes; 29.2 percent (n = 137) were sexual assaults; 9.8 percent (n = 46) were sexual molestations; and 8.3 percent (n = 39) were sexual abuse of a child. Of the remaining 21.3 percent of sexual offenses, 4.5 percent (n = 21) were categorized as sexual harassment and 4 percent (n = 19) were sexual misconduct. Only 12.8 percent (n = 60) were encapsulated by the remaining 15 attributes (sodomy, voyeurism, exhibitionism, statutory rape, unlawful sexual activity, official oppression, incest, soliciting/procuring sex, involuntary deviate sexual intercourse, malfeasance, sexual exploitation, obscene performance, obstruction of justice, official misconduct, and contributing to an illegal enterprise).

As discussed earlier in the PSV continuum, severe criminal behavior characterizes the upper range of this phenomenon. Although most of the reported cases were encapsulated by this upper range, it should be noted that sexual offense type measured only the most serious incident classification (i.e., the most serious official charge brought against the officer), meaning that lesser charges would often be omitted from the total sexual offense type. In the example that follows, if the case had been a part of our current study, the sexual offense type would have been classified solely as a rape (the most serious of the listed charges).

In January 2001, an Erie city police officer was suspended with pay after his arraignment on charges that he raped, beat, and threatened a woman. The woman told police that the officer raped her in her home, hit her in the head and chest, bit her, grabbed her throat during the attack, and threatened to kill her. The woman stated that the officer took her ripped underwear after the attack and threw it in the garbage. Police said a search of the home revealed that the apparent assailant had disconnected her phone and later threw the underwear into the basement to conceal the evidence. The officer was charged with rape, involuntary deviate sexual intercourse, sexual assault, aggravated indecent sexual assault, indecent assault, simple assault, terroristic threats, and tampering with evidence (Associated Press, 2001).

The overwhelming majority of sex offenses reported by the media were highly intrusive forms of sexual conduct that belied the "boys will be boys" characterization made by some police interviewees. Examples of these seemingly unlikely PSV offenses include officers who sexually assault crime victims, officers who molest children, officers who molest their own children/relatives, and officers who work in juvenile sex crime units, Explorer units, or other juvenile/child service programs for the purpose of sexually abusing young victims. At times these ultra-egregious offenses overlap; such is the case with the following example:

A former Denver police lieutenant who once worked with juvenile sex crime victims pleaded guilty to nearly a decade of sexual assault on a child by a person in a position of trust and to aggravated incest. The offender, Dennis Cribari, was sentenced to 8 years in prison and probation for life. Cribari began molesting his daughter from the time she was 7 years old until the time she was 16. Cribari also admitted to similar conduct over a 20-year period with other victims, including the daughter of a previous girlfriend and friends of his daughter (Lindsay, 2000).

While the percentage of very serious sex crimes reported in the articles may be an artifact of the media's desire to sensationalize rather than to provide a balanced reporting of the full range of PSV offenses, the fact that the vast majority of crimes reported were very serious sex crimes contradicts the construction of PSV as largely the product of mere misconduct. Table 5–1 lists the frequency and percentage of sexual offenses reported in the newspaper articles.

Unlike the type of sexual offense, newspaper accounts reported only the degree of intrusiveness of a sexual offense in 47.1 percent (n = 236) of the stories. Of the 236 articles that reported the intrusiveness of the conduct, 16.5 percent (n = 39) were vaginal assaults;

TABLE 5–1.   Frequency Distribution of Sexual Offense Type

Sexual Offense Type	Number	Percent
Rape/attempted rape	147	31.3%
Sexual assault/attempted sexual assault	137	29.2%
Sodomy/attempted sodomy	7	1.5%
Voyeurism/attempted voyeurism	3	0.6%
Exhibitionism/attempted exhibitionism	11	2.3%
Statutory rape/attempted statutory rape	6	1.3%
Verbal sexual misconduct/harassment	21	4.5%
Sexual molestation	46	9.8%
Unlawful sexual activity	2	0.4%
Official oppression	9	1.9%
Incest	3	0.6%
Sexual abuse of a child	39	8.3%
Soliciting/procuring sex	5	1.1%
Involuntary deviate sexual intercourse	3	0.6%
Sexual misconduct	19	4.1%
Malfeasance	3	0.6%
Sexual exploitation	2	0.4%
Obscene performance	1	0.2%
Obstruction of justice	1	0.2%
Official misconduct	1	0.2%
Contributing to an illegal enterprise	3	0.6%
Total	469	100%

TABLE 5–2. Frequency Distribution of Degree of Intrusiveness

Degree of Intrusiveness	Number	Percent
Vaginal	39	16.5%
Anal	12	5.1%
Oral	35	14.8%
Grope/touch/fondle/spank	86	36.4%
Kissing	3	1.3%
Penetration with foreign object	5	2.1%
Vaginal/anal/oral	3	1.3%
Vaginal/anal	14	5.9%
Vaginal/oral	3	1.3%
Anal/oral	3	1.3%
Oral/digital	2	0.8%
Digital	6	2.5%
Not applicable	25	10.6%
Total	236	100%

5 percent (n = 12) were anal assaults; 14.8 percent (n = 35) were oral assaults; 15.3 percent (n = 36) were a combination of vaginal, anal, oral, digital, and/or foreign object penetration, and 37.7 percent (n = 89) of the offenses consisted of groping, touching, spanking, fondling, and/or kissing. About 11 percent (n = 25) of PSV articles failed to report physically intrusive offenses; these incidents were largely sexual offenses like verbal sexual misconduct, voyeurism, or exhibitionism. Table 5–2 presents a distribution of the degree of intrusiveness of the reported forms of PSV.

In about 90 percent (n = 399) of the PSV cases, the officer used confidence tactics before assaulting the victim. Confidence tactics included officers who approached the victim openly with a subterfuge or ploy; officers who had nonviolent interactions with the victim before the attack and whose harmful intentions were realized only gradually by the victim; and officers who used deceit or false pretenses to gain access to the victim and then betrayed this trust.

Blitz attacks occurred in slightly less than 10 percent (n = 43) of PSV cases. Blitz attacks occurred when the officer suddenly surprised the victim and attacked without warning. These types of offenses occurred without prior interaction between officer and victim and were further characterized by the officer's use of direct and immediate force to subdue his victim. The majority of officers who assaulted their victims did not attempt to prolong the relationship (74.7 percent; n = 374). Where prolonging the relationship did occur, it almost always involved acquaintance relationships where the victim was assaulted over a period of months or years. In most cases, offending officers (93.6 percent; n = 469) did not attempt to dissuade the victim from reporting the offense. In other words, most of the newspaper accounts did not report that the victim was threatened by the officer into re-

maining silent about the incident. It is not known whether this was an artifact of media reporting, or whether the officer was emboldened by the assault into thinking he either did
nothing egregious (i.e., perceiving the sexual activity to be consensual), or that the victim
simply would not report the assault. Also, it is possible that the police felt that their occupation insulated them from the consequences of reporting.

As discussed later in the institutional response, the degree to which officers are protected from both departmental punishment and criminal punishment is difficult to determine using solely newspaper accounts. For example, while this study found a relatively
high number of suspensions (n = 163) and firings (n = 126) of the cases revealing departmental punishments (n = 425), newspaper accounts rarely include relevant data including
whether the officer had a prior record, the length of the suspension, the conditions of the
suspension (paid/unpaid), and the impact of the suspension or firing on the offender's future law enforcement career (transferred, demoted, reinstated by same department, reinstated by different department). These omissions in turn can safeguard recidivist agencies
and offenders who have long histories of PSV. Likewise, when media accounts fail to report final PSV case dispositions and criminal justice punishments, it becomes more difficult to assess how seriously the legal system treats PSV and the degree to which formal
sanctions impact PSV offenses.

Offender Variables

The overwhelming majority of officers alleged to have committed PSV were male (98.8
percent; n = 494), which represents a disproportionate number as compared to their representation in law enforcement agencies. Only about 1 percent (n = 6) of officers involved in
PSV were women. The mean officer age was 36, with a range from 18 to 65; the modal age
was 25. The ages were most heavily distributed in the 26–45 age category, though ages
18–25 and 46–50 each accounted for nearly 10 percent of the cases. Officers over the age
of 50 accounted for only 7 percent of PSV incidents. A majority of the officers (65.2 percent; n = 238) were on duty during the time of the PSV incident, while slightly over a third
of the officers (34.8 percent; n = 127) were off duty.

An officer's race was rarely reported unless the offender was a person of color or the
victim-offender relationship was interracial. Of the 36 articles that reported race, 27.8 percent (n = 10) of the offending officers were white, 44.4 percent (n = 16) were black, 25 percent (n = 9) were Hispanic, and 2.8 percent (n = 1) were other. Given the racial composition of American police agencies and media-reporting practices, this measure most
probably indicates the racial bias underscoring media portrayals of minorities faced with
criminal charges.

The police officers in this study represented a variety of agencies including multi-
jurisdictional, university, municipal, county, state, and federal agencies. These jurisdictions
were collapsed into municipal, county, state, federal, and special police agencies. The majority of agencies experiencing PSV (64.6 percent; n = 299) were municipal. Twenty-six
percent (n = 120) of the agencies were county, and 6.3 percent (n = 29) were state. Only 3.2
percent (n = 15) of the agencies were either federal or special police. It seems that PSV
crosses all political subdivisions of law enforcement, perhaps suggesting the systemic nature of the problem.

The offending officer's rank in the police agency was collected and coded as line officer, supervisor, or administrator. In articles where rank was reported, nearly 74 percent (n = 283) of the police offenders were line officers (patrol officers/deputies/troopers, detectives, reserves, and corporals), 16.1 percent (n = 62) were supervisors (sergeants, lieutenants, and captains/commanders), and 10.2 percent (n = 39) were administrators (chiefs, sheriffs, commissioners, constables). All alleged PSV offenders were sworn law enforcement agents at the time they were accused of the offense. The distribution of PSV cases closely mirrors the distribution of police employees across ranks of law enforcement agencies. It seems that sexual offending by police officers crosses all ranks of police agencies. Since the distribution of PSV cases falls fairly evenly across ranks of officers, it becomes difficult to assert that the occupational opportunity structure associated with routine police work is the sole or even best explanation for PSV; in addition, a significant number of police administrators were involved in this behavior.

In fact, a recent search of PSV articles using the databases Lexis-Nexis and Newspaper Abstracts dating from 1997 to 2001 had little difficulty yielding police chiefs who were either accused of or convicted of PSV. A few examples highlight this point: In Walkill, New York, a police chief whose twenty-five-member police department is responsible for a federal civil lawsuit against the city (accusing it of rampant police sexual misconduct, false arrest, harassment, and general lawlessness) is accused of having sex with a woman in the back seat of his police vehicle (Herbert, 2001); in Illinois, a former Braidwood police chief was convicted in January of 1998 and sentenced to twenty-one years in prison for sexually abusing his stepdaughter (Ziemba, 1998); in the city of Valley Park, Illinois, a former police chief stands accused of (among other nonsexual offenses) propositioning women for sexual favors in exchange for dropping charges against them while he served as chief (Little, 1999); and a former Oswego, New York, police chief was arrested on charges that while serving as chief he molested a fifteen-year-old boy. While primarily meant for descriptive purposes, these examples lend additional support for debunking the occupational opportunity structure in explaining the overwhelming majority of police sexual offenses.

Only 299 articles reported the offending officer's years of law enforcement service. The mean years of service were 10.6, with a range from 1 to 36. Thirty-three percent (n = 99) of the officers had between 1 and 5 years' experience; 25.8 percent (n = 77) had between 6 and 10; 16.7 percent (n = 50) had between 11 and 15; and 11.7 percent (n = 35) had between 16 and 20. Only 12.7 percent (n = 38) of the officers had more than 20 years of experience. With a mean of about 10 years of law enforcement service, it is difficult to argue that PSV is associated with poor selection processes that allow rogue police officers into the institution. If this were the case, one would expect that officer's sex crimes would be detected early in their careers and that organizations would remove them from the occupation. In the alternative, one could speculate that officers engage in substantial sexual offending before it comes to the attention of law enforcement officials or before official action is taken by police organizations. In either case, current police practices seem to be ineffectual in preventing PSV. A failure on the part of state officials to prevent victimization and to protect women from sexual violence suggests political and structural support for this form of violence.

The vast majority of newspaper articles on PSV failed to report whether an offending officer had a prior record. An officer's prior record included criminal offenses (both sex

TABLE 5–3.   Frequency Distribution of Officer's Prior Record

Officer's Prior Record	Number	Percent
None	30	30.9%
Sex offense	18	18.6%
Non-sex crimes	4	4.1%
Charged/dismissed/not guilty	14	14.4%
Previously disciplined by dept.	24	24.7%
Fired/forced to resign by previous dept.	7	7.2%
Total	97	100%

crimes and non-sex crimes) as well as departmental offenses. While it is tempting to conclude that the absence of reporting a prior record indicates an absence of prior offenses, newspaper articles did report the absence of prior records by officers. In all, only 97 of the 501 cases reported on prior records (see Table 5–3). Almost 31 percent (n = 30) of the officers had no prior records; 18.6 percent (n = 18) had been convicted of sex offenses; and 4 percent (n = 4) had been convicted of non-sex offenses. Roughly 14 percent (n = 14) of the officers had been charged with a crime, but either had their case dismissed or were found not guilty. Nearly 25 percent (n = 24) were previously disciplined by their department for PSV offenses, and 7.2 percent (n = 7) were either fired or forced to resign from a law enforcement agency as a result of a previous violation. At the very least, 18 of the 97 officers were convicted of sex crimes, and seven were fired or forced to resign because of PSV offenses. An additional 39 officers were either previously disciplined by their department or charged with criminal offenses. These offenses primarily pertained to PSV. In all, about 69 percent of the offending officers had a previous record of misconduct that might have alerted agencies of a problem.

It is unknown whether this variable was an artifact of newspaper reporting or whether police departments were disinclined to release potentially incriminating information against their officers. However, the fact that, minimally, twenty-five officers were permitted to continue employment in law enforcement, after having been convicted of a sex offense, or fired/forced to resign from their previous department, is telling of how police administrators respond to PSV. The extent to which this finding reflects actual police practices is suggestive of a lack of state response to PSV and possible structural support for the behaviors.

The mean number of offenses committed by officers was 1.5, with 46.5 percent (n = 232) of the officers responsible for a single offense, and 53.5 percent (n = 267) accountable for 2 or more offenses. Slightly more than 15 percent (n = 57) assaulted their victim over a period of months or years. These findings contradict the common supposition that relegates PSV to aberrant acts of poor judgment or isolated incidents of "misconduct." These results further debunk the notion that only a small number of officers commit the majority of all PSV incidents. Given the limitations of the data collected, it was impossible to estimate the frequency at which these officers committed acts of sexual violence.

Victim Variables

Most of the victims of PSV were women and girls (89.8%; n = 433); 10.2 percent (n = 49) of the victims were men and boys. While these extreme disparities in victimization rates may in part reflect lower reporting rates for males, and media coverage bias, sexual victimization is still experienced overwhelmingly by women and girls.

The victim's ages ranged from 1 to 45 and had a mean of 20.4. Females had a mean age of 21.2, and males had a mean age of 15 ($t = 4.13$, $p = .0001$) indicating statistical significance. Nine percent (n = 29) of all victims were age 10 and under. Twenty-five percent (n = 79) of the victims were between the ages of 11 and 15; 23.2 percent (n = 73) of the victims were between the ages of 16 and 20; 16.8 percent (n = 53) of the victims were between 21 and 25; and 10.5 percent (n = 33) of the victims were between the ages of 26 and 30. Only 15.2 percent (n = 48) of the victims were older than 30 years of age. Victim race was reported in just 26 cases. From those cases, 38.5 percent (n = 10) of the victims were white, 23.1 percent (n = 6) were African American, 34.6 percent (n = 9) were Hispanic, and 3.8 percent (n = 1) were other. Like officer race, these statistics were more telling of the ways in which the media configured interracial PSV incidents than they were in aggregating victimization by race.

The victim's occupational status also suffered from a dearth of reporting. Of the 150 cases that reported employment, 53.3 percent (n = 80) of the victims were employed; 20 percent (n = 30) were unemployed; 14 percent (n = 21) were students; and 12.7 percent (n = 19) were prostitutes. The victim's employment was rarely mentioned unless she was a student or a prostitute. The exception to this statement was when female victims were co-workers of the offender. None of the male victimizations revealed employment type, as 83.7% (n = 41) were children. The prostitute attribute was most revealing by its status as the only encapsulated victim occupation. It is unknown whether prostitutes were disproportionately victimized, or whether the media's focus on the victim's occupation was of greater importance than the actual PSV incident. The findings on victim occupation, however, call into question the construction of PSV victims as predominately prostitutes, teenage runaways, or women involved in serious crime. In fact, according to these media accounts of PSV, students and children were as likely to be the victims of PSV as were workers in the sex industry.

The victim's physical injury, beyond the sexual assault itself, was reported in 170 of the cases. From these cases, nearly 2 percent (n = 3) of the victims were killed; 20 percent (n = 34) of the victims had injuries to the face/body, genital area, and/or broken bones; and 78.2 percent (n = 133) of the victims were not physically injured beyond the assault. Only 6.6 percent (n = 30) of the 457 cases reported that the victim sought medical help. Because the victim's physical injury beyond assault was reported only in 33.9 percent (n = 170) of the cases, it was difficult to determine whether the victims were not seeking medical treatment because their physical injuries did not warrant it or whether the nature of sexual victimization precluded women from seeking the help they might have needed. Also, it is possible that the newspapers did not find this information significant enough to report. In any instance, it must be recalled that the power and authority vested in the police occupation may negate the necessity of physical force.

Location Variables

Of the 205 cases that reported the victim's last activity before the police encounter, 40.5 percent (n = 83) of victims were either operating or the passenger in a motor vehicle immediately before encountering the offender. The remaining 59.5 percent (n = 122) of victims were engaged in a variety of activities. Six percent (n = 13) of the victims were at a bar or restaurant before encountering the officer; 11.7 percent (n = 24) were in detention or at the police station; 11.2 percent (n = 23) were at home; 10.2 percent (n = 21) were walking; 9.8 percent (n = 20) were in a public place; and 10.2 percent (n = 21) of the victims were working before they were confronted by the officer.

The location of the initial contact between the victim and offender was compiled in an encounter site variable. Twenty-eight percent (n = 83) of the victims first encountered their offenders at a traffic stop; 13.6 percent (n = 40) were in a public place; 11.9 percent (n = 35) were encountered during a police raid or arrest; 11.9 percent (n = 35) were at the police station; 8.8 percent (n = 26) were pedestrians; 7.8 percent (n = 23) were in detention or jail; 7.1 percent (n = 21) first encountered the offenders in their home; 6.1 percent (n = 18) were at their place of employment; 2.7 percent (n = 8) were in a police program; and 2 percent (n = 6) were other. Of the 171 cases that reported location, 59 percent (n = 101) of the initial meetings between officer and victim occurred in isolated or secluded areas. As for the location of the actual victimization, in 41.4 percent (n = 122) of the reported cases, the officer went to the victim's personal property or place, for the purpose of sexually assaulting the victim. This finding was in stark contrast to Lagrange's (1993) assertion that the motivation for "easy money, drugs, and sex" forced the otherwise law-abiding officer into deviance. In other words, in many cases, it was not the occupational opportunity structure that caused the officer to deviate but, rather, a conscious decision by the officer to seek out and sexually violate his victim.

A crime site variable constructed from the data found that 22.3 percent (n = 84) of the PSV cases occurred inside the officer's vehicle; 19.6 percent (n = 74) took place on the victim's personal property; 14 percent (n = 53) transpired on the officer's personal property; 12.5 percent (n = 47) were committed in a public place; 5.3 percent (n = 20) occurred while the victim was detained or in jail; and 4.8 percent (n = 18) were eventuated in the police station or on police property. Fifteen percent (n = 57) of PSV incidents took place over a period of time and/or in many places and so could not be classified in a single site. The remaining three site variables (woods/field, victim's place of employment, and other) encapsulated only 6.4 percent (n = 24) of all crime sites.

The crime site variable is of particular interest when compared with the officer's duty status. Of all of the officers who committed PSV while on duty, 36 percent (n = 72) assaulted victims inside their police vehicle. This is of particular importance when one considers that the police vehicle is the quintessential personification of law enforcement. A woman who is assaulted in a police vehicle is not only being victimized physically and emotionally but also cognitively via the violent collision between police as protector and perpetrator.

Another piquing aspect of the crime site variable was the number of officers (22.5 percent; n = 85) who traveled to the victim's personal property or place of employment to assault her or him. As previously stated, while opportunity structure does account for some victimizations, it certainly cannot account for officers who map out their assault and commit PSV outside of their normal police activities.

Authority/Force Variables

The use of physical force was reported in 249 (49.7 percent) of the cases. In 52.6 percent (n = 131) of these cases, the officer's mere physical presence was sufficient to enable the assault; 35.7 percent (n = 89) used physical force against the victim; 6.8 percent (n = 17) displayed their weapon; and 4.8 percent (n = 12) gave verbal threats or orders to the victims. The actual type of physical force was reported in 40.7 percent (n = 204) of the cases. In 68.1 percent (n = 139) of these cases, the officer did not use physical force against the victim; 12.7 percent (n = 26) slapped, hit, beat, pushed, threw down, and/or choked the victim; 18.6 percent (n = 38) restrained the victim in some fashion (taped mouth, tied up, held down, and/or handcuffed); and less than .05 percent (n = 1) stabbed the victim.

This variable informed the study by highlighting a critical psychosociological component of victim control in PSV incidents. In the majority of cases, the offenders were able to assault their victims by way of their reception as law enforcement officers. It was often not necessary to use physical violence, as the victim already felt threatened and intimidated by the offender's status as an officer. As such, physical violence was often an auxiliary tactic used to reassert or reinforce this state-backed authority.

The sexual quid pro quo/threat variable was measured in 30.1 percent (n = 151) of the cases. Sexual quid pro quo/threats measured incidents where officers acting under official capacity used their position to obtain some sexual favor or service. Attributes ranged from coercive propositions, "offering special treatment in exchange for sexual activity," to verbal terrorism, "threatening life." Of these cases, 42.4 percent (n = 64) of the officers did not engage in sexual quid pro quo or threats; 39.7 percent (n = 60) threatened the victim; 9.3 percent (n – 14) offered special treatment in exchange for sexual activity; and 8.6 percent (n = 13) threatened the victim's life. By comparing this variable with that of crime site, we found that 82.9 percent (n = 34) of the victims who were assaulted in a police vehicle were also threatened, propositioned, or coerced before the assault. The significance of this finding was that it underscored one of the most common PSV themes; the majority of officers who commit PSV do so while on duty (65.2 percent; n = 238), against mostly female victims (89.8 percent; n = 433), most often, via traffic stops (40.5 percent; n = 83), through the extortionist tactics of sexual quid pro quo or threats (57.6 percent; n = 87).

These results, when analyzed conjointly with the officer duty status, crime site, and sexual quid pro quo/threat variables, uncovered a common theme: Most officers were on duty (65.2 percent; n= 238); the officers were more likely to assault their victims on police property (32.4 percent; n = 122) than any other crime site; and the officers' use of sexual quid pro quo/threats (57.6 percent; n = 87) was the most preferred means of gaining victim compliance.

The strength of evidence variable found support (94.3 percent; n = 297) for the victim's charge of PSV. Strength of evidence was coded as strong if the officer admitted to the offense, if the officer admitted to having consensual sex while on duty, if the incident was corroborated by another officer, or if physical evidence of a sexual assault was present (i.e., semen, fingerprints, blood stains, hair, skin samples, etc.). The presence of at least one of the above-mentioned factors is an indicator that victims had evidence to support their claims of PSV. Finally, it should be noted that the victim dropped the charges in only 0.8

percent (n=4) of all cases. These data suggest that PSV as reported by the media rarely involve unsupported allegations against police officers. This, of course, could be either the product of media reporting only cases of police violence that have strong evidence against the officer or an artifact of the charging practices of law enforcement officials.

Institutional Response

In 16.2 percent (n = 81) of the total cases, the officer's department or supervisor had knowledge of prior PSV before the officer's current offense. In 11 percent (n = 55) of the total cases, the department had prior knowledge of the officer's previous or current PSV but did nothing to discipline the officer or prevent future victimizations. These two variables were significant in that they distinguished between prior knowledge of an offense and failure to investigate an offense. For example, at times supervisors attempted to remedy a situation by either firing or forcing an offending officer to resign, but subsequently their decision was overturned by a court or police commission who then reinstated the officer. This, of course, was not the same as a department that did nothing with its knowledge of PSV. Thus, the latter variable measured negligent and/or delinquent supervisors and departments.

In 52.1 percent (n = 149) of the cases, the offending officer denied the PSV assault; 18.9 percent (n = 54) stated that the sexual activity was consensual; 25.5 percent (n = 73) admitted the offense; 2.8 percent (n = 8) committed suicide before defending themselves; and less than 1 percent (n = 2) could not recall whether they had assaulted the victim.

When departmental disciplinary actions were examined, we found that 29.7 percent (n = 126) of the officers were fired as a result of the offense; 38.4 percent (n = 163) were suspended; 20.2 percent (n = 86) resigned or retired; 5.9 percent (n = 25) received no discipline; 2.1 percent (n = 9) were reinstated by the courts or police commission; 1.9 percent (n = 8) were transferred or rehired by a different police agency; and an additional 1.9 percent (n = 8) were demoted or placed on departmental probation.

Of the 219 accumulated cases that reported a sanction by the justice system, 47.9 percent (n = 105) of the officers did not receive any penalties; 34.3 percent (n = 75) received jail or prison time; 13.2 percent were placed on probation; 3.2 percent (n = 7) were ordered to pay criminal fines and/or monetary civil damages; and less than 1 percent (n = 2; n = 1) each received life or death sentences, respectively.

Because the departmental discipline variable obtained nearly twice as many cases (n = 425) as the criminal justice variable (n = 218), it was difficult to compare agency responses. Further, nearly 56 percent (n = 278) of the total cases were reported in the initial stages of case processing (i.e., arrest, indict, file charges, etc.), meaning (1) that many of the departmental responses reflected only the stage of process that the case was at the time the newspaper reported it and (2) that over half of all criminal justice responses were not accounted for. To ensure the most accurate institutional response, we coded both of these variables by the most recent reported disciplinary action.

Although 94.1 percent (n = 400) of the police agencies addressed the particular PSV incident, it was unknown how many incidents were handled exclusively by the department's internal affairs unit. The departmental disciplinary category may have been artificially inflated by the high percentage of temporary suspensions; in other words, a more frequently used but less stringent response may have spared police departments the time, energy, and resources of ridding the agency of the offending officer. Thus, while only 52 percent (n = 114) of PSV cases received any criminal justice response, it cannot be determined how many of these incidents were even referred to the legal system.

Of the cases that were disposed of by the justice system, in 16.8 percent (n = 84) of the dispositions, the officer was found guilty of major charges or the judgment was for the plaintiff; 1.4 percent (n = 7) were found guilty of lesser charges; 5 percent (n = 25) were acquitted/deadlocked or judgment was for the defendant; 11.8 percent (n = 59) were unfounded, or there was no arrest/indictment/charges filed; 8.6 percent (n = 43) of the cases were plea bargained; 0.8 percent (n = 4) of the charges were dropped by the victim; and 55.6 percent (n = 278) were reported in the arrest/indict/file charges phase. The final dispositions were not reported for all of the cases. More than half of all articles, or article series, began and ended with an arrested or indicted officer. Consequently, this research revealed less than half of all final dispositions because of media reporting practices.

CONCLUSION

The purpose of this study was to expand on prior exploratory research of the phenomenon PSV. Sexual violence among police officers was committed overwhelmingly by men representing all ranks and political subdivisions of law enforcement. The "typical offender" was an on-duty, municipal line officer between the age of 26 and 45, with an average of 10.6 years' experience. Due to artifacts of media reporting, the officer's prior record was measured in only a small percentage of the cases; many of those however, contained officers who were previously convicted of sex offenses. In a majority of PSV cases, the officer committed more than one sexual offense, and some offended their victims over a period of months or years.

Unlike previous studies of PSV that explained the phenomenon in terms of opportunity structure, the present study found that in many cases, the officer knew the victim and went to her personal property or place of employment for the purpose of assaulting her. Also, there were a sizable number of child sexual assaults that the occupational opportunity structure could not explain. Little, if any, support was found for either the "willing women" or "police as a sexual commodity" thesis of police sexual misconduct. In most cases of PSV, the power and authority surrounding the badge and gun precluded the officer from using overt physical force against the victim. Instead, sexual quid pro quo/threats were used as a means of coercing and intimidating the victim into submission.

Although many officers were fired or suspended, it was unknown how often PSV was sanctioned by agencies exclusively, or how frequently these cases were referred to the courts. With regard to the legal system, only half of the reported cases were disposed of, and less than half of those cases were sanctioned by the criminal justice system. The distribution of PSV within the police institution and the relative lack of adequate institutional responses to PSV by state officials are suggestive of both a failure to prevent and perhaps active structural support for violence against women. These suggestions, in turn, provide some evidence of a linkage between PSV and state structural support. The dearth of critical dialogue surrounding male sexual violence and PSV negates the social reality of untold number of victims. Negligent police agencies and uncritical media accounts of PSV are only part of the problem. Every bit as egregious is, as demonstrated, the omission by the state to "actively intervene or seriously limit harms directed primarily at women" (Wonders & Caulfield, 1993: 80). Hence, neglecting to enforce laws impartially is, indeed, a political form of sanctioned violence. Though the omissions are tacit, they are precisely those that continue to be obfuscated by rotten apple, "system tinkering," and other myopic theories and explications of why male sexual violence persists.

Policy Implications

Police agencies can become more organizationally proactive by heeding the caveats of citizen complaints, working and monitoring more closely the actions of officers, and enforcing policies that disallow unauthorized females in police vehicles or stations (Kappeler & Vaughn, 1997). The sensitizing effect of organizational policies, if employed, could be quite effective, specifically against officers who commit PSV under color of authority. Nevertheless, broader structural and cultural initiatives must be taken, if we wish to attack the root causes of sexual violence.

It should be remembered that the findings in this study represent only a small slice of all female and male sexual victimizations. The findings are neither unique nor surprising. The pervasiveness and regularity with which sexual violence occurs can no longer be defended as the result of individual pathologies, occurring in only the rarest of instances.

In 1990, the United Nations called on the United States, along with numerous other countries, to take part in signing the Discrimination against Women Act. The act was drafted to prevent discrimination in a number of specific areas including political and public life, employment, education, health, marriage, and family. One hundred and one countries ratified the U.N. initiative; the United States was not one of them (Kappeler & Vaughn, 1997: 90). Until the United States seriously addresses the personal and political ramifications of gender inequality, it is unlikely that instances of PSV specifically and violence against women and children more broadly will abate.

Future Research

Because a number of important variables were not captured adequately by PSV newspaper accounts, future research in this area may wish to consider the following questions: With regard to officers who were previously disciplined by their department, what percentage were sexual offenses? How many officers charged with child sexual victimization offenses worked in adolescent and child service units? How often did police supervisors have prior knowledge of an officer's PSV, and how does this compare with supervisors who failed to investigate PSV? How often did police personnel refuse, discourage, or threaten a victim about filing a complaint? How frequently did police retaliate against a victim after filing a complaint? And last, what disposition resulted in over half of the cases that were not encapsulated at the time of this study?

Although it is apparent that newspaper articles cannot adequately account for most of these conceptualizations, legal case studies, official police records, occupational surveys, and informal interviews can all help to fill the voids in this study, as well as inform an all too scarce body of literature.

REFERENCES

ASSOCIATED PRESS. (2001, January 16). Erie police officer charged with raping, beating woman. Section State and Regional. Erie, PA: Associated Press.

Battista v. *Cannon*, 934 F. Supp. 400, MD Fla. (1996).

BRYAN, B. (1997, March 12). High-ranking police officer censured in harassment case: Major is accused by women workers. *St. Louis Dispatch*.

ERICSON, R. V., BARANEK, P. M., & CHAN, J. B. L. (1991). *Representing Order: Crime, Law, and Justice in the News Media*. Toronto: University of Toronto.

GEARTY, R. (2001, February 1). Nassau cop rearrested on new sex charge. *Daily News*.

HALE, D., & WYLAND, S. M. (1993). Dragons and dinosaurs: The plight of patrol women. *Police Forum* 3:1–8.

HANSON, E. (1999, October 27). Prisoner who said deputy raped her files suit. *Houston Chronicle*.

HERBERT, B. (2001, January 25). Police predators in America. *New York Times*.

HUNT, J. C. (1990). The logic of sexism among police. *Women and Criminal Justice* 1 (2): 3–30.

INDEPENDENT COMMISSION ON THE LOS ANGELES POLICE DEPARTMENT. (1991). Report of the Independent Commission on the Los Angeles Police Department. Los Angeles: Author.

JARRIEL, T. (1997, October 24). *ABC News 20/20*. New York: American Broadcasting Company.

KAPPELER, V. E., SLUDER, R. D., & ALPERT, G. R. (1994). *Forces of Deviance: Understanding the Dark Side of Policing*. Prospect Heights, Ill.: Waveland.

KAPPELER, V. E., & VAUGHN, M. S. (1997). Law enforcement: When the pursuit becomes criminal—Municipal liability for police sexual violence. *Criminal Law Bulletin* 33: 352–76.

KELLEY, L. (1988). *Surviving Sexual Violence*. Cambridge: Polity.

KRASKA, P. B., & KAPPELER, V. (1995). To serve and pursue: Exploring police sexual violence against women. *Justice Quarterly* 12 (1): 85–108.

LAGRANGE, R. L. (1993). *Policing American Society*. Chicago: Nelson-Hall.

LAIT, M. (1997, May 1). Group seeks outside probe of domestic abuse in LAPD; Police: Councilwoman also urges review of agency's handling of allegations about treatment of female officers. *Los Angeles Times*.

LINDSAY, S. (2000, August 16). Ex-sex-crimes investigator gets 8 years for incest: Cribari tells court that he loves daughter; she says he is "sick, manipulative" and blames her. *Rocky Mountain News*.

LITTLE, J. (1999, August 13). Valley Park adds to suit against former police chief: He is now accused of embezzlement, making deals for sexual favors. *St. Louis Dispatch*.

Lousiana cop accused of attacking prostitutes charges include murder attempt. (1998, February 12). *Times-Picayune*.

MARTIN, S. (1980). *Breaking and Entering: Policewomen on Patrol*. Berkeley: University of California.

MARTIN, S. (1990). *On the Move: The Status of Women in Policing*. Washington, D.C.: Police Foundation.

MARTIN, S. (1992). The changing status of women officers: Gender and power in police work. In Moyer, I. L., ed., *The Changing Role of Women in the Criminal Justice System* (pp. 281–305). Prospect Heights, Ill.: Waveland Press.

SAPP, A. (1986). Sexual misconduct by police officers. In Barker, T., & Carter, D., eds., *Police Deviance* (pp. 83–95). Cincinnati: Anderson.

SPILLAR, K., & HARRINGTON. P. (1997, May 16). Perspective on the LAPD: The verdict on male bias: Guilty; Two reports confirm systemic mistreatment of women cops and cover-up of domestic violence in the ranks. *Los Angeles Times*.

WONDERS, N., & CAULFIELD, S. (1993). Personal is political: Violence against women and the role of the state. In Tunnell, K., ed., *Political Crime in Contemporary America* (pp. 4–7). New York: Garland.

Ziemba, S. (1998, April 2). Braidwood's ex-top cop gets 21 years. *Chicago Tribune*.

6

The Looking-Glass World of Policing

The Ethics and Integrity of Women Police

Donna C. Hale

❖

INTRODUCTION

"Alice"[1] in Wonderland: Through the Looking Glass

On the front page of *Law Enforcement News (LEN)* ("Despite Some Gains," 2000), an article about the progress of women in police succeeded two others. The first of

---

[1]The proper name *Alice* in this subtitle refers to two Alices who entered bizarre worlds of adventure when they each respectively traveled to realms where they had not wandered before. Many things they observed had to be explained to them by the insiders of these foreign spheres, since both Alices were outsiders or strangers in these new worlds. The first Alice, created by Lewis Carroll in 1865, had two adventures: One in *Alice's Adventures in Wonderland* and in Carroll's sequel *Through the Looking-Glass* (1871). All who have read these stories, or have seen the Disney version of *Alice in Wonderland*, will agree that Alice truly experienced some phenomenal events when she entered these two worlds in her dreams.

Undoubtedly, the second Alice, Alice Stebbins Wells, also entered a world that was both foreign and hostile to women when she became the first woman to serve as a sworn policewoman in 1910 with the Los Angeles Police Department. Like the fictional Alice, Alice Stebbins Wells's experiences in an all-male society must have led her to wonder what type of land she had entered. How did the natives of her novel world explain their culture to her as an obvious intruder? Alice Stebbins Wells's story, unlike her fictional counterpart's narrative, was not a dream from which she would awaken at the end of her journey. Rather, Wells's undertaking symbolizes the first attempt of women to enter the looking-glass world of policing and as outsiders try to decipher the male culture of this adventure land.

143

the two preceding articles discussed the importance of geographic profiling for policing, and the second described the creative strategy of two police departments that traded
personnel as a way to exchange ideas on community policing techniques. I found it interesting reading that geographic profiling, which has been in use in police departments
for ten years, and community policing, implemented well over twenty years ago, are apparently both more successful innovations than the expansion of women as sworn police officers during the last three decades in the United States. As the third and last article reported some discouraging statistics from the National Center for Women and
Policing's recent 1999 report:

> There has been just a half-percent increase in the percentage of female sworn per-
> sonnel since 1998. Overall, the figure has risen just 5.3 percent since 1990, to account
> for 14.3 percent of officers nationwide. The number of women holding top ranking
> positions, the report said, is only 5.6 percent. ("Despite Some Gains," 2000: 1)

As Marion Gold (1999) writes in the preface to her book *Top Cops: Profiles of Women
in Command*, "unless attitudes and perceptions change both in the public arena and in
law enforcement agencies," (p. 9) the growth of women in police in the twenty-first century will not be significant.

However, the purpose of this chapter is not to explore the reasons why progress
has been so slow for women in policing. Rather, I begin with these disappointing statistics to suggest that because there are so few women in policing the small numbers may
actually influence policewomen's decisions regarding whether they should report or not
report any unethical practices they may witness while on or off duty. Since women are
still "breaking in"[2] to patrol as a career, they are often viewed by their male colleagues
as "outsiders" because patrol is considered a "man's job." Women may experience the
feeling of being "on the outside" because as women they are perceived by both the "ole
boys" and the "young turks" as not full members of the "club." The socialization of little boys and little girls regarding their roles in society still affects how men and women
handle life situations. The behaviors children learn on the playground carry over to the
workplace. Consequently, it should come as no surprise that women who enter any traditionally male occupation (whether white collar or blue collar) will encounter and endure many of the same experiences that women patrol officers do. Suffice it to say that
all of these women during their careers in nontraditional occupations have experienced—to some extent—skepticism, ostracism, and sexism.

Some may question why it is even necessary to examine how women police officers deal with any unethical situations they encounter in the workplace, if there are so
few of them. I believe it is important to consider this for several reasons. First, it provides the opportunity to examine how women describe the role and function of policing
in society in general. And more specifically, an examination of policewomen and ethics
provides insight regarding the attributes women believe they contribute to meet the role
and function of policing in society. For example, do they view policing as crime control,
crime prevention, or a combination of the two? How would they accomplish these roles
in the community? If their roles differ from men, how do they differ? And, if their roles
clash, how does this conflict affect levels of trust, compatibility, and performance?

---

[2]Both Susan Ehrlich Martin (1980) and Connie Fletcher (1995) use the terms *breaking and entering* in the ti-
tles of their books about the entry and experiences of women on patrol. The symbolism these terms brings to
mind is of women breaking down the barriers and entering the traditional male world of policing, i.e., patrol.
Women were breaking into an occupation that had been prohibited to them before 1972.

Another important reason to study women and integrity is to examine how they use discretion. Do their decision-making processes different from those of their male colleagues? And, if so, why? Do their limited numbers in police work affect the decisions they make? How do the attitudes of their male peers and the police department's orientation toward police work affect the judgment of the women officers?

Roles and decision making are directly related to the styles of service that women provide the public. Recent research by Susan Miller (1998: 164) describes how the styles of women police as peacemaker, negotiator, problem-solver, and cooperator are compatible with the tenets of community policing. Her research is an important addition to the typologies of police styles developed by scholars during the last thirty years to "explain how police officers perform their jobs and to explain differences between individual police officers when such differences exist" (Gaines et al., 1997: 231). Three police scholars, Gaines, Kappeler, and Vaughn (1997: 231), indicate that the typologies of Coates (1972), S. White (1972), Muir (1977), and Broderick (1987) "assist in understanding how the police interact with the community" (Gaines et al., 1997: 231–4).

Another area of the police occupational workplace that may provide insight on the impact of women police on police misbehavior is a study of the "working personality" of the female police officer. To my knowledge, the only studies to date have been on the "working personality" of the male police officer (Skolnick, 1966, in Walker, 1999: 326). For example, do policewomen handle danger and authority differently than male officers? A related topic to explore is the differences in cynicism levels of policewomen and policemen. Do women adapt differently than men do to police work? That is, are male and female police officers similar/different in the way they pass through their career stages from academy to retirement (see Barker, 1999)? How do policewomen adapt or "fit-in" to the police subculture where "the most important underlying characteristic of the police world is secrecy" (Doerner, 1998, 95)?

"NO GIRLS ALLOWED, GO HOME": THE BOYS' TREE HOUSE

When a pre-teenager, I went to my grandparents' home in the country with my brother, sister, and cousins to vacation for a couple of weeks every summer. Almost forty years later, I still remember how my brother and my cousin Charles built a tree house, and I was not allowed up. I remember climbing up, just to hear them say, "No Girls Allowed, Go Home." I climbed down because I did not want to go where I was not welcomed. I recall how belittled I felt, and perhaps I shared the "curious feeling" that Alice experienced in Wonderland after following the instructions on the little bottle to "Drink Me" (Carroll, 1960: 24) because I, too, shrank like a "telescope."

The humiliation I experienced that summer day perhaps parallels the experiences women confront when they, like Alice, also contemplate what the "looking-glass room" is like behind the ordinary "looking-glass" they see every day. If we use the "looking-glass room" as a metaphor to symbolize policing as an occupation restricted to a "room" inhabited only by men, and the ordinary "looking-glass" that hangs on the wall that women look into everyday as a metaphor for the occupations reserved for women only, we can understand how women who like Alice go through the "looking-glass" and discover that once they enter the "looking-glass room" of policing, and turn to look back through the mirror through which they came, they view their former occupations in the old room as "quite common and uninteresting" (Carroll, 1960: 131–2). Without a doubt, no one would disagree that women who penetrate the formerly restricted male professions of medicine, busi-

ness, law, engineering, and journalism, and the occupations referred to as "crafts" historically restricted to men (construction, mechanics, fire fighters, security, or policing) are
viewed as uncommon and unique by their male peers. In other words, many men still possess traditional views that women should remain on the other side of the looking-glass and
remain teachers, nurses, secretaries, or child-care or food service providers. Those women
who enter the looking-glass room and obtain nontraditional positions are considered as outsiders by the men who believe that women clearly do not have either the brains or the brawn
to do "men's work."

Indeed, until the early 1970s, few women dared to venture into any of the rooms reserved for men described previously. The few women who did encountered overt, covert,
and subtle discrimination and harassment (see Benokraitis & Feagin, 1994). It was not until 1972 with the expansion of Title VII of the 1964 Civil Rights Act by the Equal Opportunity Act that women had legal access to the looking-glass world of policing. Their positions were further protected by the Equal Opportunity Commission, which could take legal
action if women were found to be discriminated against on the basis of their sex (Gold,
1999: 23).

The historical research on women in policing supports that women have been viewed
as outsiders, especially since the early decades of the twentieth century in the United States
(Appier, 1998; Schulz, 1995). Sociologist Susan Ehrlich Martin's classic study, *Breaking
and Entering: Police Women on Patrol* (1980), was based on a "policewomen on patrol"
experiment conducted in the District of Columbia (1980: ix). Around the same time of Martin's study, another research project was underway by anthropologist Patricia Remmington
in the South. Her dissertation was published as *Policing, the Occupation and the Introduction of Female Officers: An Anthropologist's Study* (1981). Journalism professor Connie
Fletcher interviewed many of the women who entered police work during the 1970s and
1980s in her book *Breaking and Entering: Women Cops Break the Code of Silence to Tell
Their Stories from the Inside* (1995). The book organizes the women's narratives by letting
them tell their experiences in the police department from the academy to the station house
to the locker room as well as in the car. The accounts are saturated with details of the harassment and discrimination the women experienced in American police departments. The
chapters devoted specifically to the club and the code where one may expect to find more
explicit detail about corruption are steeped with anecdotes about sexual harassment and discrimination.

Autobiographies are another successful approach for policewomen to divulge first-
hand accounts regarding their ordeals in policing (Abrecht, 1976; Hays, 1992; Bristow,
1998). Chief Penny Harrington writes about her police career and how she broke through
the glass ceiling (1999) only to encounter more barriers. And, in the realm of popular culture, we have the riveting biography of Lawrencia Bembenek, *Run Bambi Run* (Radish,
1992), who was a former policewoman convicted in 1982 of first-degree murder for the
murder of her husband's ex-wife. Both the biography and the autobiography, *Woman on
Trial* (Bembenek, 1992), relate how Bembenek was "discriminated against and . . . posed a
threat to a number of corrupt officers" (Radish, 1992: 409). A quote from the back cover of
Bembenek's autobiography (1992) asked the reader to consider: "Was Lawrencia Bembenek fired then framed by the MPD [Milwaukee Police Department] because she reported
its blatant corruption to the state?"

In a myriad of publications, first-hand accounts describe the perils of women who decide to enter the looking-glass and become a police officer. But, why the resistance to women in policing? The policewomen in these first-hand accounts share personal insights on this phenomena through their own personal struggles in police work. And, a plethora of articles have been published since the mid-1970s when women entered policing as sworn patrol officers. Overall, topics researched about policewomen range from physical performance, attitudes of the public toward female police, and peers' opinions about the performance of female police officers (for a discussion of research on women in policing, see Hale, 1992; Hale & Bennett, 1995; Hale & Menniti, 1992; Hale & Wyland, 1993). Very little research describes how policewomen encounter and address police occupational deviance. The primary reason for this dearth of research regarding policewomen and ethics is the nature of the topic itself. It is equally difficult to research police deviance as either an outsider or an insider to the police organization (see Horn, 1997, for an excellent discussion of the dilemmas of women conducting research in police departments). The limitations of this research are discussed in the next section, where findings related to women and ethics are described.

MAJOR ISSUES: WHAT THE RESEARCH SHOWS ABOUT WOMEN AND ETHICS

Women and the Blue Code of Silence

> Women tend to see more in black and white instead of in all the shades of gray. That is a problem. It's a problem, yet it's one of our strengths. I think, that we're not able to do that. Men are far more forgiving of each other's weaknesses than we are. (quote from a policewoman in Fletcher, 1995, 228–9).

The greatest barrier to studying the impact of policewomen on ethics and integrity in policing is the secrecy that shrouds police misconduct (corruption and excessive use of force).[3] Both Goldstein (1975) and Stoddard (1968) describe the Blue Code of Silence, where officers are taught by their superiors and learn by experience not to "rat," "inform," or "tell" on others. The secrecy of the police is maintained by the code (Stoddard, 1968).

Generally, we find in most introductory and even advanced police college textbooks that the basic principles of the Blue Code of Silence are promulgated as the ones where a police officer does not "rat" and does not "tell"; it is an "us versus them" mentality. This dogma is perhaps the most difficult to present to students in the college classroom, to police recruits in the training academy, police officers on the street, and the police administrators and managers in the police department. Since the middle of the nineteenth century, the police creed of silence was both spoon-fed and passed on by the traditional police officers who indoctrinated each of the successive generations of "new" police with the tenets of the ancestral police code of silence. This culture of transition has continued from the

---

[3]In an earlier article that appeared in the *Quarterly Journal of Ideology*, I examined the extant literature on police corruption and excessive use of force and discussed them as subcategories of police misconduct (Hale, 1989).

nineteenth and twentieth centuries and continues into the twenty-first century. The pabulum of "don't talk, don't rat" has become the prattle, remains a remnant, and still is, unfortunately, the unofficial rhetoric of policing. Near the end of the twentieth century, police practitioner and scholar William Doerner (1998: 286) wrote that the "code of silence" is "one of the most highly valued unwritten rules among police officers . . . [where] . . . group solidarity and a sense of belonging in the form of an 'us against them' view of the world" (Doerner, 1998: 286) exists. And, he accentuates that "members of the police world cloister themselves from the view of outsiders" (Doerner, 1998: 286).

The contemporary low percentages of women in police work cited at the beginning of this chapter support that women are outsiders to policing. Although Alice Stebbins Wells entered policing as a sworn officer in 1910, her work, albeit in the police department as a sworn officer, primarily consisted of duties associated with the delivery of protective services for women and children (Appier, 1998; Schulz, 1995). Wells primarily sought the status of sworn officer because of the arrest power the position held. She believed that arrest power gave her the necessary clout to perform her job without relying on male officers to back her up and perform the arrests, if arrests were needed (for a detailed description of the early role of women in policing, see Appier, 1998; Schulz, 1995).

But, Alice Stebbins Wells and the other early policewomen were outsiders to the looking-glass world of policing in the early twentieth century because of the separate sphere that she and other early policewomen held in the police department. Appier (1998: 56) explains how the policewomen responded to the concerns that police chiefs' harbored regarding their encroachment into crime prevention—a function that the chiefs frequently acknowledged "during the 1910s and early 1920s" as the primary duty of the police department (p. 55). The chiefs believed the "stakes were simply too high" for policemen (p. 56):

> If preventing crime were indeed the primary duty of the police, and if women were indeed inherently better than men at crime prevention, then men would automatically be consigned to second-rate status within the police department. (p. 56)

The policewomen, understanding "the threat they posed to policemen" assuaged the chiefs' concerns by "repeatedly [stressing] that policewomen did not intend to take over any police function that policemen already ably performed" (p. 56). The experiences of these policewomen to justify their admission into the world of policing parallels Alice's to Wonderland. To be "the right size" to enter the little door into Wonderland's garden (Carroll, 1960, p. 24), Alice adhered to the written instructions stamped on the bottle: "Drink me." The Alices of early twentieth-century policing also obliged the police chiefs by assuring them that their work was not overstepping the function of policemen. And, not surprisingly, after both Alices humored the insiders' instructions to abide by the rules to enter Wonderland and Policeland, respectively, one can certainly identify with the Alices's utter astonishment and surprise when they had to follow even more written instructions attached to a small cake that stated: "Eat Me" just to retain the height necessary to obtain the key to open the door to Wonderland/Policeland. Alice's exclamation of "curiouser and curiouser" (Carroll, 1960: 20), when she realizes how large she grew after eating the small cake that would make her the size suitable to grasp the key from the table, represents the frustration that both she and policewomen encountered when attempting to accommodate the rules to enter territories previously off-limits to them.

Alice of Wonderland's recognition that her failure to claim the key before drinking the potion resulted in her overdue entry into Wonderland symbolizes the astonishment of the early policewomen when "the crime control model had eclipsed the crime prevention model and dominated U.S. municipal policing by the end of World War II" (Appier, 1998: 162). Appier recounts that "even though the crime prevention model never achieved dominance in police work, its existence, together with the appointment of women social workers to police departments, posed a threat to male hegemony in police work during the 1910s and 1920s" (1998: 162). According to Appier (1998), the triumph of the crime-control model succeeded in minimizing the numbers of women in policing. This transition effectively closed the door to women who wanted to be police officers, especially those who wanted to serve on patrol. Not until the affirmative action programs of the 1970s were women successful in "breaking and entering" the looking-glass room of police patrol (see S. E. Martin, 1991, in Doerner, 1998: 57).

It is important to reiterate that analogies from *Alice's Adventures in Wonderland* and *Through the Looking-Glass* (Carrol, 1960) parallel the entry of women in policing. No matter when women entered Policeland, or crossed over the frame of the looking-glass mirror, they have always adhered to the admission standards and the customs of their male superiors/counterparts. Therefore, it should come as no surprise that policewomen have contended with the code of silence in similar ways. The question remains regarding how women adapted to a code that was produced, practiced, and perpetuated by male police officers for well over 150 years in American police history. There is no doubt that policewomen have encountered the "don't rat/don't tell" adages from the beginning of their entry into the world of policing. Both historical and contemporary policewomen have learned first-hand, or even second- or third-hand, what the repercussions are if you "talk/rat" about police misconduct in any form (corruption, brutality, and sexual harassment). As one of Connie Fletcher's (1995; 225) policewomen said:

> The code *still* [emphasis in Fletcher] exists. Most definitely. The code comes from the fact that often with police officers—it's us against them. Nobody understands us. As police, we become very insular and distrustful. So the code is if somebody breaks that trust, it's not a good thing.

Another policewoman suggests that women balance the need to be ethical with the need to be accepted by members of the police culture. She remarked:

> The bottom line is everybody wants to be accepted. They want to be part of the family. And anything that threatens that acceptance, which means rocking the boat or confronting somebody on something that they've done, threatens the acceptance.

RESEARCH ON THE IMPACT OF POLICE WOMEN ON THE ORGANIZATIONAL CULTURE OF POLICING

The king in Lewis Carroll's Chapter 12, "Alice's Evidence," instructs the White Rabbitt to "Begin at the beginning, . . . and go on till you come to the end: then stop" (Carroll, 1960: 113). The king's advice serves well for a summation of the research regarding the impact of women on policing, especially since their entry into patrol work occurs after the application of Title VII beginning in the early 1970s (Gaines et al., 1997: 68).

First, Steven Ott's (1989) principles in *Organizational Culture* provide a model that may be used as an analytical tool to understand how events in American history affected the nature of the police business/work itself. His model illustrates how the founder's assumptions about the principles and functions of police work were instrumental in establishing the origins of the culture of American policing. Hale and Bennett (1995) apply this technique to explore the reasons why women have experienced such a slow entry into the world of policing.

Next, the qualitative research of Van Mannen (1978) describing the working personality of police officers, combined with anthropologist's Elizabeth Reuss-Ianni's (1983) discussion of the differences between street cops and management cops, along with Hale and Bennett's (1995) descriptive analysis of the organizational culture of police all present research that addresses how the organizational culture of policing perpetuates itself through group behavior rather than individual behavior. These studies support the assertion that over time a normative system of common beliefs and values develop that serve to provide stability and order for the members of the organization. These normative beliefs ultimately influence the behavior of the organizational members (Cartwright & Cooper, 1992).

Because of the "don't rat"/"don't talk" Blue Code of Silence, very little empirical research exists regarding whether women or men are as responsible, or not as responsible, for reporting unethical activities. One of the few studies that contains a thorough review of the research on policewomen and their attitudes regarding police misconduct is by Waugh et al. (1998), which is highly recommended to individuals who are interested in designing studies on police integrity. A few of the findings from the excellent literature review of Waugh et al. (1998: 289) are cited in the following discussion to present the most up-to-date research regarding police ethics and integrity.

Waugh et al. (1998) begin with a summary of the research by L. Miller and Braswell (1992), who concluded that "female officers gave significantly more ethical responses for both idealistic and realistic variables than did their male counterparts" (cited in Waugh et al., 1998: 289). Also included was a later study by C. Martin (1994), which found "female officers [as] more likely to report having observed unethical behaviour than their male counterparts, regardless of rank" (cited in Waugh et al., 1998: 289). A study the following year (Huon et.al., 1995), completed in Australia, described "females . . . to have higher personal ethical standards than male officers of equivalent rank . . . [and the women] . . . perceived themselves as having higher personal standards than both the typical officer and the instructor" (cited in Waugh et al., 1998: 289). However, a study by McConkey et al. (1996), modeled on an earlier study by Huon et al. (1995), did not "find any consistent gender differences" (cited in Waugh et al., 1998: 289).

Wilson and Braithewaite in Australia (1996) found female officers "were generally less coercive than male officers . . . and [the police women] preferred to use information exchange, support behavior and rejecting comments as opposed to control, threats and physical behavior" (cited in Waugh et al., 1998: 289). Wilson and Braithewaite's (1996) study also concluded that the citizens who interacted with the female police "displayed less verbal abuse and defensive behavior and participated more in the exchange of information" (cited in Waugh et al., 1998: 289). A 1997 Australian study by the Criminal Justice Commission reported that when comparing male and female police officers, policewomen who were either on or off duty "were much less likely to have complaints of assault made against them than were male officers" (cited in Waugh et al., 1998: 289).

Waugh et al., (1998) succinctly summarize their excellent literature review regarding gender differences between male and female police styles, behavior, and attitudes toward integrity and ethics as follows: policewomen "tend to see themselves as members of an 'outgroup' who are not part of the 'brotherhood' (1998: 290).

Overall, the study by Waugh et al., (1998: 295) showed: (1) "Female respondents did not show a greater propensity to report than male respondents" and (2) "Overall, very few officers of *either* gender at the rank of Constable and Senior Constable made complaints about other officers . . . and reporting rates for both male and female police officers remained consistently low over the period examined" (emphasis in original). The authors conclude that "reporting behaviour appears to be much more a function of rank than of gender" (1998: 295–6). And, third, women police officers "had a significantly lower proportion of misconduct complaints and breaches of discipline" (p. 296). Overall, the findings of Waugh et al., (1998: 298) "do not support the argument that female officers are inherently *more ethical*' in their outlook than their male counterparts" (emphasis in original). The authors indicate that the views of the police regarding ethics "appear to be shaped much more by occupational and organizational factors, especially, exposure to the police culture and task environment than by gender per se" (Waugh et al., 1998: 298).

However, Waugh et al. indicate that there are advantages to the utilization of women in policing. Their presence may result in diminished reports of use of force; women in community policing may improve the image of police overall; and community relations may be enhanced because of the more flexible, less violent style that women bring to policing (Waugh et al., 1998: 298).

In conclusion, Waugh et al., (1998: 298) remind us that in their study "the negative aspects of the police culture appear to have equal impact on males and females." The authors found:

> relatively small differences in attitudes between male and female police officers, the significant changes in how new officers judge the seriousness of various forms of misconduct and the marked differences, within a short time-frame, in the state willingness of both male and female recruits to report misconduct. (p. 298)

These authors' conclusions remind us that it is important to address the organizational culture of police to neutralize "the influence of the negative aspects of the culture on new officers" (Waugh et al., 1998: 299).

Another study by Lersch (1998: 71, 76) used data from the internal affairs office of a large police department in the Southeast to "explore for possible differences between male and female police officers accused of misconduct" (p. 76). The author concluded that:

> while women were less likely to be accused of misconduct, no significant difference was found in the type of complaint filed against male and female officers. Once an officer was accused of misconduct, both male and female officers were equally likely to be accused of misuse of force. Male and female officers named in citizen complaints did not differ significantly with respect to age, length of service, initiation circumstance, or citizen characteristics.

Lersch recommends that future research examine whether female police officers are judged "more harshly by the public when acting in an aggressive, proactive style" (p. 76). She poses the question that perhaps women are more critical of policewomen, and that women may believe that their complaints will be given more consideration by the internal affairs department because a woman filed the complaint (pp. 76–7). In conclusion, Lersch believes her findings support that more women police may improve police–community relations because "only 39 out of 682 allegations of misconduct accused a female officer of wrongdoing" (p. 78).

CONCLUSION

> "Tut, tut, child!" said the Duchess. "Everything's got a moral, if only you can find it." (Carroll, 1960: 86)

After examining the literature exploring the differences between male and female police, what can we conclude about the differences, if any, between male and female police officers regarding the ethics/integrity of policing? As the Duchess said to Alice, there is a moral, we just need to find it.

First, it is important to recall that Freud's "gender socialization theory" (Dawson, 1995: 61) contends that "gender identity, the core of personality, becomes established as early as age three through the mother–child relationship and is thereafter irreversible and unchanging (Dawson, 1995: 61). Sex differences are reinforced by the games that children learn both in the school yard and at home. Dawson (1995: 61) indicates that "[G]ender Socialization Theory predicts that as adults the sexes will bring different ethical values to their work roles, differentially shape shaping their work-related decisions."

R. D. White (1999: 4) provides a concise synopsis of Carol Gilligan's 1982 discourse *In A Different Voice: Psychological Theory and Women's Development*. He reports Gilligan's conclusion that women have a different conception of morality than men. Women, Gilligan maintains, have a morality of responsibility, whereby men have a morality of rights. Gilligan maintains that, because women affiliate with mothers and others, they are taught an ethics of care. On the other hand, men's individualism and separation from the feminine gives them an ethics of justice. Susan Miller (1998) discusses Gilligan's dichotomy in her comparative analysis of the characteristics that men and women bring to community policing. Miller believes that many of the nurturing and caring characteristics, the "ethics of care" that the early Alices practiced in American policing, are appropriate for community policing today.

Cartwright and Gale (1995, 13) suggest:

> that masculine cultures are likely to be dominated by power relationships and are results-oriented. Feminine cultures are likely to be more concerned with interpersonal relationships and be process-oriented.

Nifong (1996: 1) reports that with more women entering police "there is an emerging recognition that they bring a distinct style to policing, one that depends more on negotiation than machismo." She describes studies concluding that women rely more on verbal skills and less on physical strength. Policewomen are less confrontational when responding to calls and use physical force only if necessary (Nifong, 1996: 1). Women in policing utilize defusing skills rather than force to quell violence. As the former police chief of both Austin and Houston, Texas, Elizabeth Watson confirmed, "Women as a rule tend to be more collaborative" (quoted in Nifong, 1996: 2). And, Chief Beverly Harvard of the Atlanta Police Department stresses that she "will not tolerate police corruption or participate in a code of silence (Gregory, 1996: 1). Penny Harrington, the former police chief of Portland, Oregon, and presently the Director of the National Center for Women and Policing, was described by a ten-year veteran of the Portland Police Department as "ethical to a fault…With her, if it's right, it's right—regardless of the political consequences. That's why she became a chief, and that's why she failed. She never learned how to sell out" (Harrington, 1999: 20).

To conclude, it is important to emphasize the importance of continued research related to the different styles that men and women bring to policing. In the past several years, the media has covered truly sensational cases of police brutality, with the 1999 Diallo case in New York City and the 2000 Rampart Division corruption case in Los Angeles. The continued expansion of community policing programs also provides researchers the opportunity to study the differences in policing styles of both men and women. The groundbreaking research of Susan Miller (1998), who investigated the styles that women bring to community policing, is a primary example of a situation where Carol Gilligan's (1982) gender socialization thesis can be applied to examine the different styles/techniques that women and men may contribute to the police organizational culture.

Finally, it is important to disseminate the findings of workplace ethics research described in this text—the morals so to speak—into the college classroom, the training academy, and in-service training for police officers. Students, rookies, seasoned officers, and police managers and administrators all need a familiarity with the tenets of the organizational culture of policing. An understanding of the history of policing and the fundamental beliefs that were established early in American policing regarding ethics and integrity will provide a comprehensive understanding of why the Blue Code of Silence has existed for far too long.

As the Duchess said to Alice: "Everything's got a moral, if only you can find it."

REFERENCES

ABRECHT, M. E. WITH STERN, B. L. (1976). *The Making of a Woman Cop*. New York: William Morrow.

APPIER, J. (1998). *Policing Women: The Sexual Politics of Law Enforcement and the LAPD*. Philadelphia: Temple University Press.

BARKER, J. C. (1999). *Danger, Duty, and Disillusion: The Worldview of Los Angeles Police Officers*. Prospect Heights, Ill.: Waveland Press.

BEMBENEK, L. (1992). *Woman on Trial*. New York: HarperPaperbacks.

BENOKRAITIS, N. V., & FEAGIN, J. R.. (1994). *Modern Sexism: Blatant, Subtle, and Covert Discrimination*. Upper Saddle River, N.J.: Prentice Hall.

BRISTOW, C. (1998). *Central 822*. London: Bantam Books.

BRODERICK, J. (1987). *Police in Time of Change*. Prospect Heights, Ill.: Waveland Press.

CARROLL, L. (1960). *Alice's Adventures in Wonderland* and *Through the Looking-Glass*. New York: Signet Classic. (Originally published in 1865, 1871.)

CARTWRIGHT, S., & COOPER, C. L. (1992). *Mergers & Acquisitions: The Human Factor*. Oxford: Butterworth & Heinemann.

CARTWRIGHT, S., & GALE, A. (1995). Project management: Different gender, different culture? A discussion on gender and organizational culture, part 2. *Leadership & Organization Development Journal* 16 (4): 12–16.

COATES, R. (1972). The dimensions of police–citizen interaction: A social psychological analysis. Doctoral dissertation. University of Maryland.

CRIMINAL JUSTICE COMMISSION. (1997). *Reducing Police–Civilian Conflict: An Analysis of Assault Complaints Against Queensland Police*. Brisbane, Australia: Criminal Justice Commission.

DAWSON, L. M. (1995). Women and men, morality and ethics. *Business Horizons* 38 (4): 61–8.

Despite some gains, female cops still find too few cracks in the glass ceiling. (2000). *Law Enforcement News* 26 (535): 1.

DISNEY, W. *Alice in Wonderland* [film]. Los Angeles: Disney Enterprises, Inc.

DOERNER, W. G. (1998). *Introduction to Law Enforcement: An Insider's View*. Woburn, Mass.: Butterworth-Heinemann.

FLETCHER, C. (1995). *Breaking and Entering: Women Cops Break the Code of Silence to Tell Their Stories from the Inside*. New York: Pocket Books.

GAINES, L. K., KAPPELER, V. E., & VAUGHN, J. B. (1997). *Policing in America*. 2d ed. Cincinnati, Ohio: Anderson Publishing.

GILLIGAN, C. (1982). *In a Different Voice: Psychological Theory and Women's Development*. Cambridge, Mass.: Harvard University Press.

GOLD, M. E. (1999). *Top Cops: Profiles of Women in Command*. Chicago: Brittany Publications.

GOLDSTEIN, H. (1975). *Police Corruption: A Perspective on Its Nature and Control*. Washington, D.C.: The Police Foundation.

GREGORY, D. (1996). Beverly Harvard. *Essence* 26 (11): 56.

HALE, D. C. (1989). Ideology of police misbehavior: Analysis and recommendations. *Quarterly Journal of Ideology* 13 (2): 59–87.

HALE, D. C. (1992). Women in policing. In Cordner, G. W., & Hale, D. C., eds. *What Works in Policing?* (pp. 125–42). Cincinnati, Ohio: Anderson Publishing.

HALE, D. C., & BENNETT, C. L. (1995). Realities of women in policing: An organizational cultural perspective. In Merlo, A., & Pollock, J. M., eds., *Women, Law and Social Control* (pp. 41–54). Boston: Allyn & Bacon.

HALE, D. C., & MENNITI, D. J. (1992). Discrimination and harassment litigation of women in policing. In Muraskin, R., ed., *Women and Justice: A Critical Issue* (pp. 177–89). Englewood Cliffs, N.J.: Prentice Hall.

HALE, D. C., & WYLAND, S. M. (1993). Dragons and dinosaurs: The plight of patrol women. *Police Forum* 3 (2): 1–6.

HARRINGTON, P. E. (1999). *Triumph of Spirit: An Autobiography by Chief Penny Harrington*. Chicago: Brittany Publications.

HAYS, G., WITH MOLONEY, K. (1992). *Policewoman One: My Twenty Years on the LAPD*. New York: Villard Books.

HORN, R. (1997). Not one of the boys: Women researching the police. *Journal of Gender Studies* 6 (3): 297–308.

HUON, G., HESKETH, B., FRANK, M., McCONKEY, K., & McGRATH, G. (1995). Perspectives on ethical dilemmas: Ethics and policing—Study 1. Payneham, South Australia: National Police Research Unit.

LERSCH, K. M. (1998). Exploring gender differences in citizen allegations of misconduct: An analysis of a municipal police department. *Women & Criminal Justice* 9 (4): 69–79.

MARTIN, C. (1994). *Illinois Municipal Officers' Perceptions of Police Ethics*. Statistical Analysis Center, Illinois Criminal Justice Information Authority, Chicago, Ill.

MARTIN, S. E. (1980). *Breaking and Entering: Police Women on Patrol*. Berkeley: University of California Press.

MARTIN, S. E. (1991). The effectiveness of affirmative action: The case of women in policing. *Justice Quarterly* 8 (4): 489–504.

McCONKEY, K., HUON, G., & FRANK, M. (1996). *Practical Ethics in the Police Service. Ethics and Policing—Study 3*. Payneham, South Australia: National Police Research Unit.

MILLER, L., & BRASWELL, M. (1992). Police perceptions of ethical decision-making: The ideal vs. the real. *American Journal of Police* 11 (4): 27–43.

MILLER, S. L. (1998). Rocking the rank and file: Gender issues and community policing. *Journal of Contemporary Criminal Justice* 14 (2): 156–72.

MUIR, W. (1977). *Police: Streetcorner Politicians*. Chicago, Ill.: University of Chicago Press.

NIFONG, C. (1996). Gender revolution in precinct house. *Christian Science Monitor* 88 (124): 1.

OTT, J. S. (1989). *The Organizational Culture Perspective*. Pacific Grove, Calif.: Brooks/Cole Publishing.

RADISH, K. (1992). *Run, Bambi, Run*. New York: Penguin Books.

REMMINGTON, P. W. (1981). *Policing, the Occupation and the Introduction of Female Officers: An Anthropologist's Study*. Washington, D.C.: University Press of America.

REUSS-IANNI, E. (1983). *Two Cultures of Policing*. New Brunswick, N.J.: Transaction Books.

SCHULZ, D. M. (1995). *From Social Worker to Crimefighter: Women in United States Municipal Policing*. Westport, Conn: Praeger.

SKOLNICK, J. (1966). *Justice Without Trial: Law Enforcement in a Democratic Society*. New York: John Wiley & Sons.

STODDARD, E. (1968). The informal code of police deviancy: A group approach to blue-collar crime. *Journal of Criminal Law, Criminology and Police Science* 59 (2): 201–13.

VAN MAANEN, J. (1978). On becoming a policeman. In Manning, P., & Van Maanen, J., eds., *Policing: A View from the Street*. Santa Monica, Calif.: Goodyear.

WALKER, S. (1999). *The Police in America: An Introduction*. 3d ed. Boston: McGraw-Hill College.

WAUGH, L., EDE, A., & ALLEY, A. (1998). Police culture, women police and attitudes towards misconduct. *International Journal of Police Science and Management* 1 (3): 288–300.

WHITE, R. D. JR. (1999). Are women more ethical? Recent findings on the effects of gender upon moral development. *Journal of Public Administration Research and Theory* 9 (3): 459–71.

WHITE, S. (1972). A perspective on police professionalization. *Law and Society Review* 7 (1): 61–85.

WILSON, C., & BRAITHEWAITE, H. (1996). *Police Officer Behaviour During Interactions with Citizens: What Distinguishes the "Skilled" from the "Average" Officer? Risk Management—Study 3*. Payneham, South Australia: National Police Research Unit.

7

Drug Abuse, Corruption, and Officer Drug Testing

An Overview

Tom Mieczkowski

❖

INTRODUCTION

When the drug testing of police officers is raised as an issue, it can be considered as an extension of the issues related to drug testing of employees in general. To some degree, the generalized controversies surrounding employee testing apply to police. What is distinctive, however, about drug testing of police officers is that citizens do not generally perceive them as having ordinary standards or expectations associated with their work. Although their pay scale does not generally reflect it, police officers in carrying out their duties are almost invariably held to relatively high performance, ethical, and moral standards. In some ways, the standard is comparable to those applied to the legal, medical, and similar professional occupations. Many have made this observation, and it has been often noted that "the standard of conduct to which police officers must adhere is on a higher level than that expected of the average citizen" (O. W. Wilson quoted by Carter & Stephens, 1988). Furthermore, this principle—of a higher standard of conduct and expectations—consistently has been upheld in courts and arbitration. For example, officers who have been fired for conduct that, while not overtly illegal, is considered by their superiors to be inconsistent with the competency and fitness associated with police work have not succeeded when challenging their dismissals in court. The courts have consistently supported the concept that police officers can be held to a higher standard of conduct than the ordinary citizen (e.g., see *Thompson* v. *City of Appleton*, 1985).

Several general rationales are associated with drug testing of police officers. Some are general (i.e., apply to all employment situations, police and nonpolice), and some are specific to the police role. The general conditions associated with drug testing that apply in virtually all employment circumstances are workplace safety, workplace morale, productivity, and employer liability. Specific issues that are related to police drug testing encompass these general concerns but also include other specific issues or have a special sense of urgency when associated with policing. Since drug use is relatively widespread socially, it is expected that police will reflect to some degree the general societal patterns. Thus, one would expect some drug use by police officers. Likewise, if workers in general are impaired by drug use, then so are police officers impaired from functioning effectively and efficiently. However, as we noted, the police are perceived of as more than "workers." In considering drug testing as it applies within criminal justice, Kraska and Kappeler (1988) identify four critical factors of drug use unique to police:

1. Illegal drug by police use is seen as hypocritical and damages public confidence in the competence and quality of police services.
2. Illegal drug use by police is potentially corrupting.
3. Because they have a mandate to use violence and must exercise critical judgments under duress, the effects of drugs on police officers are even more dangerous and are of greater social concern than they would be in ordinary workplace settings.
4. Police drug use raises public safety and hazard issues, including the use of firearms, police pursuit, and interdiction and arrest of fleeing suspects.

This chapter focuses on drug testing and its application in policing and its implications for police management and administration. This chapter looks at the rationales for drug testing, the scope and types of drug testing currently associated with police administration, the technologies currently used and their advantages and limitations, and the law and legal aspects of drug testing.

DRUG TESTING AND CORRUPTION: AN OVERVIEW

Drug Testing of Workers

Many private companies test applicants for drug use at hiring or application. A substantial number also test employees on other grounds, such as a "reasonable suspicion" basis, postaccident, or even in some cases on a random basis. The motivation for this action is based on the general perception that drug use has risen among workers and is a serious problem in business operations and management. Drug testing is perceived to have a general deterrent effect on drug use in the workplace. Since the early to mid-1980s, when drug analysis technology became relatively less costly due to the development of immunoassay technology, the overall trend in self-reported workplace use of drugs has decreased and appears stabilized. Figure 7–1 shows the long-term self-reported drug use for both "current" use and use within the last year.

The basis upon which drug testing is premised in the workplace in the most general terms is that workers are likely to be more productive—and to present fewer problems to

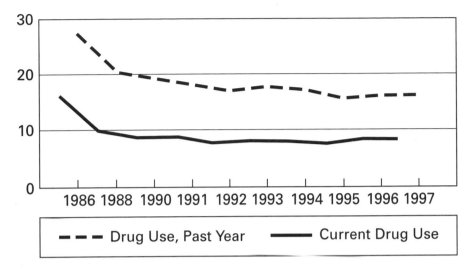

FIGURE 7–1

Trends in Percentage of Employed Persons Ages 18–49 Reporting Drug Use, 1985–97.
Source: Substance Abuse and Mental Health Services Administration, 1999.

management—if they are drug abstinent. One of the most popularly cited studies in this regard is the large-scale assessment of the costs of drugged workers done by the U.S. Postal System in 1990 (Normand et al., 1990). This study concluded, for example, that in excess of $100,000,000 would be saved on a per annum basis if drug screening was implemented, primarily due to savings in leave time, termination procedures, and overtime costs. Table 7–1 provides some estimates based on the National Household Survey on Drug Abuse (NHSDA) report of adverse employment behaviors comparing self-reported current illicit drug users and nonusers. Generally, actions considered problematic by management are reported at higher rates by persons who also self-report current drug use. Table 7–1 indicates that employee turnover, workdays skipped, quitting, and being fired are all significantly higher in drug users (Substance Abuse and Mental Health Services Administration, 1999).

When one considers the content of the police role, the impact and negative consequences of drug use go beyond the list of generalized administrative and management issues delineated in Table 7–1. The police have specific ethical standards and expectations that are unique to their work. They have unique access and exposure to drugs and drug markets, they must be prepared to exercise their authority under extreme stress, and they are authorized to use physical and even deadly force in interacting with citizens under specified circumstances. So, all these issues add urgency to the list of what might be called more mundane aspects of organizational problems such as absenteeism, turnover rates, and so on. Additionally, an important aspect of policing relationship is the concern with police corruption.

Drug corruption and drug-related corruption are other considerations that add importance to the role of drug testing in identifying, controlling, and suppressing police corruption related to drug crime. In considering this, one can subdivide drug corruption into two broad categories, modifying and adapting a conceptual approach suggested by Carter

TABLE 7–1.   Percentage of Full-Time Workers, Age 18–49, Reporting Various Workplace Outcomes by Current Illicit Drug Use, 1994 and 1997.

| | Current Illicit Drug Use | | | |
| | Yes | | No | |
Workplace Outcome	1994	1997	1994	1997
Worked for 3 or > employers in the last year?	8.9	9.3	4.0*	4.3*
Missed 2 or > days of work in the last month due to illness or injury?	10.9	12.8	9.1	8.5
Skipped 1 or > days of work in the last month?	12.1	12.9	6.0*	5.0*
Quit a job in the past year?	25.8	24.8	13.6*	15.4*
Fired in the past year?	4.6	2.3	1.4**	1.2
Had a workplace accident in the past year?	7.7	5.1	5.6	5.5

$*p = .01.$
$**p = .05.$
Source: Office of Applied Studies, 1999.

(1990b). One type of corruption is labeled "traditional." Traditional corruption primarily focuses on the police officer's illegal utilization of authority combined with structural opportunities afforded to the officer by work circumstances. The traditional motivation is the police officer's personal gain and is historically characterized by taking bribes—either money, goods and services or receiving some other commodity valued by the officer. This type of corruption is probably most widely recognized as the "Serpico" form, with active officers taking and managing a bribery system ("meat eaters" in the Knapp Commission's terms), and a larger number of passive officers accepting relatively small bribes to ignore, and in small ways facilitate the system (the Knapp Commission's "grass eaters"). The Knapp Commission in New York described this form in its investigative report in 1973 following the allegations of corruption by police officer Frank Serpico. In the Knapp Commission model of corruption, the "meat eaters"—aggressive police officers acting as the active corruption principles—are relatively small in number. A large group of semiparticipating officers (the "grass eaters") are aware of the illegal activity, but ignore it and do not consider reporting or "ratting out" their colleagues, usually in exchange for a relatively small reward. The passive officer may also choose to simply ignore the illegal conduct as a result of the "Blue Curtain," code of silence, about fellow officers (Knapp Commission, 1973; Roberg et al., 2000).

Active corruption can take many forms. Officers may seize cash, contraband, or goods of value for themselves. They may ignore criminality if bribed to ignore it. Officers may seek to extort money from persons observed to be engaged in illegal behavior and actively pursue this goal by apprehending citizens and extorting cash or goods (including drugs) under the threat of arrest and prosecution. Indeed, officers may even threaten to amplify or entirely falsify illegal behavior if citizens refuse to meet their demands. The "Miami River Cops" scandal, which involved over eighty police officers in Dade County, Florida, included charges of murder, robbery, and extortion filed and successfully prosecuted against police. In the Miami case, these behaviors were carried out in the context of drug crime, but they can also be associated with other forms of crime, such as alcohol, prostitution, or gambling and gaming. The critical feature is that the criminal activity involves buying, selling, and controlling illegal commodities or services of value for which there is a social demand and market.

Drug crime, however, may lend itself rather readily to this "traditional" corruption for a number of reasons. Since the importation and distribution of drugs follow a market/demand imperative they generate large volumes of cash in an undocumented economy. Thus, drug crime presents officers with opportunities that may be especially tempting. Purloining a warehouse full of tires, or a truck full of stolen auto parts is considerably more difficult than simply picking up a valise containing several hundred thousand dollars in cash. Indeed, since drugs are ipso facto contraband, there is no "rightful owner," which may make the temptation and rationalization of stealing "drug money" more facile (Dombrink, 1988). Drug enforcement is a fertile ground for officers setting out to enrich themselves. Drug testing is unlikely to impact this behavior, at least in any direct fashion, since it does not involve the officers' using drugs. However, if officers are involved in drug use, it represents a very potent and dangerous situation for the evolution of corruption. Furthermore, research has consistently shown that officers involved in drug use are at higher risk for corrupt behavior than nondrug involved officers.

Police Corruption and Police Drug Use

The policeman never rubs off on the street; the street rubs off on the policeman.[1]

Researchers have identified several dangers for corruption involving police officer drug use. One is that officers who are "recreational" drug users are at risk for entering what Carter (1990a) identified as a "user-driven cycle" of corrupt behavior. It usually begins when a drug-using officer ceases to buy drugs from suppliers and instead confiscates drugs, either from dealers whom he or she apprehends or from the evidence locker or storage areas where seized drugs are held. As Carter has pointed out, officers virtually universally describe how easy it is to seize drugs with a minimum of personal risk. The motivation is straightforward. First, stolen drugs are cost-free to the officer. Second, officers who attempt to buy drugs in the "regular retail drug market" run the risk of identification and possible blackmail, so it is often functionally safer for them to seize drugs encountered during arrests and keep them for their personal use rather than buying them. Carter believed that the pressure for drug-using officers to move toward this technique was inexorable:

> From officer interviews and inferences that can be drawn from depositions or statements, it
> appears that the progression from use to corruption is an evolutionary process, eventually af-

[1]Robert Leuci (1982), quoted by Marx (1988: 159). Leuci was the police officer on whom the novel and movie *Prince of the City* was based.

fecting most drug-abusing officers to some degree. . . . Most typical, the corruption involves the confiscation of drugs for personal use. (1990a: 89)

Furthermore, Carter observed that many of these officers engaged in a series of articulated rationales for their behavior, denying in effect that it was corrupt behavior. Often, they see their seizure of drugs from street dealers as accomplishing the intent of the law ("getting drugs off the street").[2] Officers also characterized this behavior as "not being theft" (since the drugs are contraband, they cannot be legally "owned" like property) and as not being corrupt behavior (since no cash was exchanged between the citizen and the officer).

Furthermore, this process is probably most common among those officers specifically assigned to narcotics enforcement, especially those who operate in plainclothes or undercover modes. Girodo (1991: 361) in his evaluation of police undercover officers noted that "although drug use is forbidden for police, it is not uncommon among undercover investigators." Girodo observed that undercover officers are always challenged by drug dealers who offer drugs under the belief that police officers will not and legally cannot consume drugs unless facing a life-threatening situation. Girodo notes that "In response, some police intent on making a case, and with knowledge that they may be tested this way, dispense with an attempted dissimulation, and pre-empt the target's tactic and gain credibility by being the one's [sic] to initiate and use drugs" (p. 362). In his assessment of 271 federal sworn law enforcement personnel, Girodo found that of the officers in his study, undercover officers had high levels of neuroticism and low levels of impulse control. He concluded that his findings add to "the accumulating evidence connecting social-role problems, adverse psychological health, behavioral maladjustment, and job dissatisfaction to accumulated undercover assignments" (p. 368). This is of critical concern because undercover assignments are very commonly utilized in narcotics enforcement operations.

Generally, it has long been recognized that a number of psychological risks are linked with undercover work. As Gary Marx (1988) noted, long-term undercover assignments are associated with high potential for erosion of the undercover officer's values and standards that differentiate legal and illegal behavior. Furthermore, prolonged undercover work is associated with increasing feelings of comradeship and sympathy for the criminal elements under investigation. Farkas (1986), for example, has argued that corruption in undercover narcotics work is linked to the development of "friendship and loyalty" to the investigated criminal group and is characterized by "actual criminal activity" while working undercover. Marx, for example, cites police graffiti he observed in a precinct station locker room:

"To Bust a Doper Be a Smoker"

Marx describes the various stresses that are a part of undercover police operations and their dangers. Among them are the corrosive effects of such assignments on the individual officers, including in some cases, a collapse of the officers' ethical and psychological barriers to engaging in the very behavior they are charged with preventing. As Marx notes, one officer in a joking manner told him, "we're here to enforce the law, not obey it."

---

[2]This phenomenon was identified by Crank and Caldero (1999) as "noble-cause corruption."

Although little has been researched and almost nothing is empirically known about the extent of police drug use, it cannot be assumed that it is insignificant. Even drug use on the job itself is a possibility that must be considered when evaluating the corrupting influences of drug use on police performance. A 1988 study on police on-duty drug use (Kraska & Kappeler, 1988) described the degree of on-duty drug use in a small police department and the rationales and attitudes of officers engaged in this conduct. Police administrators and citizens would generally concede that this form of use, actual consumption of drugs while on duty (as contrasted with off-duty drug use) is one of the most frightening and dangerous form of police drug behavior. Kraska and Kappeler noted that the topic of on-duty drug use, like police drug use in general, has received little attention and almost no empirical study, commenting that "virtually no research has been conducted in this area." Their study examined four areas focal areas: societal and occupational drug use, seriousness of police drug use, and objective and subjective aspects of particular police vulnerability to drug use. They also noted that since drug use is relatively widespread, police would likely reflect the general societal patterns of drug behavior.

Furthermore, Kraska and Kappeler argued that police have a "special vulnerability" to drug use not normally experienced by other occupations. These are objective structural issues related to work (opportunity structure, organizational structure) and unique subjective structural elements associated with the police subculture. The opportunity structure has three aspects: duration and intensity of exposure to drug using social elements, a police officer's relative freedom from supervision, and illicit drug availability to police through arrest and seizure of drugs from citizens. Additionally, there are two stress-related and bureaucratic structural elements to consider. Police officers frequently experience a high level of stress that is considered intrinsic to the police role. Drug use can be a coping response to stress and represents an extension of the elevated alcohol-consuming patterns of police officers as a group.

Systematic and Pervasive Corruption

Once drugs enter the environment of the policing role, corruption is highly likely to emerge as a significant problem. The corruption effects the individual officer as well as having unique systematic effects on policing conduct and organizational conduct. In May of 1998, the General Accounting Office (GAO) prepared a report on drug-related police corruption for Charles Rangel, member of the House of Representatives from New York. This document, entitled *Report to the Honorable Charles B. Rangel, House of Representatives, Law Enforcement Information on Drug-Related Police Corruption, Report of the GAO (GAO/GGD-98-11) to the House of Representatives* (1998) was a comprehensive examination of police drug corruption. (It will be referred to as the "Rangel Report" in this chapter.)

The Rangel Report stated that there was not a central source that would allow a reliable estimate of the extent of police corruption or of how much corruption is drug-related. However, a series of appendices to the report lists cases of drug corruption enforcement actions for several major cities detailing the scope of arrests and identifying the basic crime elements involved in the actions. Furthermore, the report lists in Appendix II a report of corruption investigations led by the Federal Bureau of Investigation (FBI) and convictions for drug-related corruption. These are summarized in Figure 7–2.

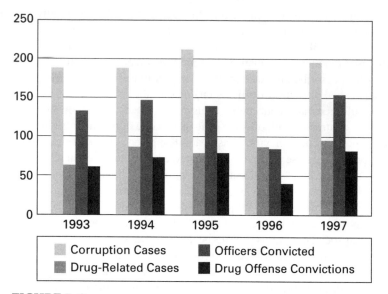

FIGURE 7–2
Total Corruption Cases and Drug-Related Corruption Cases of FBI-Led Investigations,
1993–7. *Source*: FBI Public Corruption Unit, FBI, 1998.

In characterizing drug corruption among police agencies, the GAO report stated that:

> According to a number of commission reports, academic publications, and other literature
> we reviewed and the officials and academic experts we interviewed, drug-related police cor-
> ruption differs in a variety of ways from other types of police corruption. In addition to pro-
> tecting criminals or ignoring their activities, officers involved in drug-related corruption were
> more likely to be actively involved in the commission of a variety of crimes, including steal-
> ing drugs and/or money from drug dealers, selling drugs, and lying under oath about illegal
> searches. Although profit was found to be a motive common to traditional and drug-related
> police corruption, New York City's Mollen Commission identified power and vigilante jus-
> tice as two additional motives for drug-related police corruption. The most commonly identi-
> fied pattern of drug-related police corruption involved small groups of officers who protected
> and assisted each other in criminal activities, rather than the traditional patterns of non-drug-
> related police corruption that involved just a few isolated individuals or systemic corruption
> pervading an entire police department or precinct. (*Report to the Honorable Charles B.
> Rangel, 1998: 3*)

Furthermore, the Rangel Report identifies several key aspects of drug-related police corruption and finds the mix of drug use, drugs in the environment, and the traditional norms
of police subcultural identity to be a potent combination that can exacerbate "traditional
corruption" and transform it to a unique administrative problem.

> A number of the commission reports, academic publications, and other literature we re-
> viewed and the officials and academic experts we interviewed described differences between

the nature of drug-related police corruption and the nature of other types of police corruption, however, opportunities for financial gain were a key factor in both forms of corruption. Unlike other types of corruption, officers involved in drug-related corruption were found to be actively committing crimes, not just passively ignoring them or protecting criminals. These crimes ranged from stealing drugs and money from drug dealers to lying under oath about illegal searches. Usually these activities were carried out by small groups of officers, rather than by lone individuals. Moreover, drug-related police corruption was not found to be a systemic problem that infected entire departments or precincts. Traditional police corruption usually involved a mutually beneficial arrangement between criminals and police officers (e.g., the former offered the latter bribes in exchange for immunity from arrest). In contrast, several studies and investigations of drug-related police corruption found on-duty officers engaged in serious criminal activities, such as (1) conducting unconstitutional searches and seizures; (2) stealing money and/or drugs from drug dealers; (3) selling stolen drugs; (4) protecting drug operations; (5) providing false testimony; and (6) submitting false crime reports. (*Report*, 1998: 7)

The relationship between police culture and police corruption, including drug-related police corruption, was a recurring theme articulated by our various sources. They generally concurred that although police culture may be positive (i.e., supportive of integrity), a negative culture (i.e., one that supported or generally ignored corruption) was a key factor associated with drug-related police corruption. Among the attitudes and values identified as characteristics of a police culture that supported corruption were the following: (1) a code of silence with grave consequences for those violating it; (2) loyalty to other officers above all else; (3) police cynicism or disillusionment about their jobs, the criminal justice system, and public support for those who performed properly; and (4) indoctrination on the job as to what is acceptable behavior—for example, ignoring corruption. (*Report*, 1998: 17)

There appears to be only one published study that reports both quantitative and qualitative data on police on-duty drug use. Kraska and Kappeler (1988) reported data on a police department defined as "small to medium size" (employing about 50 sworn officers) in a southern city. They were "hired as officers" for other than research purposes and report their drug data as a "serendipitous finding" of drug use on the job by fellow officers. The data are derived from forty-nine unstructured interviews, official records, and participant observation. "On-duty drug use" is defined as drug use twice or more while on duty within the last thirty days before the interview. They reported that 20 percent of the officers reported using marijuana on duty and 10 percent used other drugs, consisting of illicit hallucinogens, barbiturates, or stimulants. Twenty-eight percent of the on-duty marijuana users were relatively young officers (21–30 years old), 27 percent were "older" officers (31–38 years old). All the officers had at least 4 years of experience with the department. Nine of the 49 reported using marijuana both on and off duty, 10 reported using off duty but did not use on-duty, 1 interestingly reported using on-duty but not off-duty, and 29 reported no marijuana use on or off duty.

Kraska and Kappeler (1988) identified three types of police subcultural patterns: traditional, apathetic, and deviant. The traditional subculture (characterized as consisting of "conventional ideals of moral and ethical policing") can provide a check *against* drug use, since it sensitizes police officers to the moral and normative violations that drug use entails in the traditional perception of the police role.

The apathetic subculture is indifferent to traditional ideals and can protect or ignore drug use by individual officers. The apathetic subculture encourages individuation of conduct and discourages the emergence of group standards. It also encourages tolerance of a wide range of deviant behaviors and tends to see problems associated with deviant action as problems of detection and embarrassment. For example, drug use would not necessarily be seen as intrinsically wrong conduct by a police officer. As long as the officer disguised the drug use so that it did not become public knowledge or cause gross failures in carrying out responsibilities to other officers, it would likely be tolerated. In the literature on police drinking, tolerance for on-the-job drinking has been studied to some degree. (Reiss, 1971, for example, estimated that 3 to 18 percent of officers drank on the job, and Barker and Carter, 1986, reported an estimate of about 8 percent who drank on the job.) Apathetic or laissez-faire attitudes toward police drinking were reported as a component of the drinking/working nexus. Kraska and Kappeler noted that while the percentage of officers who test positive for drugs is "very low," this figure is based upon testing of officers who mostly receive prior warning regarding the scheduling of their drug test.

Deviant police subcultures include apathy toward ideal values but are further demarcated from the traditional view by a marked decline in traditional ideals and substitution of criminal rationalizations. This orientation not only can sustain but also can actively encourage illegal drug use or participation in drug-related criminal activity.

THE EXTENT OF WORKPLACE DRUG USE AND DRUG TESTING

An Overview

Drug testing in the workplace is becoming increasingly commonplace. Concomitant with this development, employers are increasing their sophistication in managing and responding to drug use in the workplace. Workplaces are much more likely now to have articulated policies about drug use, to spell out the specific consequences of drug use, and to offer specific procedural and substantive responses to worker drug abuse. As noted by the U.S. Government in a recent federal publication:

> About three-fourths of the full-time workers, age 18–49, reported that their workplaces provided information about drug and or alcohol use . . . about 70% reported that their workplaces had a written policy concerning drug or alcohol use . . . and about one-half of fulltime workers reported that their workplaces provided access to an Employee Assistance Program (EAP) on drug and alcohol abuse problems (Office of Applied Studies, 1999: 33)

Figure 7–3 provides an indication of the scope of drug-testing activity in the workplace, the circumstances and conditions under which testing takes place, and a comparison of these changes from 1994 and 1997 (Office of Applied Studies, 1999).

Figure 7–3 shows that the percentage of workplaces that drug test employees has risen overall, and this rise has occurred in all testing circumstance categories. The Office of Applied Studies at the Substance Abuse and Mental Health Services Administration (SAMHSA) (1999) estimates that 70 percent of all current users of illicit substances are employed full-time. This translates in 1997 figures to about 7.7 percent of full-time workers reporting current illicit drug use (defined as use within the past thirty days). This means in actual numbers that approximately 6.3 million full-time workers currently use illicit drugs,

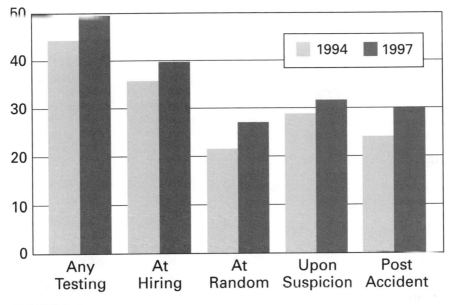

FIGURE 7–3
Percentage of Full-time Workers, Age 18–49, Reporting Workplace Drug-Testing Programs, 1994 and 1997. *Source*: Office of Applied Studies, 1999.

about 6.2 million are currently heavy users of alcohol, and about 1.6 million report both behaviors.

Table 7–2 reports the amount of self-reported current illicit drug use and heavy alcohol use currently estimated by SAMHSA based on the NHSDA data set. "Current use" is again defined as use within the last thirty days.

One can make several interesting observations based on the data in Table 7–2:

- Overall, workplace drug use has held relatively steady over this period, while alcohol use has dropped slightly.
- In considering age, reduced rates of alcohol use are characteristic of younger respondents, who show a contrary increase in illicit drug use. The middle age grouping (26–34) shows decreases in both areas. Older respondents show small increases in reported drug use and no change in alcohol use.
- A dramatic change difference is shown by gender, with women showing substantial decreases in both drug and alcohol use. Men show increases in reported drug use and a decrease in alcohol use.

The Extent of Police Drug Testing

So far, the data presented have looked at general trends of workers, which include police officers, of course, but are not specific to police officers. This chapter has already covered

TABLE 7–2.   Percentage of Full-Time Workers Reporting Current Illicit Drug and Current Heavy Alcohol Use

Demographic Characteristics	Percent of Illicit Drug Use		Percent of Heavy Alcohol Use	
	1994	1997	1994	1997
Total	7.6	7.7	8.4	7.6
Age group				
18–25	12.4	13.5	13.6	11.7
26–34	8.6	7.2	8.9	7.9
35–49	5.4	6.3	6.3	6.3
Gender				
Male	9.3	9.8	11.9	11.1
Female	5.2	4.6	3.3	2.5
Race/ethnicity				
White, non-Hispanic	8.3	8.5	8.9	8.1
Black, non-Hispanic	6.5	6.2	5.2	4.4
Hispanic	5.6	5.2	8.8	9.8
Education				
> High school	9.7	11.2	13.2	14.7
High school graduate	8.3	7.9	10.0	7.1
Some college	7.5	8.7	8.3	7.3
College graduate	6.1	5.2	4.7	5.8

Source: Office of Applied Studies, 1999.

to some degree the kinds of risks and circumstances that characterize the specifics of potential police drug abuse. For the purposes of this chapter, it is necessary to focus on police
specifically, but I do not mean to imply that police are immune from the same social trends
and behaviors as citizens at large. Thus, I will evaluate how the police rate relative to other
workers, examine issues related to drug use in the workplace, and present and evaluate the
estimates for the prevalence of illicit drug use by the police. Unfortunately, little is known
about actual police drug use, because such data are either not collected or, if collected, are
withheld from public distribution. Even if one tries to examine the more broad scope of
police-involved drug corruption, there is little information. As the Rangel Report noted:

> Regarding the extent of drug-related police corruption, data are not collected nationally. Fed-
> eral agencies either do not maintain data specifically on drug-related police corruption or
> maintain data only on cases in which the respective agency is involved. Thus, it was not pos-
> sible to estimate the overall extent of the problem. However, the academic experts and vari-

TABLE 7–3   Number of Policing Agencies and Sworn Full-Time Officers

Type of Agency	Number of Agencies	Number of Full-Time Sworn Officers
All state and local	18,769	663,535
Local police	13,578	410,956
Sheriff	3,088	152,922
Special police	1,316	43,082
Texas constable	738	1,988
Federal		74,493
Total		738,028

ous officials we interviewed, as well as the commission reports, expressed the view that, by and large, most police officers are honest. (*Report*, 1998: 3)

In 1996 there were about 738,000 full-time sworn law enforcement officers in the United States. Table 7–3 provides a breakdown of the distribution of these officers by the state entities for which they work.

Nearly 90 percent of all sworn officers in the United States work for state and local governments, and around 10 percent work for federal agencies. This is important because it means that the vast majority of police are subject to policies that are individuated by state and local law and administrative regulation. As is true with all aspects of policing, it means that there is a substantial amount of variability in the specifics of actions that govern police and the kinds of data gathered about police practice. This chapter describes a generalized picture. Bear in mind that there will be a fair amount of local variations in specific policies and practices.

Police departments typically have drug-testing policies and consequently have several common points or circumstances at which drug testing is likely to be carried out. For example, police departments commonly test job applicants for sworn positions or test on a regular or randomized basis those officers involved specifically in vice and narcotics operations. The most universal application of drug testing as it is currently practiced in policing agencies is in the testing of job applicants. Data on the use of drug testing by state agencies published by the Bureau of Justice Statistics reveal that, of all fifty state-level law enforcement agencies, forty-two use a drug screen for applicants or new officer recruits. Eight states do not routinely test new applicants (Colorado, Kentucky, Maine, Nebraska, Oklahoma, South Carolina, Vermont, and West Virginia). Examination of *local* law enforcement agencies (cities, counties, townships, etc.) reveals that in excess of 80 percent of local law enforcement agencies also test applicants.

In 1986 McEwen, Manili, and Connors published data from a National Institute sponsored survey on employee drug testing policies in 33 police departments around the United States (McEwen et al., 1986). They reported that at the time 24 of the 33 departments (72.7 percent) had testing programs. These 24 all tested job applicants. All 33 departments had a written policy and procedure to follow in the event they suspected drug use by an officer. The McEwen et al. 1986 data are reported in Table 7–4.

TABLE 7–4.   The 1986 McEwen Survey on Drug Testing Practices by Thirty-Three Police Departments

Job Categories and Events Tested in Surveyed Departments

Job Categories and Events Tested	Number of Departments	Percent
Job applicants	15	62.5
Probationary officers	5	20.8
Officers seeking transfer to sensitive jobs	3	12.5
Officers in sensitive jobs	4	16.7
Officers suspected of drug use	18	75
After auto accidents	2	8.3
Scheduled testing	1	4.2

Source: McEwen et al., 1986.

Generally, McEwen et al. identify three situations that were identified as "testing points." These are:

- Testing job applicants
- Testing probationary officers
- Testing tenured officers in special circumstances

About one-fourth of the departments surveyed indicated that clinical treatment would be the organizational response to an officer's failed drug test rather than summary dismissal from the job. However, the referral to treatment would not be automatic, but contingent on the circumstances and severity of the drug abuse problem of the officer. Furthermore, when considering testing, either probationary or tenured officers they note that testing may be done as a scheduled protocol or can be a random testing system. Scheduled testing has been the least objectionable from the perspective of infringement of individual rights but is the easiest for a determined drug user to evade. For most drugs, abstinence for just a few days before the scheduled test will ensure a negative result. A random test protocol (i.e., an officer can potentially be asked to produce a urine specimen at any time) is more effective in identifying drug use. However, random testing programs have raised the most serious objections by personnel and unions, and when legally challenged, have been the least sympathetically viewed by the courts.

In 1997 the Bureau of Justice Statistics (BJS) conducted an updated survey on drug-screening policies and practices by police departments. BJS collects data under the Law Enforcement Management and Administrative Statistics (LEMAS) program (Reaves & Goldberg, 1999). It is conducted every 3 to 4 years and collects data from over 3,000 state and local police agencies, including all those that employ 100 or more sworn officers. Additionally, it collects data from a nationally representative sample of smaller agencies. Data are obtained on many topics related to police management including employee drug-testing policies. Table 7–5 reports the results of the LEMAS survey in 1997 about police department drug-testing policies toward job applicants.

TABLE 7–5　Screening for Drugs for New Recruits in Local Law Enforcement Agencies, 1997

Drug Testing Policy	Number of Agencies	Percent
Tests all applicants	564	86.6
Tests some but not all applicants	35	5.4
Does not test or no information	52	8.0
Total	651	100.0

Source: Bureau of Justice Statistics, 1997, Table 4a.

As Table 7–5 shows, more than 90 percent of all surveyed policing agencies test some or all job applicants. This represents an increase over the 1986 percentage by about 27 percent.

Comparing Police Officer Drug Testing to Other Occupations

How do police officers fare compared to other categories of workers in various dimensions of drug testing? The next series of tables compares police officers (under the job category labeled "protective services") to a select group of other occupational types. First, I will present the degree to which police officers are tested compared to other job categories and then present data showing how police officers compare in drug test results compared to other workers.

Table 7–6 reports the type of drug-testing programs (limited to a four-selection sequence) by a series of occupational categories. These categories are derived from the standardized series of occupational categorizations developed by the Bureau of Labor Statistics (Zhang et al., 1999). Police officers are identified as "protective services" workers in this table and in the subsequent comparison tables. Table 7–6 compares the prevalence of these reported testing protocols for the years 1994 and 1997.

Table 7–6 reveals that, generally, police officers are more frequently tested than other job categories. The only job category that exceeded protective services' rate of testing was the transportation industry, which in 1994 had higher rates of testing in random protocols and postaccident testing. However, as Table 7–6 shows, by 1997 protective services emerged as the highest percentage category.

Table 7–7 lists the self-reported drug and alcohol use patterns for each of the occupational categories. In Table 7–7, the category with the *lowest* reported percentage is in boldface type. Table 7–7 compares the self-reported drug and alcohol use for the years 1994 and 1997.

Table 7–7 shows several interesting patterns. Protective services have the lowest percentage of self-reported drug use for both 1994 and 1997. But in neither year do the police have the lowest heavy alcohol use. For alcohol use, the "professional" category (in 1994) and the "sales" category (for 1997) showed the lowest reported heavy alcohol use. Protective services in 1994 were fifth in rank and in 1997 sixth in rank in rating the job categories from lowest to highest percentage of heavy alcohol use. Bear in mind that these are self-reported data. One factor that could bear upon the accuracy of this self-reported use is that

TABLE 7–6.   Percentage of Full-Time Workers, Age 18–49, Reporting Workplace Drug-Testing Programs, by Occupational Categories and Type of Program, 1994 and 1997

	Type of Testing Program							
	At Hiring		Random		Upon Suspicion		Post Accident	
Occupation	1994	1997	1994	1997	1994	1997	1994	1997
Executive managerial	30.1	33.3	18.3	24.1	25.5	30.3	17.7	27.2
Professional	24.2	26.9	12.4	14.3	19.7	17.9	11.8	15.2
Technical	35.9	38.0	20.5	19.5	34.8	30.3	20.7	26.4
Sales	25.9	28.9	14.0	18.7	19.0	23.9	16.2	19.8
Protective services[*]	**67.1**[†]	**74.0**	38.7	**60.4**	**62.1**	**68.9**	37.3	**56.0**
Transportation	61.7	62.7	**51.3**	52.9	47.9	47.6	**56.9**	54.7
Construction	29.8	25.8	23.9	25.7	23.5	22.4	24.7	27.2
Total	34.5	38.5	20.1	25.3	27.4	29.9	22.3	28.6

[*]Protective service occupations (BLS classification): firefighting and fire prevention occupations; police and detectives; guards; firefighting occupations; public service; sheriffs, bailiffs, and other law enforcement officers; correctional institution officers; crossing guards.
[†]Highest percentages are boldfaced.
Source: Zhang et al., 1999.

TABLE 7–7.   Percentage of Full-Time Workers, Age 18–49, Reporting Current Illicit Drug and Heavy Alcohol Use, by Occupational Categories, 1994 and 1997

	Current Illicit Drug Use[*]		Heavy Alcohol Use[†]	
Occupation	1994	1997	1994	1997
Executive managerial	5.5	8.9	6.5	7.1
Professional	5.1	5.1	**4.3**[‡]	4.4
Technical	5.5	7.0	6.2	5.1
Sales	11.4	9.1	8.3	**4.1**[§]
Protective services[11]	**3.2**[‡]	**3.0**[§]	6.3	7.8
Transportation	5.3	10.0	13.1	10.8
Construction	15.6	14.14	17.6	12.4
Total	7.6	7.7	8.4	7.5

[*]Use of any illicit substance within the last 30 days.
[†]Heavy alcohol use is defined as drinking five or more drinks on the same occasion on each of at least 5 days in the previous 30 days.
[‡]Low percentages are boldfaced.
[§]Lowest percentages reported.
[11]Protective service occupations (BLS classification): firefighting and fire prevention occupations; police and detectives; guards; firefighting occupations; public service; sheriffs, bailiffs, and other law enforcement officers; correctional institution officers; crossing guards.
Source: Zhang et al., 1999.

alcohol use is legal, while drug use is not. For example, although research on these data is extremely limited, some reports indicate that the amount of drug use among police departments may be more serious than the SAMHSA data indicate.

An earlier section reviewed Marx's (1988) conceptual position on the potential for drug abuse by undercover police officers, as well as Girodo's comments on this phenomenon. Orvis (1994: 289) reports that "of 520 police agencies recently surveyed, 262 reported discovering police officers abusing drugs, with 39.3 percent reporting that marijuana was the most frequently abused drug and 35.9 percent reporting cocaine as the most abused drug." However, the problem, while perhaps relatively widely dispersed, appears to involve a small percentage of sworn officers. Orvis notes that for those departments reporting a problem with drug-abusing officers, the mean value for investigations was seven per year.

Another measure of the degree to which police agencies have an administrative focus on illegal drug use and abuse as well as alcohol abuse is the extent to which written policies and procedures are in place in these organizations. Furthermore, it is well documented that generally workplaces that have such policies and procedures in place, and disseminate these to workers, have lower rates of reported alcohol and drug use (Office of Applied Studies, 1999: 65). Table 7–8 reports the percentage by occupational category of policies, information, and employee assistance programs (EAPs).

Table 7–8 indicates that by a very substantial margin policing and protective services workers have access to information and employee assistance, and this has been the case in

TABLE 7–8. Percentage of Full-Time Workers, Age 18–49, Reporting Their Workplace Provides Information, Has a Written Policy, or Maintains an EAP Concerning Drug or Alcohol Use, by Occupational Categories, 1994 and 1997

Occupation	Information about Drug or Alcohol Use		Written Policy about Drug or Alcohol Use		Employee Assistance Program	
	1994	1997	1994	1997	1994	1997
Executive managerial	76.9	71.5	71.6	68.6	54.6	53.6
Professional	83.4	75.2	76.7	72.4	60.5	56.4
Technical	83.5	78.6	81.1	75.3	62.1	61.7
Sales	63.8	62.2	59.2	59.3	36.7	43.3
Protective services[*]	**97.0[†]**	**95.2**	**94.4[†]**	**92.6**	**85.5[†]**	**79.7**
Transportation	87.2	85.9	84.6	83.3	54.6	46.5
Construction	56.8	60.0	54.7	55.6	24.5	30.3
Total	73.9	73.5	69.3	70.3	49.6	49.7

[*]Protective service occupations (BLS classification): firefighting and fire prevention occupations; police and detectives; guards; firefighting occupations; public service; sheriffs, bailiffs, and other law enforcement officers; correctional institution officers; crossing guards.
[†]Highest percentages are boldfaced.
Source: Zhang et al., 1999.

the past as well as in recent times. Construction workers, in contrast, appear to have the least information and assistance access.

Some of the general points regarding drug use, alcohol use, and drug testing established in this chapter follow:

- In considering overall rates of drug use in the workplace, the trend from the mid-1980s until the present shows that, generally, workplace drug use has fallen or stabilized.
- Drug use in the workplace has been documented to be costly. Comparing drug-using to non–drug-using workers shows higher rates of absenteeism and turnover associated with drug use.
- In general, the amount of drug testing conducted in the workplace has increased.
- Police departments are among the leading institutions in conducting drug testing of employees.
- Applicants for police officer positions are nearly universally drug tested, and police officers in probationary status are aggressively tested.
- Drug testing of police officers has increased since 1990, especially the incorporation of random and postaccident testing.
- Police officers have the lowest rates of self-reported drug use compared to other comparable job categories.
- Police officers have relatively higher rates of heavy alcohol abuse than they do of drug use.
- Police departments are the leaders in providing written policies and procedures regarding drug use in the workplace.
- Police officers have high access to EAPs at rates higher than other occupational groups.

LEGAL ASPECTS OF DRUG TESTING

A General Overview

In general the courts have given wide latitude to drug testing in the private sector, since no state authority is involved in the requirement to submit to a drug test. That is, under most circumstances, the drug testing of an employee is a civil or tort issue. However, even in the private sector, employer-mandated drug testing must follow accepted constitutional standards for due process, equity, and reasonableness (McEwen et al., 1986). Additionally, the testing must be done in accordance with other rules, arrangements, and agreements that may impinge on the employer, such as union–employer contracts. Typically, courts have permitted drug testing of a urine sample when done as a part of general preemployment health screening. As well, courts have permitted an employer to request a drug test from an employee when reasonable suspicion is raised regarding drug activity that can compromise an employee's ability to safely and effectively carry out his or her work assignments. Courts have not squelched random testing, nor have they suppressed postaccident testing. However, the courts are always at liberty to impose standards and practices that may, in the view of the bench, be requisite for protection of the rights of citizens under the general concept of due process and equity before the law. In addition, the courts may consider other constitutional issues, such as reasonableness of search, privacy, and self-incrimination protections. Furthermore, the court may consider other issues plaintiffs may raise in a tort action against an employer. An employee may also bring actions on the basis of common law, such as libel or slander associated with the divulging of drug-testing information, or malfeasance resulting in an injury.

It is also important to bear in mind that drug addiction and alcoholism are generally considered protected handicaps in the law. This typically requires employers to offer treatment and counseling to workers who admit to or are discovered to be drug addicted or alcoholic. Any dismissal action taken by an employer must follow due process. This usually requires a hearing or proceeding giving the employee an opportunity to express his or her explanation of the drug test result and its circumstances. Generally, the courts have utilized a "balancing test" in determining the reasonableness of testing demands and sanctions applied to drug-positive employees versus the invasiveness and infringement on privacy of the individual. The competing interests in the balance are the employee's right to expectations of privacy and protection from unreasonable search and seizure versus the employer's rights to a safe and effective workplace and a workforce free from intoxication (Orvis, 1994).

An employee who is drug tested and "fails" a drug test (i.e., has a positive result for a drug test), or an employee who refuses to submit to a drug test and is fired as a consequence may have an actionable tort in the civil law. Generally, an employer who refers the employee into some form of employee assistance (which is often premised on the employee admitting drug use) and offers a return to work on successful completion of treatment/counseling can escape any legal liability. However, failure to pay attention to due process (both procedural and substantive), failure to provide some counseling or treatment alternative, and failure to have an equitable, declared drug use policy may result in a loss in a civil law suit.

An employee may have several avenues for redress under tort law, depending on the specifics of the drug testing and the type of injury the plaintiff alleges to have suffered. This is especially true if the employee alleges that a positive test is in error (i.e., a false-positive). An employer who divulges the results of a false test or fails to take due diligence to secure accurate and reliable drug test results may be liable for defamation. This is most likely to arise in a situation where the employer releases the false test result to another party that consequently results in an injury to the employee. Furthermore, relatively well-defined procedural expectations are in place in the evaluation of a drug test. For example, it is advisable that any drug test on which a job action will be taken should be "confirmed" (that is, the matrix retested) by a second, independent technique. Furthermore, an independent medical review officer should review the test results to ascertain whether there are medical reasons that could explain the positive result and should have the opportunity to consult with the person who has tested positive.

Currently, there is no federal statutory basis for requiring or mandating that a private employer must drug test employees. However, as we noted previously, the private sector has with some dispatch initiated a substantial amount of drug testing of employees, especially at the application stage, and in some probationary, early stage of employment. Furthermore, private employers also have instituted drug testing in safety-sensitive positions, in circumstances defined as suspicious, or in the investigation of workplace accidents. For example, drug testing is particularly intense in gas and electric utilities companies, where workers are often working with dangerous materials and in dangerous circumstances (Orvis, 1994). There are also "indirect" methods by which the government, while not requiring an employer to drug test, may encourage it. For example, the government may require an employer working under government contract to certify that the employer has a "drug-free workplace" or face a loss of the contract. Likewise, states have passed legislation that gives employers who have in-place drug testing programs a discounted rate for worker's compensation taxes.

The federal government encouraged the development and application of workplace drug testing in the public under Executive Order 12564, signed by President Ronald Reagan in 1986. Under this order, the president mandated that the heads of federal agencies must develop plans for ensuring that the federal workplace was drug-free, including the use of drug-testing technologies as one way toward furthering that goal. In 1986 the Drug-Free Workplace Act (DFWA) was passed by Congress, which extended the principles of Executive Order 12564 to cover federal contractors and federal grant recipients. However, the DFWA did not require that contractors and grantees carry out drug testing; they were only required to certify that they operate drug-free workplaces. They were allowed to carry out testing if they wished. Over time, the agencies that most aggressively pursued the establishment of mandatory drug testing was the Department of Defense and the Department of Transportation. These agencies, however, did not require carte blanche testing of all employees, but identified certain safety-sensitive positions for which testing was mandatory. The National Institute on Drug Abuse was the lead agency in establishing federal guidelines for the application of testing in these circumstances.

Drug Testing of Public Sector Employees

State agencies that require a drug test from a citizen are acting under the authority of the state, and the courts have recognized that they are in a distinct and special legal posture. Generally speaking, the state argues that it has an interest or even a compelling interest in drug testing. This is usually to ensure public safety, to guard against liability, and to meet the requirement that it exercise diligence in protecting public interests. The single biggest negative factor in the use of drug tests is the perception by many that it is invasive, intrusive, and presumptive of guilt. An additional aspect of this controversy is the degree to which drug testing is (or should be) directed at measuring impairment versus to what extent drug testing reveals drug use that has occurred during nonwork time. This issue is directed toward privacy of conduct and an employer's right to access information about private activities of employees.

Privacy, Searches, and Seizures: The Constitutional Issues

Regardless of an employer's views on drug testing, the legality and limitations of drug testing practices ultimately rest with the judicial system and its review of practices. In regard to state agencies requiring a drug test, the courts have generally found this to be a Fourth-

Amendment search and also to involve aspects of due process and the rights to expectation of privacy. As well, in a few cases, the legality of drug testing has been challenged on the grounds of Fifth-Amendment self-incrimination and also the Fourteenth Amendment by invoking the equal protection of law.

An examination of the constitutional principles that govern drug testing on the job show that the courts have considered four general principles:

- The justification or need for testing
- The nature of the intrusion of the testing into the expectation of privacy
- The likelihood of on-the job impairment by the employee
- The reliability of the test and what procedural safeguards are used to ensure accuracy

The courts have generally acknowledged the notion that drug testing under several circumstances is reasonable under the Fourth Amendment. Under *Terry* v. *Ohio,* (1968), the courts have generally acknowledged that a "reasonable expectation of privacy" is a constitutionally protected right of citizens. Furthermore, the courts have also generally held that the taking of biological specimens, such as blood, for the purposes of testing for the presence of materials such as intoxicants are searches and seizures protected under the Fourth Amendment (e.g., *Schember* v. *California,* 1966). Because drug-testing programs have, until recently, relied almost exclusively on urinalysis, this has raised special concern regarding the nature of intrusion. The collection of a urine specimen raises particular issues in regard to verification of the origin of the specimen as well as chain-of-custody questions. Generally, the "forced, observed collection of urine has been strongly disapproved" by the courts (Carper & McCamey, 1989). However, drug testing per se is not unreasonable, so the courts have reviewed the circumstances listed previously as part of a "balancing test" to determine the reasonableness issue in particular cases that have come before it. The degree to which facts underlying individual suspicion compete against the degree to which the government has a "compelling interest" in ensuring a drug-free work environment. The courts have found that it is reasonable in the case of the police role that drug use by an officer is a valid public concern, and therefore the issue of public safety is a reasonable and compelling one (e.g., *Turner* v. *Fraternal Order of Police*, 1985). In *Turner*, for example, the government held that "the police is a paramilitary organization dealing hourly with the public in delicate and often dangerous situations . . . police officers may, in certain situations, enjoy less constitutional protection than the ordinary citizen."

This is primarily because the justification of testing is premised on an attempt by government authorities to ensure public safety. In essence, police officers can be drug tested, since officers who are intoxicated are a threat to public safety as well as to their fellow officers. Furthermore, the courts have ruled that there are security and enforcement situations when the government has "compelling interests" and that persons who enter into police positions have a "diminished expectation of privacy" due to the nature of the work itself (*National Treasury Union* v. *Von Raab*, 1989). Such a compelling interest has also been upheld for transportation workers who are regulated by federal law (*Skinner* v. *Railway Labor Executives Association*, 1989), military personnel (*Committee for G.I. Rights* v. *Callaway*, 1975), and Department of Justice employees (*Harman* v. *Thornburgh*, 1989). The courts have also held that the distinction between "off-duty" and "on-duty" drug use—and the failure of a drug test to distinguish between these two events—is not a basis for denying the legality of a drug-testing program (*American Federation of Government Employees* v. *Skinner*, 1989).

However, absent such specific circumstances as the carrying of firearms or direct involvement in the interdiction of drugs as a police practice, the courts have generally held that there must be a reasonable suspicion to support the demand that an employee submit to a drug test. Reasonable suspicion requires "factual, specific, objective" indicators of job performance that appear to be drug-affected. The courts have rejected broad notions of rationalization such as "we want to drug test because there is a nationwide drug problem" or "we want to bolster the public confidence in police." Generally, the courts have not seen these reasons as sufficient grounds for testing individuals (Carper & McCamey, 1989). However, within those occupations where the courts have found a "compelling interest" for the government, such as policing, transportation, and the military, the courts have permitted random drug screening. Generally, the courts have held that if the government has interests in guaranteeing public safety, governmental safety, or security, then random screening is acceptable and does not require the establishment of individual suspicion (Orvis, 1994).

Police-Specific Issues

The generalized "compelling interest" that focuses primarily on public safety is not the only consideration taken up by the courts. The courts have recognized that police officers are citizens who also have rights, and therefore the use of drug testing must be circumscribed by the constraint of reasonable suspicion (*Policemen's Benevolent Association of New Jersey, Local 318* v. *Washington Township*, 1987). The notion of reasonable suspicion has been balanced against the "diminished expectation of privacy" that the courts have also applied to police and law enforcement employees. Over time, the "reasonable suspicion" criteria have been eroded to some degree. Initially, the standard of "reasonable suspicion" was accepted as a requirement to meet the court's criteria of a lawful use of drug testing of police officers. The reasonable suspicion had to be based on "an objective, factual indication that a particular officer's job performance is affected by drugs" and cannot be a capricious or unsubstantiated suspicion (Carper & McCamey, 1989). Such rationales as statistical data indicating increasing levels of drug use or generalized views such as "there's a lot of drug use in society" could not be used as justifications for specific drug tests (*Fraternal Order of Police Lodge 12* v. *City of Newark*, 1987). Furthermore, the courts had generally held that information leading to "reasonable suspicion" upon which a drug-testing program could be established must be specific, must transcend casual allegation, and must have sufficiency beyond curiosity or isolated events as justifiers (e.g., *Bostie* v. *McClendon*, 1986, *Penney* v. *Kennedy*, 1986).

Since 1989, the courts have given greater weight to the "diminished expectation of privacy" component in determining the balance between private rights and "compelling" government interests (Orvis, 1994). In a series of decisions, the courts generally permitted mandatory random screening of police personnel without individual suspicion being established (*American Federation of Government Employees* v. *Derwinski*, 1991; *Copeland* v.

Philadelphia Police Department, 1988; *McKenna* v. *City of Philadelphia*, 1991). In this series of decisions, the courts generally held firm to the "diminished expectations of privacy" concept that applies to persons engaged in law enforcement activity and linked it to the "compelling interests" argument. The government, generally, need show only that drug testing is in the interests of ensuring public safety and the security of government information or data and is consistent with the "professional competence" that the public can expect from persons in law enforcement positions (Sorensen & del Carmen, 1991a). This list of "compelling interests" can become quite long. The interests have been argued to include six areas: public safety, public trust, potential for official corruption, official credibility, worker morale, and worker safety. The implication is that the government has a compelling interest in all these areas (Higginbotham, 1986). However, the courts have generally held that the suspension of "reasonable suspicion" is not blanket dismissal of the concept. In several cases, the courts have held that where a "compelling interest" does not justify a mandatory, random, suspicionless search, the "reasonable suspicion" test remains in effect (Sorensen & del Carmen, 1991b). The only points at which drug testing can be done in these noncompelling situations are (1) at job application, (2) as a matter of a routine physical health examination, or (3) with consent.

A proviso that the courts have imposed on drug testing, even if random and/or mandatory, is that any such program must provide due process in its execution and in any resulting consequences, such as job termination and demotions. *Due process* is a general term that does not have a specific and inflexible definition. In general, it addresses the legal principle of fairness and equity. Normally, due process addresses issues of the procedures available to a person undergoing some form of legal charge, investigation, or scrutiny. Due process is a way to characterize the processes used to arrive at a legally meaningful judgment, decision, or determination. That an accused person has knowledge of and enjoys access to all the avenues of review and appeals, for example, are elements of procedural due process. In drug testing, these would include issues such as chain-of-custody, employee notification, test confidentiality, and similar aspects of the drug-testing procedure. Substantive due process touches upon issues of "fundamental fairness." Examples of substantive due process would include concern for coercion of testimony, the use of brutal methods in effecting an arrest, and similar matters (Felkenes, 1988).

As due process applies to drug-testing programs, the courts have established a set of guidelines to which drug-testing programs are expected to conform. Employees must be notified in a timely and reasonable manner of the date, time, and place of specimen collection. They must also be told how the testing will be done, and how the chain of custody of the specimen will be ensured. The testing organization must exercise due diligence to ensure that test results are valid and reliable. The employer must ensure that results are held in confidence and that any disclosure of results is made only to persons legally authorized to have the information. Last, in situations where the test matrix (e.g., urine) can be used to reveal other medical information, the employer must make certain that the specimen is used for the stated purpose only and for no other medical assessment or diagnosis. The courts have held strongly to the standards of procedural due process. In *Capua* v. *City of Plainfield* (1986), the court ruled against a drug-testing program specifically because it failed to notify employees of the intent to drug test, had no written policy on the drug-testing procedure itself, had no mechanism to protect confidentiality, did not confirm the test results, did not allow the employees to see the laboratory results, and terminated all positive employees immediately and filed criminal charges against them (Sorensen & del Carmen, 1991b).

The basic guidelines that have been established regarding drug testing within police agencies reflect the court's guidance in establishing both procedural and substantive due process. There should be a rationale for testing classes of employees, and carte blanche testing should be avoided. Any testing program should be announced well in advance of its onset, and any employee who withdraws from a designated pool for testing should be allowed to do so without retribution or reaction. At the time of testing, a relevant history should be taken from the employees so that they may reveal the taking of medicinals or other substances that may interfere with the drug test outcome. The employer needs to have clear and strict chain-of-custody procedures for all specimens collected. All tests that are performed by a "screening method" (such as enzyme-multiplied immunoassay [EMIT] or radioactive immunoassay [RIA]) need to be confirmed by a second technology, preferably gas chromatography-mass spectrometry (GC/MS) or an analogous procedure. Employees should be allowed to use an independent laboratory of their choice to confirm any positive outcome identified by the employer's laboratory. Last, any employer reaction to a positive drug test should be in an administrative role only and not a criminal one. In their analysis of the drug testing of police officers, Sorensen and del Carmen (1991b) list a number of procedural suggestions to consider when implementing a drug-testing program among criminal justice employees:

- Avoid random mandatory screening unless there is a clear and compelling governmental interest. This is usually only acceptable to the courts when the position can be shown to be "sensitive" or to involve overt public safety, such as the carrying of firearms.
- Always try to obtain consent. If a test is demanded of an individual, be prepared to establish a reasonable suspicion. Generally, except for job applicants, persons in probationary employee status, or as part of a routine physical, the courts will require some form of substantiated suspicion.
- Have written policies that cover all aspects of the drug-testing program, and distribute these policies to all employees.
- Maintain all test results as confidential, and use them solely to make administrative decisions. Do not pursue any criminal charges on the basis of a drug test.
- Instead of automatic termination for persons who test drug positive, utilize EAPs where it is possible and does not jeopardize organizational or public safety.

This list of recommended practices follows fairly closely the current practices that typify large, urban police departments. There are variations, however, due to the decentralized nature of American policing. As the Rangel Report on drug-related police corruption observed:

In addition, according to our sources, drug use was a reported concern and drug testing—whether targeted or random—was a practice employed by some police departments to detect drug use, although such use was not necessarily found to be an indicator of drug corruption. However, how departments treated positive test results varied. For example, in Chicago, drug use is treated as a medical problem. In New York City, according to NYPD officials, an offi-

cer who (1) fails a drug screening test; (2) is found in possession of illegal drugs; or (3) refuses to take a drug screening test is dismissed. In either case, positive drug test results are
typically not treated as a crime. (*Report to the Honorable Charles B. Rangel*, 1998: 25)

DRUG-SCREENING TECHNOLOGIES

How Is Drug Screening Done?

Drug screening is a term that refers to the use of a chemical identification technology to detect the presence of a drug in a specimen of matrix. In addition to looking for the drug (often referred to as the "parent drug"), the drug test may also seek to identify a drug metabolite or even several drug metabolites (Karch, 1996; Perrine, 1996).

What Do You Test? What Are Test Matrices?   In theory, one can test almost any kind
of biological specimen for the presence of a drug or related metabolite. However, the selection of a particular specimen type is usually based on a series of practical considerations
(Yinon, 1995). For example, in the application of "Breathalyzer" type testing to determine
the blood alcohol concentration of a person operating a car, the Breathalyzer actually tests
the exhaled breath and its associated water vapor to evaluate the plasma alcohol concentration. This test is popular because the exhaled breath is convenient to collect and does not
represent an "invasive" collection process, such as collecting blood with a hypodermic needle (McKim, 2000). In addition to appropriateness and invasiveness, other considerations
that govern the selection of a matrix include possible sepsis, ease of transportation and storage, and specimen stability. The commonly used test specimens/matrices when testing for
psychoactive drugs include blood, urine, sweat, saliva, and hair.

Why Are the Different Test Matrices Important?   Several factors influence the selection of a particular matrix. Some are practical issues as discussed above. However, very
critical additional factors are the limitations, especially time limitations, that are associated
with particular types of specimens. In effect, the selection of a specimen automatically im-
poses a time window that is associated with that specimen (Cone et al., 1996). Drugs pass
through the body in a dynamic process. From the time they are ingested until the time they
are excreted, they are involved in a dynamic process of change. Different specimens reflect
different stages of this dynamic process (Liska, 1997; McKim, 2000). In the simplest example, for instance, consider a person smoking crack cocaine.

Crack cocaine, delivered to the surface of the lungs, quickly moves large concentrations of the drug into blood plasma. Indeed, the rapidity of absorption through the alveoli
is very near to intravenous injection. Thus, a blood sample, harvested just a few minutes after a person smokes crack will have cocaine present in it. However, it will take twenty to
thirty minutes for appreciable amounts of cocaine or cocaine metabolite to appear in the
urine. And after cocaine is removed via metabolism from the circulating plasma, it will still
be present in the urine stored in the bladder. Thus, blood and urine have different time windows. The longest time window (or one that "looks back" the longest) is hair analysis.
While it will take three to five days for cocaine, for example, to appear in the hair of a cocaine user, the cocaine appears "locked" into the hair virtually permanently. Unless or un-

til the hair is removed or dissolved, the cocaine will be detectable, even months after the ingestion of the drug. The same long-term appearance also is true for fingernails or toenails.

So, a major factor in selecting a particular specimen, or matrix, on which to perform the analysis is the *time window* of detection (Mieczkowski et al., 1991). Another major factor to consider is the extent to which one wishes to have a quantitative assessment of the amount of drug detected in the analysis. Most assays performed can produce either a "positive or negative" categorical reading (using some preselected threshold, or cutoff, value) or can give a concentration value of the amount of drug or drug metabolite recovered from the specimen (cutoff values will be discussed in more detail later). When the test reports concentration of an analyte, it is usually in some standardized per-unit-volume or per-unit-mass basis. For example, in urine testing, the concentration is usually reported in nanograms per milliliter of urine; for hair analysis, it is usually in nanograms of analyte per milligram of hair. In general, the concentration value bears a rough relationship to the exposure rate for the material being analyzed. The greater the exposure, the greater the concentration is a general toxicological principle (Hawks & Chiang, 1986). However, it is not generally considered accurate to make a simple statement such as one person who has a higher concentration of drug in their urine has used more drug than a person who has a lower concentration. This is because the excretion curves may have started at different times (i.e., they did not consume their drugs at the same start time), and there is considerable biovariability in the rates of excretion between individuals, as well as changes in the excretion efficiencies of the body as it ages. So, while under theoretically ideal conditions, it may be possible to compare two individuals and assess their relative drug use, as a practical matter, this is not done in most clinical circumstances, since there are problems with interpreting the meaning of the outcomes (Burke et al., 1990: Ellis et al., 1985; Weiss & Gawing, 1988). With hair analysis, and possible sweat patch analysis, which measures the cumulative effect of taking drugs over a long period, it is possible to make a relative assessment of intensity of drug use, but only in a rough categorical manner, such as high, medium, and low. This is because the hair (or sweat patch) will sequester drugs over several weeks or months, and this dampens down the dynamic change problems associated with urinalysis. However, even under these circumstances, the interpretation should be made cautiously, and it is probably best to use the person as their control. This means, in effect, that multiple testing of the same person over a long time frame can be compared to evaluate the relative abundance of the material in the specimen. For example, in using hair analysis in a drug rehabilitation program (which requires drug abstinence), we expect to see a diminishing concentration of drugs in the subject's hair as they undergo progressive testing over a long time frame.

What Are the Advantages and Limitations of Different Matrices?   As mentioned, time and concentration determination are issues in selecting a particular type of specimen. The fluid-based specimens (blood, urine, and sweat) are most effective for measuring quite recent drug use. Hair and nail shavings, clippings, or scrapings are very good for long-term assessment. Sweat patches, which are worn on the skin like an adhesive bandage, are also effective for relatively long-term drug use detection, since they act like cumulative dosimeters (Baer & Booher, 1994). Two additional points should be evaluated when considering hair specimens or nail clippings or shavings as matrices. The hair specimen is collected by clipping the hair at the level of the scalp, not by "pulling out" the hair as is sometimes claimed. The use of a finger or toenail specimen is based upon either a conventional clipping of the nail, as one would do in any trimming of the nails, or very small shavings or scrapings from the surface of the nail.

General advantages and limitations of the specimen beyond these time window considerations are generally related to practical issues. The most important one of these is *invasiveness*. In the general medical connotation, the term *invasiveness* applies to a procedure's intrusion into or invasion of the person, whether biologically invasive (e.g., drawing blood with a hypodermic needle) or psychologically invasive (e.g., collection of a urine specimen or the collection of a hair specimen). Ideally, a test that requires a specimen collected by the least intrusive or invasive method is the preferred approach, provided all other needs are met by that specimen's analysis parameters. Other practical matters in considering a particular specimen type are the convenience or ease of handling, storing, or transporting the specimen, and the degree to which the specimen may constitute a biohazard as a disease vector.

What Can Be Learned from Drug Screens?   A drug test is a chemical assay that indicates the presence or absence of a particular chemical compound or family of compounds as present in a specimen. As we have already noted, an assay in the real world inevitably involves some level of *interpretation*. Some of these interpretation issues have already been discussed, for example, the relationship of *time windows* to the particular test and the specimen type (Weiss & Gawing, 1988) and that the test, in addition to looking for the drug itself (the *parent drug*), may also show the presence of the drug metabolite.

A very important aspect of test interpretation is the issue of the particular *cutoff values*, or *thresholds*, that are used in test interpretation. The decision to use a particular threshold, or cutoff value, can have a dramatic effect on test interpretation and should be carefully considered in any clinical setting or application.

To understand the nature of cutoff values, it is necessary to review again some of the fundamental ideas of chemical analysis. Detecting a chemical species present in a test specimen involves several interesting factors. One is, how much of a particular chemical must be present in a specimen for the test to have the ability to detect its presence? This is an issue of test *sensitivity*. For all chemical assays, there is an ultimate limit that is a technical function of the test, which is referred to as the *limit of detection (LOD)*. It is very rare in clinical applications to use this lowest possible threshold. Instead, some value is selected that is greater than this value. This is usually called the *cutoff value (COV)* and may vary under a variety of circumstances and clinical settings. A higher cutoff value (higher than the LOD) is selected for a variety of reasons, all of which center around being conservative in interpreting the test result. That is, in clinical settings, individuals may be classified as "drug negative" even though they have some amount of drug in their urine, or hair, or whatever specimen the program is using to test its clients. This occurs because they may have a value in the specimen higher than the LOD but lower than the COV. This interesting outcome is sometimes called the difference between a forensic positive, which is based on the LOD and an evidentiary positive, which is based on the COV. Thus, a person might be a forensic positive but an evidentiary negative. A curious outcome, indeed! It also means that shifting the COV threshold can modify the number of persons who are classified as "drug positive." In any given target group or population, lowering the COV will tend to increase the number of positive clients; raising it will decrease that number.

Why are COVs selected that are greater than the LOD? As noted, this choice is made primarily for conservative assay interpretation. One thing to bear in mind is that a person may ingest small amounts of a drug inadvertently by contact with contaminated materials, such as foodstuffs or dishware. Also persons may inhale drugs as particulate matter such as dust or smoke that result from the use of the drug in their environment. This is especially important for police officers, who may be environmentally exposed to drugs more frequently and more intensely than ordinary citizens. So, cutoffs and other procedures are used to try to control for this effect.[3] Controversy arises, however, in trying to determine exactly where the COV should be set and in trying to determine the amount of contamination a person can reasonably expect to find in "innocent" (i.e., nonwillful) drug ingestion. This is not an easy problem to resolve. COVs for urinalysis, for example, have been modified several times by governmental agencies, sometimes quite dramatically.

In this regard, drug testing and its cutoff values are often evaluated by the potential for what are often called false-positives and false-negatives. First, it is important to bear in mind that a false result can occur if the assay procedure is done incorrectly. This type of false result is not based on some property of the assay itself but, rather, is tied to the competence and care of the laboratory that conducts the test. Thus, for example, the inadvertent contamination of a true-negative specimen by sloppy handling can produce a false result. Mislabeling or other procedural error can also lead to a true-positive being called a negative. Control for this type of false result depends on quality-control and assurance actions taken by the laboratory and relevant regulatory and licensing agencies.

However, if for the sake of argument, we assume the laboratory has not made an error in the processing of the specimen, we still have a remaining issue. These true and false terms can have different meanings depending on whether *forensic* or *evidentiary* criteria are used in assessing the assay outcome. A false-negative, in this sense, is one that can be considered to be a forensic positive (assay value above LOD) but an evidentiary negative (assay value below COV). If the LOD and COV are the same value, then this problem disappears. A false-positive is possible if the interpreter of the assay used a COV that was below the LOD. Thus, if the COV is always at or above the LOD, and the test is done correctly from a procedural point of view, then you can eliminate false-positive outcomes.

WHAT ABOUT COMPLICATIONS?

Officer Denial of a Positive Test Result

One of the more difficult clinical situations is the denial of drug use by an officer in the face of a positive drug test. Generally, this is not a frequent occurrence in most treatment and criminal justice programs. Most clients in these circumstances will admit to drug use when they are confronted with confirmed positive results (Harrison & Hughes, 1997). Repudiation or denial of a positive result is more likely to arise in employee testing and perhaps with

---

[3]This has been most intensely debated regarding hair analysis. Specimens like hair are washed by special procedures to remove environmental contaminants (see Mieczkowski, 1997).

criminal justice testing in particular. In most programs, internal affairs and personnel administrators can expect police officers frequently to claim that the positive result is "impossible" because they have never used or taken the drug in question or often that they have never used any drugs.

Test Error: Can the Test Just Be Wrong?

The possibility that the test result is wrong has already been briefly discussed. Of course, it is possible for the test to be wrong, since it is always possible that an operational error or mistake occurred. To minimize this likelihood, it is important to use a certified laboratory that has professional standards of quality assurance and quality control and is both inspected and evaluated by participation in some type of "challenge" program. It is also possible—especially worth considering when using a laboratory with which the consumer lacks experience—for the agency to send "known" negative, positive, and contaminated samples blindly to the laboratory to enhance institutional confidence in their performance. However, one must recognize that inevitably people with positive test results will periodically deny drug use, and no readily identifiable or compelling evidence will allow an absolute determination of the truth of the denial. In such cases, the most pragmatic course is to repeat the test (which is a problem for fast-excretion matrices such as urine), even though the time window is violated and the results are not actually comparable. Also, if it is a urine, blood, or sweat matrix, hair analysis may prove a good alternative, since it will permit a longer retrospective period to be evaluated. This also illustrates the difficulties inherent in putting great emphasis on the outcome of a single drug test. Programs are generally better served by looking for patterns of positive outcomes in a series of tests. Programs are even better served by using more than one test specimen and by relying on the outcome of several different indicators such as urine, hair, and sweat.

Interpretation Error: Can the Test Be Misinterpreted?

Interpretation is often overlooked in the process of drug testing, since we tend to think of the drug-testing process as mechanical. But, in reflecting on what has been discussed, it is clear that the test must be "interpreted" or a meaning assigned to the result. The test tells us that a drug or drug metabolite is present in the matrix examined, but it does not tell us how this drug got there. Interpretation involves assigning some meaning to the test in terms of its implications. Sometimes, the interpretation seems relatively easy, sometimes it is not (Yinon, 1995).

Typically, the interpretation placed on a drug test is that individuals who test positive have consumed the detected drug. And we normally assume they have done so willfully and knowingly. Thus, they are a "drug user," or "drug abuser," or "violator," or some such status is assigned to them. However, returning to the issue of COVs, remember that a test may show traces of a drug, but the drug concentration is below the selected COV. Those persons are "negative," that is, evidentiary negative, but have drug levels above the LOD in their sample, or forensic positive. These results have several important implications.

One of the most important is that the percentage of persons who are positive or negative can be manipulated by moving the threshold. While the lower limit of the COV is fixed at LOD, the upper limit can be any value. And over time, these values have been manipulated. Following are two examples. In the early uses of immunoassay urinalysis testing, there was great concern that, since marijuana was generally consumed by smoking, many persons would be exposed to marijuana smoke passively, that this passively consumed marijuana and its metabolites would appear in the urine, and that these persons would be classified as "marijuana users," a clear misinterpretation. So the threshold for marijuana was set rather high. However, after a period of time, many programs using urinalysis testing reported frequent cases of persons who admitted to marijuana use "passing" their urinalysis; that is, they were getting a "negative" urinalysis outcome even though they readily admitted smoking marijuana, often quite consistently. An examination of these cases showed marijuana was present in the urine, but below the COV. Eventually, the recommended COV was lowered (it is now about one-third the value that was originally proposed!) until a consensus was reached that the value was low enough to detect "real users" but still high enough to rule out marijuana inhalation from environmental smoke.

Thus, the development and application of COVs are designed to deal with some of the problems of test interpretation and the assignment of meaning to the test result. COVs are higher than LODs in most cases to help distinguish passive contamination, inadvertent ingestion, and contamination from environmental sources.

CURRENT DIMENSIONS OF THE PROBLEM

A Look at Real-World Results

As noted, the amount of information of police officer drug use is very limited. A thorough review of the literature failed to uncover any explicit data on the results of drug tests of police officers. However, a limited amount of general self-report drug use data pertinent to police officers are available, as well as some anecdotal or case study data.

This final section reviews some data from preemployment drug screening done by a police department in a major midwestern city. What is interesting about these data is that they provide information on the possible dimensions of the problem of drug use among applicants for police positions. Bear in mind that the persons who appeared for the drug screening were informed in the solicitation for applicants that all persons applying for the police officer positions would undergo drug tests. What makes this situation additionally interesting is that the department used both urinalysis and hair analysis for the drug-screening process. Thus, we have the opportunity to assess the differences in detection when using the two techniques. Recall that urine testing is very good for short-term detection, having a time window of roughly forty-eight to seventy-two hours for rapidly excreted drugs (e.g., cocaine, heroin, amphetamine), but urinalysis does not do well at detecting long-term patterns of drug use. Hair assays cannot detect drugs until three to five days after ingestion, but provided the hair is not cut from the scalp, they can detect drug use retrospectively for several months, dependent on the length of the recovered hair.

General Outcome

Table 7–9 contains the outcomes for both urine and hair drug tests for the applicant pool as a whole. The urinalysis procedure covered ten drugs (cocaine, opiates, marijuana, PCP, am-

TABLE 7–9. Comparing Positive and Negative Outcomes for Urinalysis and Hair Assay for the Applicant Pool

	Test Result		
Test Type	Negative	Positive, Any Drug	Total
Urinalysis	2,253 (97.1%)	66 (2.9%)	2,319
Hair assay	2,164 (93.3%)	155 (6.7%)	2,319

phetamines, diazepines, methadone, propoxyphene, methaqualone, and barbiturates), and the hair assay evaluated five drugs (cocaine, opiates, marijuana, PCP, and amphetamines). All drug screen tests were confirmed by GC/MS, and the tables exclude any drugs that were prescribed medicines. Tables reflect only drugs that were detectable by both urine and hair assays. The results in Table 7–9 are dichotomized into negative and positive for any drug.

As Table 7–9 reveals, the number of applicants testing negative is quite high, regardless of test type. Of course, one would reasonably expect that this group would not likely be one heavily involved in drug use. Not only are these persons applicants for a police position, but they also have been notified that a drug test would be done. Table 7–10, details the particular patterns of positive test results. The number of positive assays for each drug is shown, along with the row percentage, which is in parentheses.

Table 7–10 indicates that cocaine was the most frequently identified drug by hair analysis and marijuana the most frequently identified drug by urinalysis. This makes sense in light of what is known about the pharmacology of the respective drugs and the characteristics of each drug screen method. Cocaine is relatively rapidly excreted from the body. In contrast, cannabinoids (the psychoactive chemicals in marijuana) are relatively slowly excreted, taking anywhere from five days to as long as several weeks to disappear from the urine. Interestingly, cannabinoids concentrate very poorly in the hair (on the order of about 10^3 less than cocaine or opiates) and are difficult to recover and confirm because of the low concentrations. Thus, the major contribution that hair assays are likely to make in this context is in the detection of cocaine, and Table 7–10 is consistent with this conjecture.

TABLE 7–10. Positive Tests by Drug Type and Screening Method for the Applicant Pool

	Test Result			
Test Type	Cocaine Positive	Marijuana Positive	Positive, Other Drug	Total
Urinalysis	19 (28.8%)	33 (50.0%)	14 (21.2%)	66
Hair assay	104 (67.1%)	45 (29.0%)	6 (3.9%)	155
Total	123	78	20	221

Drug Screening of the Applicant Pool

Results by Gender.   Table 7–11 provides drug screen outcomes for the applicant pool, reporting each gender separately. Row percentages are in parentheses. An interesting observation can be made regarding the outcome of the urinalysis screening. Men tested positively for cocaine at a much higher rate than women (2.96 times more frequently), and women tested marijuana positive more frequently than men by a rate of 1.65 times. Both genders had virtually identical negative rates by urinalysis. When considering the results from the hair assays, a slightly different result is apparent. Like the urinalysis, cocaine detection is greater for men than women at a rate similar to the urine test. Men test hair positive for cocaine at 2.2 times the rate of female applicants, which is close to the rates identified by urinalysis. However, the relative marijuana detection for hair is the reverse of the urine results. Marijuana detection by hair assay, like cocaine, is higher for men than women. Male applicants test positive at about 1.4 times the rate of female applicants.

Results by Race/Ethnicity.   Table 7–12 presents the results of both screening types for the four most prevalent race/ethnic groups in the applicant pool. Overall observation indicates that there a few apparent patterns, but most of the comparisons of positive rates across these categories do not reveal any great consistency. Persons who self-identified as Asians had no detection by urinalysis for any drug. Hispanics had low rates of detection for cocaine by urinalysis compared to black or white applicants (whites had a 2.3 times greater rate, blacks a 6.03 times greater rate). However, for marijuana detection by urinalysis, the patterns differed. Blacks had the most frequent rate of detection (1.96%), followed by Hispanics (1.52%), and whites (1.1%). Considering hair assay results, Hispanics had the highest positive rate (7.05%) followed by blacks (6.7%), Asians (4.3%), and whites (2.02%). No group had lower than a 90% negative rate by any test type. As true of all other comparisons, overall, more negative outcomes are observed when examining urinalysis test outcomes than when examining hair assay outcomes.

TABLE 7–11.   Drug Screen Results by Gender, Drug Type, and Screening Method for the Applicant Pool

Test Type/ Gender	Cocaine Positive	Marijuana Positive	Positive, Other Drug	Negative	Total
Urinalysis					
Men	17 (0.98%)	21 (1.2%)	11 (0.64%)	1,669 (97.14%)	1,718
Women	2 (0.33%)	12 (1.99%)	3 (0.49%)	584 (97.17%)	601
Hair assay					
Men	90 (5.24%)	36 (2.09%)	5 (0.29%)	1,587 (92.4%)	1,718
Women	14 (2.33%)	9 (1.49%)	1 (0.17%)	577 (96.01%)	601

TABLE 7–12. Drug Screen Results by Race/Ethnicity, Drug Type, and Screening Method for the Applicant Pool

	Test Result				
Test Type/ Race, Ethnicity	Cocaine Positive	Marijuana Positive	Positive, Other Drug	Negative	Total
Urinalysis					
White	6 (0.6%)	12 (1.1%)	7 (0.64%)	1,064 (97.7%)	1,089
Black	12 (1.57%)	15 (1.96%)	7 (0.92%)	729 (95.5%)	763
Hispanic	1 (0.26%)	6 (1.52%)	0	390 (98.2%)	397
Asian	0	0	0	70 (100%)	70
Hair assay					
White	22 (2.02%)	23 (2.11%)	2 (0.18%)	1,042 (95.7%)	1,089
Black	51 (6.7%)	19 (2.50%)	3 (0.39%)	690 (90.4%)	763
Hispanic	28 (7.05%)	3 (0.76%)	1 (0.25%)	365 (91.9%)	397
Asian	3 (4.3%)	0	0	67 (95.7%)	70

CONCLUSION

Clearly, there is a justifiable concern with the use of drugs by police officers. As noted in this chapter, police officers are a part of society and will reflect society's norms and values, both good and bad. Drug use is a concern because it can impair an officer's ability to function appropriately and effectively, because it heightens and potentiates the possibilities of corruption, because it represents an ethical and legal breach of trust, and because it corrodes the public's confidence in the police and their integrity.

Police agencies have moved aggressively in implementing policies and practices to identify and respond to drug abuse by police officers. This movement is characterized by a series of administrative actions, ranging from creating written work rules to providing counseling, to stress management programs and assistance for the drug-addicted officer. However, often identified as most dramatic of these policy decisions is the implementation of a bioassay-based drug-testing program. This chapter has described how such programs operate, and the technical drug assays that are available to police agencies. It has also reviewed the possible questions, problems, and issues related to interpreting and responding to a positive drug assay. This review has also placed police drug-testing programs and policies in the context of general workplace testing and identified those elements that it shares with these programs as well as the unique issues that police agencies face. Last, data on the outcome of an applicant-screening process using both a traditional technology (urinalysis) and a recent technology (hair analysis). Review of these data indicates that while the vast majority of applicants can pass a drug test, there is a meaningful group of people seeking work in policing that appears to be drug involved. Furthermore, the data support the idea that policing agencies may want to consider using multiple drug-testing modalities to maximize the identification of different drugs whose characteristics can be an important consideration in interpreting drug test results.

REFERENCES

American Federation of Government Employees v. *Derwinski*, 777 F. Supp. 1493 N.D. Cal. (1991).

American Federation of Government Employees v. *Skinner*, 885 F. 2d. 884 D.C. Cir. (1989).

BAER, J., & BOOHER, J. (1994). The Patch: A new alternative to drug testing in the criminal justice system. *Federal Probation* 58 (2): 29–33.

BARKER, T., & CARTER, D. (1986). *Police Deviance*. Cincinnati, Ohio: Anderson Publishing.

Bostie v. *McClendon*, 650 F. Supp. 245 (1986).

BURKE, W., NARISPUR, V., VASANT, D., VENDEGRIFT, B., & IRADJ, M. (1990). Prolonged presence of metabolite in urine after compulsive cocaine use. *Journal of Clinical Psychiatry* 51 (4): 145–8.

Capua v. *City of Plainfield*, 643 F. Supp. 1507 D.N.J. (1986).

CARPER, G., & McCAMEY, W. (1989). Drug testing in police agencices. *Journal of Contemporary Criminal Justice* 5 (2): 89–100.

CARTER, D. L. (1990a). An overview of drug-related misconduct of police officers: Drug abuse and narcotic corruption. In Weisheit, R., ed. *Drugs and the Criminal Justice System* (pp. 79–109). Cincinnati, Ohio: Anderson Publishing.

CARTER, D. L. (1990b). Drug-related corruption of police officers: A contemporary typology. *Journal of Criminal Justice* 18: 85–98.

CARTER, D. L., & STEPHENS, D. W. (1988). *Drug Abuse of Police Officers: An Analysis of Critical Policy Issues*. Springfield, Ill.: Charles C. Thomas.

Committee for G.I. Rights v. *Callaway*, 518 F. 2d 466 D.C. Cir. (1975).

CONE, E., JUFER, R., DARWIN, W., NEEDLEMAN, S. (1996). Forensic drug testing for opiates. VII. Urinary excretion profile of intranasal (snorted) heroin. *Journal of Analytical Toxicology* 20: 379-92.

Copeland v. *Philadelphia Police Department*, 840 F. 2d 1139 3d Cir. (1988).

CRANK, J., & CALDERO, M. (1999). *Police Ethics: The Corruption of Noble Cause*. Cincinnati, Ohio: Anderson Publishing.

DOMBRINK, J. (1988). The touchables: Vice and police corruption in the 1980's. *Law and Contemporary Problems* 51: 201–32.

ELLIS, G., MANN, M., JUDSON, B., SCHRAMM, N., & TASHCHIAN, A. (1985). Excretion patterns of cannabinoid metabolites after last use in a group of chronic users. *Clinical Pharmacology and Therapeutics* 38 (5): 572–78.

FARKAS, G. M. (1986). Stress in undercover policing. In Reese, J. T., & Goldstein, H. A., eds. *Psychological Services for Law Enforcement* (pp. 433–40), Washington, D.C., U.S. Government Printing Office.

FELKENES, G. (1988). *Constitutional Law for Criminal Justice*. Upper Saddle River, N.J.: Prentice Hall.

Fraternal Order of Police Lodge 12 v. *City of Newark*, 524 A. 2d 430 (1987).

GIRODO, M. (1991). Drug corruption in undercover agents: Measuring the risk. *Behavioral Sciences and the Law* 9: 361–70.

Harman v. *Thornburgh*, 878 F. 2d 170 D.C. Cir. (1989).

HARRISON, L., & HUGHES, A. (1997). *The Validity of Self-Reported Drug Use: Improving Accuracy of Survey Estimates*. NIDA Research Monograph 167. Washington, D.C.: U.S. Department of Health and Human Services.

HAWKS, R., & CHIANG, C. (1986). *Urine Testing for Drugs of Abuse.* NIDA Research Monograph 73. Washington, D.C.: U.S. Department of Health and Human Services.

HOFFMAN, J., LARISON, C., SANDERSON, A. (1997). *An Analysis of Worker Drug Use and Workplace Policies and Programs.* Washington, D.C.: Office of Applied Statistics, Substance Abuse and Mental Health Services Administration.

KARCH, S. (1996). *The Pathology of Drug Abuse.* 2d ed. Boca Raton, Fla.: CRC Press.

KNAPP COMMISSION OF POLICE CORRUPTION. (1972). *Report on Police Corruption.* New York City: George Braziller.

KRASKA, P., & KAPPELER, V. (1988). Police on-duty drug use: A theoretical and descriptive examination. *American Journal of Police* 7 (1): 1–28.

LISKA, K. (1997). *Drugs and the Human Body.* 5th ed. Upper Saddle River, N.J.: Prentice Hall.

MARX, G. (1988). *Undercover: Police Surveillance in America.* Berkley: University of California Press.

McEWEN, T., MANILI, B,. & CONNORS, E. (1986). *Employee Drug Testing Policies in Police Departments.* National Institute of Justice Research in Brief, October. Washington, D.C.: National Institute of Justice.

McKenna v. *City of Philadelphia,* 771 F. Supp. 124 E.D. Penn. (1991).

McKIM, W. (2000). *Drugs and Behavior: An Introduction to Behavioral Pharmacology.* 4th ed. Upper Saddle River, N.J.: Prentice Hall.

MIECZKOWSKI, T. (1997). Distinguishing passive contamination from active cocaine consumption: Assessing the occupational exposure of narcotic officers to cocaine. *Forensic Science International* 84 (1): 87–111.

MIECZKOWSKI, T., BARZELAY, D., GROPPER, B., & WISH, E. (1991). Concordance of 3 measures of cocaine use in an arrestee population: Hair, urine and self-report. *The Journal of Psychoactive Drugs* 23 (3): 241–9.

National Treasury Union v. *Von Raab,* 109 S.Ct. 1384 (1989).

NORMAND, J., SALYARDS, S., & MAHONEY, J. (1990). An evaluation of preemployment drug testing. *Journal of Applied Psychology* 75 (6): 629–39.

OFFICE OF APPLIED STUDIES. (1999). *Worker Drug Use and Workplace Policies and Programs: Results from the 1994 and 1997 NHSDA.* Substance Abuse and Mental Health Services Administration. Washington, D.C.: Office of Applied Studies.

ORVIS, G. (1994). Drug testing in the criminal justice work place. *American Journal of Criminal Justice* 18 (2): 289–305.

Penney v. *Kennedy,* 648 F. Supp. 815 (1986).

PERRINE, D. (1996). *The Chemistry of Mind-Altering Drugs: History, Pharmacology, and Cultural Context.* Washington, D.C.: American Chemical Society.

Policemen's Benevolent Association of New Jersey, Local 318 v. *Washington Township,* 672 F. Supp. 779 (1987).

REAVES, B., & GOLDBERG, A. (1999). *Law Enforcement Management and Administrative Statistics, 1987: Data for Individual State and Local Agencies with 100 or More Officers.* NCJ# 171681. Washington, D.C.

REISS, A. (1971). *The Police and the Public.* New Haven, Conn.: Yale University Press.

Report to the Honorable Charles B. Rangel, House of Representatives, Law Enforcement Information on Drug-Related Police Corruption, Report of the GAO [GAO/GGD-98-11] to the House of Representatives. (1998, May). Washington, D.C.: U.S. Government Accounting Office.

ROBERG, R., CRANK, J., & KUYKENDALL, J. (2000). *Police and Society.* Los Angeles: Roxbury Publishing.

Schember v. *California,* 384 U.S. 757 (1966).

Skinner v. *Railway Labor Executives Association,* 109 St.C. 1402 (1989).

SORENSON, J., & DEL CARMEN, R. (1991a). Legal issues in drug testing offenders and criminal justice employees. In Weisheit, R., ed. *Drugs, Crime and the Criminal Justice System* (pp. 329–60). Cincinnati, Ohio: Anderson Publishing.

SORENSON, J., & DEL CARMEN, R. (1991b). Legal issues in drug testing police officers. *Police Liability Review* 3 (Spring): 1–4.

SUBSTANCE ABUSE AND MENTAL HEALTH SERVICES ADMINISTRATION. (1999). *Worker Drug Use and Workplace Policies and Programs.* Analytic Series A-11. Washington, D.C.: U.S. Government Printing Office.

Thompson v. *City of Appleton*, 366 N.W. 2d 326 (1985).

Terry v. *Ohio*, 392 U.S. 1 (1968).

Turner v. *Fraternal Order of Police*, 500A. 2d 1005 (1985).

WEISS, R., & GAWING, F. (1988). Protracted elimination of cocaine metabolites in long-term, high-dose cocaine abusers. *JAMA* (85): 879–80.

YINON, J. ed. (1995). *Forensic Applications of Mass Spectrometry*. Boca Raton, Fla.: CRC Press.

ZHANG, Z., HUANG, L., & BRITTINGHAM, A. (1999). *Worker Drug Use and Workplace Policies and Programs: Results from the 1994 and 1997 National Household Survey on Drug Abuse.* Substance Abuse and Mental Health Services Administration, U.S. Department of Health and Human Services, Office of Applied Studies, Analytic Series A-11. Washington, D.C.: U.S. Department of Health and Human Services.

8

Community Policing and Police Corruption

Joseph A. Schafer

❖

INTRODUCTION

During the last quarter of the twentieth century, several prominent buzzwords rose to prominence in describing how American policing should be conducted. *Community policing, problem-oriented policing, problem solving*—all of these terms refer to an alternative strategy to policing our communities. They represent a movement away from the traditional police practices that emerged during the professionalization movement. This movement to professionalize American policing influenced how police services were provided during the first three-quarters of the twentieth century.

Police leaders, community advocates, and scholars have spent countless hours discussing, researching, and writing about community policing.[1] Largely absent from this dialogue has been consideration of why the professionalization movement altered American police organizations. There were clear reasons why reformers worked to professionalize police departments, and the shift to community policing may create a degree of tension between these styles of policing. According to a common cliché, we are reminded that forgetting history may doom us to repetition of the past. Although it may offer many promises, we must recognize and acknowledge that community policing has the potential to generate unintended consequences, some of which may be undesirable.

---

[1]Although I acknowledge that there are some distinctions between these concepts, for the purpose of this chapter, I will use *community policing* as an umbrella term for the sake of brevity.

This chapter examines the potential intersection of community policing and corruption. It contrasts how police agencies have been organized and have operated during the professional and community policing eras. The impact of corruption is considered in the context of community policing. The relationship between traditional causes of corruption and the benefits of community policing are discussed. Finally, consideration is given to the management of police officers in a community policing context and whether community policing may reduce or increase the probability of corrupt conduct.

NATURE OF THE TOPIC

Too often, discussions about American policing lack a historical context; they fail to consider how various past experiences have resulted in current practices. Overlooking why police agencies are organized and operate in specific manners may result in inappropriate conclusions being drawn about the appropriate future of policing in America. This chapter is intended to acquaint the reader with salient historical and contemporary issues pertaining to police corruption and misconduct, specifically in the context of community policing.

Other chapters in this text have acquainted the reader with historical issues relating to police corruption (e.g., see Chapter 2). This section discusses the historical development of both professional and community policing structures in American police organizations. It also acquaints the reader with the concept of community policing by elaborating on some of the concept's central tenets.

The Development and Reform of American Police Organizations

The early decades of the nineteenth century were times of tremendous change and transformation in America. Populations were increasing rapidly as immigrants flowed into growing urban communities such as New York City (Miller, 1977). Tensions between various racial and ethnic groups, significant economic failures, and conflicting political developments all led to clashes and conflicts in urban communities (Uchida, 1997). Concurrently, the popular perception was that crime was rising. In response to these problems, crime and public safety were being addressed using methods of "policing" rooted in tribal customs developed during the Roman Empire (Reith, 1948). Originally, these tribal systems considered the enforcement of laws and norms to be the responsibility of every able-bodied male. With time, this notion had evolved to the point where "parish constables" were appointed or elected to oversee this function in villages and small segments of larger communities.

Cities such as London relied on a patchwork of parish constables and members of the night watch to address rising levels of urban disorder (Miller, 1977). Parish constables and their deputies served communities during the daytime. They were notoriously corrupt and incompetent. Members of the night watch, charged with combating crime and disorder, were often the old and feeble who could no longer perform other useful functions (Reith, 1948). These officials were ill-equipped, untrained, and little more than a source of public amusement. The impact of this outdated method of policing on crime and disorder was negligible. London and its outlying villages attempted to address this situation by increasing the number of deputy constables, but crime, disorder, and fear persisted. While the parish constable system had worked well for agrarian communities, the Industrial Revolution rendered this approach outdated.

In 1829, nearly fifty years after it was originally recommended, the first modern police organization was established to provide services in the London metropolitan area. The new London police were based upon the notion that crime and disorder could be prevented; their existence was rooted in a set of core principles developed by Sir Robert Peel (Carter & Radelet, 1999). Included in these core principles were the ideas that the police must seek public support, cooperation, and compliance in order to effectively perform their duties and achieve their crime prevention mandate. Although they faced initial opposition, these new police gained respect within the London metropolitan area; other regions of the United Kingdom established similar forces in the subsequent decades (Reith, 1948).

By the 1840s and 1850s, the Industrial Revolution was sweeping through America. One of the by-products of this dramatic socioeconomic transformation was an increase in urbanization and a decrease in the efficacy of existing control mechanisms. News of the successes achieved by the London police encouraged American communities to copy their organizational structure and guiding principles. Modern police forces began emerging in major American communities before the Civil War, although their adoption was not without resistance. After the war, the guiding principles of the London Metropolitan Police became a fixed feature of American police organizations (Fosdick, 1920). Many major American cities date their police forces to the decades immediately before and after the Civil War.

In the early decades of their existence, American police officers enjoyed a close relationship with the citizenry they served (Fogelson, 1977; Walker, 1977). Unlike their British counterparts, however, American police organizations were closely allied with local politics (Carter & Radelet, 1999). On the one hand, this close relationship between the police, the community, and local politics had advantages. In larger communities, such as New York, police officers were originally required to have been a resident of the ward they were to serve (Miller, 1977). This ensured that officers had an intimate knowledge of the neighborhood and its residents (lawful and otherwise). Alternatively, linking police officers with local political leaders had a tendency to make the police a tool that could be used to further an elected official's agenda.

In the early decades of their existence, policing was typically viewed as "casual labor" rather than as a career (Walker, 1977). In large cities, officers were often political appointees who were being rewarded for their loyalty and service to the dominant political interests. Despite working long hours, officers had few real duties. In the absence of effective communication systems, officers could not be alerted of "crimes in progress" in a timely fashion. Much of their patrol time was undirected, and they were generally free from supervision. Walker notes that in the absence of direction, supervision, and training, officers often found "alternative" ways to spend their working hours. Such alternatives might range from relatively innocuous activities, such as hanging out in barber shops or saloons, to serious corruption and abuses of authority. Corruption and misconduct were in no way unique behaviors exhibited by police officers; these problems were endemic in many aspects of municipal politics during this era.

Efforts to reform corruption in police organizations, as well as politics in general, began to emerge during the latter decades of the nineteenth century. Consequently, during the first decades of the twentieth century, there was a push to professionalize police officers and to remove them, at least symbolically, from the community they served. One of the ways in which police reform was brought about was through modifications in the structure of police organizations and the imposition of controls on officers. The traditional structure of police organizations emerged during the reform era to create greater accountability and oversight of police officers to minimize opportunities for misconduct, graft, bribery, and corruption.

During the early decades of the twentieth century, American police departments underwent tremendous organizational transformation. Previously, operational styles and organizational structures had varied widely between different jurisdictions. Prominent police executives such as August Vollmer and O. W. Wilson advocated for a professionalization of American police organizations. Incumbent in the notion of professionalization is that a one-size-fits-all organizational structure was the ideal way to structure and operate a police agency. For the first time, American police organizations began to adopt management principles to guide their daily operations. The traditional structure of police organizations emerged from this application of the principles of scientific management to police organizations (Walker, 1999).

This traditional structure has been characterized as bureaucratic, hierarchical, and paramilitary (Cordner, 1978; Franz & Jones, 1987). Police organizations adopted rigid structures; communication and direction flowed down the chain of command. Officers were expected to follow orders given by their supervisors and were disciplined for disobedience. Detailed policies and procedures were developed to restrict officer discretion in performing routine functions. Accountability was created to ensure that officers were on the job and were not involved in corruption or misconduct. Police officers were selected based upon civil service criteria, rather than as a result of political patronage. Police leaders were chosen based upon their qualifications. The influence of external political considerations was eliminated from the management of police organizations (Walker, 1999). All of these elements were intended to preserve the integrity of police organizations.

The Rise of Community Policing

Robert Merton (1936) writes of the "unanticipated consequences of purposive social action." Merton contends that well-intended efforts often produce unforeseen results; this is an apt description of the movement to reform and professionalize American police organizations. Reform initiatives were undertaken to remove the police from political control, to create public confidence in the integrity of the office of "police officer," and to reduce opportunities for officers to engage in undesirable behavior. While such intentions are certainly benevolent, they resulted in a fundamental transformation in the relationship between the police and the communities they served. In effect, removing the police from political control and corruption was achieved by imposing a rigid organizational structure that created a wedge between the police and the public. This separation from the community was reinforced by historical circumstances, including the development and proliferation of automobiles, telephones, and two-way radios.

By its very nature, policing is an occupation that requires that the line-level employee (the patrol officer working a beat) be granted a certain degree of discretion. Consequently, administrators in traditional organizations sought to maintain a high degree of internal control by creating detailed policies to define the parameters of officer behavior and to control their discretion (Weisburd et al., 1988). In addition, the widely scattered nature of a police workforce makes it more difficult to oversee the activities and behaviors of employees. Unlike a factory setting, police employees are not in one central location where their actions may be closely monitored. Because of this, administrators have traditionally employed written policies, procedures, directives, and rules in an attempt to control officer conduct and action.

The traditional model of policing resulted in an established style of operational behavior for patrol officers. Officers typically engaged in preventive patrol (Reiss, 1971). Officers spent their free time attempting to spot some sign of trouble, be it a traffic violation or suspicious activity. When officers were given a call for service, they were typically sent to "take a complaint" from a citizen. All too often, these encounters resulted in police officers finding themselves cast as the adversary in their contacts with citizens (Wilson, 1968). When the police were called to intervene in a situation, the result was often that someone was arrested or given a citation. The person on the receiving end of this sanction might feel animosities toward the officer, even though the officer was only doing his job by enforcing the law. As a result, officers often felt a sense of isolation from, and antagonism toward, the community they served (Manning, 1997; Rubinstein, 1973; Skolnick, 1994).

For better or worse, police reformists were successful in their efforts to bring about change in American police organizations. According to Walker:

> By the end of the 1930s the dominant feature of modern American police administration had taken shape . . . large bureaucratic structures organized along hierarchical, semi-military lines, increasingly drawn into a tight knit subculture. (1977, p. ix)

The effect of these reform efforts was not limited to altering the relationship between the police and the public. The impact of the traditional structure on employees was often counterproductive for organizations. Gary Cordner observes that frequently the traditional organizational structure resulted in negative consequence for employee morale and motivation.

> Among these feelings are demoralization and powerlessness in the lower ranks, a conception of top command as arbitrary, a growing cynicism among supervisory and middle-management personnel, and the subsequent development of a we/they attitude toward top management. . . . Ideas are stifled, officers are not confident of the support of top management, and the CYA syndrome takes hold. (1978: 30)

Suspicion is engendered between the ranks. Communication within the organization slows to a trickle. Distrust begins to grow, particularly of higher echelons in police departments. Morale problems emerge at all levels of the organization, most prominently among line-level officers (Franz & Jones, 1987).

As the educational level of employees increases, employees experience a greater desire to be involved in the decision-making process within their organization (Angell, 1971). The traditional model does not allow for such autonomy and input, leaving officers feeling frustrated, alienated, and resentful. The traditional structure, while well intentioned, created profoundly negative consequences for line-level police officers. Such consequences included feeling isolated from police administrators and disenfranchised from the public they served.

The various tensions resulting from the traditional model of policing may be a powerful force in socializing officers to adopt particular attitudes and behavioral patterns. By virtue of their social role, police officers are granted unique powers and rights that tend to set them apart from other members of society (Bittner, 1970; Kobler, 1975). This status also tends to reinforce the idea among police officers and organizations that the police have a monopoly on expertise about crime and community safety (Trojanowicz et al., 1998).

The net impact of the traditional model was a dysfunctional structure that created control and accountability at the expense of community alliances and employee morale. In addition, research indicated that traditional policing approaches were largely ineffective (Skolnick & Bayley, 1986). Although many employees entered policing with the hopes of "changing the world," few were able to maintain a positive outlook on their chosen occupation. The essence of this situation is best captured by Trojanowicz et al., who remarked that "thwarted idealists may struggle against becoming cynics, but cynicism toward the community and toward the police hierarchy may be so potent that few can resist" (1998: 269).

A Brief Overview of Community Policing

The first three-quarters of the twentieth century saw several substantial efforts to modify police operations and practices. Attempts were made to professionalize policing, to improve police–community relations, and to promote crime prevention. Despite these efforts, crime rates and public perceptions of safety seemed to fluctuate independently. In the aftermath of the President's Commission on Law Enforcement and the Administration of Justice of 1967, police practitioners and scholars had begun to question the fundamental assumptions upon which traditional police operations were based. The result of these inquiries was that the "research had shown repeatedly that traditional police strategies were not working effectively" (Skolnick & Bayley, 1986: 3). If the accuracy and validity of these findings are accepted, the tried-and-true methods of policing employed by virtually every law enforcement agency in the county in the mid-1970s were doing nothing to reduce crime or foster a feeling of safety among the public.

Police agencies had taken steps to insulate their officers from excessive contact with the public out of fear that such interactions might produce undesirable behavior. Citizens, however, were not satisfied with the distant relations they had with police officers under the traditional style of policing (Bracey, 1992). In addition, police officers were dissatisfied with control mechanisms that deprived them of the opportunity to get to know neighborhoods and citizens, to establish trust and cooperation with the community, and to develop long-term solutions to persistent community problems (Bracey, 1989).

A redefinition of American policing occurred during the last quarter of the twentieth century. Community policing emerged on the tail end of this effort. During that time, there was a growing realization that professional policing inadvertently "left people out of policing" (Trojanowicz & Carter, 1988: 1). This omission occurred both in terms of the people that police organizations served and the people they employed. Police–community relations, crime prevention, and team policing all attempted to reintegrate people into the process of policing. Each of these successive efforts moved police organizations away from the strict control and rigid structure of the traditional model of policing. In addition, each effort was less programmatic and more philosophical than its predecessor.

Community policing is a reform innovation that finally moved beyond a program and crossed over to the realm of organizational philosophy. In its pure form, community policing is carried out by an organization, not by select members. It is an idea that is integrated into the beliefs, values, and actions of all members of an organization. Community policing requires police organizations to rethink their relationship with their community. Citizens are viewed as being "co-producers" of police services; as such, they play an important role in directing and supporting police activities aimed at reducing crime and disorder (Trojanowicz et al., 1998). Community policing is rooted in the belief that "effective policing requires lengthy, stable, *personal* involvement of police officers in the community and with its residents" (Bracey, 1992: 179) (emphasis in the original).

While community policing holds the promise to bring about a positive transformation in American policing, some view it with skepticism because it has emerged from a line of other failed evolutions (Trojanowicz & Carter, 1988). Perceived as the latest installment for managers who subscribe to the "paradigm of the month club," many line-level officers do not take this philosophy seriously. It is perceived as a temporary phase that will pass in favor of the next wave of innovative (and federally funded) policing. This perception has made it difficult for many agencies to shift to a community policing paradigm, regardless of good intentions among police executives.

Despite the abundance of attention it has received since the mid-1970s, community policing is still a concept that many do not fully understand. Wilkinson and Rosenbaum observe that:

> community policing represents a fundamental change in the basic role of the police officer, including changes in his or her *skills, motivations,* and *opportunity* to engage in problemsolving activities and to develop new partnerships with key elements of the community. (1994: 110) (emphasis in original)

Community policing is based on the concept that police officers and private citizens can work together to creatively solve community problems (Trojanowicz et al., 1998). While these problems may relate to crime, they may also relate to the fear of crime, neighborhood disorder (either social or physical), or quality-of-life conditions. Rather than viewing themselves as the resident experts on crime, police organizations and officers are required to take a more democratic approach in the community policing model; organizations, officers, and community residents collaboratively identify problems, establish priorities, and develop and enact solutions.

Community policing epitomizes a new organizational strategy that allows police agencies to decentralize services and realign the patrol function (Skogan & Hartnett, 1997). Under the traditional model of policing, organizations have historically emphased staffing specialized units, often at the expense of the patrol division. Community policing renews emphasis on staffing and supporting the patrol division. By reallocating personnel from specialized functions into the more generalized patrol division, agencies engaging in community policing can support more community-based efforts (Greene et al., 1994).

The focus of the community policing strategy is supporting the line officer who is assigned to work closely with people and problems in a designated geographic area (Trojanowicz et al., 1998). Community policing may place a heavy emphasis on "establishing geographic responsibility and accountability to police officers, establishing relatively permanent shifts and beats for personnel assignments, and limiting cross-dispatching of officers away from assigned areas" (Weisel & Eck, 1994: 65). It is a way for the police to strengthen their ties with the citizens and community they serve (Greene et al., 1994). The traditional model of policing emphasized controlling officer discretion and creating distance between them and the public. Community policing, in contrast, emphasizes building alliances with the public and encouraging officers to be creative and innovative in addressing persistent community problems.

The late Robert Trojanowicz did more than any other scholar or practitioner to define what constitutes "true" community policing and to further the cause of community policing. According to his work (see generally, Trojanowicz & Carter, 1988; Trojanowicz et al., 1998), community policing is:

- *A philosophy and an organizational strategy, not just a tactic or a program:* True community policing is reflected in the attitudes and actions of all officers in a police organization, not just a select few who are relegated to a specialized unit. It shapes all aspects of police operations, not just narrow tasks in limited geographical areas.
- *Problem-oriented:* The police proactively seek out long-term solutions to the conditions that are contributing to crime and disorder. This problem focus cannot occur without input and involvement from the community.
- *Working together and sharing power:* Citizens are viewed as partners in the process of bringing about positive change within a community. As such, they have knowledge and resources that can make cooperative efforts more successful than police efforts alone.
- *Developing trust:* Incidents of corruption and abuses of power, no matter where they occur, can harm the image of the police in their community. Community policing gives a name and a face to the police so that residents will feel that the police are people they can trust and work with.
- *Creativity and innovation:* Community policing is not a static program; it is a fluid response to dynamically changing needs and issues. To succeed, it must seek out new and different ways to address these problems.
- *Broadly focused:* While traditional policing was focused strictly on quantitative outputs (response time, arrests made, crimes reported, crimes cleared), community policing also considers qualitative outputs (the fear of crime, the level of neighborhood disorder, the quality of community life, the degree of citizen satisfaction).
- *Geographically focused:* Because officers are placed in the same geographic area every time they work, it is expected that officers will come to know the people and problems in that area and will develop a feeling of ownership. As officers become involved in the life of a neighborhood on a day-to-day basis, they will become more invested in that area and its quality of life.

Despite the vast amount of literature written about community policing in the last quarter century, there is still a great deal of confusion over what it is and is not. In addition to defining what community policing is, Trojanowicz et al. (1998) also defined what it is not:

- *Community policing is not a technique:* "Community policing is not a technique that departments can apply to a specific problem, but an entirely new way of thinking about the role of the police in the community" (p. 15).
- *Community policing is not public relations:* Although improved relations with the public are welcome by-products of community policing, they are not conscious objectives. Prior attempts at improving police–community relations were largely appearance, while community policing is substance.
- *Community policing is not soft on crime:* Community policing does not restrict officers from making arrests or enforcing the law. Officers involved in community policing may make fewer arrests than their traditional counterparts, but this is because they are dealing with a broad range of community concerns and issues, not all of which are criminal in nature.
- *Community policing is not an independent entity within a police department:* Although not every officer in a community policing organization will work an assigned beat area every day, they may still operate in a manner consistent with the philosophy.
- *Community policing is not cosmetic:* "Community policing broadens the police mandate to focus on proactive efforts to solve problems" (pp. 17–8). Officers concern themselves not just with matters of crime but also with noncriminal matters of concern to the community they serve.
- *Community policing is not just another name for social work:* The police already perform a wide variety of services that have little to do with serious crime. Government as a whole has a moral obligation to serve its constituents; as the only government social agency in operation twenty-four hours a day, seven days a week, the police must be responsive to requests for information and service that are noncriminal in nature.
- *Community policing is not a panacea:* Social problems are dynamic, making it difficult to correct them with simple solutions. Although it will not fix every problem, community policing is the most responsive policing philosophy developed to date.

Despite periodic criticism of community policing by uninvolved officers, those who spend time working in such an assignment often find it to be a rewarding experience and may be more supportive of community policing as a philosophy of policing (Trojanowicz et al., 1998). Officers may find that a community policing assignment increases their overall job satisfaction (Wycoff & Skogan, 1994). Officers working in community policing assignments report that they get to know the "good people" on their beat and felt that they had better relationships with the community (Skogan & Hartnett, 1997).

Community policing may also enhance relationships within police departments (More, 1998). Cooperation and communication may increase between various units within a department as these units all work together to respond to neighborhood problems and community concerns. Supervisor–subordinate relationships also improve. Line officers feel that they have a voice in their organization and perceive that their contributions are being recognized. Community policing affords officers the opportunity to exercise creativity and innovation, while developing a sense of ownership; however, it should be noted that not all police officers want to be creative or innovative. Based on evaluative and descriptive studies by others, it is generally expected that officers who have held a community policing assignment view this philosophy more favorably than do those who have performed only traditional policing duties.

The professional model dominated American policing for the majority of the twentieth century. Despite its virtues, this model had serious negative consequences for those officers on the receiving end of its command and control. Community policing has emerged as an alternative way for police organizations to operate. The major differences between traditional and community policing paradigms are clear. While it has been defined and operationalized differently from agency to agency, a community policing philosophy emphasizes partnership, prevention, and problem solving. Police officers with experience in community policing typically report having a greater sense of satisfaction in the job they perform and view citizens as partners, rather than adversaries.

MAJOR ISSUES

Concern over the level of police misconduct and corruption was among the most prominent motivations for the reform movement, which changed the face of American policing in the first three-quarters of the twentieth century. Reformists and progressive police managers believed that major factors contributing to this problem included the lack of control over police officers and the close ties between officers and the public. As a result, the traditional structure for police organizations emerged to control officer conduct, to restrict employee discretion, to create accountability, and to limit opportunities for corruption and misconduct. More recently, scholars and practitioners have questioned whether this traditional structure has created a healthy environment for police employees and whether it was an effective means to address crime problems in American communities.

Despite all of the dialogue and writings in support of community policing, little attention has been given to the possibility that this organizational approach may allow officers to engage in corruption with greater ease. There is no indication that agencies that have embraced community policing have different rates of corruption or misconduct (Kelling, 1988). It does not appear that agencies that have made the transition to a community policing philosophy have either more or less corruption than agencies structured in a traditional fashion. In addition, there is no indication that agencies that embrace community policing will see an effect (either positive or negative) on the rates of undesirable officer behavior. This lack of evidence, however, does not nullify the need for more discussion of this topic.

Corruption and misconduct by a few employees have the tendency to brand entire agencies, or police in general, with these undesirable labels. As Sherman remarks, "police corruption scandals successfully define the entire police department as a corrupt organization" (1978: 206). In the eyes of the public, the guilt and stigma associated with wrongdoing may extend well beyond those few officers who committed these acts. When the general public thinks of New York City police officers, do they envision the faceless officers who operate "by the book?" It may be more likely that the term "New York City police officer" conjures up images of officers such as Justin Volpe, who used a broken broomstick handle to commit an act of sodomy on Abner Louima. The act of this one officer (and his apparent co-conspirators) created a stigma that tens of thousands of other officers must bear on a daily basis.

Incidents such as the assault on Louima create negative consequences for entire organizations (and to some extent, police officers everywhere). The acts of a very few, however aberrant, may unravel police–community alliances that have been painstakingly constructed over the course of many years. Dantzker captures the essence of this situation, observing that:

> From a community standpoint, corruption among police officers leads to a loss of respect and trust for all members of the police agency. An unfortunate phenomenon is that it only takes one corrupt officer to cause community distrust of the whole police agency, severely hampering the agency's effectiveness. (1995: 160)

In addition to causing strains in police–community relationships, major scandals have a deleterious impact on the morale of other officers. The actions of their co-workers force officers to endure media scrutiny, public resentment, and a general stigmatization of their agency and their profession. Regardless of their own guilt or innocence, other officers must bear the burden created by the corruption and misconduct of their peers.

The birth of community policing may have enhanced the negative repercussions of major scandals on police organizations and officers. In the past, when incidents of misconduct and/or corruption came to light, these incidents made it more difficult for officers to pursue their goals. Enforcing the law became more challenging because the institution of policing had lost some status in the eyes of the public, and officer morale would suffer as a consequence. In addition, officers might face greater restrictions on their behavior as agencies struggled to regain control of their employees (Sherman, 1978; Wilson, 1968). The behavior of the few would frequently result in restrictions on the conduct and freedom of the many.

This challenging situation is compounded in agencies embracing a community policing philosophy. Acts of corruption or misconduct erode the very foundation of what agencies are hoping to achieve: increased public trust and cooperation. While such trust and cooperation were helpful for traditional agencies, they are a fundamental necessity if community policing agencies are to achieve their goals and objectives. If agencies lose the partnership and goodwill they have cultivated within their community, they will not be able to operate successfully under a community policing philosophy. In community policing, the police and the public are co-producers of services. Acts of corruption or misconduct by officers may eliminate, or at the very least stymie, cooperation between the police and the citizenry they serve.

Acts of misconduct, whether real or perceived, may pose a significant challenge to fostering understanding and support between the police and the public. Relationships that have historically been weak may be even more susceptible to this problem. For example, allegations of "racial profiling" create a point of contention between the police and minority groups. These minority groups are the very segments of the population with whom the police must work the hardest in order to establish improved relations. When relationships are established between the police and the minority community, they may be strained by allegations of wrongdoing. Agencies must be conscious of how various members of the community perceive their tactics and operations. Although the police may understand the rationale behind their conduct, the same might not always be said about community residents.

Community policing has the capacity to help residents better understand police operations and tactics, and in this way it may help reduce public perceptions of abuse and misconduct. Such perceptions, while fallacious, may still harm relationships between the police and segments of the population. For example, youths and members of minority groups may perceive certain police actions as having improper motivations. The impetus behind an officer's decision to search a vehicle's passengers during the course of a traffic stop may be legitimate (e.g., based upon an observed traffic violation, not the driver's race/ethnicity, gender, or age). Further, an officer's conduct may be based upon lawful and reasonable considerations, such as personal safety.

Community policing allows agencies to establish dialogue with disenfranchised members of their community. By educating the public about the motives that drive officer conduct in public interactions, citizens may better understand police actions. In the traffic stop example, if these citizens understood that the officer's search was a result of the officer's concern for their personal safety, they might be less likely to view the interaction as having been negative. In turn, they would be less likely to speak ill about the police as a result of this contact.

CAUSES

Other chapters in this text have addressed the causes of specific forms of police misconduct and corruption. This section considers these and other perspectives and demonstrates how they relate to community policing. Certain specific forms of corruption may have unique causes. In general, however, prior research suggests several enduring perspectives on factors that motivate officers to engage in misconduct and corrupt behavior.

Few police officers begin a career in policing with the preconceived notion that they will pursue personal gains through corruption, graft, and misconduct. In fact, research suggests that most people pursue a career in policing out of a sense of benevolence; they wish to help others in times of need (Meagher & Yentes, 1986). Unfortunately, too many officers find their way to a corrupt lifestyle over the course of their career. The critical issue that administrators and scholars seek to understand is how an honest and law-abiding citizen may come to rationalize the need to engage in corruption or misconduct. Is such behavior a product of individual weaknesses, occupational socialization, organizational culture, or some combination thereof? If the general causes of corruption are understood, appropriate solutions may be developed and implemented.

Sherman (1974) describes the "evolution of the moral career" of police officers as it relates to corruption. He suggests that there is a progression that corrupt officers generally follow in the process of "becoming bent." New officers are socialized into a peer group that accepts (and perhaps encourages) some level of graft. Sherman (1978) argues that an officer starts by taking small bribes or gratuities (e.g., free meals, discounts at a store, or free liquor), which seem harmless. Over time, officers learn to neutralize their conduct, particularly if they find themselves becoming cynical or disillusioned about their occupation. This situation may be compounded when an officer is faced with economic hardship, either due to poor personal financial planning, unforeseen family situations, or poor pay. Eventually, officers may be able to rationalize taking sizable bribes to ignore or protect serious criminal offenses, or they may even engage in crimes themselves.

Legendary police executive O. W. Wilson was vehemently opposed to officers' accepting any form of gratuity from the public, no matter how small (Bopp, 1977). Wilson subscribed to the "slippery slope" perspective of corruption and misconduct (Smith, 1974) Much like Sherman's "moral career" hypothesis, this school of thought believes that once officers begin to take small gifts or bribes (even though they may seem insignificant), it becomes easier to accept more significant gratuities. In time, the proverbial free cup of coffee may lead an officer to accept money in exchange for turning a blind eye to prostitution or gambling. In other words, once an officer begins slipping down the slope of corruption, it is easy to keep sliding into more significant forms of misconduct.

Neiderhoffer's (1969) work supports these perspectives. He suggests that most officers enter policing with good intentions and often see little or no harm in their first acts of misconduct or corruption. Their first infraction may be unintentional, for example, accepting a free meal to avoid a visible argument with a waitress over a bill. Once this first infraction occurs, however, other problems may develop. "Often the first transgression is inadvertent. Or, they may be gradually indoctrinated by older policemen. Step by step they progress from a small peccadillo to outright shakedown and felony" (1969: 70). After an officer has made the leap by accepting minor gratuities it is easy to incrementally progress into more serious forms of deviant behavior.

Organizational culture plays a strong role in the development of corrupt behavior among police officers (Gardiner, 1970). When an agency encourages, or at the very least accepts, misconduct or corrupt actions, it is not surprising to see large segments of the officers engaged in this undesirable behavior. In addition, Gardiner, among others, contends that corruption problems are often not limited to police organizations but are endemic in the local government in general. In the minds of police officers, this broader culture of corruption may reinforce that such behavior is acceptable ("if a building inspector can get rich ignoring violations in the construction code, why can't I get rich ignoring traffic violations?"). In addition, community residents may resign themselves to the idea that a certain amount of cash is required to "grease the wheels" of city government.

It must be recognized that neophyte officers do not make the decision to accept a gratuity or small bribe in a vacuum. They struggle with such decisions in an occupational environment that may influence the outcome of their deliberations. Knowing that other officers accept money to ignore parking laws in front of certain businesses, rookie officers may feel that they are being watched by their peers. The act of accepting a bribe or gratuity becomes a litmus test among one's peers. New officers may feel that such actions are necessary to be accepted by their co-workers (Delattre, 1996; Neiderhoffer, 1969). Accepting free meals is not a matter of pursuing personal gain but a display of solidarity; evidence that an officer is "one of the boys." For officers already involved in misconduct, involving new officers in such behavior ensures that the rookies have a vested interest in not "ratting them out" within the organization. The act reaffirms the new officers are dependable because they share some degree of culpability.

Rookie officers may also struggle with the contradictions and paradoxes they confront on a daily basis in the community they police. Westley (1970) describes how officers frequently become cynical, disillusioned, and pessimistic as a result of the immorality, injustices, and abuses that are the stuff of a police officer's work environment. Leuci (1989) elaborates on this point, describing how his ideals about justice, truth, and fairness became distorted as a result of his occupational experiences. These distortions ultimately lead him to take his first step onto the slippery slope of corruption and misconduct. This first infraction led to far more serious behavior. "It was, by later comparison, minor" (1989: 187).

It is not being suggested that community policing results in an actual decrease in corruption and misconduct among police officers. Kelling (1988) disputes this contention, noting that no evidence indicates that community policing caused an increase in negative behavior in many major cities that have experimented with this innovation. It must, however, be recognized that certain elements of community policing (decreased supervision and control, increased freedom and autonomy) have historically been associated with corruption and misconduct problems in American policing. The key difference between the problems of the past and the circumstances of the present is the broader organizational and community contexts that are incumbent in community policing.

A by-product of community policing is a change in the job satisfaction and occupational experiences of police officers involved in these initiatives. This philosophy modifies how officers interact with the public, allows them to make a difference in addressing persistent community problems, and enables them to feel as if they have a meaningful career. Consequently, while feelings of cynicism, pessimism, and disillusionment still exist, they may not be as profound. Theoretically, an organizational culture that accepts or encourages corruption and/or misconduct would be incompatible with community policing's philosophy of enhanced service through collaboration and problem solving. This is not to say that corruption and misconduct will not exist in organizations espousing community policing. Rather, such an organizational philosophy removes two of the powerful elements that may motivate officers to engage in such unwanted behavior.

As noted earlier, the historical response to endemic corruption and misconduct has been the development of a rigid organizational structure. It was hoped that these reforms would create a structure that would limit an officer's opportunity to engage in corruption or misconduct. The implicit assumption motivating such reforms is that officers will naturally drift toward deviant conduct if their behavior is not strictly regulated. There are many anecdotal examples of a rigid organizational structure emerging in response to a major scandal. In considering the communities he studied, Wilson observes that "invariably a legalistic [formal] department was once a corrupt or favor-doing department" (1968: 180).

This reaction was further typified by the way in which the New York City Police Department has typically dealt with internal scandals. Sherman provides this description of the Department's response to the revelation that hundreds of officers were paid off to overlook an illegal gambling operation:

> A succession of reform commissioners tried to control corruption by tightening the central control over the department. Rigid bureaucratic procedures were established for almost every phase of police activity, with a heavy emphasis on maintaining written records of every official action. (1978: xxvi)

Control was achieved by increasing supervision. Police operations were centralized and bureaucratized; rules and regulations were devised to govern officer discretion and freedom in the performance of their duties. Officers were given even more paperwork to complete in order to document all of their activities and encounters with the public.

There is, however, an obvious tension between such increases in control and regulation and the spirit of community policing. For community policing to be successful, line-level officers must be granted a certain degree of freedom and autonomy. If officers are to be effective, they cannot be burdened with unnecessary procedures, documentation, and policies. Alternatively, agencies must still take steps to create parameters to guide the behavior of their employees. If agencies wish to pursue community policing while still ensuring that their employees behave in an appropriate manner, they must rethink the control mechanisms that they have traditionally employed.

SOLUTIONS

Community policing does not, in and of itself, solve problems of corruption and misconduct. Such solutions may, however, be an unanticipated consequence (Merton, 1936) of adopting a community policing philosophy within a police organization. Alternatively, the freedom and independence incumbent in community policing may create more opportunities for officers to engage in undesirable behavior. It also poses new challenges for effectively supervising and monitoring officers. Corruption and misconduct are still issues that police agencies must confront, even if they are pursuing community policing objectives. Traditional control mechanisms and corruption responses, however, must be expanded to be more holistic in limiting occurrences of unwanted conduct.

Community Policing and Misconduct

The literatures on police corruption and misconduct frequently indicate that these behaviors emerge through a combination of situations. Typically, officers make a slow progression from minor forms of graft, bribery, or criminal activity into more serious forms of deviant conduct. This behavior is often supported or overlooked by the formal and informal organizational culture in which the officers work. The officers may be able to rationalize their behavior as their worldview changes due to their occupation. Employment in the criminal justice system has been likened to working in a "toxic environment" (Bartollas & Braswell, 1997); even the most optimistic and good-natured people may find themselves becoming cynical, pessimistic, and apathetic. The combination of these situations may create an environment ripe for misconduct that even an ethical and moral officer may find very tempting.

If the theory of community policing is correct, this organizational philosophy should reduce actual incidents of corruption and misconduct for two reasons (although opportunities for such behaviors may be increased). First, a corrupt organizational culture is incompatible with the philosophy of community policing. Community policing suggests that organizations should be committed to collaboration and partnership in an effort to address crime and disorder issues. If an agency genuinely has such a commitment, it cannot also support misconduct and corrupt behavior. Graft and bribes are frequently offered to allow criminal conduct to persist without police interference. An agency cannot espouse community policing while it has an organizational culture that supports or encourages corruption or misconduct.

Second, research indicates that community policing ameliorates many of the negative effects of policing as an occupation (disillusionment, cynicism, pessimism, apathy, etc.). Certain forms of corruption and misconduct are the product of frustration officers have with police organizations and the broader criminal justice system (Bracey, 1992). Officers involved with community policing frequently indicate that they are more satisfied with their jobs, have different views of the public they serve, and believe they can make a difference in addressing crime and disorder. Thus, community policing removes much of the frustration and negative feelings officers have toward their occupation and their community. In the absence of these elements, corruption and misconduct may still occur; however, it becomes more aberrant behavior by individuals rather than an accepted institutional practice.

Community policing cannot completely eliminate corruption or misconduct in a police organization. It may, however, reduce the likelihood that officers will tumble down the slippery slope of negative behavior. Although community policing decreases the probability that an officer will engage in corrupt behavior, it should be acknowledged that it does increase opportunities for such conduct. Therefore, agencies must still make efforts to combat and address these behaviors among their employees. Past experiences in corruption control suggest that agencies must rethink and expand the measures they have taken to respond to this issue in a more proactive manner. While past control techniques may still have some value, agencies need to be more creative and holistic in their approaches.

In responses to corrupt conduct by police officers, community and departmental leaders have historically taken steps to create bureaucratic and structural barriers to reduce or eliminate opportunities for future misconduct. These barriers were typically erected as reactive responses to the emergence of major scandals. A primary objective of the reform movement in American policing was to impose greater controls on officers to regulate their behavior and restrict their discretion.

Some have questioned whether community policing does too much to relax these controls and whether it may contribute to a resurgence in corruption and misconduct (Bracey, 1992). This is an important consideration that has been largely overlooked by proponents of community policing. Despite this general lack of consideration, a few have addressed this question and have, for a variety of reasons, rejected such contentions. Weisburd et al., respond to such implications by noting that:

> Putting patrol officers in cars, rotating working shifts and breaking continuity in the assignment of officers to particular units and neighborhoods, were policies intended not only to increase efficiency but also to reduce the likelihood of familiarity and special relationships developing between the officers and the public. Such relationships were thought to increase the likelihood of corrupt behavior. . . . On the contrary, citizen familiarity with police officers may very well serve to make those officers more visible and vulnerable to discovery and complaint. (1988: 42)

In other words, under community policing, officers lack the anonymity that might allow them to engage in corruption or misconduct. Citizens will know the officers who police their neighborhood. This familiarity will allow citizens to recognize inappropriate behavior, and they may even know the name of the officer who committed such an offense, enabling police leaders to take disciplinary action.

In addition, community policing may alter how officers view their job and the community they police.

[One of community policing's supposed drawbacks may actually be one of its greatest strengths. Because CPOs spend so much time working with citizens . . . they are more likely to identify with the needs of the people they serve. CPOs are less likely to adopt the traditional police mind-set of us (the police) against them (everybody else). (Trojanowicz et al., 1998: 226)

The traditional "code of silence" typically found in police organizations (Kappeler et al., 1998) may not be as strong under these circumstances. Officers may come to see the public as their partners and peers. Officers operating under a community policing philosophy may develop a higher sense of duty—the belief that corruption and misconduct would be an abrogation of the trusting relationship they enjoy with the public. It should not, therefore, be automatically assumed that a transition to a community policing paradigm will cause an increase in corruption and misconduct in a police organization.

Supervision

Supervision becomes more difficult in an organization pursuing community policing objectives. The role of a supervisor is significantly different under a community policing paradigm, and the supervisor–subordinate relationship will have to be redefined if community policing is to be effective. Police supervisors have traditionally employed authoritarian measures to regulate and monitor the activities and behaviors of their subordinates. Community policing necessitates that supervisors grant subordinates more independence. In addition, the supervisor acts as a resource to support the actions of those personnel carrying out community policing for an organization (Trojanowicz et al., 1998).

Community policing alters how officers spend their time, making it more difficult for supervisors to ensure that they are being productive and behaving in an acceptable manner. Community policing seeks out alternative measures to reduce crime and disorder in communities; issuing citations and making arrests are not always the best solutions to a problem. This notion is reminiscent of O. W. Wilson's "Square Deal Code," which instructed officers to "never arrest if a summons will suffice; never to summons if a warning would be better" (Delattre, 1996: 54). Given this belief, it is more difficult to quantify the outcomes of community policing efforts (e.g., attending community meetings, interacting with neighborhood leaders, etc.) than the outcomes of traditional policing efforts (e.g., arrests, citations, reports, etc.). The distinction between an officer who is "goofing off" and an officer who is performing his or her duties may not be clearly evident on a daily basis.

The best solution to this challenging and changing role of supervision is not an authoritarian approach but a more innovative management style (Weisburd et al., 1988). Officers who have been given community policing assignments should set long-term goals defining what they expect to achieve in their assigned area. Although productivity may not be entirely evident on a given day, officers should be expected to demonstrate their efficacy over time. On a daily basis, officers should be required to document how they spend their time and should be prepared to justify how such an allocation contributes to the achievement of their long-term goals. This grants officers the autonomy to operate in a largely self-directed manner, while maintaining a degree of supervisory control and oversight.

Addressing Corruption under Community Policing

Police power and authority have been compared to a double-edged sword. "On the one edge is the authority and power necessary to protect life and do 'justice.' On the other edge is the ability to abuse power and authority, to injure individuals, to damage the community, and to affect the social order negatively" (Kappeler et al., 1998: 216). The double-edged sword analogy might also be applied to community policing and possible occurrences of corruption and misconduct. One edge of the sword is the capacity for community policing to grant officers the flexibility, freedom, and independence to be creative and productive in forming community partnerships and addressing persistent community problems. The other edge is the risk that the requisite freedom and autonomy might create too many opportunities for officers to engage in misconduct and corrupt behavior. The challenge for police leaders is to balance this sword, to grant officers independence while preserving control and organizational integrity.

Sherman (1978) divides policies for controlling police corruption into two categories. The first consists of those policies that block opportunities for corruption. Examples include policies barring the acceptance of gratuities, limiting officer discretion, and mandating that officers periodically rotate the time of day they work and the geographic areas they police. Sherman's second category includes elements that aid investigators in detecting and apprehending corrupt officers. Such elements include the development and operation of internal affairs units to receive complaints, investigate officers, and, where necessary, conduct "sting" operations. While these are important elements of a comprehensive corruption and misconduct reduction effort, they are not sufficient by themselves. Although they may have been efficacious and pragmatic under a traditional approach to policing, they are ill-suited for addressing corruption and misconduct under community policing.

More recently, scholars and practitioners have begun to define internal corruption control measures more broadly. These alternative definitions view corruption and misconduct as problems that need to be addressed on multiple levels throughout the course of an officer's career. More suggests that:

> The anti-corruption control apparatus has to be strengthened to include improving the quality of recruits, enhancing police training, strengthening supervision, and upgrading methods of prevention. Additionally, there must be a strengthening of internal investigations, enforcement of command accountability, and the causes and conditions that spawn corrupt acts need to be addressed. (1998: 289)

Others have also defined necessary internal control measures more broadly to include the selection of quality employees; provision of proper training and policies to guide conduct; promulgation and enforcement of rules and regulations that define the parameters of acceptable behavior; and provision of sufficient supervision to hold personnel accountable (Kappeler et al., 1998).

These perspectives view corruption control as a synthesis of the traditional measures described by Sherman (1978), as well as more proactive measures taken by police leaders to select, train, and socialize officers. Such a synthesis is crucial in agencies pursuing community policing objectives. If community policing is to be effective, agencies must take a risk by relaxing some of the controls they had enacted to reduce opportunities for corrupt conduct. For agencies to avoid incurring negative repercussions as a result of this relaxation, they must create officers who will resist potential temptation. The solution, then, is instilling employees with strong ethical bearings. Such an ethical attitude cannot be instilled as a one-time inoculation given to employees during their initial training. Instead, ethics are matters that must be discussed and readdressed on an ongoing basis throughout officers' careers.

Effective Ethics Education

Ethical policing is a topic found in the curriculum of virtually every police academy in the United States. In addition, many colleges offer courses dedicated entirely to the subject of ethics and criminal justice. These educational efforts are certainly motivated by good intentions, but some have contended that they fail to achieve their full potential. Martinelli (1999) suggests that most police ethics programs fail to instill a sense of duty and obligation among police officers. New recruits are given a few hours of ethics training in the academy with the assumption that they will require no further guidance. Unfortunately, this training fails to adequately prepare officers for the temptations they may face once they are working on their own.

Martinelli (1999) argues that ethical issues need to be an ongoing element of a department's annual in-service training curriculum. Agencies do a disservice by discussing ethics only during academy training and then (perhaps) every few years during an officer's career. If an agency wishes to set an ethical tone for its employees, ethics need to be discussed on a routine basis. He suggests that the overall tone of an ethics awareness program needs to get "back to basics," that simply telling officers to "do the right thing" is not sufficient to convey how and why unethical behavior may have negative consequences. Martinelli proposes an approach that he labels the Police Legal Ethics Awareness Training (PLEAT) program. The unique element of the PLEAT program is its reliance on case law and administrative rulings to communicate the importance of ethical conduct.

The PLEAT program is based upon the notion that officers will learn to see the value in ethical behavior when a curriculum appeals to pragmatic considerations. By using case studies of situations where officers have been disciplined for their conduct, both off- and on-duty, students may better understand how their behavior might impact their financial and occupational security. For example, the standard *Code of Ethics* for police officers instructs officers to "keep their private life unsullied"; unfortunately, the exact meaning of this phrase is ambiguous and subjective. This notion becomes more concrete when placed in the context of an officer who lost his job for an off-duty affair (especially when his dismissal was upheld by the state supreme court).

The key, Martinelli (1999) proposes, is linking abstract and ambiguous codes of conduct with concrete and real-life examples of how such codes will be used to judge officers. Martinelli believes that a PLEAT program should be customized to communicate such issues to different target audiences (i.e., academy trainees, veteran officers, managers, and administrators). The specific information presented to a new employee will be different from that communicated to a unit commander. While patrol officers need to understand ethical conduct for patrol operations, supervisors need to understand how they may be held liable for the conduct of their subordinates. He also suggests that the content of the case studies used in a PLEAT program will vary between jurisdictions. Agencies would want to select examples that reinforce issues relevant to their specific Code of Ethics; in addition, the salient case law is often dependent upon local courts, making the development of a universal curriculum problematic.

The PLEAT program is only one element of the strategies agencies may use to combat corruption and misconduct. Certainly, other elements require attention if agencies wish to create a positive organizational culture and to mold officers who will resist the temptation of corruption and misconduct. In addition to ethical awareness training, agencies must also confront other issues, including, but not limited to selecting quality employees who possess the skills and attributes to succeed in a particular agency; ensuring that occupational socialization reinforces academy training through the development of a reliable field training program; creating an organizational culture that, at the very least, does not condone corruption and misconduct; and continually working to reinforce the notion that deviant behavior is an unacceptable violation of the public's trust in their local police. The PLEAT program is discussed here to demonstrate how agencies may take a more holistic approach to limit deviant behavior among their personnel.

A Brief Note on Gifts and Gratuities

It is important to be mindful of the fact that at least two parties are involved in corrupt acts: the police and the public. It has been noted that "the public is an essential ingredient in police corruption" (National Advisory Commission on Criminal Justice Standards and Goals, 1973: 473). Although there are certainly circumstances where corrupt acts by police officers might be better classified as extortion, in many situations, citizens are willing and active participants in the corruption process. "Honest" citizens may willingly offer money to avoid receiving a traffic citation. Other citizens may be willing to pay an officer a regular sum of money so the officer will turn a "blind eye" to criminal activity.

Despite the pernicious motive of the citizens in these examples, in many situations, a gift may be offered with benign intentions. Goldstein contends that many gratuities offered by citizens are "made in sincere appreciation for a service rendered" (1977: 208). A liquor store owner offers a free bottle of wine because an officer frequently drives by the establishment on the night shift. A citizen offers an officer a small reward in exchange for finding and returning her purse. Although the officers in these examples are only doing their job, the citizens may feel compelled to offer a small gift as a sign of their appreciation.

Consequently, in addition to maintaining a degree of internal control, police administrators "have a particular responsibility to make citizens aware of how their individual actions affect the quality of police service" (Goldstein, 1977: 208). Beyond simply educating officers that certain conduct is unacceptable, agencies must strive to inform the public that gratuities are not necessary. While this matter has always been important, it is a particularly acute consideration in agencies involved in community policing efforts. The higher degree of interaction between the police and the public may increase the likelihood that citizens will befriend particular officers. As a token of their friendship and appreciation, citizens may wish to bestow gifts upon officers who have helped them improve the quality of life in their neighborhood.

Advocates of police reform and professionalism have historically viewed gratuities as unacceptable (Bopp, 1997; Delattre, 1996). Many departments have had some form of "no-gratuity" policy during their existence (although actual enforcement may have varied).

Even in recent years, there has been a resurgence in barring gratuities in some major American police departments. In 1990, the New York City Police Department reinstated a policy prohibiting the acceptance of all forms of gratuities; even the proverbial "free cup of coffee" can result in punitive actions against an officer. Similar measures were implemented by the Fort Worth, Texas Police Department in 1991; the agency ordered that discounted and free meals and beverages could not be accepted from local convenience stores or restaurants (Dantzker, 1995).

A citizen's impulse to offer a gift presents an unusual challenge for agencies pursuing community policing. In fact, some have suggested that community policing may increase the likelihood that officers will be offered various forms of gratuities by the citizens they serve.

> [It] is reasonable to believe that frequent friendly contact with local residents and merchants may increase the temptations toward the softer forms of corruption such as the free lunch, the "professional" discount, or the gift of appreciation for effective service. (Weisburd et al., 1988: 43)

In the past, police agencies might have dealt with this situation with the knee-jerk response of banning officers from accepting gratuities. This matter, however, does become more complicated in agencies seeking to improve community relationships and alliances.

> Even honest members of the community may wish to express and strengthen what they see as a personal relationship with personal gifts. Simply forbidding such exchange may weaken the very relationships community policing is designed to produce. (Bracey, 1992: 180)

A "no-gratuity" policy may create an uncomfortable, tense, and even hostile situation for officers who must turn down the offer of a small token or a free meal. Agencies that are making the transition to community policing may need to reconsider whether a comprehensive ban on gratuities is actually in their best interests.

Bracey (1992) proposes that gratuities need to be considered in the context in which they are given. A citizen may feel indebted to a police officer for addressing a problem that has plagued their neighborhood for some time. As a sign of appreciation (not as a means of bribing or demeaning) toward that officer, the citizen might wish to offer a small gift. This gratuity is offered as a sign of appreciation, not as a tool to influence an officer's future behavior. Having a policy forbidding an officer from accepting such a gift may insult the citizen and erodes the goodwill the officer worked so hard to establish.

Agencies involved with community policing may be wise to create a more flexible policy that allows for the integration of contextual factors in helping officers decide whether it is appropriate to accept a gratuity. Such policies, however, do create potential problems in their enforcement. Imputing a citizen's intent may be a subjective process; an officer and a supervisor may not agree on such matters. In addition, agencies may be concerned with how other members of the community might react when they see officers receiving small gifts from business owners or other residents.

There was a time when agencies could simply address the matter of gratuities by simply banning officers from accepting all gifts and bribes. Community policing may increase public appreciation of the police, increasing the possibility that citizens may feel compelled to show their gratitude. A strict ban on gratuities may result in tense moments of conflict as citizens offer (and perhaps insist) that officers accept gifts that they are not allowed to accept. The refusal of an offer of a free meal may cause tremendous damage on fragile and newly established community alliances. Alternatively, agencies must be concerned that allowing gratuities may lead officers to expect such benefits and could lead some down the slippery slope toward misconduct and corruption. Members of the public, practitioners, and academics should engage in greater dialogue to define acceptable parameters for gratuities within a community policing context.

Summary

As agencies are proactive in carrying out community policing, they must also be proactive in using multiple approaches to address corruption and misconduct. There was a time when police organizations addressed misconduct only when a citizen complaint could be substantiated by ample evidence of wrongdoing. Until such an allegation arose, misconduct was largely ignored; after all, what we do not see cannot harm us. This era has ended; agencies should no longer reactively confront corruption and misconduct in response to complaints (Bracey, 1989). While such reactive responses are necessary, they must be supplemented by appropriate policies and regulations, efforts that educate officers, a willingness to discipline officers who commit violations, and the creation of an organizational culture that does not support or tolerate corruption or misconduct.

CONCLUSION

Community policing has, at least on the surface, altered the face of American policing since the early 1980s. Some have been critical of community policing, suggesting that decentralization, relaxed supervision, and increased freedom may create an environment that will allow for more corruption and misconduct. Despite such speculation, no evidence exists that community policing has an impact (either positive or negative) on rates of such behavior. While it is wise to view community policing reforms with some degree of caution, it must also be remembered that this philosophy results in a fundamental transformation in the relationship between the police and the public.

Research into corruption suggests that a key ingredient is a sense of cynicism and pessimism among police officers. With their ideals and beliefs distorted by the harsh realities of "the real world," officers become disillusioned about matters of crime and justice, and what is right and wrong. Taking a small bribe or accepting minor gratuities seems harmless. In time, officers may engage in increasingly serious forms of corruption and misconduct as they develop new ways to neutralize their behavior. Neiderhoffer (1969) sees the situation as akin to Durkheim's idea of "anomie." Social norms of moral, just, and acceptable behaviors seem meaningless in defining the parameters of acceptable conduct (Delattre, 1996). The implication of most corruption studies is that officers generally do not engage in such negative conduct in the absence of this anomic outlook.

Research into community policing, however, suggests that those who spend time working in such an assignment often find it to be a rewarding experience (Trojanowicz et al., 1998). Officers may find that a community policing assignment increases their overall job satisfaction (Wycoff & Skogan, 1994) and report that they enjoy developing relationships with the community (Trojanowicz & Pollard, 1986). They get to know the "good people" on their beat and feel that they have better relationships with the community (Skogan & Hartnett, 1997).

Despite its many promising advantages, community policing does not eliminate the need for police organizations to be conscious of possible misconduct by officers. Agencies must continue to seek out new ways to minimize the risk that their employees will succumb to temptation. Community policing does, however, change the ways in which agencies pursue corruption control. Strict policies and regulations need to be replaced with education programs and increased awareness of the negative consequences that corruption and misconduct create for the entire agency. New officers need to be aware that there will be times when they will be faced with temptations. Agencies must also define what the acceptable parameters of gifts and gratuities will be within their community and organizational context.

Reality suggests that there will always be problems with corruption and misconduct in policing; these problems are as old as the occupation itself. Community policing, however, may reduce this problem by nullifying the cynicism and disillusion that seem to contribute to negative behavior. Police departments have historically addressed these problems by creating structures and procedures that regulate and control the behavior of line-level officers. In making the transition to community policing, it is possible that reductions in oversight and control may provide sufficient freedom to allow some officers to pursue personal gain. This may, however, be an acceptable risk. As some have pointed out, "the potential benefits from community policing far outweigh its potential problems" (Trojanowicz et al., 1998: 236).

REFERENCES

ANGELL, J. E. (1971). Toward an alternative to the classic police organizational arrangements: A democratic model. *Criminology* 9 (2/3): 185–206.

BARTOLLAS, C., & BRASWELL, M. (1997). *American Criminal Justice: An Introduction.* Cincinnati, Ohio: Anderson.

BITTNER, E. (1970). *The Function of Police in Modern Society.* Washington, D.C.: National Institute of Health.

BOPP, W. J. (1977). *"O.W.": O.W. Wilson and the Search for a Police Profession.* Port Washington, N.Y.: National University Publications.

BRACEY, D. H. (1989). Proactive measures against police corruption: Yesterday's solutions, today's problems. *Police Studies* 12 (4): 175–9.

BRACEY, D. H. (1992). Police corruption and community relations: Community policing. *Police Studies* 15 (4): 179–83.

CARTER, D. L., & RADELET, L. A. (1999). *The police and the community.* 6th ed. Upper Saddle River, N.J.: Prentice Hall.

CORDNER, G. W. (1978). Open and closed models in police organizations: Traditions, dilemmas, and practical consideration. *Journal of Police Science and Administration* 6 (1): 22–34.

DANTZKER, M. L. (1995). *Understanding Today's Police.* Upper Saddle River, N.J.: Prentice Hall.

DELATTRE, E. J. (1996). *Character and Cops: Ethics in Policing.* 3d ed. Washington, D.C.: AEI Press.

FOGELSON, R. (1977). *Big-City Police.* Cambridge, Mass.: Harvard University Press.

FOSDICK, R. (1920). *American Police Systems*. New York: Century.

FRANZ, V., & JONES, D. M. (1987). Perceptions of organizational performance in suburban police departments: A critique of the military model. *Journal of Police Science and Administration* 15 (2): 153–61.

GARDINER, J. A. (1970). *The Politics of Corruption: Organized Crime in an American City*. New York: Russell Sage Foundation.

GOLDSTEIN, H. (1977). *Policing a Free Society*. Cambridge, Mass.: Ballinger Publishing Co.

GREENE, J. R., BERGMAN, W. T., & MCLAUGHLIN, E. J. (1994). Implementing community policing: Cultural and structural change in police organizations. In Rosenbaum, D. P., ed. *The Challenge of Community Policing: Testing the Promises* (pp. 92–109). Thousand Oaks, Calif.: Sage.

KAPPELER, V. E., SLUDER, R. D., & ALPERT, G.P. (1998). *Forces of deviance: Understanding the dark side of policing*. 2d ed. Prospect Heights, Ill.: Waveland Press.

KELLING, G. L. (1988). Police and communities: The quiet revolution. *Perspectives on Policing, no. 1*. Washington, D.C.: National Institute of Justice.

KOBLER, A. (1975). Police homicide in a democracy. *Journal of Social Issues* 31 (1): 163–84.

LEUCI, R. (1989). The process of erosion: A personal account. In Kenney, D. J., ed. *Police and Policing: Contemporary Issues* (pp. 181–7). New York: Praeger.

MANNING, P. K. (1997). *Police Work: The Social Organization of Policing* 2d ed. Prospect Heights, Ill.: Waveland Press.

MARTINELLI, T. J. (1999). *Critical Trends in Policing Regarding Officer Unethical Behavior from a Risk Management Perspective*. Unpublished manuscript, Michigan State University.

MEAGHER, M. S., & YENTES, N. A. (1986). Choosing a career in policing: A comparison of male and female perceptions. *Journal of Police Science and Administration* 14 (4): 320–7.

MERTON, R. K. (1936). The unanticipated consequences of purposive social action. *American Sociological Review* 1, 894–904.

MILLER, W. R. (1977). *Cops and Bobbies: Police Authority in New York and London, 1830–1870*. Chicago: University of Chicago Press.

MORE, H. W. (1998). *Special Topics in Policing*. 2d ed. Cincinnati, Ohio: Anderson.

NATIONAL ADVISORY COMMISSION ON CRIMINAL JUSTICE STANDARDS AND GOALS. (1973). *Police*. Washington, D.C.: U.S. Government Printing Office.

NEIDERHOFFER, A. (1969). *Behind the Badge: The Police in Urban Society*. Garden City, N.Y.: Doubleday Company.

REISS, A. J., JR. (1971). *The Police and the Public*. New Haven, Conn.: Yale.

REITH, C. (1948). *A Short History of the British Police*. London: Oxford University Press.

RUBINSTEIN, J. (1973). *City Police*. New York: Farrar, Straus & Giroux.

SHERMAN, L. W. (1974). Becoming bent: Moral careers of corrupt policemen. In Sherman, L. W., ed. *Police Corruption: A Sociological Perspective* (pp. 191–208). Garden City, N.Y.: Anchor Books.

SHERMAN, L. W. (1978). *Scandal and Reform: Controlling Police Corruption*. Berkeley, Calif.: University of California Press.

SKOGAN, W. G., & HARTNETT, S. M. (1997). *Community Policing, Chicago Style*. New York: Oxford University Press.

SKOLNICK, J. H. (1994). *Justice without Trial: Law Enforcement in a Democratic Society*. 3d ed. New York: Macmillan.

SKOLNICK, J. H., & BAYLEY, D. H. (1986). *The New Blue Line: Police Innovation in Six American Cities*. New York: Free Press.

SMITH, R. L. (1974). *The Tarnished Badge*. New York: Arno Press.

TROJANOWICZ, R. C., & CARTER, D. (1988). *The Philosophy and Role of Community Policing*. Available on-line: http://www.cj.msu.edu/~people/cp/cpphil.html [accessed September 16, 1999].

TROJANOWICZ, R. C., KAPPELER, V. E., GAINES, L. K., & BUCQUEROUX, B. (1998). *Community Policing: A Contemporary Perspective.* 2d ed. Cincinnati, Ohio: Anderson.

TROJANOWICZ, R. C., & POLLARD, B. (1986). *Community Policing: The Line Officers' Perspective.* Available on-line: http://www.cj.msu.edu/~people/cp/communit.html [Accessed September 16, 1999].

UCHIDA, C. D. (1997). The development of the American police: An historical overview. In Dunham, R. G., & Alpert, G. P., eds. *Critical Issues in Policing: Contemporary Readings.* 3d ed. (pp. 18–35). Prospect Heights, Ill.: Waveland.

WALKER, S. (1977). *A Critical History of Police Reform.* Lexington, Mass.: D. C. Heath.

WALKER, S. (1999). *The Police in America: An Introduction.* 3d ed. New York: McGraw Hill.

WEISBURD, D., McELROY, J., & HARDYMAN, P. (1988). Challenges to supervision in community policing: Observations on a pilot project. *American Journal of Police* 7 (2): 29–50.

WEISEL, D. L., & ECK, J. E. (1994). Toward a practical approach to organizational change: Community policing initiatives in six cities. In Rosenbaum, D. P., ed. *The Challenge of Community Policing: Testing the Promises* (pp. 53–72). Thousand Oaks, Calif.: Sage Publishing.

WESTLEY, W. A. (1970). *Violence and the Police: A Sociological Study of Law, Custom, and Morality.* Cambridge, Mass.: MIT Press.

WILKINSON, D. L., & ROSENBAUM, D. P. (1994). The effects of organizational structure on community policing: A comparison of two cities. In Rosenbaum, D. P., ed. *The Challenge of Community Policing: Testing the Promises* (pp. 110–26). Thousand Oaks, Calif.: Sage Publishing.

WILSON, J. Q. (1968). *Varieties of Police Behavior: The Management of Law & Order in Eight Communities.* Cambridge, Mass.: Harvard University Press.

WYCOFF, M. A., & SKOGAN, W. G. (1994). Community policing in Madison: An analysis of implementation and impact. In Rosenbaum, D. P., ed. *The Challenge of Community Policing: Testing the Promises* (pp. 75–91). Thousand Oaks, Calif.: Sage Publications.

9

Early Warning Systems as Risk Management for Police

Samuel Walker and Geoffrey P. Alpert

❖

INTRODUCTION

Police departments in the United States are increasingly concerned with the problem of the cost of civil litigation arising from police officer misconduct and in developing strategies for reducing their financial exposure (Newell et al., 1992). Beh (1998) argues that emerging case law indicates that police agencies may increase their financial exposure by failing to take proactive steps to address alleged misconduct, for example, by failing to have an effective procedure for investigating citizen complaints.

Managing risk in a police department can take many forms and procedures. First, an accurate recruitment and screening process should identify those applicants who are likely to succeed. Second, quality preservice and in-service training should orient those successful applicants to the work required of police officers. Third, proper policies that guide officers must be in place. Fourth, strong supervision must augment policies and training, and fifth, a system of accountability needs to be instituted that disciplines officers for behavior that deviates from the acceptable. This system of up-front risk management is modeled after other professions that prepare their managers for possible problems, setbacks, and mistakes. This chapter looks at one aspect of managing risk in police agencies by developing and implementing an Early Warning (EW) system. Be-

Research for this chapter was supported by Grant No. 98-IJ-CX-0002 by the National Institute of Justice Grant, Office of Justice Programs, U.S. Department of Justice. Points of view in this document are those of the authors and do not necessarily represent the official position or policies of the U.S. Department of Justice.

219

fore exploring the specifics of the EW system, we review its history and place as a risk-management tool. We then make suggestions for improving EW systems.

THE CONCEPT OF RISK MANAGEMENT

Actuarial statisticians and safety engineers have been estimating the likelihood of illness, accidents, injuries, and their related costs for a variety of professions (American Society of Insurance Management, 1954–present). In many of these arenas, estimated costs are plowed back into the bids for construction, product development, and even program administration. This concept of risk management has also reached into policing. The concept of calculated risk refers to the ratio of costs and benefits. When the potential benefits outweigh the risks, then a planned course of action can be followed. If the risks outweigh the benefits, then a change or modification in the planned course is necessary. To understand risk analysis, the organizational contexts in which they exist must be understood. In the construction industry, quality and profits are primary concerns. In the arena of policing, it is necessary to attempt to reduce a variety of problems, including civilian complaints about the police and physical risk to officers and civilians. As noted, the risk management approach requires that expected values of events and the undesirable consequences be measured and evaluated. Probabilistic risk assessments attempt to predict the likelihood of safety failures of complex systems. That is, by using fault-tree or event-tree analyses, assessments can show failure probabilities for various components and their links to the system structure.

EARLY WARNING SYSTEMS

One method to track and assess the risks of police officer behavior is the implementation of an Early Warning (EW), or early identification system (Walker et al., 1999). The early identification of "problem" police officers has developed as an important way to curb police misconduct through accountability. Early Warning systems were endorsed in 1981 by the U.S. Commission on Civil Rights (1981) and the 1996 Justice Department conference on Police Integrity (U.S. Department of Justice, 1997) and have been incorporated as part of several consent decrees negotiated by the Civil Rights Division of the Justice Department (*United States* v. *City of Pittsburgh*, 1997). By 1999, about 27 percent of all municipal and county police agencies serving populations greater than 50,000 people had EW systems in place, and another 12 percent were planning to implement one (Walker et al., 1999).

An EW system is a data-based management tool that is created to identify officers whose behavior has reached a preestablished level and that has some kind of intervention designed to address any problematic behavior that is identified. The system is "early" in the sense that a department acts on the basis of performance indicators that do not necessarily warrant formal disciplinary action but suggest that an officer may be having problems on the job. In that sense, the system "warns" the officer's supervisors of the potential problem.

The growing popularity of EW as a remedy for police misconduct raises questions about its effectiveness and the various program elements that are associated with effectiveness. To date, however, little has been written on the subject (Kappeler et al., 1998).

THE PROBLEM OFFICER: EMPIRICAL EVIDENCE

Interest in EW systems has increased in response to growing evidence that in most police agencies a small percentage of officers are responsible for a disproportionate share of citizen complaints and other concerns. The phenomenon of the "problem officer" who receives a high rate of citizen complaints was first recognized in the 1970s. Herman Goldstein (1977: 171) was perhaps the first authority to discuss "Identifying Officers with a Propensity for Wrongdoing." He cited a program developed by Hans Toch (Toch et al., 1975) in which Oakland, California, police officers with records of use of force incidents were counseled by peer officers. The U.S. Commission on Civil Rights (1981) was the first authoritative body to recommend the creation of EW systems in all police departments. The aftermath of the 1991 Rodney King beating heightened national awareness of the phenomenon of the problem officer. The Christopher Commission (1991) identified forty-four "problem officers" in the Los Angeles Police Department (LAPD) with extremely high rates of complaints. The commission commented that these officers were "readily identifiable" on the basis of existing LAPD records. Investigative journalists have found the problem officer phenomenon in other police departments (Walker et al., 1999).

FROM INFORMAL KNOWLEDGE TO MANAGEMENT TOOL

Theoretically, EW systems are consistent with the basic principles of personnel management and human resource development (Mathis & Jackson, 1999; Poole & Warner, 1998). Effective personnel management makes the assumption that employee performance is assessed, evaluated, and reported regularly. Systematic performance evaluations and supervisors' first-hand knowledge of employees should be sufficient to identify those employees whose performance is inadequate or problematic (Redeker, 1989).

Unfortunately, police personnel evaluation systems have generally failed to provide meaningful assessments of performance that provide supervisors with the necessary information to identify officers with problematic behavior. Police departments have been punishment oriented, with few formal programs for helping individual officers improve performance and little organizational attention to officers with recurring performance problems. Oettmeier and Wycoff (1997: 5) argue that "Most performance evaluations currently used by police agencies do not reflect the work officers do." The formal categories for performance assessment are often vague and global (e.g., "initiative," "dependability") (Landy, 1977). In particular, these "systems" fail to address the most critical aspects of police work, notably, the exercise of discretion under conditions of uncertainty and stress, with the most important decisions involving the use of force. The neglect of these aspects of the job is particularly important because of the unique role of the police. Unlike other professions, police officers carry weapons and have the power to use coercive force, even to the point of using deadly force (Bittner, 1970). Failure to correct misuse of force can and often does result in serious violations of citizens' rights and creates serious police–community relations problems (U.S. Commission on Civil Rights, 1981).

The recognition of the problem-officer phenomenon spread in the 1990s to the point where it increasingly became a cliché among police chiefs that "10 percent of your officers cause 90 percent of your problems." Although it may have been conventional wisdom among insightful police officers, it was not until the advent of the formal EW concept that police managers made an attempt to use this knowledge in any systematic fashion as part of the personnel evaluation process. The basic purpose of EW is to translate records of officer performance into a formal management tool for monitoring officers' actions, identifying potentially problem officers, and implementing an intervention strategy to correct problematic behavior, where necessary.

INITIAL EXPERIMENTS

The first EW programs developed independently in several departments in the late 1970s. The process of development was ad hoc and experimental, without the guidance of recommended or model programs. Unfortunately, none of these initial experiments appears to have survived for very long, and little in the way of records survives.

Several departments began using indicators of activities to monitor officers' involvement in citizen contacts that involved specified activities, such as the use of deadly force (Milton et al., 1977). Some of these initial approaches also included the review of arrest reports to identify the use of force by officers. In Oakland, for example, records were kept on individual officers to determine if any officers showed early signs of trouble. Additionally, computers were used to determine if any officer characteristics such as age, length of service, or education correlated with their use of force (Milton et al., 1977: 96). In New York, information on each officer's use of force, use of firearms, complaints, discipline, sick leave, and off-duty employment was used to determine if that officer needed further monitoring or intervention. The "system" included a reporting link from officers who entered the information into the files to an officer's supervisor (Milton et al., 1977: 96). Kansas City cross-referenced officers with their supervisors "on the theory that particular supervisory officers may be tolerating abusive behavior" (Milton et al., 1977: 97).

Although some agencies had methods available to identify violent-prone officers or those in need of monitoring, many apparently ignored the early warning signs. In 1981, the U.S. Commission on Civil Rights report *Who is Guarding the Guardians* included data on Houston police officers indicating that a small percentage of officers received a disproportionate share of complaints. The commission recommended that police agencies establish EW systems to control misconduct:

> The careful maintenance of records based on written complaints is essential to indicate officers who are frequently the subject of complaints or who demonstrate identifiable patterns of inappropriate behavior. Some jurisdictions have "early warning" information systems for monitoring officers' involvement in violent confrontations. The police departments studied routinely ignore early warning signs. (U.S. Commission on Civil Rights, 1981: 159)

MIAMI AND MIAMI DADE: THE FIRST FORMAL SYSTEMS

The first formal EW systems known to have survived to the present developed in the Miami and the Miami-Dade police departments in the late 1970s.

City of Miami

In 1979, The City of Miami Police Department became concerned with its officers' behavior that generated citizen complaints. In a May 29, 1979, memorandum to the chief, the commander of the internal security unit suggested an EW system based on organizational development. His suggestion was for a "cyclical model where the problem is diagnosed, external professionals are consulted, strategies are developed, programs are implemented and evaluated, and results are fed back to begin the cycle again" (Ross, 1979: 1). To demonstrate his idea, Commander Ross had identified a list of officers, by assignment, who had two or more citizen complaints during a two-year period (1976–78). He also compiled a list of officers who had received five or more civilian complaints during that period. Armed with those data and the Internal Security Monthly Activity Reports, Commander Ross computed some interesting statistics. He found that the average number of complaints filed against a Miami police officer was .65 per year and 1.3 complaints for two years. He found that 5 percent of the officers accounted for 25 percent of all complaints. He noted, "That is, if this group were suddenly removed from our department, our complaint picture could be reduced by as much as one-fourth. Obviously, this group should warrant some special attention, if we are to reduce our complaint incidence" (Ross, 1979: 2–3). At the mid point in the study, the average Miami police officer was 32 years old with 8 years of service. The officers with the 5 or more complaints were 27 1/2 years old with 4.2 years of service. These officers with the most complaints were disproportionately assigned to midnight shift. The complaint of excessive force made up 9 percent of complaints against all officers, but for those with 2–4 complaints, it increased to 13 percent of the complaints, and for those with 5 or more complaints, it was 16 percent of their complaints. A similar relationship was found with complaints for harassment.

Commander Ross suggested that commanders and supervisors should be systematically provided with information "that can be used to identify problem officers" (Ross, 1979: 7). He also noted that off-duty employment, including rock concerts, wrestling matches, and football games, generated a high number of citizen complaints. He reasoned that fatigue may "heighten an officer's opportunity to react in an aggressive manner" (Ross, 1979: 10). He suggested that the department should respond to these officers before they become involved in self-destructive activities or develop a trend of violating departmental orders. His proposal included more intensive supervision, counseling by outside professionals, and training in tactics and strategies. He concluded that (1979: 12), "The problem will not vanish, but it can be reduced through constant attention. The solutions will not be cheap, they will be time consuming, and may be difficult to implement. However, the potential is there to make a significant impact on the citizen complaint's [sic] against police officers."

The Miami EW system evolved into one of the most comprehensive approaches to monitoring police officers in the United States. As officers are included, their supervisors are informed. It is the supervisor's responsibility to meet with the officers and to determine if they need any assistance, counseling, training, or other intervention. The Miami EW system uses four categories of behavior to identify officers (Departmental Order 2, Chapter 8):

1. Complaints—A list of all officers with 5 or more complaints, with a finding of sustained or inconclusive, for the previous two years.

2. Control of Persons (Use of Force)—A list of all officers involved as principals in 5 or more control of persons incidents for the previous two years.
3. Reprimands—A list of all employees with 5 or more reprimands for the past 2 years.
4. Discharge of Firearms—A list of all officers with 3 or more Discharge of Firearms within the past 5 years.

Officers who are placed on the EW system, according to the established criteria, are informed by their supervisor, who must investigate the situation and write a memorandum with a recommendation. Internal Affairs provides the supervisor with a report of each incident, which must be reviewed as well as the officer's assignment when the incident occurred. After evaluating the reports, the supervisor must make a recommendation, which may include one of the following:

1. Reassignment
2. Retraining
3. Transfer
4. Referral to an employee assistance program
5. Fitness for duty evaluation
6. Dismissal pursuant to civil rules and regulations

The memorandum goes to the commander of internal affairs through the chain-of-command. Each reviewing supervisor must agree or disagree with the recommendation. The Miami Police Department has had an EW system since the early 1980s. Since the early 1990s, few officers are identified by the criteria. At the end of 1998, one officer was on EW I, sixteen officers were on EW II, no (0) officer was on EW III, and four officers were on EW IV.

Miami-Dade Police Department

Several events took place in the Miami area during the late 1970s that created problems for police officers in the Miami-Dade Police Department, formerly the Metro-Dade Police Department, and Dade County Sheriff's Office. The beating of an African American school teacher and the beating death of another African American (Insurance Agent Arthur McDuffie) by Miami-Dade officers, peaked racial tensions in the Miami area. On May 17, 1980, the four officers accused of the death of Arthur McDuffie were acquitted by an all-white jury in Tampa. Upon notification of the verdict, three days of riots broke out that resulted in civilian deaths and millions of dollars in property damage. As a result of the problems, the Dade County Commission enacted local legislation that made public the internal investigations conducted by the Miami-Dade Police Department. In addition, an Employee Profile System was adopted to track formally all complaints, use of force incidents, commendations, discipline, and disposition of all internal investigations.

As an off-shoot of the Employee Profile System, the Miami-Dade Police Department implemented the Early Identification System (EIS) under the supervision of the Internal Review Bureau. This system was created because early signs of potential problems are often not apparent to officers and may be missed by some supervisors. It is not clear what role the City of Miami's EW system had in the development of the system for the Metro-Dade department.

In 1981, quarterly and annual reporting systems were made operational. The quarterly reports listed officers who had received two or more complaints that had been investigated and closed or who were involved in three or more use of force incidents during a three-month reporting period. The annual system listed employees who had been identified in two or more quarterly reports. The requirement that complaints had to be investigated and closed before they would qualify to be included in the quarterly report created a timing problem, as many complaints took months or a year before they were investigated and closed. Because of this problem, monthly reports were issued in 1992, which listed employees who had received two or more complaints during the past 60 days (regardless of disposition). It is these monthly reports that have identified officers with the most recent complaints or behavioral concerns. Major Dan Flynn (nd.: 2) has reported that:

> patterns of certain kinds of officer behavior, such as serious disputes with citizens and/or co-workers, or an above-average rate of using force, can be very predictive of more serious stress-related episodes to follow. Even though not all complaints and disputes are the fault of the involved officer, a process that enables a review of those events is invaluable. It makes it possible to reach officers who may be experiencing an escalating level of stress, before it gets out of hand and results in serious misconduct.

The monthly, quarterly, and yearly reports are disseminated to the supervisors of the listed officers. The information on the list is "utilized by supervisors as a resource to determine if job stress or performance problems exist. They are designed as a resource in evaluating and guiding an employee's job performance and conduct" (Charette, nd.: 5). The information included in the reports should be used by supervisors as one resource to determine if an officer is experiencing stress or performance problems. The EIS data must be used in conjunction with other information to provide a comprehensive understanding of an officer's performance. It is important to recognize that the information contained in the reports does not form conclusions concerning job stress or performance. The reports are designed solely as a resourse to assist supervisory personnel in evaluating and guiding the officer.

The officer's immediate supervisor receives a copy of a report listing his or her officers. The supervisor can discuss the report with the officer and determine that no further action is needed and can make referrals to departmental or outside programs, including Psychological Services, Stress Abatement Programs, or Specialized Training Programs. In 1981, 150 employees were identified in the two initial reports. In 1982, 46 employees were identified in all four quarterly reports. This decline is due to a number of factors, including the improved recruitment and selection procedures in the agency, and not just the EIS. Between 1981 and 1992, departmental strength increased approximately 96 percent, but complaints remained at an average of approximately 300 per year. Charette (nd.: 12) concluded his report by noting: "A department's ability to monitor and control its employees [sic] conduct in a formalized tracking system, instills confidence in the employees, the organization, and the public it serves."

ISSUES RELATED TO EW SYSTEM ADMINISTRATION

Implementation

The most important EW administration issue concerns the implementation of an EW system in a particular agency. Early Warning systems are complex, expensive, and high-maintenance operations that require a significant investment in personnel, data collection, and administrative oversight (Walker et al., 1999). A significant concern is that some police departments may create EW systems but then fail to provide sufficient administrative oversight to ensure that the program remains vital.

Program Elements

There are three basic elements to EW systems: selection criteria, intervention, and postintervention follow-up (Walker et al., 1999).

Selection Criteria.
Early Warning systems can vary greatly according to their selection criteria. Some systems rely solely on citizen complaints (Minneapolis Civilian Review Authority, 1990), while others rely on a broader range of performance indicators, including use of force reports, involvement in civil litigation, and violations of administrative rules (e.g., neglect of duty). The use of multiple indicators provides a broader base of information than the sole reliance on a single indicator such as citizen complaints or use of force. Relying on a single indicator may result in failure to identify officers whose behavior legitimately requires intervention. Multiple indicators, by definition, are more likely than single ones to identify officers whose performance is problematic and may be in need of intervention.

Intervention.
The intervention phase begins with an informal counseling session between the officer and his or her immediate supervisor. The outcome of that discussion may result in no further action or may lead to the next step, formal intervention. In any case, the results of the informal counseling should be documented, even if the supervisor finds no reason to move to the next step. The intervention can include individual counseling, remedial training, or group sessions to work on a particular issue.

Postintervention Follow-up.
The final issue involves follow-up monitoring of officers after the intervention. This process has the effect of putting supervisors on notice that their behavior is being monitored. And as noted, this approach requires a considerable departmental investment in administrative attention, paperwork, and data collection. Some EW systems have relatively informal follow-up procedures, relying on supervisors to monitor officers' behavior but without any formal record keeping, while others require elaborate documentation (Walker et al., 1999).

Goals and Expectations

Early Warning systems are generally directed toward so-called problem officers: to identify them on the basis of problematic performance indicators and to provide some intervention designed to correct their behavior. The refinement of the goals and expectations of EW systems should have more than one target and should focus on officers, supervisors, and departments.

Individual Officers.   The expected impact of EW systems on individual officers involves a form of deterrence and/or learning theory. It is assumed that, through the process of simple deterrence, officers who are subject to an EW system will perceive a threat of punishment if their present behavior continues and change that behavior to conform to the standards that are explained to them. In this respect, EW systems are designed to be "early" and informal in order to communicate the threat and give officers an opportunity to change before formal disciplinary action becomes necessary. It is also assumed that an EW system may have a general deterrent effect on officers not subjected to the system. Perceiving the EW system as at least labeling if not actually punishing officers, other officers may make an effort to perform according to department standards to avoid inclusion in the EW system.

Deterrence is only one goal of an EW system. These systems are officially intended to help rather than punish officers. The intervention phase is designed provide the counseling or remedial training to improve an officer's performance.

Supervisors.   Although EW systems are generally conceived as a system for correcting the behavior of individual problem officers, a properly functioning system will be directed toward supervisors as well as individual officers. That is, an EW system places supervisors on notice that it is their responsibility to monitor closely officers who have been subject to the program. Thus, the behavior of the supervisor is as much at issue as is the behavior of the officers.

The impact of an EW system on supervisors is potentially twofold. First, if an officer slips through the cracks and the problematic behavior is not noticed, the supervisor will be informed through the EW system. Second, supervisors often find themselves assigned to officers about whom they know very little. An EW system can provide a readily accessed source of data on past performance history that might warrant special attention.

Departments.   The final impact of an EW system is on the organization. In theory, information derived through the EW system (e.g., frequent citizen complaints related to a particular enforcement practice or a specific unit) is used to effect changes in policies and procedures and/or training. Presumptively, such changes can help reduce the existing problems and help the organization achieve its official goals. In this respect, an EW system can contribute to a police department becoming a "learning organization" (Geller, 1997). Similarly, Perez (1994) defines organizational "learning" as one of the criteria for evaluating citizen complaint systems.

In a police department that has no serious commitment to accountability and integrity, where serious forms of misconduct are not punished, an EW system will probably have little, if any, impact. In this context, the program will become just another formal bureaucratic procedure, empty of meaningful content. The potential contributions of an EW system will simply be overwhelmed by the failure of the department to investigate alleged misconduct and discipline officers appropriately. An EW system should be thought of as an administrative tool designed to support a properly functioning system of accountability. In the absence of a properly functioning system, it cannot make any real contribution by itself. At the other end of the scale, in a hypothetically ideal police department with the highest standards of integrity, an EW system is unnecessary. In such an organization, potential problems are already being addressed. Obviously, the ideal does not exist in any known police department, any more than it exists in any other public or private organization.

The vast majority of police departments fall in the broad middle category, with some on-the-street problems with some commitment to accountability. To repeat the essential point made earlier, an EW system is an administrative tool that supports the basic system of accountability. The impact will vary from department to department, according to the strength of the existing system of accountability. In departments with a recent history of accountability problems (e.g., frequent corruption allegations; recurring civil litigation and high damage awards), the EW system will serve as notice to officers that the department is serious about eliminating improper conduct. It will also serve to identify and intervene with officers with recurring serious performance problems. In departments with comparatively high standards of accountability and relatively rare instances of serious misconduct, the EW system will primarily serve an integrity maintenance function. That is, the impact will fall primarily on supervisors to ensure that potential problems do not "slip through the cracks."

CONCLUSION

Early Warning systems have emerged as a popular remedy for police misconduct. They are a potentially important management tool for the control of police officer misconduct and for promoting standards of accountability within a police agency. An evaluation of the impact of EW systems found that they were effective in reducing citizen complaints and other problematic behavior in officers subject to intervention (Walker et al., 1999). This evaluation suggests that EW systems can be an effective risk management tool for police agencies.

The evaluation also found, however, that EW systems are expensive, complex, high-maintenance operations, requiring a significant investment of administrative resources (Walker et al., 1999). The following elements are necessary for an effective EW system:

1. The criteria for identifying "problem" officers should encompass a broad range of performance indicators and should not be limited to just citizen complaints.
2. The intervention should involve more than just an officer's immediate supervisor, in order to ensure that individual supervisors do not covertly undermine the goals of the program.
3. Postintervention monitoring of officers by supervisors is needed. Postintervention monitoring is designed not only to identify cases where patterns of serious misconduct continue, but also communicates a message to subject officers that their performance is being closely scrutinized and, equally important, places immediate supervisors on notice that their responsibilities include the close monitoring of officers whose performance is problematic.

The evaluation of EW systems also concluded that they cannot function effectively apart from the larger organizational culture in which they exist. An EW system is not likely to be effective in a department that has not made a larger commitment to accountability. Or, to put it in crude terms, an EW system cannot "save" a badly managed department. An EW system should be seen as one part of a system of risk management and accountability. In an agency that has made a commitment to accountability, an EW system can serve as one of several management tools designed to curb misconduct and raise the quality of services delivered to the public.

REFERENCES

AMERICAN SOCIETY OF INSURANCE MANAGEMENT. (1954–present). *Risk Management*. New York: Risk and Insurance Management Society.

BEH, H. G. (1998). Municipal liability for failure to investigate citizen complaints against police. *Fordham Urban Law Journal* 25 (2): 209–54.

BITTNER, E. (1970). *The Functions of the Police in Modern Society*. Washington, D.C.: National Institute of Mental Health.

CHARETTE, B. (nd.). *Early Identification of Police Brutality and Misconduct*. Miami: Metro-Dade Police Department.

CHRISTOPHER COMMISSION. (1991). *Report of the Independent Commission on the Los Angeles Police Department*. Los Angeles: Christopher Commission.

FLYNN, D. (nd.). *Reducing Incidents of Office Misconduct: An Early Warning System*. Miami: Metro-Dade Police Department.

GELLER, W. (1997, November). Suppose we were really serious about police departments becoming learning organizations? *NIJ Journal* No. 234.

GOLDSTEIN, H. (1977). *Policing a Free Society*. Cambridge, Mass.: Ballinger.

KAPPELER, V., SLUDER, R., & ALPERT, G. (1998). *Forces of Deviance: Understanding the Dark Side of Policing*. Prospect Heights, Ill.: Waveland Press.

LANDY, F. (1977). *Performance Appraisal in Police Departments*. Washington, D.C.: The Police Foundation.

MATHIS, R. L., & JACKSON, J. H., eds. (1999). *Human Resource Management: Essential Perspectives*. Cincinnati: Southwestern College Publishing.

MILTON, C., HALLECK, J., LARDNER, J., & ALBRECHT, G. (1977). *Police Use of Deadly Force*. Washington, D.C.: The Police Foundation.

MINNEAPOLIS CIVILIAN REVIEW AUTHORITY. (1990). *Administrative Rules*. Minneapolis: CRA.

NEW ORLEANS POLICE DEPARTMENT. (1998). *Professional Performance Enhancement Program (PPEP)*. New Orleans: NOPD.

NEWELL, C., POLLOCK, J., & TWEEDY, J. (1992, March/April). Financial aspects of police liability. *International City Management Association, Baseline Data Report* 24 (2).

OETTMEIER, T. N., & WYCOFF, M. A. (1997). *Personnel Performance Evaluations in the Community Policing Context*. Washington, D.C.: Police Executive Research Forum.

PEREZ, D. W. (1994). *Common Sense about Police Review*. Philadelphia, Pa.: Temple University Press.

POOLE, M., & WARNER, M. (1998). *The IEBM Handbook of Human Resource Management*. London: International Thomson Business Press.

REDEKER, J. (1989). *Employee Discipline: Policies and Practices*. Washington, D.C.: Bureau of National Affairs.

REISS, A. J. (1971). *The Police and the Public*. New Haven, Conn.: Yale University Press.

ROSS, J. S. (1979, May 29). Memorandum from Commander John Ross to Chief Kennith I. Harms. *Citizen Complaints Against Police Officers*. Miami, Fla.

TOCH, H., GRANT, J. D., & GALVIN, R. T. (1975). *Agents of Change*. New York: John Wiley.

U.S. COMMISSION ON CIVIL RIGHTS. (1981). *Who Is Guarding the Guardians*. Washington, D.C.: The U.S. Commission on Civil Rights.

U.S. DEPARTMENT OF JUSTICE. (1997). *Police Integrity: Public Service with Honor.* Washington, D.C.: U.S. Government Printing Office.

U.S. DEPARTMENT OF JUSTICE. (1997). *Police Use of Force: Collection of National Data.* Washington, D.C.: U.S. Government Printing Office.

United States v. *City of Pittsburgh*, W.D. Pa. (1997).

WALKER, S., ALPERT, G. P., & KENNEY, D. J. (1999). *Responding to the Problem Police Officer: A National Evaluation of Early Warning Systems.* Draft Final Report. Submitted to the National Institute of Justice.

10

The Existence of Police Misconduct

Forever Present?

M. L. Dantzker and Kenneth Bolton, Jr.

❖

INTRODUCTION

As this volume on police misconduct was being prepared, a trial stemming from the worst corruption scandal in the history of the Los Angeles Police Department (LAPD) came to a conclusion. Three of four police officers who had been accused of framing individuals were convicted of conspiracy.[1] These officers were part of the Rampart division where officers had been accused of shootings, beatings, and planting evidence on individuals. From the time the investigations began, more than twenty officers have left the LAPD. While the LAPD employs over 5,000 police officers, the small group of officers who stand accused or convicted tarnish the reputation of all LAPD police officers, as does any police officer who engages in any form of police misconduct.

Police misconduct has existed since the beginning of policing. Although often viewed as corruption, "Police misconduct can be defined as a wrongdoing committed by a police officer. This wrongdoing can be a criminal act or a violation of departmental policies and procedures. Misconduct can be unethical or amoral and yet not be considered criminal" (Palmiotto, 2001: 32). By this definition, the possibilities for police misconduct are abundant. However, this does not mean that misconduct has to occur, yet it does despite all the changes that have occurred in policing.

---

[1]Interestingly enough, before this chapter was published, the convictions of the three officers where thrown out by an appellate court. However, the LAPD police chief and the county district attorney vowed to retry the officers.

Attempts to explain police misconduct, in any form, continue among police practitioners and scholars. Because much of the interest tends to focus on corruption, explanations have centered on this phenomenon. However, those same explanations that are used for explaining corruption can also be used for explaining misconduct.

Dantzker (2000) offers three perspectives for corruption that are applicable to the broader category of misconduct: individuality, society, and the police environment. The individuality perspective takes into account that every officer brings with him or her a differing "set of morals, values, and norms under which he or she operates" (p. 175). Because misconduct could be attributed to a flaw in the officer's character, it is easier to simply blame the actions on "a bad officer." Yet, "individuality does not account for the consistent appearance" (p. 176) of "bad officers" in policing.

Since police officers do not work in a bubble but within a broad expanse we label society, we cannot overlook how society can contribute to police misconduct. While politics has been the most recognized contributor to police misconduct (i.e., patronage and payoffs), societal members cannot escape blame. Willingness to look the other way, offer gratuities, or refuse to cooperate are nourishment to police misconduct. Last, one cannot ignore laws, and their broadness and ambiguities can offer police officers an opportunity to engage in misconduct.

Finally, the police environment may be guilty of assisting in police misconduct. As Walker (1999) has indicated, the police environment includes the general nature of policing, the other components of the criminal justice system, and police agency characteristics. As a result, there are ample opportunities and contributors to police misconduct. This volume has offered just one avenue of understanding but through a myriad of perspectives.

SUMMARY

Beginning with Chapter 1, Barker begins the journey into understanding police misconduct by examining early policing in England, focusing on the bribery and brutality that were an easily accepted part of early policing. He continues with a discussion of how policing is ripe for misconduct and requires ethical police conduct, reinforcing this with an examination of professional and occupational ethics and the existence of a law enforcement Code of Ethics.

Barker continues his discussion with a look at the various organizational and rule violations, the reactions both internally and externally, and what may be involved in misconduct, such as money, sex, abuse of authority, and use of force. He concludes by offering various mechanisms of control that include self, peers, supervisors, Early Warning systems (which is discussed in greater detail by Alpert and Walker in Chapter 9), administrational reactions, and review boards. Furthermore, he encourages and emphasizes the need for training and additional research to help better understand and control misconduct. Ultimately, it is Barker's perspective that ethical policing will lead to a lack of police misconduct.

To better understand its existence, in Chapter 2, Bolton traced police misconduct historically and concluded that any act of misconduct should be analyzed by looking at the "complex intertwining of social processes" in which it occurs. He begins by offering how structural economic conditions are analytically central in understanding the production and persistence of police misconduct. To illustrate, he outlines the historical impact of economics from the creation of police agencies to break down the social institutions of minority groups perceived as barriers to dominant group hegemony, to the emergence of technologies adopted by police agencies that foster alienation and conflict between police and communities. Further, Bolton illustrates how dominant ideologies, social institutions such as politics and the courts, components of policing such as administration and subcultures, communities, and the individuality of officers all play roles in shaping policing and fostering misconduct. Ultimately, he suggests that misconduct is not a recent phenomenon and that it is not a "thing" in and of itself easily observed and explained. Rather, he argues, misconduct can only be understood historically, having existed for the duration of policing, and as the outcome of intertwining "social processes." How to address this situation is discussed later in this chapter, in the section entitled, "Thinking about Solutions."

One of the most recognized problems in today's society is the presence and continued market for illegal drugs. Considering that the illegal drug business is perceived as a multibillion-dollar industry, that kind of economics cannot help but affect some police officers. In her chapter, "All Is Fair in Love and War," the volume editor, Kim Lersch, offers an in-depth look at drugs and police misconduct. She begins with a history of drug problems in the United States and the legislation created to try to address the problems. This is followed by a discussion of police corruption and drugs, citing two widely publicized incidents as examples: LAPD's Rampart Division and Miami Police Department's Riverside scandals. In both cases, police officers committed various criminal offenses in the name of profit from drugs. To address this issue, Lersch takes an interesting criminological approach by applying the theories of differential association (who one associates with influences one's behavior) and differential reinforcement (basically, the ends justifying the means). Both theories applied to police misconduct and drugs offer a very interesting perspective.

In Chapter 4, Worden and Catlin examine the uses and abuses of force by police officers. They begin with four major police use-of-force incidents in the 1990s—King, Green, Louima, and Diallo—which, in reality, are more the exception than the rule. As Worden and Catlin point out, the use of force in general is more the exception than the rule, but the police do have a legal right to use force when necessary. However, they note that the police can abuse their coercive authority either by using a higher degree of coercion than that which is necessary or to use less than the situation requires.

Worden and Catlin continue their discussion, looking at the form of force that police could apply. They identify the six common levels of force as being presence, verbal, control and restraint, chemical agents, "tactics and weapons," and firearms. This discussion continues with a description of when each level is appropriate. Furthermore, they differentiate between such terms as lethal force, improper force, unnecessary force, and excessive force. From this point, they review the examination of use and abuse of force in the social science research.

They begin the research component by pointing out that research into police use and abuse of force generally relies on obtaining data one of four ways: records produced by police; direct, systematic observation; surveys of the public; and surveys of the police. They discuss the advantages and disadvantages of each source. In addition to sources of the research, they look at the research as it applies to the following:

1. The incidence of police use of force, which the research shows does not occur nearly as often as perceived.

2. Race and disrespect, for which the results are mixed, but with one consistent finding: Police officers are more likely to use force against someone who is disrespectful.
3. Problem officers: The research shows that force is used disproportionately by some officers. As to why, the research is ambiguous.
4. Organizational factors for which there is minimal empirical evidence to determine how certain factors affect use of force. The factors identified are rules and regulations, selection and training, bureaucratization, organizational climate, and civilian review.

Worden and Catlin conclude their chapter with what we know: Social science evidence provides a sound basis for few firm generalizations about the use and abuse of force by police. Basically, much more research is needed.

While it is unfortunate that police officers do engage in various forms of misconduct, sometimes the media's portrayal of the misconduct could cause misperceptions by the public as to the degree of the misconduct. To gain a clearer picture of how the media reports police sexual violence, McGurrin and Kappeler conducted an interesting study, the results of which are reported in Chapter 5.

In their chapter, McGurrin and Kappeler begin with a true story of a Massachusetts State Trooper who stopped women and then sexually assaulted them. This leads into the crux of the chapter, an examination of police sexual violence (PSV), particularly as it is reported in the media. They build up to their study and its results by first defining PSV as "those situations in which a citizen experiences a sexually degrading, humiliating, violating, damaging, or threatening act committed by a police officer, through the use of force or police authority." This is followed by a brief discussion of the background of PSV, which has been given little attention or is more often referred to as "sexual misconduct."

The chapter continues with a look at linking PSV to structural and cultural forms of gender discrimination. They report that the studies and investigations that have been conducted find that hundreds of cases of PSV have occurred. This leads to the description of their study, which was conducted to explore possible linkages between PSV and state power as well as to examine various media constructions of PSV. To accomplish this task, they conducted a content analysis of newspaper accounts of PSV.

McGurrin and Kappeler initially located over 11,000 articles that mentioned sexual violence, with 1,255 relating to police. After eliminating duplicate stories, they eventually had 501 unique articles. While they report a variety of findings, the bottom line was that they found that the typical offender was an on-duty municipal line officer between the ages of twenty-six and forty-five and with an average of ten or more years of experience. It seems that the power and authority of the badge and uniform were often enough to gain access and accomplish their sexual assaults. McGurrin and Kappeler also found that not much had been done by the agencies or the courts against those officers accused of such behavior.

Overall, while cautioning readers about generalizing their findings to all of policing, McGurrin and Kappeler believe that what they report is sufficient enough to warrant policy review by most police agencies. The authors state that police agencies need to take a more serious stance and approach to officers who are accused of and commit sexual violence.

Policing has long been a male-dominated occupation. However, since the mid-1970s, female police officers have increased their numbers enough that attention should be paid to their activities in the same manner as has been done with their male counterparts for decades. In Chapter 6, Donna Hale presents an interesting examination of the integrity and ethics of female police officers. She does this using an analogy based on *Alice in Wonderland*, where the protagonist Alice enters an unfamiliar world. Hale compares women's entry into policing in the same fashion.

Hale begins by noting that, like Alice, women were viewed and continued to be viewed as outsiders. As such, very little has been done regarding research on women and misconduct. She notes that policing has long supported a Blue Code of Silence and that, by abiding by it, women were more likely to be accepted into the male police world. She continues her discussion with an examination of the limited research that has been conducted on women and police misconduct, noting that findings have been mixed regarding comparisons between male and female integrity and misconduct. Yet she indicates that no support has been offered that indicates whether women are no more or no less ethical or likely to be involved in misconduct than male officers. Hale contends that the police organizational culture tends to affect both genders equally. She concludes that, in theory, gender may make a difference as to who will commit misconduct, but in practice gender does not appear to make a difference despite the appearance that women do seem to have less episodes of misconduct.

In Chapter 3, as mentioned, Lersch discusses the problems for police misconduct and drugs. In Chapter 7, Tom Mieczkowski takes the examination of drugs and misconduct a step further by looking at abuse, corruption, and a need for officer drug testing. He begins with an overview of drug testing, comparing general employee use of drugs to police employee use. Regarding the relationship to policing, he notes that the two basic modes of misconduct are the traditional activities (stealing, shakedowns, etc.) and the actual use of drugs, on and off duty, both of which seem to stem from increased exposure to drugs and the stress of the job. Despite its presence, he advises that little data on police drug use exist.

Since it is recognized that drug use can exist among police officers, Mieczkowski discusses the use of drug testing in the workplace. This discussion begins with the review of the 1999 Substance Abuse and Mental Health Services Administration's study (Office of Applied Studies, 1999), which indicated that use of drugs is holding steady, although a slight increase in use among men was demonstrated, and that age is related to use. Furthermore, with more and more employers requiring drug testing, many police agencies have drug-testing policies for time of hiring, during probation, and for tenured officers in special circumstances. Actually, it appears that police officers might be tested more often than any other occupation and that policing is the leader in providing written policies and procedures regarding employee drug testing.

Mieczkowski concludes his chapter by summarizing the legal aspects of drug testing, noting the Americans with Disabilities Act's issues for addicts and alcoholics, the 1986 Drug-Free Workplace Act, and Executive Order 12564 for a federal drug-free workplace. He further notes how the courts have upheld public drug testing when there are compelling interests, it is circumscribed by the constraint of reasonable suspicion, and it avoids random mandatory testing. Finally, he discusses the various means of conducting the drug tests, and, based on his own study, he suggests which test might be most appropriate for police officer drug testing.

One of the most popular "changes" in policing since 1980 has been in the direction of community policing. Despite its popularity, some are concerned that community policing may increase police misconduct. Joe Schafer, in Chapter 8, examines this potential problem. He starts with a brief history of police change to the "professional" model from a traditional model that was believed to be a dysfunctional structure that led to strict controls and accountability at the expense of community alliances and employee morale. He explains that community policing is the current phase of the professional model. Unfortunately, he claims that community policing is still a concept not fully understood, and there is confusion as to what it is or is not. This aside, Schafer offers some major issues associated with community policing and its relationship to misconduct.

Schafer begins by noting that there is a lack of attention to how this approach may allow officers to engage in misconduct with greater ease, how misconduct can taint all officers, and the importance of making community policing work and how it can be affected by police misconduct. Furthermore, he suggests that the misconduct can result from socialization, progression, and the organizational attitude and culture. Despite the prospects and concerns some might have about the potential for misconduct under community policing, Schafer insists that community policing should reduce misconduct because (1) a culture of misconduct is incompatible with the philosophy of community policing; (2) research indicates that community policing ameliorates many of the negative effects of policing as an occupation; and (3) community policing brings officers more into public view and awareness, making misconduct more difficult to accomplish anonymously. While it could lead to more problems, he believes that community policing can offer more than enough to outweigh the negatives.

The truth is never easy to face. Nevertheless, the truth is that police misconduct exists. However, it is probably not nearly as widespread as perceived. Still, we know that it does exist and is often associated with a small handful of officers. Therefore, in Chapter 9, Walker and Alpert suggest a need for police agencies to recognize and short circuit misconduct through the use of an Early Warning (EW) system. They begin their discussion with a brief history and the liability concerns for agencies when officers engage in misconduct. They explain that the EW system is a data-based management tool that is used to identify officers whose behavior has reached a preestablished level and that has some kind of intervention designed to address any problematic behavior identified. While this appears to be a very reasonable and useful idea, little has been written about it. However, it has been implemented in agencies that have had the misfortune of major misconduct scandals. For example, they identify the Miami Police Department's EW system, which tracks complaints, reports, reprimands, and discharges of firearms. While EW systems make sense in theory, some practical issues must be addressed. For instance, Walker and Alpert suggest how implementation can be complex, expensive, and high maintenance. Still, they conclude that EW systems can be effective, provide clear criteria for recognizing misconduct, offer interventions beyond that of an immediate supervisor, and offer postintervention capabilities. In sum, they support the implementation and use of an EW system for addressing police misconduct.

THINKING ABOUT SOLUTIONS

Each chapter of this text has offered some exploration of solutions to police misconduct. Social science has always sought to relate an understanding of a social phenomenon to the development of adequate solutions that allow for its control. A problem arises, however, because social behavior is dynamically resistant to full understanding, and, consequently, solutions produce contradictory and unintended consequences. Rather than resembling Sisyphus, perpetually pushing a boulder up a hill only to have it simply roll back down, human "development" is more like tumbleweeds spinning uncontrollably across the desert of time entangled in the wind of our own actions.

The remainder of this chapter emphasizes the necessity of critically reflecting on proposed solutions to police misconduct in light of the full range of social processes that shape its emergence and persistence. Our discussion illustrates how solutions consistently promote contradictory outcomes in which some aspect of misconduct is alleviated, only to have the behavior manifested in other forms, shaped by other processes. We suggest that those wishing to understand and address police misconduct, therefore, must consciously analyze the phenomena relationally and resist the temptation to rely on one-dimensional explanations that promote facile solutions.

Attempting to understand police misconduct is a complex undertaking with definitional and methodological difficulties. First, much of what we understand about police misconduct comes from descriptive accounts of police–community interactions in the 1960s, early 1970s, and again in the 1990s. Limiting our understanding of misconduct to these criminal acts and/or policy violations ignores that police have historically engaged in behavior considered misconduct as well as legitimated, socially accepted acts against minority groups that most observers retrospectively regard as misconduct. Second, and intertwined with the first, is the lack of records kept on police misconduct, limiting our ability to fully understand its depth and breadth.

Additionally, the overwhelming majority of accounts of misconduct come from large, urban areas. This tendency has resulted in the behavior of police officers in New York, Chicago, and Los Angeles being used as a model to understand the behavior of officers in smaller agencies, in smaller cities and rural areas. Discourse on misconduct consequently assumes an understanding of all misconduct without actually examining the processes that shape misconduct in these areas. Conclusions are typically drawn and solutions proposed that ignore differences in behavior based on temporal and contextual social factors.

To further a historical understanding of police misconduct by reviewing scholarly discourse on the subject is clearly, therefore, a problematic endeavor. The effort is, however, useful when factors that shape police misconduct identified by scholars are rejected as self-sufficient realities, explanatory in and of themselves, and, instead, are positioned relationally. This allows for the creation of a fuller model of the analytical dimensions of police misconduct, furthering our ability to understand how these factors come together in a specific context, in a specific instance of police misconduct.

As an example, consider an analytical model developed from the scholarly findings previously discussed in Chapter 2. The model emphasizes the relationship between societal power—economic and political—and consequent struggles for power between diverse groups and individuals; the organizational structure of competing (and cooperating) institutions and the positions occupied by relevant agents within these institutions; and, finally, the stratified biographies of the agents themselves including their dispositions, activities, and potentialities. The strength of this model is that it promotes a contextual and temporal understanding of acts of misconduct in relation to the multidimensional processes that shape them. It further allows students of policing to identify relevant analytic dimension(s) in a specific context while exploring whether the explanation for a specific act of misconduct is generalizable to other acts. Further, rather than being complete and exhaustive, this model is flexible and is sufficiently general to allow the inclusion of other factors as they emerge as part of society's collective understanding of police misconduct. Finally and importantly, this model can be used to determine the adequacy of proposed solutions to misconduct.

Solutions to police misconduct actively sought in the 1960s and early 1970s were assumed, for a time, to have achieved some measure of success. The Supreme Court of the early 1960s was active in creating and interpreting law as it applied to the activities of officers. By the early 1970s, solutions that were to be developed from within police agencies were being promoted by scholars and administrators. A good summary of the most frequently proposed solutions was outlined in Cooper (1975). These included (1) minority recruitment; (2) community relations units; (3) psychological screening; and (4) police review boards. All proposed changes sought to improve the quality of individual officers as well as agencies' relationship with community members.

Although never conclusive, some evidence that these solutions had desired effects exists. Examining minority recruitment, for example, Lersch (1998) found that although there was no significant difference in the type of complaints filed against male and female officers, female officers were less likely to be accused of misconduct. She concluded that this finding supports the idea that hiring more female officers may improve police–community relations. Blumberg (1991) echoed this conclusion with evidence that female officers, as well as male officers from a middle-class background, are less likely to use their weapons against members of the public. Similarly, and further examining community–police relations, Walker et al. (1996) concluded that the significant decline in police shootings of black citizens from 1975 to 1990 implied better police–minority group relations.

Recently, this optimism has waned due to numerous, very public acts of misconduct. Given societal recognition of misconduct and decades of largely unsuccessful attempts to find solutions to control it, it is crucial to understand why solutions have not been fully successful and to determine how best to proceed in the coming years. We feel that the reemergence of police misconduct as a national social problem should not be very surprising, given that it is an outcome of dynamic social processes. Therefore, piecemeal solutions, although positive in and of themselves, are not sufficient to address the totality of the problem.

For example, focusing on the culture and organization of police officers and their relationship to other institutions, Bittner foreshadowed this concern by warning that any critique of police would unavoidably alienate them, "will strengthen their defensive and distrustful posture, and will cause, at best, a patchwork of reform, the main effect of which will be to shift malpractice from one form to another" (1970: 2).

Problems arising from attempts to change policing through affirmative action and mass hiring of officers were detailed in Dorschner's (2000) account of the chaos that dominated Miami police agencies in the 1980s. He links proposed solutions to the simultaneous rise of the drug trade, local political infighting, and departmental conflict—painting a convincing picture of the contradictions involved in trying to address concerns about police misconduct. Responding to similar agency chaos and police misconduct in other cities, scholars and administrators at all levels of government have fine-tuned reforms and promoted internal accountability of departments by addressing training, promotion, supervisor accountability, discipline, and citizen oversight while holding agencies liable for the actions of their officers.

Similarly, the courts and legislatures have become increasingly involved in addressing, for example, issues of departmental and municipal liability in an attempt to strengthen agencies' internal supervision of their officers. These law-making bodies argue that:

> cities take on a degree of responsibility by deciding to allocate these powers to a police force and therefore, must be held accountable for the entity they have created. The individual police officers of this nation are vested with such vast discretion that effective disciplinary procedures to dissuade abusive conduct must exist. (Marcus, 1994: 677)

However, problems arise when confusing mandates from both the legislature and the courts make the job of officers tougher. Wilzbach (1997), in his analysis of the Illinois Supreme Court's decision to suppress evidence gained under previously valid statutes later ruled to be unconstitutional, illustrates how differences between the courts and the police can foster mistrust and a lack of confidence and can potentially become a source of future misconduct. When legislators pass laws that shape the daily activities of police officers, who act on those laws in good faith only to see the courts rule that the legislators erred and the laws are, in fact, violations of constitutionally mandated rights, police officers see months and sometimes years of hard work diminished, feel betrayed and confused, and lose confidence in "cooperating institutions."

Further, Martin (1993) suggests that responding to charges of brutality in the past may have allowed departments and their officers to become better prepared to deal with the public and handle its concerns. Consequently, the increasing use of civil suits that hold municipalities liable, although a promising solution, may result in greater solidarity between local government, the department, and its officers in attempting to cover up and or vigorously defend their actions rather than recognize existing problems and work for acceptable solutions. More importantly, legal strategies, contradictorily, only work on narrowly defined, very public instances of misconduct. The courts focus on brutality, for example, defining and delineating it as a social problem worthy of attention and effort to address it, while other forms of conduct persist with little real response.

Each proposed solution seemingly has a potentially negative caveat that allows police misconduct to persist in some form. Somewhat more interesting, while promoting internal and civil solutions, legislators, the courts, other governmental agencies, media, and police agencies simultaneously foster an environment ripe for misconduct by promoting a "war" climate. This contradiction is readily apparent in the growing symbiotic relationship between Community-Oriented Policing (COPS) programs and Police Paramilitary Units (PPUs), as outlined by Kraska and Kappeler (1997), who detail how funding for COPS programs have been sometimes rerouted to facilitate the militarization of police agencies.

With donated military hardware, military training, and organization, police agencies are looking more like military agencies. Simultaneously, COPS programs are becoming an integral phase of a domestic "Operation Phoenix," in which PPUs first move to suppress and pacify a community and COPS teams follow up by increasing control and surveillance through increased community–police cooperation. The recent examples provided by the tragic case of Amadou Diallo in New York and the rampant misconduct of officers in the Rampart Division in Los Angeles illustrate how a "war" atmosphere fosters brutality and misconduct, although, as in the Diallo case, the actions of officers may be ultimately judged as legitimate by agencies and/or the courts.

The globalization of the world's economy further promotes these types of programs on the international stage and allows our government to similarly police other areas of the world, entrenching a siege mentality in the minds of the public and creating a climate ripe with opportunities for abuse. Witness the recent billion-dollars-plus program to fight the production of cocaine in Colombia, for example.

It should not be surprising, therefore, that some scholars now argue that the main reason for these contradictions is that police reform is not a substitute for social reform. It is clear that internal departmental controls fail in the face of personal, organizational, and subcultural ideas of race, class, gender, and justice, allowing systemic misconduct to persist. As predicted in 1972, changing police behavior may not improve relations unless it is coupled with a program of social renovation so penetrating and effective that it shatters the barriers that make up coherent social groups (Bayley & Mendelsohn, 1969).

Recognizing and addressing the structure of economic and political power in American society and understanding how its ideological justifications shape the attitudes and behaviors of all individuals, including police officers, clearly are important in addressing misconduct. Solutions should go beyond the mere identification of individual "problem officers" and include more than management issues of accountability, training, and supervision. Without societal reform, any attempts to reform police are, at best, a piecemeal solution, argues Cohen, because:

> in a society that constantly competes for resources and wealth . . . the police are inherently called upon to preserve the status quo. When that status quo is fraught with class bias and racial oppression, the police will function to protect only upper- and middle-class white interests at the expense of all others. (Cohen, 1996: 173, 200)

Acting on this understanding, some scholars have undertaken efforts in their communities to address the full range of social processes and dimensions that shape police misconduct. Dianne Martin, for example, concludes from her work in Toronto that police misconduct is so resistant to a solution that the only way to solve it is an innovative, community-based initiative that has as its ultimate goal fundamental structural change:

> Popular misbeliefs about police misconduct include, for example, the belief that police misconduct is the result of the odd "bad apple" or that it will be eliminated through better training. These kinds of beliefs serve a common end and are building blocks of that hegemony. Thus, exposing the fallacies in these "common sense" propositions is a first step in a strategy that attempts to build a different consensus with different values. This strategy highlights tactics such as community outreach and education and coalition-building around policing issues between groups frequently divided by existing power relations: racial minorities, working-class whites, feminist activists working against violence and pornography, and neighborhood activists working against drugs and prostitution, for example. (Martin, 1993: 137)

Students can also be actively part of the process of addressing misconduct, as described in Cyril D. Robinson's community study in Memphis. Students discovered that to solve problems, communication between police officers and community members must involve looking "deeply into the historical, economic, political, and social underpinnings of the neighborhood to connect these with national trends, and thus create links with current neighborhood problems" (Robinson, 1987: 195). Students learned through action and became a part of the solution.

Continuing frustration fostered by the contradictions inherent in addressing police misconduct forces scholars to employ a fuller model that allows for a relational analysis of all of the dimensions of misconduct. It is, however, certainly a time-consuming endeavor, permitting few results in the short term. It may be asked, therefore, if it is worthwhile expending the immense time, effort, and agony necessary to carry out small changes when the root of the problem lies outside policing in the organization of society. We respond that, although small steps alone cannot create definitive, long-term alterations in police practices, such action does bring small advances and creates political consciousness within and solidarity among communities who struggle for just treatment while revealing the full nature of misconduct through continued legislative and police resistance to "reasonable" demands. Though piecemeal actions and small changes within one social institution do not fully address the economic, political, and ideological issues crucial for social justice, because policing is at the front line of the criminal justice system, even small changes undertaken with a fuller understanding of the complex dimensions of the problem may ultimately have a relatively large effect on altering existing social relations.

CONCLUSION

Although a specifically identifiable group and/or individual engages in police misconduct, we must remember that, analytically, how we understand this range of behaviors is similar to how we understand human behavior in general. Consequently, to develop a full analysis of police misconduct, we must simultaneously focus on the structural conditions of American society at a given point in history, the cultural and ideological constructions of meaning that guide actions and attitudes of the citizenry, institutional and organizational processes that specifically function to socialize and control behavior, and interactions between individuals and groups.

We must always keep in mind that human behavior is flexible, dynamic, and contradictory, and, more frequently than not, attempts to explain it seem to raise more questions than provide answers. One reason, perhaps, is that social scientists have historically overlooked human agency: the active, creative, imaginative abilities of humans. While it is important to describe, as most social scientists have done, how people learn and internalize their social systems, culture, and institutions and are therefore shaped, it is further important to describe how people also reflect, interpret, and act on the processes that shape them and ultimately have the ability to transform these processes.

With this in mind, the goal of this chapter has not been to provide a definitive, final analysis, but rather to provide an overview of the basic analytical dimensions that students of police behavior must discuss when trying to understand the history and current prevalence of police misconduct.

REFERENCES

BAYLEY, D. H., & MENDELSOHN, H. (1969). *Minorities and the Police: Confrontation in America.* New York: The Free Press.

BITTNER, E. (1970). *The Function of the Police in Modern Society: A Review of Background Factors, Current Practices, and Possible Role Models*. Chevy Chase, Md.: National Institute of Mental Health.

BLUMBERG, M. (1991). Police use of deadly force: Exploring some key issues. In Barker, T., & Carter, D. L., eds. *Police Deviance* (pp. 219–39). Cincinnati, Ohio: Anderson Publishing.

COHEN, D. S. (1996). Official oppression: A historical analysis of low-level police abuse and a modern attempt at reform. *Columbia Human Rights Law Review* 28 (1): 165–201.

COOPER, L. B. (1975). Controlling the police. In Viano, E. C., & Reiman, J. H., eds. *The Police in Society* (pp. 241–7). Lexington, Mass.: Lexington Books.

DANTZKER, M. L. (2000). *Understanding Today's Police*. 2d ed. Upper Saddle River, N.J.: Prentice Hall.

DORSCHNER, J. (2000). The dark side of the force. In Hancock, B. W., & Sharp, P. M., eds. *Criminal Justice in America: Theory, Practice, and Policy*. 2d ed. (pp. 117–36). Upper Saddle River, N.J.: Prentice Hall.

KRASKA, P. B., & KAPPELER, V. E.. (1997). Militarizing American police: The rise and normalization of paramilitary units. *Social Problems* 44 (1): 1–17.

LERSCH, K. M. (1998). Exploring gender differences in citizen allegations of misconduct: An analysis of a municipal police department. *Women and Criminal Justice* 9: 69–80.

MARCUS, J. M. (1994). Up against the wall: Municipal liability for police brutality under respondeat superior. *Osborne* v. *Lyles*, N.E.2D. 825 (Ohio 1992). *Southern Illinois University Law Journal* 18: 655–84.

MARTIN, D. L. (1993). Organizing for change: A community law response to police misconduct. *Hastings Women's Law Journal* 4 (1): 131–74.

OFFICE OF APPLIED STUDIES. (1999). *Worker Drug Use and Workplace Policies and Programs: Results from the 1994 and 1997 NHSDA*. Washington, D.C.: Office of Applied Studies, Substance Abuse and Mental Health Services Administration.

PALMIOTTO, M. J. (2001). Police misconduct: What is it? In Palmiotto, M. J., ed. *Police Misconduct: A Reader for the 21st Century* (pp. 32–41). Upper Saddle River, N.J.: Prentice Hall.

ROBINSON, C. D. (1987). Community relations through community history. *Social Justice* 15 (3/4): 179–96.

WALKER, S. (1999). *The Police in America*. 3d ed. New York: McGraw-Hill.

WALKER, S., SPOHN, C., & DELONE, M. (1996). *The Color of Justice: Race, Ethnicity, and Crime in America*. Belmont, Calif.: Wadsworth Publishing.

WILZBACH, M. S. (1997). Search and seizure and the lockstep doctrine: Illinois deviates from the lockstep doctrine in telling the police that they cannot rely on Illinois' laws. *Southern Illinois University Law Journal* 22: 181.